1952 by Langston Hughes. Reprinted by permission of Harold Ober Associates.

Ted Poston, "The Revolt of the Evil Fairies." Reprinted by permission of the author.

Random House, Inc., excerpts from *A Raisin in the Sun*, by Lorraine Hansberry. Copyright © 1958, 1959, 1966 by Robert Nemiroff as Executor of the Estate of Lorraine Hansberry; excerpt from *Invisible Man* by Ralph Ellison. Copyright 1947, 1952 by Ralph Ellison. Reprinted by permission of the publishers.

Paul R. Reynolds, Inc., "The Man Who Lived Underground," by Richard Wright, copyright © 1944 by L. B. Fischer Publishing Corporation. Reprinted by permission of Paul R. Reynolds, Inc.

Flora Roberts, Inc., "The Pocketbook Game" by Alice Childress in *Best Short Stories by Negro Writers*, edited by Langston Hughes. Reprinted by permission of Flora Roberts, Inc.

The Sterling Lord Agency, "A Poem for Black Hearts," from *Dark Symphony*. Copyright © 1965 by LeRoi Jones. Published by The Free Press. Reprinted by permission of The Sterling Lord Agency.

Twayne Publishers, Inc., excerpts from *Harlem Gallery* by Melvin B. Tolson; "The White House," "If We Must Die," and an excerpt from "Baptism," from the *Selected Poems of Claude McKay*. Reprinted by permission of the publishers.

Yale University Press, from *For My People* by Margaret Walker. Copyright © 1942 by Yale University Press. Reprinted by permission of the publishers.

To my husband, Murray, who makes all things seem possible.

Foreword

To say that learning flourishes and wisdom grows in a climate of sympathetic understanding between teacher and taught is to state a truism, but it is a truism too often ignored by those whose experience should confirm it. Too many teachers have sought to establish their reputations and professional security on the accumulation and dissemination of facts and objective information that can be measured, quantified, and verified. The "scientific method" and the use of technical aids have so mechanized the teacher's function that "humanism," unhappily, has come to seem quite beside the point, and the prospect of computers and other electronic devices taking over classrooms is not as appalling as it should be. The depersonalization of teaching has been especially noticeable in urban ghetto schools, where sympathetic understanding is not even an occasional condition of the intellectual climate, which, students complain (in earthy language), is fouled by teacher–student alienation, irrelevance, and prejudice.

A Gift of the Spirit is a response to these complaints which at the same time goes far beyond them. As a response, Dr. Karel Rose's book is addressed to teachers. It assumes, rightfully to be sure, (1) that there are severe limitations to the accumulation of facts; (2) that science and art are alternate and complementary ways of knowing; and (3) that literature provides insights that are not only useful but, if teaching and learning are to occur, indispensable. In *A Gift of the Spirit* these assumptions are basic to a new approach to teaching the ghetto child. The first part of the book is a deeply concerned professional teacher's assessment of the emotional, cultural, and intellectual disabilities which measure the distance between teacher and taught, but it is also a perceptive explication of how the distance can be bridged and why it must be bridged. It is addressed specifically, though not exclusively, to teachers.

The rest of *A Gift of the Spirit* is for everyone. An anthology of black writing, the selections were chosen not only for their literary merit but for their significance as revelation and analysis. What does it mean to be black in America? There are many answers. From the autobiographical narrative of Gustavus Vassa, which was published in 1791, to Eldridge Cleaver's *Soul on Ice* and LeRoi Jones' "A Poem for Black Hearts," the selections have that specificity that is characteristic of both the best imaginative writing and the truest personal statement.

Taken all together, the selections constitute a history of the black experience and of the ways blacks have dealt with that experience in America.
It is a history that Americans can no longer afford to ignore.

Saunders Redding

A Gift of the Spirit

READINGS IN BLACK LITERATURE FOR TEACHERS

Karel Rose

Brooklyn College
City University of New York

With a foreword by Saunders Redding, Cornell University

HOLT, RINEHART AND WINSTON, INC.

New York   Chicago   San Francisco   Atlanta
Dallas   Montreal   Toronto

Acknowledgments

For permission to reprint copyrighted materials, the editor is indebted to the following:

John Henrik Clarke, "The Boy Who Painted Christ Black." Reprinted by permission of the author.

The Dial Press, reprinted from *Go Tell It on the Mountain* by James Baldwin. Copyright © 1953, 1952 by James Baldwin and used by permission of the publisher, The Dial Press, A Division of Dell Publishing Co., Inc.

Dodd, Mead & Company, "Dark Symphony," from *Rendezvous with America* by Melvin B. Tolson. Copyright 1944 by Dodd, Mead & Company, Inc.; "We Wear the Mask," from *The Complete Poems of Paul Laurence Dunbar*. Reprinted by permission of the publishers.

Grove Press, Inc., excerpt from *The Autobiography of Malcolm X*. Reprinted by permission of the publishers. Copyright © 1964 by Alex Haley and Malcolm X. Copyright © 1965 by Alex Haley and Betty Shabazz.

Harper & Row, Publishers, Inc., first four lines of "From the Dark Tower," in *On These I Stand* by Countee Cullen. Copyright 1927 by Harper & Row, Publishers, Inc. Renewed 1955 by Ida M. Cullen; "Yet Do I Marvel," from *On These I Stand* by Countee Cullen. Copyright 1925 by Harper & Brothers. Renewed 1953 by Mrs. Ida M. Cullen; from pp. 19–22, 160–169, *Black Boy* by Richard Wright. Copyright 1937, 1942, 1944, 1945 by Richard Wright; from pp. 7–25, 44–73, *Native Son* by Richard Wright. Copyright 1940 by Richard Wright. Renewed 1968 by Ellen Wright; "As Seen by Disciplines," from *In the Mecca* by Gwendolyn Brooks. Copyright © 1968 by Gwendolyn Brooks Blakely. Reprinted by permission of the publishers.

Hill & Wang, Inc., "Census" and "Coffee Break," from *Simple's Uncle Sam* by Langston Hughes. Copyright © 1965 by Langston Hughes. Reprinted by permission of the publishers.

Alfred A. Knopf, Inc., "A Dream Deferred" (formerly titled "Harlem"). Copyright 1951 by Langston Hughes. Reprinted from *The Panther and the Lash* by Langston Hughes; excerpt from "Cross," from *Selected Poems* by Langston Hughes. Reprinted by permission of the publishers.

Liveright, Publishers, excerpt from *Cane* by Jean Toomer. Permission of Liveright, Publishers, New York. Copyright © 1951 by Jean Toomer.

McGraw-Hill Book Company, excerpt from *Soul on Ice* by Eldridge Cleaver. Copyright © 1968 by Eldridge Cleaver. Used with permission of the publishers.

Henry Morrison, Inc., excerpts from *The Me Nobody Knows*, edited by Stephen Joseph. Reprinted by permission of Henry Morrison, Inc.

Harold Ober Associates, "Good Morning," from *Lenox Avenue Mural*. Copyright 1952 by Langston Hughes; "Same In Blues," from *Lenox Avenue Mural*. Copyright 1951 by Langston Hughes; "One Friday Morning." Copyright

Preface

This book assumes that confrontations with literature can convey human feelings and provide students with an intense experience of how it feels to be black in America. Since good writers are skilled in conveying, through the literary medium, the essence of a situation, their compositions may inaugurate individual revelations as the reader confronts what for him is a "truth." It is only the black writer, in most cases, who is able to tell the world "the way it is" for the Negro. "No white man, however brave and well-intentioned, can ever sing the Negro song." [1] There are those who might dispute this point. Nevertheless, the black man, because of the immediacy of his situation (the creative talent is implied), can provide insights into the "life of feeling" that may otherwise be concealed from the white man.

In the past ten years, education has been in a state of ferment and many experimental projects have been initiated in order to develop programs that bridge the gap between the middle-class teacher and the ghetto child. Very frequently, this child has been Negro and the problem takes on a greater complexity as social class differences muddle and sometimes obscure the realities of the situation. Middle-class teachers (both Negro and white) have to be helped to come closer to children from deprived backgrounds, and to recognize that their attitudes may be rooted in racial prejudices that are fortified by cultural and intellectual disabilities. This is the nature of the chain of circumstances, and every link is dependent upon a previous one. Teachers, whether they are black or white, in many cases have adopted middle-class values and cannot be counted on to accept a group which has difficulty "getting in step" with the establishment. Teachers should recognize the cyclical nature of the problems of the deprived black child in terms of social class as well as racial disparities.

My purpose in this book is to identify more clearly for those involved in the educational process how the black man feels about his experiences. What are the factors which have intimidated him? What are the causes of his alienation? How does he see the world that is institutionalized in the schools? It is anticipated that black literature will serve as a sensitizing catalyst, and will therefore open the gates to new vistas of awareness for the reader.

The book is divided into two parts. In the first part, the first chapter focuses on the nature of the literary experience and suggests the

[1] Colin MacInnes, as quoted in Doris Abramson, "Negro Playwrights in America," *Columbia Forum*, 12:11, Spring 1969.

potentialities of literature for inspiring human concern. The second chapter provides guidance for the introduction of black literature into education courses. The third chapter is concerned with assisting the teacher in training who wishes to supplement the selections in the anthology. Bibliographical aids and criteria are suggested as a means of further exploring the burgeoning field of black literature.

In the second part—the anthology—there are five chapters. Each chapter focuses on one thematic unit which the teacher, if he chooses, may follow in sequence. These thematic units emerged from the content of the literary selections included in the anthology. It should be noted that many of the literary selections are excerpts and, in this form, are best termed "symbolic instances" with the recognition that when less than a complete work is offered there is an alteration of the author's aesthetic design.[2]

Because of the sensitivity of the area of race relations, readers may have some concern as to how the selections were chosen after the initial screening and basic literary criteria were established. A board of black educators (see page x) was selected to provide additional reaction and comment on the choice of literary works. For it is acknowledged that racial differences may constitute a curtain through which certain lights cannot pass. Therefore the black man, considering the literature written by and about his people, brings into play fundamental responses which may be obscured for white people. In this way the board enlarged my vision and helped me to identify literature that was multidimensional, honest, and appreciative of the existing cultural motifs in the lives of black people. Mutual respect and regard formed the cornerstone of the invitation to this board to participate in this project.

The total group of readings should not be regarded as a definitive survey of black American literature, for there are many excellent works which have not been included. Rather than a conclusive statement, the anthology should be viewed as a point of departure and a *modus vivendi* for expanding the horizons of teachers. My major concern is with what literature can do to increase sensitivity, and my intent is to utilize the aesthetic medium for heightening the awareness of those who may have had relatively little sophisticated training in the literary way of knowing.

It is in this spirit of exploration of human experience through an art form that Dr. Leland B. Jacobs so graciously gave of his time and assisted me to think though the development of this book. His insights and guidance were invaluable, and I am indebted to him for helping to make this undertaking an exciting and enriching experience.

---

[2] For this insight I would like to acknowledge the guidance of Dr. Francis Shoemaker, Director of the Office of International Programs and Services, Teachers College, Columbia University, New York City.

My debt to Dean Louis E. Rosenzweig of Brooklyn College must be acknowledged for his continuing encouragement in my career. His educational philosophy has served as a touchstone and a perpetual source of inspiration.

Great Neck, New York   Karel Rose
December 1970

Contents

You think your pain and your heartbreak are unprecedented in the history of the world, but then you read. It was books that taught me that the things that tormented me the most were the very things that connected me with all the people who were alive, or who had ever been alive.

James Baldwin

from "My Childhood," *School Library Journal,*
September 1964, p. 23.

chapter 1

IMAGINATIVE LITERATURE AS A WAY OF KNOWING

The teacher who seeks to explore imaginative literature recognizes the implications of aesthetic experiences for professional growth. This book is intended for the person who is prepared to consider seriously the contributions of art as an intellectual tool for understanding. It is anticipated that it will assist the teacher to "entertain" the literature of black artists to the goal of the reader's knowing what a professional should comprehend about the Negro experience in America. The significance of black literature for educators is that it provides them with an interior look at race through the black man's perception of himself and his condition. Though the material may not explicitly confront the school situation, it does attempt to inform the reader who is willing to be informed of the variety of human feelings. The literary way of knowing focuses on the human as well as on the professional implications of being a teacher.

Somehow educators frequently have demonstrated in their practices that the accumulation of information about the field is more efficiently accomplished through reading expositional materials where the emphasis is on the accumulation of facts. There is a small center of security generated because some of these facts can be objectively verified. On the other hand, it is exceedingly difficult to validate what the well-written play can tell the teacher about logical thinking, the passionate poem about interpretive skills, and the existential novel about practical classroom procedures.

Admittedly, education—with its ambiguous roots and its limited body of scientific evidence to guide its activities—is in a difficult situation. Reluctant to consider practices that do not feed the scientific "trunk," practitioners searching for evidence frequently find themselves pigeonholing instructions and rewarming "proven" procedures. As the clients of the education system—students and parents—make demands on the schools, very often the response is to "tighten up" and to add further structure onto the one that is already being charged with "irrelevancy."

There has been a fear that if we explore the commonplace in a variety of ways, if we do not prematurely impose regularity on an irregular world, then our very existence as a profession is challenged. As George Homans observes, "We have much anxiety about opening

1

ourselves to the charge that we have discovered at infinite pains what everybody knows."[1]

This discussion in no way suggests that the scientific mode is inappropriate for education. On the contrary, the form and process that science imposes on reality are essential, if we are to understand our own experience in relation to the larger world. The focus here is to help the educator recognize the limitations of a purely factual approach to teacher-training and to become more mindful of the field of aesthetic experience as a way of knowing and as a source of information.

The impersonality of society, the pace of change, and the explosion of factual information often outdistances man's ability to orient himself, and may lead to what C. Wright Mills terms "a sense of being trapped." Teachers are aware that students, with their new-found freedom, are reacting negatively to curricula stuffed with objectives but irrelevant to their understanding of the larger world. Professionals can no longer ignore the rejection of the purely factual approach to learning, for too many students are articulating their need to become aware of a different kind of fact—a "feeling fact," an "artistic fact." There is an appreciation of the idea that by becoming aware of another person, whose life pattern may be different from one's own but whose "feeling life" bears striking similarities, personal experience can be better understood. Many students see Camus' literary reality as a fact; they understand their own experience in terms of Pinter's images, and they see a way out of their *anomie* by reading Eldridge Cleaver.

We are living through a societal revolution, and it is not only the students who are taking issue with the established procedures. Education, a cultural barometer, is feeling the pressure from forces within and external to the establishment. There is a growing reexamination of objectives, methodology, and curriculum. Not infrequently there is the recognition that the arts must be joined with the sciences, with respect for the contributions of each to process and information, if students are to be educated—educated for an understanding of the larger scene in terms of its personal meaningfulness for the conduct of life. Toward this end William E. Hocking, in his essay, "What Man Can Make of Man," optimistically states that,

> . . . The new conscience is finding its courage because man's soul is recovering the sight of both its eyes! It is taking the scientific conscience into the house, not as master but as partner.

---

[1] George C. Homans, *The Human Group* (New York: Harcourt Brace Jovanovich, Inc., 1950), p. 5.

Many teachers cognizant of the role of the factual and informational heritage of the culture are not adequately sensitized to the potentialities of the art experience for increasing their identification with others, their empathic competence, and their knowledge of the varieties of human emotion. It is these qualities, largely determined by a teacher's "feeling-ness," that have the greatest impact on children in the classroom.

SCIENCE AND ART— ALTERNATE WAYS OF KNOWING

Imaginative literature and informational writing offer complementary as well as alternate ways of knowing. Though each mode may produce in the reader a dedication, an excitement, even a passion for the subject, it is imaginative literature, addressed to man's sensibilities, that has the potential for inspiring human concern. It is the "intuitive and imaginative powers, [which] are the midwives to new forms of thought and conduct, new vistas, and even new social institutions and systems."[2]

This book seeks to bring forth in the reader an awareness of the potentialities of imaginative literature for increasing man's way of knowing about the world, by emphasizing the human capacity to identify with another individual or situation. The scientific statement, in contrast, more precisely orders logic and facts, and stresses careful documentation which may be verified by others. Kenneth B. Clark, a social scientist, describes ghetto conditions in this manner:

> Poor housing conditions, malnutrition and inadequate health care are undoubtedly responsible for the high infant death rate, where flies and maggots breed, where the plumbing is stopped up, and not repaired, where rats bite helpless infants: the conditions of life are brutal and inhuman.[3]

From the perspective of the literary artist who describes slum housing and the terror of rat-infested quarters, the focus of attention is on communicating the *feelings* of those individuals who live under these conditions. Richard Wright helps the reader to know this feeling (or his thought about this feeling) when he describes Bigger's encounter with a rat:

---

[2] Earl S. Johnson, "Ways of Knowing," *Readings in Curriculum*, Glenn Hass and Kimball Wiles, eds. (Boston: Allyn and Bacon, Inc., 1965), p. 308.

[3] Kenneth B. Clark, *Dark Ghetto: Dilemmas of Power* (New York: Harper & Row, Publishers, 1965), p. 31.

Buddy extended his hand. Bigger caught the skillet and lifted it high in the air. The rat scuttled across the floor and stopped again at the box and searched quickly for the hole; then, it reared once more and bared long yellow fangs, piping shrilly, belly quivering.

Bigger aimed and let the skillet fly with a heavy grunt. There was a shattering of wood as the box caved in. The woman screamed and hid her face in her hands. Bigger tiptoed forward and peered.

"I got 'im," he muttered, his clenched teeth bared in a smile. "By God, I got 'im."[4]

Both Clark and Wright have made accurate observations; both excerpts have the ring of truth, but in each case it is a different order of truth. The social scientist speaks in terms that are objectively verifiable, while the artist's description encourages a subjective interpretation of the "facts" that he presents. It is Wright's picture of reality that impresses us with a kind of universal truth about a *feeling*. Through this human appeal to our own feelings of fear he heightens our perception of ghetto life. Though slum life is not common to all men, feelings of fear are. There was never a Bigger Thomas in the sense that there is a New York City ghetto, yet for the serious reader Bigger is as real and as true as his own existence.

Works of imaginative literature present facts in a different way than do essays. Though the novel, the play, or the poem must also be specific in describing the conditions of existence, the furniture of reality in these genres is subject to the writer's personal rendering of the facts and is conditioned to some extent by his desire to communicate with the reader. Claude McKay's poem, "The White House," presents certain facts about racist attitudes in our society, but its value as an explanation of racism or as a framework for developing broader concepts is questionable. McKay's appeal is an emotional one.

Your door is shut against my tightened face,
And I am sharp as steel with discontent;
But I possess the courage and the grace
To bear my anger proudly and unbent.[5]

Racism, a fact, is handled sensuously, for the poet is imposing his feelings on the fact. It should be recognized that this presentation of

---

[4] Richard Wright, *Native Son* (New York: Harper & Row, Publishers, 1966), p. 10.

[5] Claude McKay, "The White House," *Selected Poems of Claude McKay*, (New York: Bookman Associates, 1953), p. 78.

"fact" may have a greater ring of truth for some than the factual description that follows:

> The color cult has been injurious to the personality develop-ment of the masses. It has saddled them with a "self-hate" complex and a sense of impotence and inferiority which tends to destroy upward aspiration . . . They resent the continuous portrayal of their community as an inherently inferior neighborhood. The total atmosphere eventually becomes characterized by bitterness.[6]

This selection from sociology brings into focus many additional factors which should be considered in appreciating the black man's anger and, therefore both McKay and Smythe do increase our understanding. For the artist and the researcher are necessary for a total view and a balanced perspective. Without one or the other we limp along with a kind of partial perception that produces, at best, an insulated view of the world.

THE RESPONSIBILITY OF THE READER

The writer of imaginative literature begins with an idea, a feeling about life, that he wishes to order and express. This idea is given aesthetic form as characters, situations, and actions are ordered into relationships designed to engage the reader. In one sense the artist is making a presentation; he is offering his thoughts about feeling within the framework of a literary reality. He is confronting his reader with a perspective that is structured by and responsible to the demands of his art.

There is also a responsibility on the part of the reader to enter into and become aware of the artist's intent and so to entertain his purposes and share, for the moment, whatever mood he seeks to create. Enter-tain is not used in the casual sense, but here means to earnestly consider what the writer desires the reader to feel. It involves a kind of intellectual and emotional strenuousness implying that the reader is, at the very least, taking the artist seriously. This means being alert to the author's field of vision, recognizing the essential spirit of his work, and permitting one's imagination to experience the facts of the fictional world. This does not imply the acceptance of the writer's outlook, but it does suggest the need for a kind of aesthetic involvement on the part of the reader.

While the reader may be making a conscious effort to appreciate

---

[6] Lester D. Crow, Walter I. Murray, and Hugh H. Smythe, eds., *Educating the Culturally Disadvantaged Child: Principles and Programs* (New York: David McKay Company, Inc., 1966), p. 35.

the tensions inherent in a problem, posed both by the subject matter and the medium itself, it should be recognized that he must have had personal experience that has prepared him to recognize the implications of the literary work. René Wellek and Austin Warren observe that, "We have to have a knowledge independent of literature in order to know what the relation of a specific work to 'life' may be."[7] The artist, more frequently, is caught up in the process of the creation itself. His concern is not usually to solve or answer the problems generated by his work.

In the case of the black artist, however, the problem becomes more compelling, and polemics and social protest often play a powerful role. Nevertheless, for many writers, the demands of their art still take precedence. "Even a cry of anguish," Robert Bone states, "can be highly organized and rendered with style and form."[8] There is indeed a concern for tension; but the way in which it is handled is determined by literary considerations. If the aesthetic requisites become too cumbersome the writer, as in the case of James Baldwin, may at certain times turn his talents to the essay form. Inasmuch as an artist seeks to define a problem in personal terms, however, he becomes involved in the creative process. In this context, S. Alexander observes that,

> . . . the artist's work proceeds not from a finished imaginative experience to which the work of art corresponds, but from passionate excitement about the subject matter; that the poet sings as the bird, because he must; that his poem is wrung from him by the subject that excites him.[9]

It is in this spirit that the literature presented in the anthology should be approached. The writer's success in making his literary statement should be measured by the excitement, the intensity, the fire of the response that it evokes in the reader. Is the reader caught up in the author's insights? Does the literary work communicate its intentions? Is it believable? Furthermore, is there an awareness of process that is really at the heart of storytelling? Is there, on some level, a recognition with the artist of the changes that influence the outcome?

A further word might be said about the reader's receptivity to the literary experience. There can be no question of the many powerful forces that mitigate against engagement with the author's statement.

---

[7] René Wellek and Austin Warren, *Theory of Literature*, 3d Ed. (New York: Harcourt Brace Jovanovich, Inc., 1956), p. 212.

[8] Robert A. Bone, *The Negro Novel in America*, Rev. Ed. (New Haven: Yale University Press, 1968), p. 251.

[9] S. Alexander, *Art and the Material* (New York: Longmans, Green and Company, 1925), p. 11.

Resistance may be the result of an emotional unwillingness to confront that which illuminates life in a painful way. This is particularly relevant when discussing black literature since so many works reflect a racial protest. Rejection of literature may also be the outgrowth of an individual's stance that literature is not serious study. There also are those who repudiate the strenuousness necessary for enjoyment. Margaret Early speaks of the reader's *duty* to enjoy himself. "Enjoyment," she says, "must be won by conscious effort."[10]

In substantial agreement with this approach, the encounters with literature which follow recognize the relationship between enjoyment and effort. The focus is on experiences that will help the reader to develop a sensitivity to literary feelings; feelings that may serve as springboards to a greater awareness of the human condition. It is assumed that the strenuousness necessary to identify with a writer's struggle or to empathize with a literary character is a response that can be developed.

It is important to grant, nevertheless, that the extent, if any, to which these responses are nurtured is very much a private affair. The level at which the readings are contemplated is a highly individual matter and the conclusions that can be drawn are relevant only in a personal way. Very often they may never be publicly voiced by a reader. For exposure to the literature of the Negro is a kind of individual education of the imagination, and the extension of perceptions that may be very distressing. David Littlejohn observes, "The real pain of reading Negro literature of the race war is as oppressive as it is beneficial. If a new truth does not really hurt—not 'literarily' but really—it is probably no truth."[11]

LIMITATIONS OF THE LITERARY WAY OF KNOWING

Along with the enormous potential of the literary art comes limitations. Highly personal aesthetic statements cannot be exploited for the establishment of moral or scientific codes of action. Literature is not an objective case history; it is personally selective and bound by the artistic considerations and purposes of the writer. We must turn to informational writing rather than imaginative literature when we need verifiable facts and logical arguments. Leland Jacobs notes that for

---

[10] Margaret J. Early, "Stages of Growth in Literary Appreciation," *English Journal*, XLIX:167, March 1960.

[11] David Littlejohn, *Black on White: A Critical Survey of Writing by American Negroes* (New York: Grossman Publishers, 1966), p. 20.

thought about thought we go in search of the essay, the treatise; for thought about feeling we seek out the poem, the play, the novel.

Why is it necessary to justify art by assuming that its purpose is to provide an answer or to say something about values? Or, as Joseph Brennan asks: Why is the novel viewed as "an aesthetic doughnut from which the moral jelly, cleverly inserted and covered by the novelist, must be extracted and exposed to public view?"[12]

The literary work is not a Double-Crostic; its essence cannot be unraveled by piecing together remote clues, or by doing some shrewd guessing. A work of art has a special tone, an essential life of its own that distinguishes it from didactic writing. As a creative piece of work it can only be appreciated if it is analyzed on the terms in which it was ordered. Therefore it is the literary elements that have to be examined; the similes, the metaphors, and the images which are the aesthetic tools that frame the writer's thought about feeling.

Though moral ideas are woven into the fabric of the work and a value scheme may be implicit, moral ideas are not the objective of a work of art. For the creative writer is not seeking to write an ethical code; he is producing an aesthetic statement most often bound by the rules of his art, not his morality. If teachers utilize literature primarily for the purpose of discussing moral issues, they should make it clear that they are not teaching literature. There is of course a very real place in education for a dialectic on moral principles; but to tease out of the literary text a moral catechism is hopelessly confusing. As Brennan summarizes: "For then, not only are we talking about morals instead of literature (What is success? What is the worthwhile life?) but we cannot even discuss morals if the questions are put into these yawning categories."[13] If the literary artist chooses to write about thought, he will not use imaginative literature as his vehicle. When feeling is the root metaphor, however, the demands and restrictions that bind the aesthetic statement provide the clues to the artist's meaning.

The literary tone is not moral; it is ironic. The writer in control of the art form, and disciplined by his medium, maintains an aesthetic distance from his material and balances his judgment and his imagination. In the same way that literature appeals to and embodies both thought and emotion, the artist prepares his creation in control of the struggle between his own passions and the subject matter itself. It is this distance, this creation of a world with a different kind of reality,

---

[12] Joseph Gerard Brennan, "Morals or Literature: The Abstractive Fallacy," *English Journal*, LVIII:226, February 1969.

[13] Joseph Gerard Brennan, "Morals or Literature: The Abstractive Fallacy," *English Journal*, LVIII:228, February 1969.

this ironic tone, that permits the reader to see over the head of the situation and say, "Yes, that is a true feeling. I know because I have felt that way." Literature may grant to the reader a new perspective, and as the artist stands guard over his emotions, so too, the reader may balance the rational and the emotional. In other words, he may be led to consider, through the insights that the literature offers, whether the beliefs that he has long accepted have only emotional roots with little or no grounding in his thinking. Similarly, for those students who do not permit themselves to become emotionally involved, the passion of the artist may serve to vitalize a purely intellectual approach.

There is another limitation imposed by the nature of the readings in this anthology. Some of the selections are total works; others are excerpted pieces. The latter might best be defined as "symbolic instances," and it should be recognized that, as such, they cannot provide a complete *literary* experience. Any length less than the total work of art deprives the reader of the aesthetic design. Nevertheless these excerpts do have considerable potential for illuminating the human condition, and it is anticipated that the serious reader will avail himself of the opportunity to read the complete work.

THE POTENTIALITIES OF LITERATURE

The literary selections and the questions that precede them should encourage the reader to focus on the author's perceptions of the pathos, the humor, and the incongruities of life. Through another's vision the reader is assisted in becoming more astute in his observation of feelings, and is guided away from a simple, subjective, sentimental picture of the world. Through literature, the reader can test his feelings about life by recognizing the ambiguities that pervade his responses to fictional characters. As in life, he may condemn on the one hand, yet applaud on the other. Beneatha, the heroine of Lorraine Hansberry's play, *A Raisin in the Sun*, may arouse in the reader such contradictory feelings. But this has enormous value, not only for professional growth as a teacher, but more importantly for human growth. It is recognized that growth cannot be imposed, but it can be encouraged and subtly trained. At the very least, its ramifications and ambiguities can be explored, for "To come to grips with that full personality made up of coexistent forces that drive us to contradictory responses is to be inducted into some understanding of humanity."[14]

---

[14] Robert B. Heilman, "Literature and Growing Up," *English Journal*, XLV:308, September 1956.

With this orientation, the reader should concentrate on the evidence presented by the work itself. It is his personal responsibility to refer to the text during discussion, no matter how appealing it may be to generalize. He must allow himself to be exposed to a kind of aesthetic discipline, not unlike the kind that is imposed upon the artist by his material. For the teacher who appreciates the essential tone of this book will make every attempt to maintain distance, suspend judgment, and substantiate his opinions by reference to the literature. In this way, he is in a better position to recognize his own bias and feelings, and separate them from those of the literary artist. Examination of the textual material will be particularly helpful to those readers who are at the mercy of their emotions, and who do not usually attempt to take the writer seriously.

The introduction of black literature into teacher education gives the professional an opportunity to consider and appreciate what it feels like to be a Negro in America, and thus to be someone who has been denied access to many sources of satisfaction. By responding to the literature the teacher has the opportunity to contemplate his own "feelingness," and this may, in turn, permit him to identify with human experiences quite different from his own. The whole process is engulfed in a kind of reciprocity; the awareness of another's reality increases the sense of one's own.

SUMMARY

1.   Imaginative literature is a way of knowing and a source of stimulating one's feelings.
2.   Imaginative literature, addressed to man's sensibilities, has the potential for inspiring human concern.
3.   Imaginative literature develops thought about feeling.

Recognizing the potentialities of literature, the guidelines in this book seek to encourage in the reader and the prospective teacher the following:

1.   Awareness of one's own feelings.
2.   Awareness of the feelings of other individuals.
3.   Awareness of the essential spirit of literature which implies the recognition of what is happening, not merely the outcome.
4.   Awareness of the nature of the aesthetic mode which should preclude the necessity for exploiting literature for the purposes of teaching moral principles.
5.   Awareness of the seriousness and intent of the artist.
6.   Awareness of what it feels like to be a Negro in the American culture.

chapter 2

THE MESSAGE OF BLACK LITERATURE FOR TEACHERS

There was a time, not long ago, when the very existence of a worthwhile body of black literature was questioned. Many blacks, unaware of their own literary heritage, too often assumed that image-makers were not, and could not be black. The white-power structure, on the other hand, accepted and encouraged those images of the Negro that were essentially in harmony with their preconceptions: that is, the noble savage, the Uncle Tom, and the Aunt Jemima. Despite this long history of shrunken perceptions, the vitality of Negro art is being recognized, and there is a burgeoning awareness of the contributions of the black writer to the literary scene. Frequently utilizing his own social conditions as the catalyst for aesthetic statements, the black artist is challenging American society to consider a bold new vision. From the time of the early black writers there has been identifiable direction, though the social climate has undergone tremendous change. The seeds of self-determination on the part of the Negro were sown by men like Frederick Douglass, in 1852, who when crying out against the injustices and hollow shouts of liberty wrote,

> For it is not light that is needed, but fire; it is not the gentle shower, but thunder. We need the storm, the whirlwind, and the earthquake. The feeling of the nation must be roused; the propriety of the nation must be startled; the hypocrisy of the nation must be exposed.[1]

The roots of black pride were articulated by Jean Toomer and Claude McKay, when the latter wrote in 1919,

> If we must die—oh, let us nobly die.
> So that our precious blood may not be shed
> In vain; then even the monsters we defy
> Shall be constrained to honor us though dead![2]

---

[1] Frederick Douglass, "What to the Slave Is the Fourth of July?" *Black on Black: Commentaries by Negro Americans*, Arnold Adoff, ed. (New York: Crowell-Collier and Macmillan, Inc., 1968).

[2] Claude McKay, "If We Must Die," *Selected Poems of Claude McKay*, (New York: Bookman Associates, 1953), p. 36.

There is, currently, a trend among contemporary black writers to cele-brate the beauty of blackness and in so doing to create a black vision for America. John Oliver Killens, among others, looks to the Negro artist to lead black people on a pilgrimage back home to their Black Consciousness.[3]

The racial revolution has confronted the Negro artist with enormous pressures and demands. He is forced to consider the ancient controversy of political versus aesthetic allegiance. But the old question takes on a new dimension for those black writers who recognize that racial issues are their central concern and that their emotional vitality and talent are often permanently focused on this aspect of the social scene. Further-more, to paraphrase Doris Abramson, the Negro artist is in the unenviable position of presenting insights about black reality that frequently attack the prevailing mores and may be rejected by many Negroes and whites.[4] Artistry and social analysis need not be polar concepts. "The pertinent dichotomy is not between art and social protest but rather between creativity and mere craftsmanship, between the construct of an imagina-tively valid world and a pasteboard bloodless one."[5]

For this reason, in the selection of the material for this anthology, there has been an assumption that works of literary merit will more effectively communicate the human condition. Good writers are skilled in conveying images, pictures, and feelings. The suitability of a work does not hinge on its literary merit alone, for there are criteria to be reckoned with that are over and beyond literary considerations. It has also been deemed appropriate to include readings that, though not falling into the category of imaginative literature, are, nevertheless, powerful personal statements. The question of what teachers can learn from the experience of reading black literature has guided the choice of selections, and it is the writer's belief that the dedicated reader can get an education in at least two areas:

1.   He can become more aware and proficient in the literary way of knowing.
2.   He can become aware, through the content of black literature, of how the Negro writer views his experiences in America.

Furthermore, there is a relationship between literary awareness and con-tent awareness, for without certain skills the reader is unable to recognize

---

[3] John Oliver Killens, "The Black Writer and the Revolution," *Arts in Society,* V:397, Fall–Winter 1968.

[4] Doris Abramson, "Negro Playwrights in America," *Columbia Forum,* XII:11, Spring 1969.

[5] Edward L. Kamarck, "Art or Social Protest," *Arts in Society,* V:9, Fall–Winter 1968.

or explore those meanings which lie beneath the surface. The connection may very well be reduced to the old dichotomy between form and content, but it should be recognized that both are essential for the critical interpretation of a literary selection. Let us discuss literary awareness initially.

FOSTERING LITERARY AWARENESS

Though this book does not purport to be a manual for the development of interpretive reading abilities, those who have acquired some of the insights which feed literary understanding have greater access to the content of a selection. For both content and feeling are revealed through certain structural arrangements, and the recognition of these contributes to the reader's sensitivity to the work's implications. The tone, the symbolism, the choice of language, and a host of other elements provide clues that increase the quality of the communication between the writer and the reader. The awareness of these subtleties enables the reader better to comprehend the feelings of another, and thus derive greater pleasure from the reading experience.

It is from this vantage point that attention to literary awareness is significant for teachers. If the reader can increase his engagement with literature, through greater awareness of the artistic elements that permeate the texture of the work, then he may feel more actively involved and closer to the feelings, the values, and the attitudes of the Negro writers who are telling their story.

The guidelines that follow will direct the reader's attention to literary clues that should assist him to become aware of the feelings and meanings that lie beneath the surface. The major objective of this analysis is to make the literary work more available to the teacher.

SYMBOLS

A symbol is a concrete way of communicating an idea or concept in literature. Working by indirection, the symbol is best appreciated when the reader recognizes its suitability to the textual material. For example: The Blue Vein Society in Charles Chesnutt's short stories is a most effective symbol. On some levels, it lasts long after the details of the plot are forgotten. At first reading, "Blue Veins" has a very literal meaning: it calls to mind the picture of an individual who is white enough to show blue veins. Yet the implications of being a "Blue Vein" go far beyond physical qualities. Membership in the society demands a certain behavioral code; it connotes a specific value system and reflects a whole cluster of feelings. Taken in the context of the stories themselves, the Blue Vein Society symbolizes a group of Negroes who seek to establish a caste system among their own people. The symbol, in turn, gives rise to other symbolic patterning in the story that serves to strengthen the impact of the meanings Chesnutt wished to express.

One obvious use of symbolism is a title. It must be brief but, as in *A Raisin in the Sun*, it suggests in its succinctness, a multiplicity of meanings under one umbrella. A symbol should encourage the reader to consider why it was selected, and to reflect on its relationship to the literary work. Langston Hughes' poem suggested the symbol to Lorraine Hansberry. Both have used it differently; both have used it powerfully.

> What happens to a dream deferred?
> Doe it dry up
> like a raisin in the sun?
> Or fester like a sore—
> And then run?
> Does it stink like rotten meat?
> Or crust and sugar over—
> like a syrupy sweet?
> Maybe it just sags
> like a heavy load.
> Or does it explode?[6]

The utilization of cane, referring to sugar cane, as a symbol, provides the *leitmotif* for Jean Toomer's book. On the title page of *Cane*, the following words appear:

> Oracular,
> Redolent of fermenting syrup,
> Purple of the dusk,
> Deep-rooted cane.[7]

Throughout the book that which is embedded in the earth and in the black background of slavery and primitivism is celebrated. Freedom and identity for the Negro are associated with his recognition of the special quality of his heritage.

IMAGES

The skillful writer uses images to describe more concretely his own ideas so that the reader may be able to perceive his characters, his situations, and his meanings. He may do this by careful detailing or by

---

[6] Reprinted by permission of Alfred A. Knopf, Inc. from *The Panther and the Lash*. © Copyright 1967 by Langston Hughes.

[7] Jean Toomer, *Cane* (New York: University Place Press, 1923).

the use of figurative language. Nevertheless, the primary objective of the creative artist is not merely to assist the reader in a photographic reconstruction but, as Mary Ryan notes, "to heighten the emotional effect—to bring the reader into the story as an active participant."[8]

Images are not only the result of the ideas about life that the author wishes to explore. To paraphrase Sheila O'Connell, images are conditioned by the previous experiences of the reader, his emotional involvement with the work, and by the attitudes and experiences of the author. Frequently, characters may give "the reader the impressions that the author intended to give but also others—impressions that were never intended."[9]

From the author's perspective, images are directly related to the ideas about life that he wishes to explore. The image of the Negro as an underground man pervades much of black writing. In "The Man Who Lived Underground," Richard Wright is developing the concept of the Negro's underground existence. The story has as its setting a sewer, and the images of filth, marginality, and confinement enhance the author's construct. Therefore, he speaks of "the odor of rot," "the wet gloom glowing greenishly," "a soundless cry," "the ripples of veined water skimming over the shriveled limbs," and "the somber shadows."[10]

Similarly, *Invisible Man*, the classic by Ralph Ellison, begins "in a section of the basement that was shut off and forgotten during the nineteenth century."[11] The underlying concept of invisibility is fed by the images of hibernation and homes that are holes in the ground. In many selections in the anthology, the reader will recognize through the descriptive sensuous images the emotional implications of living in an underground world.

Related to invisibility are the images of masking, central to much Negro writing. An early poet, Paul Laurence Dunbar, develops an important poem around this image and writes of "a mask that grins and lies."[12] Similarly, Melvin S. Tolson, a contemporary poet, though using images somewhat differently in *Harlem Gallery*, masks his meaning with

---

[8] Mary Ryan, *Teaching the Novel in Paperback* (New York: Crowell-Collier and Macmillan, Inc., 1963), p. 53.

[9] Mary Sheila O'Connell, "Images of Canadians in Children's Realistic Fiction," Doctor of Education Project Report (New York: Teachers College, Columbia University, 1966), p. 35.

[10] Richard Wright, "The Man Who Lived Underground," *Eight Men* (New York: Pyramid Books, 1969).

[11] Ralph Ellison, *Invisible Man* (New York: New American Library of World Literature, Inc., 1952), p. 9.

[12] Paul Laurence Dunbar, "We Wear the Mask," *Complete Poems of Paul Laurence Dunbar* (New York: Dodd Mead & Company, Inc., 1965), p. 112.

difficult references and oblique symbols. He expresses his intent when he writes,

> Metaphors and symbols in Spiritual Blues
> have been the Negro's Manna in the Great White World.[13]

It is readily apparent how the process of masking is particularly painful to those whose very art demands that they be their "own man." Countee Cullen's image of the poet communicates this agonizing dilemma:

> Yet do I marvel at this curious thing:
> To make a poet black, and bid him sing![14]

The black writer is particularly aware of the power of images to control perception. For hundreds of years the Negro people have been "imagized" by others, but the contemporary black artist is recognizing that one of his major functions is to do the naming and the defining for his own people. This is not to say that he writes only about the black experience; the main thrust of many Negro artists is to make their writing universal. Playwright Charles Gordone, winner of the 1970 Pulitzer Prize, observes that he is an "American writer," and therefore chooses to write about the human and spiritual isolation of black and white.[15]

EXTENDED METAPHORS

The simple metaphor contributes to the forming of images by providing an abstraction with concrete qualities. Many readings in the selected literature utilize the extended metaphor, and within this device there are related symbols. Another means of identifying the extended metaphor is to think of it as "the feeling about life named through the events of the story."[16]

Invisibility, an extended metaphor pivotal in black writing, names the feeling further by explicating the symbols of invisibility, for example, masks, tombs, speechlessness, namelessness. Specific events may con-

---

[13] Melvin B. Tolson, *Harlem Gallery* (New York: Twayne Publishers, 1965), p. 91.

[14] Countee Cullen, "Yet Do I Marvel," *On These I Stand: An Anthology of the Best Poems of Countee Cullen* (New York: Harper & Row, Publishers, 1947), p. 3.

[15] Charles Gordone, "Yes, I Am a Black Playwright, But . . . ," *New York Times*, January 26, 1969, p. 11.

[16] Elizabeth Ann Parker, "A Manual for Elementary-School Teachers on Teaching Prose Fiction Reading Abilities," Doctor of Education Project Report (New York: Teachers College, Columbia University, 1966), p. 162.

tribute to the impact of the extended metaphor. In *Invisible Man*, when the white paint is being mixed, ten drops of dead-black liquid are added, but then stirred until they disappear. Another illustration of the metaphor is from an anonymous slave journal that describes how invisibility was guaranteed:

> A Negro has got no name. My father was a Ransom and he had a uncle named Hankin. If you belong to Mr. Jones and he sell you to Mr. Johnson, consequently you go by the name of your owner. Now where you got a name?[17]

To the same point, James Baldwin has written a collection of essays entitled, *Nobody Knows My Name.*

Suppression, as an extended metaphor, pervades black writing because it is a truth of the Negro experience. Its symbols and images are jails, chains, caged birds, and sewers.

The Black Christ, with its implications and rejections of the white man's Christianity, is metaphorically treated by many writers. Countee Cullen entitles a poem "Black Magdalens"; John Henrik Clarke has a story included in this anthology, "The Boy Who Painted Christ Black." Through the use of religious symbols, the black writer is able to raise questions about the white man's value schemes.

Ambiguity becomes an extended metaphor for some writers. Living in the midst of a society of contradictions, questions about appearance and reality loom large. Langston Hughes asks,

> My old man died in a fine big house.
> My ma died in a shack.
> I wonder where I'm gonna die,
> Being neither white nor black.[18]

Plot is often contrived to contribute to the feeling of ambiguity. In *Native Son*, the reader is never completely certain that Bigger has murdered Mary. Sometimes the characters are unable to distinguish the dream world from the world of here and now, as in Robert Hayden's poem "In Light Half Nightmare and Half Vision." People speak in ambiguities. The protagonist in *Invisible Man* is advised to "look beneath the surface. . . . Play the game, but don't believe in it. . . . You're hidden right out in the open."[19] That ambiguities pervade the lives of

---

[17] Julius Lester, *To Be a Slave* (New York: Dial Press, 1968), p. 77.

[18] Langston Hughes, "Cross," *Selected Poems by Langston Hughes* (New York: Alfred A. Knopf, 1967), p. 158.

[19] Ralph Ellison, *Invisible Man* (New York: New American Library, 1952), p. 137.

all men is evident. But the Negro writer presents to his audience further dimensions of the hypocrisy and duplicity that he alone inherits.

IRONY

The ironic element appears in many literary selections. It is evident in imaginative literature as well as in expository works. Irony may simply be sarcasm, or it may form the foundation for the entire mood and tone. "Irony of situation derives from a particular set of circumstances containing contradictory elements with the contradiction in some sense revealed."[20] Charles Chesnutt very often adopts an ironic tone toward his material. In "The Wife of His Youth," he satirizes the "Blue Veins," yet he endows their leader with certain positive qualities. As the author takes the aesthetic distance that the ironic tone grants, social and racial distinctions are highlighted. Chesnutt ironically juxtaposes Tennyson's classic portrayal of Queen Guinevere against a description of the little black woman in a blue calico dress. "She looked like a bit of the old plantation of life," indeed unlike "the gracious shapes of which Mr. Ryder had just been reading."[21]

Similarly, Richard Wright offers an ironic note in his description of Mrs. Dalton, Bigger's employer. "That was Mrs. Dalton," the man said, "she's blind. . . . She has a very deep interest in colored people."[22]

In many cases, writers have structured their works to point out the irony implicit in the situation. This is the approach in *A Raisin in the Sun* when Mr. Lindner, the white representative of the Clybourne Park Improvement Association, "a sort of welcoming committee," lectures the Younger family on the "matter of caring about the other fellow," and therefore suggests that for the happiness of all concerned it is better for Negro families to live in their own communities.[23]

Dramatic irony and satire are meshed in a character created by Langston Hughes—the not-so-simple Jesse B. Semple. In one of his "flights of fancy," Simple, reflecting on survival from an atomic explosion, observes:

> "Negroes are very hard to annihilate. I am a Negro—so I figure, I would live to radiate and, believe me, once charged, I will take charge."

[20] Margaret Ryan, *Teaching the Novel in Paperback* (New York: Crowell-Collier and Macmillan, Inc., 1963), p. 59.

[21] Charles Chesnutt, *The Wife of His Youth* (Ann Arbor: University of Michigan Press, 1968), p. 10.

[22] Richard Wright, *Native Son* (New York: Harper & Row, Publishers, 1966), p. 49.

[23] Lorraine Hansberry, *A Raisin in the Sun* (New York: New American Library, 1958), pp. 95, 97.

"If Negroes can survive white folks in Mississippi, said Simple,
we can survive anything."[24]

The double-edged quality of irony is apparent in this character. As
Langston Hughes observes, "Simple might be 'laughing to keep from
crying.' "[25]

The ironical situation, like the ambiguous one cited previously, seems
to have particular significance for the black artist. The Negro writer,
often anxious to foist a shock of recognition on his reader, may see in
the ironic mode a parallel to the experiences of his people. It is interesting
to note that many important works by black artists have titles with
ironic implications. Some of the more obvious ones are: *Native Son, Soul
on Ice,* "The Pocketbook Game," *The Living Is Easy, The Outsider,* and
God Is for White Folks.

FOSTERING CONTENT AWARENESS

Though no one individual or group speaks for the Negro, the reader
of black literature can acquire considerable awareness about Negro
life. He can get the feel of the Afro-American heritage, the black ghetto,
the child's school experiences, "the ethics of living Jim Crow," and "the
Negro caste system."

The thematic units in the following chapters are designed to highlight matters of import in these areas. In addition, the reader of black
literature is offered an education in Negro attitudes, for certain main
currents of feeling pervade the readings. The prospective teacher should
be aware of these feelings while recognizing their subjective nature.
Literary analysis may be a valuable assist to the reader in detecting
the author's feelings about his subject.

Imaginative literature can offer certain "truths" about the black
experience, and though this content is not verifiable in the scientific
sense, it may very well provide for some readers, the only way of coming
to grips with "the way it is."

Certain themes pervade. Over and over, many Negro writers are
expressing the depth of their resentment and the unbearable tensions
they feel. One does not necessarily have to read LeRoi Jones or Eldridge
Cleaver to recognize the pressures. In 1829, David Walker wrote, in
an *Appeal* included in this anthology:

---

[24] Langston Hughes, *The Best of Simple* (New York: Hill & Wang, 1961),
pp. 212–213.

[25] Langston Hughes, *The Best of Simple* (New York: Hill & Wang, 1961), p. 8.

> Remember Americans, that we must and shall be free and enlightened as you are, will you wait until we shall, under God, obtain our liberty by the crushing arm of power?[26]

The black artist is and has been telling us many things, and it is the responsibility of the professional to be aware of what is being said. The degree to which the individual utilizes this information is directly related to his point of departure, as well as his psychic willingness to permit the material to engage him. Nevertheless, the teacher who reads these selections might do well to consider the kind of informational awareness that this exposure provides. Though the material may not necessarily reflect the beliefs of the man on the street, it should shed light on the views held by many black writers who may prove to be in the vanguard of society.

Many black writers seek to increase the awareness of the reader to the following:

1. The contradictions between racism and the tenets of religion and democracy

Frederick Douglass in his Fourth of July speech in 1852 stated:

> What to the American slave is your Fourth of July? I answer, a day that reveals to him more than all other days of the year, the gross injustice and cruelty to which he is the constant victim. To him your celebration is a sham.[27]

As recently as July 7, 1968, James Baldwin received a standing ovation after telling the Fourth Assembly of the World Council of Churches, ". . . that Christian Churches had betrayed the black man by their identification with racist institutions in society and that in doing so they had lost touch with their own principles."[28]

2. The myths that have been perpetuated that appear to question the Negro's basic humanity by doubting his capacity for refined feelings

---

[26] *Walker's Appeal, in Four Articles: Together with a Preamble, to the Colored Citizens of the World, but in particular, and very expressly, to those of the United States of America, written in Boston, State of Massachusetts, September 28, 1829;* Milton Meltzer, ed., *In Their Own Words: A History of the American Negro, 1619–1865* (New York: Thomas Y. Crowell Company, 1964), pp. 25–27.

[27] Frederick Douglass, "What to the Slave Is the Fourth of July?", *Black on Black: Commentaries by Negro Americans,* Arnold Adoff, ed. (New York: Crowell-Collier and Macmillan, Inc., 1968).

[28] James Baldwin, as quoted in Edward B. Fiske, "Baldwin Accuses Christian Churches of Betraying Negro," *New York Times,* July 8, 1968, p. 1.

One need only read the slave journals to refute the question of refined feelings. For here we see many examples of the Negro's outcries against the emotional assaults to his being. The following excerpt is from Charles Ball's slave narrative:

> When they put us in irons to be sent to our place of confinement in the ship, the men who fastened the irons on these mothers took the children out of their hands and threw them over the side of the ship into the water. When this was done, two of the women leaped overboard after the children—the third was already confined by a chain to another woman and could not get into the water, but in struggling to disengage herself, she broke her arm and died a few days after of a fever.[29]

3.   The perspective that the attitudes of today's Negroes are not the result of a drastically revised mental set

The black man has consistently demonstrated through his activities and his writing that the condition of servitude is obnoxious and unbearable. One only has to look at the elaborate restraints imposed upon the slave to be convinced that "slaves did not become the puppets that their owners would have liked."[30] Restrictions were placed on the slave's mind as well as his body. He had no legal rights, he could not assemble, he was not allowed to learn to read, and he could attend religious services only if accompanied. Rather elaborate arrangements for a people whose desire for freedom has been so consistently questioned.

The Negro has been prepared for today's racial crisis by a long series of experiences. What is different today is his relative strength and determination in challenging the existing order. The Negro's self-confidence has been nourished by the emergence of a new nationalistic feeling among his people, in this country, as well as by the newly won freedom of several African nations.

Beginning with Frederick Douglass, the Negro deprecated "men who wanted crops without plowing up the ground,"[31] and Countee Cullen, in a more contemporary vein, has beautifully phrased the same idea:

> We shall not always plant while others reap
> The golden increment of bursting fruit,

---

[29] Charles Ball, as quoted in Julius Lester, *To Be a Slave* (New York: Dial Press, 1968), p. 25.

[30] Ball, p. 102.

[31] Frederick Douglass, West India Emancipation Speech, August 1857, as quoted in *Black on Black: Commentaries by Negro Americans*, Arnold Adoff, ed. (New York: Crowell-Collier and Macmillan, Inc., 1968), p. 1.

> Not always countenance, abject and mute,
> That lesser men should hold their brothers cheap.[32]

4.   The right of the Negro people to self-determination with its implications for taking hold of decision-making and image-making powers that presume a rightful share of the "action"

Those who claim to be the spokesmen for the black people are themselves divided as to how this objective is to be accomplished. For there are many vocal groups who do not wish to be "integrated into a burning house"; while others feel that the Negro must become an essential current in the American mainstream. Whatever the prospects, change is the only certainty, for the Negro is not likely to settle back into his old role. No longer apologetic, the blacks, after a long underground experience, are demanding their right to a place in the sun— their right to create their own images. There is a "New Negro," in the prophetic words of Alain Locke, with which the white man must negotiate. As has been noted, this is not a contemporary idea, for "Black Power may be simply translating into the American idiom what the English talked about years ago, namely self-determination."[33]

When the literary artist writes to break free from his chains, he is seeking a new attitude, a new sense of self. The motto of the Southern Christian Leadership Conference states the position simply:

> Black is beautiful,
> And it's so beautiful
> To be black.

Similarly, John Oliver Killens in exploring the dimensions of racial equality writes, "I work for the day when my people will be free of the racist pressures to be *white like you*; a day when 'good hair' and 'high yaller' and bleaching cream and hair-straighteners will be obsolete."[34]

The relationship between manhood and self-determination has been recognized by many spokesmen. Ossie Davis in eulogizing Malcolm X wrote:

> He would make you angry as hell, but he would also make
> you proud. It was impossible to remain defensive and apologetic

---

[32] Countee Cullen, "From the Dark Tower," *On These I Stand* (New York: Harper & Row, Publishers, 1947), p. 47.

[33] James Baldwin, as quoted in Edward B. Fiske, "Baldwin Accuses Christian Churches of Betraying Negro," *New York Times*, July 8, 1968, p. 23.

[34] John Oliver Killens, "Explanation of the Black Psyche," *Black on Black: Commentaries by Negro Americans*, Arnold Adoff, ed. (New York: The Macmillan Company, 1968), p. 143.

about being a Negro in his presence. He wouldn't let you. And you always left his presence with the sneaky suspicion that maybe, after all, you were a man![35]

This concept was propounded much earlier with the publication in 1903 of *The Souls of Black Folk*. In this moving and scholarly study of his people, W. E. B. DuBois says: "The history of the American Negro is the history of this strife—this longing to attain self-conscious manhood, to merge his double self into a better and truer self."[36]

The new social posture, as exemplified in the works of many writers, celebrates the beauty of blackness. This is an integral part of the process of positive self-identification.

> Oppressed people cannot remain oppressed forever. The yearning for freedom eventually manifests itself, and that is what has happened to the American Negro. Something within has reminded him of his birthright of freedom, and something without has reminded him that it can be gained.[37]

THE MEANING OF "SOUL"

In essence, could it be that in exploring the content of the black experience we are considering the meaning of "soul"? DuBois eloquently spoke of three Negro gifts to America ". . . a gift of story and song . . . the gift of sweat and brow to beat back the wilderness . . . the third, a gift of the Spirit."[38] This "gift of the Spirit" may be a clue to the meaning of soul as used today. It may not be essential accurately to define the term; "caneness" with its implications of earthiness, may be another way of saying the same thing. What is significant is the concept. " 'Soul,' no matter how many ways you define it, expresses the growing Negro reaction against oppression and rejection on one hand, and against assimilation or absorption on the other."[39]

The selections in this anthology should be viewed as "gifts of the Spirit" from the black writer. For it is through these distinctive, artistic, and spiritual contributions that the Negro culture may exercise its most

---

[35] Ossie Davis, "On Malcolm X," in Malcolm X, *The Autobiography of Malcolm X* (New York: Grove Press, 1966), p. 458.

[36] W. E. Burghardt DuBois, *The Souls of Black Folk* (Greenwich, Conn.: Fawcett Publications, 1968), p. 17.

[37] Martin Luther King, "Letter from Birmingham Jail," *Black on Black: Commentaries by Negro Americans*, Arnold Adoff, ed. (New York: Crowell-Collier and Macmillan, Inc., 1968), p. 185.

[38] W. E. Burghardt DuBois, *The Souls of Black Folk* (Greenwich, Conn.: Fawcett Publications, 1968), pp. 189–190.

[39] Dorothy Sterling, "The Soul of Learning," *The English Journal*, CLVII:180, February 1968.

potent influence on the American consciousness. Yet the reader, too, has an obligation. Frequently the literature is a brutal attack on accepted value systems and behavioral patterns. But it is important that the reader not be "morally intimidated," as David Littlejohn observes. "It is all too easy to grovel, to cringe beneath the lash . . . and then discrimination and moral sensibility is paralyzed."[40] The American Negro experience is painful for the author and for the reader because it demands an honest self-examination. However, the very best writing, whether it be by men of color or not, does make significant statements about the emotional experiences of all humanity.

ORGANIZING READINGS
IN BLACK LITERATURE

There is surely no one best way to organize one's reading experiences in this field. No matter what organizational pattern is selected, the underlying challenge is to make the literature available by engaging the intellectual and emotional responses of the reader. If education seeks to counter the charges of "irrelevancy," and seeks to help the student to discover what is meaningful for him, then the learning process must be viewed as the ebb and flow of emotional and intellectual interaction. Literary learning may be looked at in this way; for the writer has the power to appeal to the total human being. Maxine Greene, recognizing the potentialities of literature for relating learning and self-understanding states that ". . . learning how to engage with works of literature entails a process of patterning the materials of the self."[41] It would appear that this is a particularly vital consideration for educators.

When we want to direct attention to an appreciation of human experience and values, thematic units may provide a helpful framework. The teacher or the student presented with a large group of readings, who is unfamiliar with the field of black literature, needs certain procedures for focusing the meanings of the materials. Without some conceptual framework on which the reader can anchor his ideas, many learnings may be lost.

The thematic approach, as an organizing device, emerged from the reading materials. There was an intersecting of ideas and a commonality of thinking among some writers. Among others, the relationship existed in terms of the subject matter that pervaded their writing. John

---

[40] David Littlejohn, *Black on White: A Critical Survey of Writing by Negro Americans* (New York: Grossman Publishers, 1966), p. 19.

[41] Maxine Greene, "Against Invisibility: English for the Probing Black and White Young," *Negro American Literature Forum*, II:39, Fall 1968.

Brown, Frederick Douglass, and Melvin Tolson all write about the experience of slavery. However, they do so in different genres, with stress on distinct literary moods and with attention to varying elements of the writer's craft. Therefore, it seemed helpful to develop a structure around which similar information could be grouped.

One caution should be kept in mind. The guidelines in the introductory chapters and the questions at the conclusion of each unit strive to limit unnecessary generalizing by encouraging close adherence to the author's text. For certainly, one of the gravest injustices perpetuated on the Negro has been the tendency to stereotype his reactions and behavior. Through this simplistic approach, man fed his own need to impose order—a quality very often, too deeply ingrained in the human psyche.

In the analysis of black literature, it is important to proceed cautiously. For though black artists are being anthologized with greater frequency, and the paperback market has recognized the economic potential of Negro writing, there is still a considerable degree of inequity paraded under the guise of order.

> If sophisticated white Americans (and Europeans) have out-grown the singin'-and-dancin'-fool concept of the Negro, they have not learned a great deal in the process if they now rush to adopt each Negro novelist's new agonized, hate-filled hero as the norm.[42]

Though there may be a certain vortex of experiences among many Negroes, we cannot presume without careful qualification to define the Negro on the basis of a literary sampling. For this in essence is denying the distinctiveness, not only of the individual black man, but more specifically of the black writer. In a sense, we are categorizing and thus negating the very wellspring of his art—his own creative responses to personal experience.

While organizational patterns have many assets and are often conducive to good teaching situations, they tend to be restricting. For this reason, supplementary references are provided for each unit so that the teacher, on his own, may explore the body of Negro literature. The reader may choose to follow the sequence in the anthology, but should recognize that there is nothing sacred about the order. The units are independent entities and, therefore, the person who finds only one chapter of the thematic units relevant for his work may conveniently extract this material. For those, however, who choose to work with the complete anthology, it is anticipated that they will discover the many relationships that exist among the units. In the last analysis, nevertheless,

---

[42] David Littlejohn, *Black on White: A Critical Survey of Writing by American Negroes* (New York: Grossman Publishers, 1966), p. 157.

the organizational structure disappears when the reader becomes im-
mersed in a work of art. In the act of reading, the receptor is turned
inward and is not aware of categories.

The major areas that have been selected for the anthology were
developed to direct the reader's attention to the content of the literature
in the following thematic units:

The Black Heritage

The Urban Slum

Social Factors of Influence

Psychological Responses

School Experiences and Educational Attainment

In order to encourage the teacher who utilizes this book to think
independently and to contemplate the vast quantity of black literature,
certain procedures and sources of literature, both for children and
adults, will be suggested. For as Negro writers of the past are discovered
and young blacks turn toward the literary art as a means of self-expression, the teacher may find himself in a literary fog. Within a year or
two, the amount of material will have multiplied in this burgeoning
field, and the reader may seek to augment the anthology of readings.
How does he go about finding what he wants? What guideposts does
he establish? It is the purpose of the following chapter to provide
guidance in these matters.

chapter 3

ASSISTING THE TEACHER IN THE SELECTION OF BLACK LITERATURE

This book, if properly used, will not serve as a restrictive device; rather, it is anticipated that its guidelines and suggestions will draw attention to the wealth and potentialities of Negro writing for teacher education. An assumption is made that prospective teachers will need some assistance in the selection and use of literary materials, for their backgrounds would more likely include comprehensive education in the social sciences. Since literature is infrequently included in teacher-training programs, except for those who plan careers in English, this chapter outlines some sources and criteria suggested by the nature of the literary art that may prove fruitful in helping prospective teachers, both black and white, come closer to appreciating the Negro experience in America. Black literature can serve as a fertile field for building understanding and respect among peoples of different ethnic backgrounds.

SOURCES FOR THE SELECTION OF LITERATURE

The teacher can turn to a number of publications which provide information on literature by and about Negroes. *The Negro in Print*, available in most libraries, is published six times a year by The Negro Bibliographic and Research Center, Inc. in Washington, D.C. Two other bibliographies worthy of mention are *The Negro in American Literature* by Abraham Chapman, and *The Negro in America: A Bibliography*, compiled by Elizabeth W. Miller. Chapman's work is particularly helpful because it provides a literary history of the American Negro, as well as a bibliography divided into twenty categories. Elizabeth Miller's work is considerably less comprehensive in the field of the literary arts. A selective but extremely valuable bibliography is included in *Dark Symphony*, edited by James A. Emanuel and Theodore L. Gross.

On the current publishing scene, anthologies seem to command attention and offer the reader a selection of literary materials of many categories of writing. A review of the anthologies dating back to Alain Locke's *The New Negro*, published originally in 1925, and Sterling Brown, Arthur P. Davis, and Ulysses Lee's landmark anthology *The Negro Caravan*, will suggest many literary works. More contemporary collections will be helpful, but the bias and particular purposes of the anthologist should be recognized. There is considerable duplication in many anthologies; however this core of unanimity may be helpful to the reader in the choice of selections.

ANTHOLOGIES

Among the best of the modern anthologies is Abraham Chapman's *Black Voices*. In this varied collection the reader is exposed to fiction, autobiography, poetry, and literary criticism. It is a vitally exciting group of readings. Similarly, *Black on Black*, edited by Arnold Adoff, offers persuasive literature dating back to 1852 and develops themes that are current today. The illustration of the continuity of thinking among the Negroes of yesterday and today is a significant content learning for teachers.

In Their Own Words, a three-volume anthology edited by Milton Meltzer, provides excerpts that date back to pre-Civil War days and continues to the present time. Though the collection is helpful in compiling early works, for the most part, the selections are too brief. More effective is Julius Lester's *To Be a Slave*, a collection of moving narratives, faithfully reproduced, with additional commentary by the editor. The parallels in the life of the black man today are very obvious, and provide the reader with an appreciation of the impact of myth-making on Negro literature.

Dark Symphony, mentioned previously for its bibliography, is equally comprehensive in its excerpts from black literature. It begins with Douglass' famous Fourth of July Speech, and ranges through the works of the most contemporary poets and critics.

Black Fire, a compilation of the writing of some seventy Afro-Americans, edited by LeRoi Jones and Larry Neal, is frankly polemical in intent and expresses the point of view of many contemporary black writers.

Some anthologies utilize a specific literary form as their central focus. Two good references for the short story are *American Negro Short Stories*, edited by John Henrik Clarke, and *The Best Short Stories of Negro Writers*, edited by Langston Hughes. For new trends in Negro poetry, *Beyond the Blues*, by Rosey E. Pool, is an exciting collection. A definitive anthology of Negro poetry from 1746 through 1949 entitled *The Poetry of the Negro* has been edited by Langston Hughes and Arna Bontemps.

The teacher may wish to consider collections of the works of a single writer. Notable among these is *Annie Allen* by Gwendolyn Brooks, which won the Pulitzer Prize for poetry in 1950. *On These I Stand*, by Countee Cullen, is a selection by the poet himself. *The Best of Simple*, by Langston Hughes, is a group of sketches culled from three other volumes about this famous Negro folk character.

LITERARY CRITICISM

The teacher may wish to turn to any one of a number of books that critically analyze the literary expression of the American Negro. *The Negro Novel in America* by Robert A. Bone is particularly helpful as a critical study, and serves to highlight the social as well as the literary ramifications of a particular work. This study also provides valuable insights into the prevailing concepts of assimilation and Negro Nationalism, pivotal for appreciating much thematic material in Negro literature.

A broader range of Negro literary expression is covered in *Black on White: A Critical Survey of Writing by American Negroes* by David Littlejohn. The author reviews the essay, the novel, poetry, and the drama, and suggests how the reading of this literature may provide a vast education in the history and folklore of the American Negro. Though Dr. Bone's work provides a greater analysis-in-depth, Littlejohn's book is helpful in highlighting, once again, the unique problems surrounding racial identity, and the black writer's ability to transcend and make a statement meaningful for all men.

Two works of literary criticism by black writers are particularly valuable: *Negro Voices in American Fiction*, by Hugh M. Gloster, and *To Make a Poet Black*, by Saunders J. Redding.

Herbert Hill's *Anger, and Beyond: The Negro Writer in the United States*, is an historical critical survey of Negro writing examined by different critics. It is an eminently readable collection and suggests a variety of perspectives for the examination of black writing. The introduction by the author is particularly noteworthy, as is the essay by Arna Bontemps on the Negro Renaissance.

PERIODICALS

The teacher may turn to periodical offerings that provide bibliographic as well as critical analysis of trends and approaches to the study of black literature. *The Education Index* and *The Reader's Guide to Periodical Literature* offer the teacher many current references.

It should be noted that with the current interest in Negro culture many of the more popular periodicals contain pertinent articles. However, there are a few publications that emphasize the literary scene and usually include a number of articles on the relevancy of black literature for education. These are listed below:

Afro-American Studies: An Interdisciplinary Journal

This publication is aimed at filling professional needs and provides a forum for the communication of methods, curricula, and programs in the field.

Amistad

A new quarterly magazine. It is the first periodical to be devoted to black writing and is designed for college courses as well as for the interested general reader who wishes to know and understand "the basis, workings, and implications of Western (especially American) culture and civilization, past and present."

The Crisis

A publication of the National Association for the Advancement of Colored People.

Freedomways: A Quarterly of the Negro Freedom Movement

This publication has a decidedly literary emphasis. Book reviews are included in every issue and a number of articles are devoted to analyzing the contributions of Negro authors.

Journal of Negro Education

A publication that frequently contains a number of articles on the relevancy of Black Studies for education. It is published by Howard University.

Negro American Literature Forum

This journal is published by the School of Education of Indiana State University and is, to the writer's knowledge, the only periodical of its kind to emanate from a School of Education.

Black World

A monthly publication that has original poetry and fiction, as well as articles on the many issues that surround the black consciousness.

BLACK LITERATURE FOR CHILDREN

If the teacher seeks to become acquainted with children's literature written by Negro authors, the following sources are helpful. *We Build Together*, in its third revision, edited by Charlemae Rollins, is the most comprehensive bibliography of Negro life and literature for elementary and high school students. The introduction by Charlemae Rollins and Marion Edman is helpful in analyzing the current trends in literature for youngsters.

Though not nearly as complete, and limited to elementary grades, Minnie W. Koblitz's *The Negro in Schoolroom Literature* is an annotated guide to books that contribute to the understanding of the Afro-American heritage. The bibliography contains over 250 books in nine different categories.

A shorter and much earlier bibliography should be noted: Augusta Baker's *Books about Negro Life for Children*. Since the publication of this listing, the children's literature market has been flooded with new interracial trade books, but Mrs. Baker's introduction is still very helpful in suggesting criteria for judging books about the Negro.

In the general area of human relations, Muriel Crosby's *Reading Ladders for Human Relations* offers an annotated list of books for teachers to use with elementary school children. The theme of each book is noted.

The most recent and by far the most comprehensive bibliography in this field is *A Bibliography of Negro History and Culture for Young Readers*, edited by Miles M. Jackson, Jr. Spencer Shaw has written an introduction that is both informative and inspiring.

Though limited by intent to use in the high school, Barbara Dodds' *Negro Literature for High School Students* includes a few books of which both elementary and college teachers should be aware. The historical survey suggests many adult-level books that might be welcome additions to a teacher's reading list. The thematic units, however, are too limited in scope and treatment.

Hopefully, many opportunities will arise for the teacher to include children's literature by and about the Negro in his course of study. However, to paraphrase Emma Gelders Sterne's comment, bibliographies such as the ones cited will be unnecessary when skin color becomes irrelevant on the American and world scenes.

The bibliographies, anthologies, and critiques that have been cited by no means exhaust the field. What is most apparent is the wealth of available material written by the Negro that remains relatively unknown to both black and white educators. Furthermore, there still remains a tremendous need for teaching aids and resource materials to be developed that might provide assistance for working in this field.

THE ESTABLISHMENT OF CRITERIA

It has been stressed that how effectively a piece of literature illuminates and provides insights into another's feelings is often related to aesthetic and literary factors. Aesthetically distinctive literature will also provide a better total picture in the domain of truth. Too often, in the area of race relations, this matter of "truthfulness" becomes an individual value judgment. To avoid stereotyping and to expand the reader's horizons, every effort should be made to lay the groundwork for choosing selections that present the broad spectrum of Negro life in an honest way.

One of the objectives in using literature in teacher education is to expand the professional's awareness of the black experience in America. However, though aesthetic standards are very important, they should not provide the only basis for evaluating a selection. In the choice of his readings, the professional might recall the potentialities of literature detailed in Chapter I, and seek out those materials that encourage greater awareness of the feelings of others through empathy and identification.

The selection should suggest many avenues for discussion. Rather than the presentation of solutions, the reading should generate thinking.

One cannot read black literature without confronting antagonism and resentments; but the author's presentation should not intimidate or blunt the judgment of the reader. Though the truth may be disturbing, it is important that the selection does not "turn the reader off." A highly hostile or alienated work may provoke and disturb in such a way that the reader will lose his courage in facing himself. Arthur Jersild has observed that, "In order to achieve understanding of self, one must have the courage to seek it, and the humility to accept what one may find."[1]

The selection should present the ambiguities of life in a helpful way. That is to say: that the beautiful community does not always produce beautiful people, and that difficult and trying circumstances often develop not only good people but incomparable heroes, who come from awful darkness but bring sweetness and light.[2]

The selection should provide a truthful account of "the way it is" by the recognition of the social and psychological factors involved in behavior and communication. Another assist to truthfulness is provided when there is acknowledgment of the effects of traditional and historical commitments on personality development.

Reading book reviews in magazines and newspapers, as well as browsing in libraries, will bring to light many interesting additions to this anthology. The teacher in the New York area should consult the superb Schomburg Collection of the Countee Cullen Regional Branch of the New York Public Library. The Trevor Arnett Library at Atlanta University also has an extensive collection, as well as the Hall Branch of the Chicago Public Library.

In conclusion, it should be recognized that to a large extent Negro

---

[1] Arthur T. Jersild, *When Teachers Face Themselves* (New York: Teachers College Press, 1955), p. 83.

[2] Albert Murray, "Something Different, Something More," *Anger, and Beyond: The Negro Writer in the United States*, Herbert Hill, ed. (New York: Harper & Row, Publishers, 1968), p. 121.

culture in America has survived because of the creative efforts of the the black artist who can play a powerful role in defining the cultural nationalism of the Negro. Harold Cruse observes that the Negro has been a mere commodity on the cultural market and that it is the Negro creative intellectual, if he can master a literary and cultural critique of his own, who has the potential for rehabilitating the Negro image in the eyes of the world.[3]

The very conception of this book gives further credence to the role of the Negro writer as image maker. It is anticipated that the literature in the anthology and those readings that will be selected by individual teachers will not widen the gulf between white and black, but rather will encourage mutual respect by identifying and subsequently understanding the separating myths.

SUGGESTED SOURCES

ADOFF, ARNOLD, ed. *Black on Black: Commentaries by Negro Americans* (New York: Crowell-Collier and Macmillan, Inc., 1968).

BAKER, AUGUST. *Books about Negro Life for Children*, Rev. Ed. (New York: The New York Public Library, 1961).

BONE, ROBERT A. *The Negro Novel in America*, Rev. Ed. (New Haven: Yale University Press, 1966).

BROOKS, GWENDOLYN. *Annie Allen* (New York: Harper & Row, Publishers, 1949).

BROWN, STERLING, ARTHUR B. DAVIS, AND ULYSSES LEE, eds. *The Negro Caravan* (New York: The Dryden Press, 1943).

CHAPMAN, ABRAHAM, ed. *Black Voices* (New York: New American Library, 1968).

CHAPMAN, ABRAHAM, ed. *The Negro in American Literature* and *A Bibliography of Literature by and about Negro Americans* (Oshkosh: Wisconsin State University, 1966).

CLARKE, JOHN HENRIK, ed. *American Negro Short Stories* (New York: Hill & Wang, Inc., 1966).

CROSBY, MURIEL, ed. *Reading Ladders for Human Relations*, 4th Ed. (Washington, D.C.: American Council on Education, 1963).

CULLEN, COUNTEE. *On These I Stand: An Anthology of the Best Poems of Countee Cullen* (New York: Harper & Row, Publishers, 1947).

DODDS, BARBARA. *Negro Literature for High School Students* (Champaign, Ill.: National Council of Teachers of English, 1968).

EMANUEL, JAMES A., AND THEODORE L. GROSS, eds. *Dark Symphony: Negro Literature in America* (New York: Free Press, 1968).

---

[3] Harold Cruse, *The Crisis of the Negro Intellectual* (New York: William Morrow and Company, 1967), p. 518.

GLOSTER, HUGH. *Negro Voices in American Fiction* (New York: Russell and Russell, 1965).

HILL, HERBERT, ed. *Anger, and Beyond: The Negro Writer in the United States* (New York: Harper & Row, Publishers, 1968).

HUGHES, LANGSTON. *The Best of Simple* (New York: Hill & Wang, 1961).

HUGHES, LANGSTON, ed. *The Best Short Stories by Negro Writers, An Anthology from 1899 to the Present* (Boston: Little, Brown and Company, 1967).

HUGHES, LANGSTON, AND ARNA BONTEMPS, eds. *The Poetry of the Negro, 1746–1949* (Garden City, N.Y.: Doubleday and Company, Inc., 1949).

JACKSON, MILES M., JR., ed. *A Bibliography of Negro History and Culture for Young Readers.* (Pittsburgh, Pa.: University of Pittsburgh Press, 1960, for Atlanta University).

JONES, LEROI, AND LARRY NEAL, eds. *Black Fire: An Anthology of Afro-American Writing* (New York: William Morrow and Company, 1968).

KOBLITZ, MINNIE W. *The Negro in Schoolroom Literature: Resource Materials for the Teacher of Kindergarten Through Sixth Grade* (New York: Center for Urban Education, 1966).

LESTER, JULIUS. *To Be a Slave* (New York: Dial Press, 1968).

LITTLEJOHN, DAVID. *Black on White: A Critical Survey of Writing by American Negroes* (New York: Grossman Publishers, 1966).

LOCKE, ALAIN, ed. *The New Negro, an Interpretation* (New York: Johnson Reprint Corporation, 1968).

MELTZER, MILTON, ed. *In Their Own Words: A History of the American Negro: 1619–1865* (New York: Thomas Y. Crowell Company, 1963), 3 vol.

MILLER, ELIZABETH, comp. *The Negro in America: A Bibliography* (Cambridge: Harvard University Press, 1966).

POOL, ROSEY E., ed. *Beyond the Blues: New Poems by American Negroes* (London: Headley Brothers Ltd., 1962).

REDDING, SAUNDERS. *To Make A Poet Black* (Chapel Hill: University of North Carolina Press, 1939).

ROLLINS, CHARLEMAE, ed. *We Build Together: A Reader's Guide to Negro Life and Literature for Elementary and High School Use* (Champaign, Ill.: National Council for Teachers of English, 1967).

READINGS IN BLACK LITERATURE

SLAVERY
John Brown, *Slave Life in Georgia* (1855)
Frederick Douglass, *Narrative of the Life of Frederick Douglass* (1845); "What
    to the Slave Is the Fourth of July?" (1852)
Gustavus Vassa, *The Interesting Narrative of the Life of Olaudah Equiano or
    Gustavus Vassa the African* (1791)
David Walker, *Walker's Appeal* (1829)

POST–CIVIL WAR
Charles Chesnutt, "The Sheriff's Children" (1899); "The Wife of His Youth"
    (1899)
Paul Laurence Dunbar, "We Wear the Mask" (1895)

THE NEGRO RENAISSANCE
Countee Cullen, "Yet Do I Marvel" (1925)
Claude McKay, "If We Must Die" (1919); "The White House" (1922)

THE CONTEMPORARY SCENE
James Baldwin, *Go Tell It on the Mountain* (1952)
Alice Childress, "The Pocketbook Game" (1956)
John Henrik Clarke, "The Boy Who Painted Christ Black" (1940)
Eldridge Cleaver, *Soul on Ice* (1968)
Ralph Ellison, *Invisible Man* (1947)
Lorraine Hansberry, *A Raisin in the Sun* (1959)
Langston Hughes, "Lenox Avenue Mural" (1951); "One Friday Morning"
    (1941); *Tales of Simple* (1965)
LeRoi Jones, "A Poem for Black Hearts" (1965)
Stephen M. Joseph, editor, *The Me Nobody Knows: Children's Voices from the
    Ghetto* (1969)
Malcolm X, *The Autobiography of Malcolm X* (1964)
Ted Poston, "The Revolt of the Evil Fairies" (1941)
M. B. Tolson, "Dark Symphony" (1944); *Harlem Gallery* (1965)
Margaret Walker, "For My People" (1942)
Richard Wright, *Black Boy* (1937); *Native Son* (1940); "The Man Who Lived
    Underground" (1942)

chapter 4

THE BLACK HERITAGE

There are two ways in which a man can be enslaved.

One is through force. He can be penned behind fences, guarded constantly, punished severely for breaking the slightest rule, and made to live in constant fear.

The second is to teach him to think that his own best interests will be served by doing what his master wishes him to do. He can be taught that he is inferior and that only through slavery will he eventually rise to the "level" of his master.

The southern slave owner used both.

—Julius Lester,
To Be a Slave

The readings in this section seek to sensitize the teacher to the American Negro's quest for identity. Confronting the cry of anguish as Negro writers describe how they were stripped of their African traditions, separated from their families, and sold into bondage, the reader has an encounter with the *feelings* of the black man. The implications of these early experiences for the development of an identity are placed in bold relief when reading the literature of the past.

Ambivalence has characterized the Negro's attitude toward his own background, and he has been forced to view himself from a dual perspective. Many ask, along with the poet, Countee Cullen, "What is Africa to me?" For this "mother country" does not attract a large number of blacks. Most Negroes, their roots firmly planted in native soil, see themselves as Americans who are determined to play a role in deciding the future of their country. Nationalism, a term meaning many things, serves as a kind of umbrella. There are those who would return to Africa, others who seek to establish Negro enclaves within the United States, and another group who see political power and community control as a resolution. Likewise, assimilation has many adherents who feel that they can become an integral part of the mainstream while maintaining their own identity. The appreciation of the questions surrounding assimilation and nationalism are pivotal to developing an understanding of the black experience in America.

Contemporary Negro leaders recognize the repercussions of feeling like an "Invisible Man" yet being born a "Native Son." There has been a concerted attempt in recent years to develop the Negro's identification with the vigorous, successful black man in many fields. Negro authors have a particularly significant role to play in this regard, for they can help to create the images and myths with which their people can identify.

The struggle of the Negro people has become a critical issue in America. The readings that are offered suggest the continuity as well as the strength of that struggle. In essence, it is a search for identity which encompasses the African heritage, the experience of slavery, and the distinctive contributions of the Negro to American culture. With intent to neither intimidate the white reader nor to patronize the Negro reader, the following selections, by black writers, are presented to provide an accurate account of the black man's experience in America and his attempt to extract from that heritage a sense of dignity which can transcend racial values and celebrate the universal elements in human behavior.

I.   The readings in this chapter were selected for their relevance to the unit topic, *Black Heritage*. Some of the subthemes which are given voice in the selections are:

1.   The African heritage
2.   Slavery
3.   The plantation tradition
4.   Conditions of living in the South
5.   Assimilation versus nationalism

II.   The following readings are suggested as supplementary references for the unit on *The Black Heritage*:

1.   Countee Cullen, "Heritage (For Harold Jackman)," Arna Bontemps, ed., *American Negro Poetry* (New York: Hill & Wang, 1968), pp. 83–86. (poetry)
2.   W. E. Burghardt DuBois, *The Souls of Black Folk* (Greenwich, Conn.: Fawcett Publications, 1968). (social commentary)
3.   Robert Hayden, "Middle Passage," Abraham Chapman, ed., *Black Voices* (New York: New American Library, 1968), pp. 444–449. (poetry)
4.   Julius Lester, *To Be a Slave* (New York: Dial Press, 1968). (social commentary)
5.   Jean Toomer, "Song of the Son," Abraham Chapman, ed., *Black Voices* (New York: New American Library, 1968), p. 377. (poetry)

QUESTIONS FOR DISCUSSION

1.   What do these selections suggest about the historical continuity of feelings and attitudes among Negroes from the days of slavery to the present time?

2.   What value patterns and perceptions come into conflict on a slave ship?

3.   What were the critical moments of decision for Frederick Douglass?

4.   In Douglass' narrative, what did you note about the treatment and behavior of slaves in the city as compared with those in the country?

5.   After reading the selections in this unit, what is your interpretation of the meaning of "living Jim Crow?"

The Life of Olaudah Equiano

GUSTAVUS VASSA

From The Interesting Narrative of the Life of Olaudah Equiano, or Gustavus Vassa the African. Written by Himself, 1791.

The first object which saluted my eyes when I arrived on the coast was the sea, and a slave ship, which was then riding at anchor, and waiting for its cargo. These filled me with astonishment, which was soon connected with terror, when I was carried on board. I was immediately handled, and tossed up to see if I were sound, by some of the crew; and I was now persuaded that I had gotten into a world of bad spirits, and that they were going to kill me. Their complexions too differing so much from ours, their long hair, and the language they spoke (which was very different from any I had ever heard), united to confirm me in this belief. Indeed, such were the horrors of my views and fears at the moment, that, if ten thousand worlds had been my own, I would have freely parted with them all to have exchanged my condition with that of the meanest slave in my own country. When I looked round the ship too and saw a large furnace or copper boiling, and a multitude of black people of every description chained together, every one of their countenances expressing dejection and horror, I no longer doubted of my fate; and quite overpowered with horror and anguish, I fell motionless on the deck and fainted. When I recovered a little, I found some black people about me, who I believed were some of those who had brought me on board, and had been receiving their pay; they talked to me in order to cheer me, but all in vain. I asked them if I were not to be eaten by those white men with horrible looks, red faces, and long hair. They told me I was not: and one of the crew brought me a small portion of spirituous liquor in a wine glass; but being afraid of him, I would not take it out of his hand. One of the blacks therefore took it from him and gave it to me, and I took a little down my palate, which, instead of reviving me, as they thought it would, threw me into the greatest consternation at the strange feeling it produced, having never tasted any such liquor before. Soon after this, the blacks who brought me on board went off, and left me abandoned to despair. I now saw myself deprived of all chance of returning to my native country, or even the least glimpse of hope of gaining the shore, which I now considered as friendly; and I even wished for my former slavery in preference to my present situation, which was filled with horrors of every kind, still heightened by my ignorance of what I was to undergo. I was not long suffered to indulge my grief; I was soon put down under the decks, and there I received such a salutation in my nostrils as I had never experienced in my life: so that with the loathsomeness of the stench and crying together, I became so sick and low that I was not able to eat, nor had I the least desire to taste anything.

I now wished for the last friend, death, to relieve me; but soon, to my grief, two of the white men offered me eatables; and, on my refusing to eat, one of them held me fast by the hands, and laid me across, I think, the windlass, and tied my feet, while the other flogged me severely. I had never experienced anything of this kind before; and although, not being used to the water, I naturally feared that element the first time I saw it, yet nevertheless, could I have got over the nettings, I would have jumped over the side, but I could not; and, besides, the crew used to watch us very closely who were not chained down to the decks, lest we should leap into the water: and I have seen some of these poor African prisoners most severely cut for attempting to do so, and hourly whipped for not eating. This indeed was often the case with myself. In a little time after, amongst the poor chained men, I found some of my own nation, which in a small degree gave ease to my mind. I inquired of these what was to be done with us? They gave me to understand we were to be carried to these white people's country to work for them. I then was a little revived, and thought, if it were no worse than working, my situation was not so desperate: but still I feared I should be put to death, the white people looked and acted, as I thought, in so savage a manner; for I had never seen among any people such instances of brutal cruelty; and this was not only shewn towards us blacks, but also to some of the whites themselves. One white man in particular I saw, when we were permitted to be on deck, flogged so unmercifully with a large rope near the foremast, that he died in consequence of it; and they tossed him over the side as they would have done a brute. This made me fear these people the more; and I expected nothing less than to be treated in the same manner. I could not help expressing my fears and apprehensions to some of my countrymen; I asked them if these people had no country, but lived in this hollow place (the ship)? They told me they did not, but came from a distant one. 'Then' said I, 'how comes it in all our country we never heard of them?' They told me because they lived so very far off. I then asked where were their women? Had they any like themselves? I was told they had: 'And why,' said I, 'do we not see them?' They answered, because they were left behind. I asked how the vessel could go? They told me they could not tell; but that there were cloth put upon the masts by the help of the ropes I saw, and then the vessel went on; and the white men had some spell or magic they put in the water when they liked in order to stop the vessel. I was exceedingly amazed at this account, and really thought they were spirits. I therefore wished much to be from amongst them, for I expected they would sacrifice me: but my wishes were vain; for we were so quartered that it was impossible for any of us to make our escape. While we stayed on the coast I was mostly on deck; and one day, to my great astonishment, I saw one of these vessels coming in with the sails up. As soon as the whites saw it, they gave a great shout, at which we were amazed; and the more so as the vessel appeared larger by approaching nearer. At last she came to an anchor in my sight, and when the anchor was let go I and my countrymen who saw it were lost in astonishment to observe the vessel stop; and were now convinced it was done by magic. Soon after this the other ship got her boats out, and they came on board of us, and the people of both ships seemed very glad to see each other. Several of the strangers also shook hands with us, black people, and made motions with their hands, signifying I suppose, we were to go to their country; but we did not understand them. At last, when the ship we were in had got in all her cargo, they made ready with many fearful noises, and we were all put under deck, so that we could not see how they managed the vessel. But this disappointment was the least of my sorrow. The stench of the hold, *while we were on the coast was so intolerably loathsome that it was dangerous to remain there for any time,* and some of us had been permitted to stay on the deck for the fresh air; but now that the whole ship's cargo were confined together, it became absolutely pestilential. The closeness of the place, and the heat of the climate, added to the number in the ship, which was so crowded that each had scarcely room to turn himself, almost suffocated us. This produced copious perspirations, so that the air soon became unfit for respiration, from a variety of loathsome smells, and brought on a sickness among the slaves, of which many died, thus falling victims to the improvident avarice, as I may call it, of their purchasers. This deplorable situation was again aggravated by the galling of the chains, now become insupportable; and the filth of the necessary tubs, *into which the children often fell, and were almost suffocated.* The shrieks of the women, and the groans of the dying, rendered the whole a scene of horror almost inconceivable. Happily perhaps for myself I was soon reduced so low here that it was thought necessary to keep me almost always on deck; and from my extreme youth *I was not put in fetters.* In this situation I expected every hour to share the fate of my companions, some of whom were almost daily brought upon deck at the point of death, which I began to hope would soon put an end to my miseries. Often did I think many of the inhabitants of the deep much more happy than myself. I envied them the freedom they enjoyed, and as often wished I could change my condition for theirs. Every circumstance I met with served only to render my state more painful, and heightened my apprehensions, and my opinion of the cruelty of the whites. One day they had taken a number of fishes; and when they had killed and satisfied themselves with as many as they thought fit, to our astonishment who were on the deck, rather than give any of them to us to eat, as we expected, they tossed the remaining fish into the sea again, although we begged and prayed for some as well as we could, but in vain. Some of my countrymen, being pressed by hunger, took an opportunity, when they thought no one saw them, of trying to get a little privately; but they were discovered, and the attempt procured them some very severe floggings.

One day, when we had a smooth sea and moderate wind, two of my wearied countrymen who were chained together (I was near them at the time), preferring death to such a life of misery, somehow made through the nettings and jumped into the sea: immediately another quite dejected fellow, who on account of his illness was suffered to be out of irons, also followed their example; and I believe many more would very soon have done the same if they had not been prevented by the ship's crew who were instantly alarmed. Those of us that were the most active were in a moment put down under the deck, and there was such a noise and confusion amongst the people of the ship as I never heard before, to stop her, and get the boat out to go after the slaves. However two of the wretches were drowned, but they got the other, and afterwards flogged him unmercifully for thus attempting to prefer death to slavery. In this manner we continued to undergo more hardships than I can now relate, hardships which are inseparable from this accursed trade—Many a time we were near suffocation from the want of fresh air, which we were often without for whole days together. This, and the stench of the necessary tubs, carried off many. During our passage I first saw flying fishes, which surprised me very much: they used frequently to fly across the ship, and many of them fell on the deck—I also now first saw the use of the quadrant. I had often, with astonishment, seen the mariners make observations with it, and I could not think what it meant. They at last took notice of my surprise: and one of them, willing to increase it, as well as to gratify my curiosity, made me one day look through it. The clouds appeared to me to be land, which disappeared as they passed along. This heightened my wonder; and I was now more persuaded than ever that I was in another world, and that every thing about me was magic. At last we came in sight of the island of Barbadoes, at which the whites on board gave a great shout, and made many signs of joy to us. We did not know what to think of this; but as the vessel drew nearer we plainly saw the harbour, and other ships of different kinds and sizes; and we soon anchored amongst them off Bridge-Town. Many merchants and planters now came on board, though it was in the evening. They put us in separate parcels, and examined us attentively. They also made us jump and pointed to the land, signifying we were to go there. We thought by this we should be eaten by these ugly men, as they appeared to us; and, when soon after we were all put down under the deck again, there was much dread and trembling among us and nothing but bitter cries to be heard all the night from these apprehensions, insomuch that at last the white people got some old slaves from the land to pacify us. . . .

We were not many days in the merchant's custody before we were sold after the usual manner, which is this:—On a signal given (as the beat of a drum), the buyers rush at once into the yard where the slaves are confined, and make choice of what parcel they like best. . . . In this manner, without scruple, are relations and friends separated, most of them never to see each other again. . . Is it not enough that we are torn from our country and friends, to toil for your luxury and lust of gain? Must every tender feeling be likewise sacrificed to your avarice? Are the dearest friends and relations, now rendered more dear by their separation from their kindred, still to be parted from each other, and thus prevented from cheering the gloom of slavery, with the small comfort of being together, and mingling their sufferings and sorrows? Why are parents to lose their children, brothers their sisters, or husbands their wives? Surely this is a new refinement in cruelty, which, while it has no advantage to atone for it, thus aggravates distress, and adds fresh horrors even to the wretchedness of slavery.

Walker's Appeal

DAVID WALKER

From Walker's Appeal, in Four Articles: Together with a Preamble, to the Colored Citizens of the World, but in particular, and very expressly, to those of the United States of America, written in Boston, State of Massachusetts, September 28, 1829.

MY BELOVED BRETHREN: The Indians of North and of South America —the Greeks—the Irish, subjected under the king of Great Britain—the

Jews, that ancient people of the Lord—the inhabitants of the islands of the sea—in fine, all the inhabitants of the earth (except however, the sons of Africa), are called *men*, and of course are, and ought to be free. But we (coloured people), and our children are *brutes*!! and of course are, and *ought to be* SLAVES to the American people and their children forever!! to dig their mines and work their farms; and thus go on enriching them, from one generation to another with our *blood* and our tears!!!! . . . .

Now I appeal to heaven and to earth and particularly to the American people themselves, who cease not to declare our condition is not *hard* and that we are comparatively satisfied to rest in wretchedness and misery under them and their children. Not, indeed, to show me a coloured President, a Governor, a Legislator, a Senator, a Mayor, or an Attorney at the Bar.—. . .

They think because they hold us in their infernal chains of slavery, that we wish to be white, or of their color—but they are dreadfully deceived—we wish to be just as it pleased our Creator to have made us, and no avaricious and unmerciful wretches have any business to make slaves of, or hold us in slavery. How would they like for us to make slaves of, and hold them in cruel slavery, and murder them as they do us?. . .

Fear not the number and education of our *enemies*, against whom we shall have to contend for our lawful right; guaranteed to us by our Makers; for why should we be afraid, when God is, and will continue (if we continue humble), to be on our side?

The man who would not fight under our Lord and Master, Jesus Christ, in the glorious and heavenly cause of freedom and of God—to be delivered from the most wretched, abject and servile slavery, that ever a people was afflicted with since the foundations of the world, to the present day—ought to be kept with all of his children or family, in slavery, or in chains, to be butchered by his *cruel enemies*. . . .

If you commence, make sure work—do not trifle, for they will not trifle with you—they want us for their slaves, and think nothing of murdering us in order to subject us to that wretched condition—therefore, if there is an attempt made by us, kill or be killed. Now, I ask you, had you not rather be killed than to be a slave to a tyrant, who takes the life of your mother, wife, and dear little children? Look upon your mother, wife, and children, and answer God Almighty; and believe this, that it is no more harm for you to kill a man, who is trying to kill you, than it is for you to take a drink of water when thirsty; in fact, the man who will stand still and let another murder him, is worse than an infidel, and, if he has common sense, ought not to be pitied. . .

Remember Americans, that we must and shall be free and enlightened as you are, will you wait until we shall, under God, obtain our liberty by the crushing arm of power? Will it not be dreadful for you? I speak Americans for your own good. We must and shall be free I say, in spite of you. You may do your best to keep us in wretchedness and misery, to enrich you and your children, but God will deliver us from under you. And wo, wo, will be to you if we have to obtain our freedom by fighting. Throw away your fears and prejudices then, and enlighten us and treat us like men, and we will like you more than we do now hate you, and tell us no more about colonization, for America is as much our country, as it is yours.

Treat us like men, and there is no danger but we will all live in peace and happiness together. For we are not like you, hard hearted, unmerciful, and unforgiving. What a happy country this will be, if the whites will listen. What nation under heaven will be able to do any thing with us, unless God gives us up into its hand?

But Americans, I declare to you, while you keep us and our children in bondage, and treat us like brutes, to make us support you and your families, we cannot be your friends. You do not look for it, do you? Treat us then like men, and we will be your friends. And there is not a doubt in my mind, but that the whole of the past will be sunk into oblivion, and we yet, under God, will become a united and happy people. The whites may say it is impossible, but remember that nothing is impossible with God. . .

Are we MEN!!—I ask you, O my brethren! are we MEN? Did our Creator make us to be slaves to dust and ashes like ourselves? Are they not dying worms as well as we? Have they not to make their appearance before the tribunal of Heaven to answer for the deeds done in the body, as well as we?

Have we any other Master but Jesus Christ alone? Is He not their Master as well as ours?—

What right then, have we to obey—call any other Master, but Himself? How we could be so (submissive) to a gang of men, whom we cannot tell whether they are (as good) as ourselves or not, I never could conceive. However, this is shut up with the Lord, and we cannot precisely tell—but I declare, we judge men by their works.

Slave Life in Georgia

JOHN BROWN

From Slave Life in Georgia: A Narrative of the Life Sufferings and Escape of John Brown, A Fugitive Slave.

The morning after our arrival, my mother was set to plough, and I was put to grub and hoe. She also had other very hard work to do, such as making fences, grubbing bushes, fetching and burning brush, and such like. I had the same kind of work to do, though being small, I could only help my mother a very little, except in the tobacco-fields, where I was of most use, picking off tobacco-worms from the leaves. This was, also, the principal occupation of the children, from the time they could get about to do any thing at all, until they grew old and strong enough to go to harder work.

I said our master was very cruel. I will give one instance of the fact. I and my little brother Curtis were sent up one day to the house. Passing through the grounds, where there was a large number of water-melons, they tempted us, we being very thirsty. So we took one and ate it. The value of it was not half a farthing. We did not know we were seen. James Davis, however, was not far from us, and soon overtook us. He swore at us for thieving his property, and as I was the biggest and had taken the fruit, he at once set to flogging me with the cow-hide, and continued doing so until he was tired out, and I could scarcely move. I did not get over that beating for a very long while.

I remained at James Davis's for nearly eighteen months. Once during that period, I remember he took me into the town to a tavern kept by one Captain Jemmy Duprey. There was a negro speculator there, on the look-out for bargains, but he would not have me. I did not know where I was going, when my master took me with him, but when I got back I told my mother, who cried over me, and said she was very glad I had not been sold away from her.

But the time arrived when we were to be finally separated. Owing to a considerable rise in the price of cotton, there came a great demand for slaves in Georgia. One day a negro speculator named Starling Finney arrived at James Davis's place. He left his drove on the highway, in charge of one of his companions, and made his way up to our plantation, prospecting for negroes. It happened that James Davis had none that suited Finney, but being in want of money, as he was building a new house, and Finney being anxious for a deal, my master called me up and offered to sell me. I was then about or nearly ten years of age, and after some chaffering about terms, Finney agreed to purchase me by the pound.

How I watched them whistling whilst they were driving this bargain! and how I speculated upon the kind of man he was who sought to buy me! His venomous countenance inspired me with mortal terror, and I almost felt the heavy thong of the great riding-whip he held in his hand, twisting round my shoulders. He was a large, tall fellow, and might have killed me easily with one blow from his huge fist. He had left his horse at the gate, and when the bargain for me was struck, he went out and led him to the door, where he took the saddle off. I wondered what this was for, though suspicious that it had something to do with me; nor had I long to wait before I knew. A ladder was set upright against the end of the building outside, to one rung of which they made a stilyard fast. The first thing Finney did was to weigh his saddle, the weight of which he knew, to see whether the stilyard was accurately adjusted. Having satisfied himself of this, a rope was brought, both ends of which were tied together, so that it formed a large noose or loop. This was hitched over the hook of the stilyard, and I was seated in the loop. After I had been weighed, there was a deduction made for the rope. I do not recollect what I weighed, but the price I was sold for amounted to three hundred and ten dollars. Within five minutes after, Finney paid the money, and I was marched off. I looked round and saw my poor mother stretching out her hands after me. She ran up, and overtook us, but Finney, who was behind me, and between me and my mother, would not let her approach, though she begged and prayed to be allowed to kiss me for the last time, and bid me good bye. I was so stupified with grief and fright, that I could not shed a tear, though my heart was bursting. At last we got to the gate, and I turned round to see whether I could not get a chance of kissing my mother. She saw me, and made a dart forward to meet me, but Finney gave me a hard push, which sent me spinning through the gate. He then slammed it to and shut it in my mother's face. That was the last time I ever saw her, nor do I know whether she is alive or dead at this hour.   .

We were in a lane now, about a hundred and fifty yards in length, and which led from the gate to the highway. I walked on before Finney, utterly unconscious of anything. I seemed to have become quite bewildered. I was aroused from this state of stuper by seeing that we had reached the main road, and had come up with a gang of negroes, some of whom were hand-cuffed two and two, and fastened to a long chain running between the two ranks. There were also a good many women and children, but none of these were chained. The children seemed to be all over ten years of age, and I soon learnt that they had been purchased in different places, and were for the most part strangers to one another and to the negroes in the coffle. They were waiting for Finney to come up. I fell into the rank, and we set off on our journey to Georgia.

An American Slave

FREDERICK DOUGLASS

From the Narrative of the Life of Frederick Douglass, An American Slave.

CHAPTER I

I was born in Tuckahoe, near Hillsborough, and about twelve miles from Easton, in Talbot County, Maryland. I have no accurate knowledge of my age, never having seen any authentic record containing it. By far the larger part of the slaves know as little of their ages as horses know of theirs, and it is the wish of most masters within my knowledge to keep their slaves thus ignorant. I do not remember to have ever met a slave who could tell of his birthday. They seldom come nearer to it than planting-time, harvest-time, cherry-time, spring-time, or fall-time. A want of information concerning my own was a source of unhappiness to me even during childhood. The white children could tell their ages. I could not tell why I ought to be deprived of the same privilege. I was not allowed to make any inquiries of my master concerning it. He deemed all such inquiries on the part of a slave improper and impertinent, and evidence of a restless spirit. The nearest estimate I can give makes me now between twenty-seven and twenty-eight years of age. I come to this, from hearing my master say, some time during 1835, I was about seventeen years old.

My mother was named Harriet Bailey. She was the daughter of Isaac and Betsey Bailey, both colored, and quite dark. My mother was of a darker complexion than either my grandmother or grandfather.

My father was a white man. He was admitted to be such by all

I ever heard speak of my parentage. The opinion was also whispered that my master was my father; but of the correctness of this opinion, I know nothing; the means of knowing was withheld from me. My mother and I were separated when I was but an infant—before I knew her as my mother. It is a common custom, in the part of Maryland from which I ran away, to part children from their mothers at a very early age. Frequently, before the child has reached its twelfth month, its mother is taken from it, and hired out on some farm a considerable distance off, and the child is placed under the care of an old woman, too old for field labor. For what this separation is done, I do not know, unless it be to hinder the development of the child's affection toward its mother, and to blunt and destroy the natural affection of the mother for the child. This is the inevitable result.

I never saw my mother, to know her as such, more than four or five times in my life; and each of these times was very short in duration, and at night. She was hired by a Mr. Stewart, who lived about twelve miles from my home. She made her journeys to see me in the night, travelling the whole distance on foot, after the performance of her day's work. She was a field hand, and a whipping was the penalty of not being in the field at sunrise, unless a slave has special permission from his or her master to the contrary—a permission which they seldom get, and one that gives to him who gives it the proud name of being a kind master. I do not recollect of ever seeing my mother by the light of day. She was with me in the night. She would lie down with me, and get me to sleep, but long before I waked she was gone. Very little communication ever took place between us. Death soon ended what little we could have while she lived, and with it her hardships and suffering. She died when I was about seven years old, on one of my master's farms near Lee's Mill. I was not allowed to be present during her illness, at her death, or burial. She was gone long before I knew any thing about it. Never having enjoyed, to any considerable extent, her soothing presence, her tender and watchful care, I received the tidings of her death with much the same emotions I should have probably felt at the death of a stranger.

Called thus suddenly away, she left me without the slightest intimation of who my father was. The whisper that my master was my father, may or may not be true; and, true or false, it is of little consequence to my purpose whilst the fact remains, in all its glaring odiousness, that slaveholders have ordained, and by law established, that the children of slave women shall in all cases follow the condition of their mothers; and this is done too obviously to administer to their own lusts, and make a gratification of their wicked desires profitable as well as pleasurable; for by this cunning arrangement, the slaveholder, in cases not a few, sustains to his slaves the double relation of master and father.

I know of such cases; and it is worthy of remark that such slaves invariably suffer greater hardships, and have more to contend with than others. They are, in the first place, a constant offence to their mistress. She is ever disposed to find fault with them; they can seldom do any thing to please her; she is never better pleased than when she sees them under the lash, especially when she suspects her husband of showing to his mulatto children favors which he withholds from his black slaves. The master is frequently compelled to sell this class of his slaves, out of deference to the feelings of his white wife; and, cruel as the deed may strike any one to be, for a man to sell his own children to human flesh-mongers, it is often the dictate of humanity for him to do so; for, unless he does this, he must not only whip them himself, but must stand by and see one white son tie up his brother, of but few shades darker complexion than himself, and ply the gory lash to his naked back; and if he lisp one word of disapproval, it is set down to his parental partiality, and only makes a bad matter worse, both for himself and the slave whom he would protect and defend.

Every year brings with it multitudes of this class of slaves. It was doubtless in consequence of a knowledge of this fact, that one great statesman of the south predicted the downfall of slavery by the inevitable laws of population. Whether this prophecy is ever fulfilled or not, it is nevertheless plain that a very different-looking class of people are springing up at the south, and are now held in slavery, from those originally brought to this country from Africa; and if their increase will do no other good, it will do away the force of the argument, that God cursed Ham, and therefore American slavery is right. If the lineal descendants of Ham are alone to be scripturally enslaved, it is certain that slavery at the south must soon become unscriptural; for thousands are ushered into the world, annually, who, like myself, owe their existence to white fathers, and those fathers most frequently their own masters.

I have had two masters. My first master's name was Anthony. I do not remember his first name. He was generally called Captain Anthony— a title which, I presume, he acquired by sailing a craft on the Chesapeake Bay. He was not considered a rich slaveholder. He owned two or three farms, and about thirty slaves. His farms and slaves were under the care of an overseer. The overseer's name was Plummer. Mr. Plummer was a miserable drunkard, a profane swearer, and a savage monster. He always went armed with a cowskin and a heavy cudgel. I have known him to cut and slash the women's heads so horribly, that even master would be enraged at his cruelty, and would threaten to whip him if he did not mind himself. Master, however, was not a humane slaveholder. It required extraordinary barbarity on the part of an overseer to affect him. He was a cruel man, hardened by a long life of slave-holding. He would at times seem to take great pleasure in whipping a slave. I have often been awakened at the dawn of day by the most heart-rending shrieks of an own aunt of mine, whom he used to tie up to a joist, and whip upon her naked back till she was literally covered with blood. No words, no tears, no prayers, from his gory victim, seemed to move his iron heart from its bloody purpose. The louder she screamed, the harder he whipped; and where the blood ran fastest, there he whipped longest. He would whip her to make her scream, and whip her to make her hush; and not until overcome by fatigue, would he cease to swing the blood-clotted cowskin. I remember the first time I ever witnessed this horrible exhibition. I was quite a child, but I well remember it. I shall never forget it whilst I remember any thing. It was the first of a long series of such outrages, of which I was doomed to be a witness and a participant. It struck me with awful force. It was the blood-stained gate, the entrance to the hell of slavery, through which I was about to pass. It was a most terrible spectacle. I wish I could commit to paper the feelings with which I beheld it.

This occurrence took place very soon after I went to live with my old master, and under the following circumstances. Aunt Hester went out one night—where or for what I do not know,—and happened to be absent when my master desired her presence. He had ordered her not to go out evenings, and warned her that she must never let him catch her in company with a young man, who was paying attention to her belonging to Colonel Lloyd. The young man's name was Ned Roberts, generally called Lloyd's Ned. Why master was so careful of her, may be safely left to conjecture. She was a woman of noble form, and of graceful proportions, having very few equals, and fewer superiors, in personal appearance, among the colored or white women of our neighborhood.

Aunt Hester had not only disobeyed his orders in going out, but had been found in company with Lloyd's Ned; which circumstance, I found, from what he said while whipping her, was the chief offence. Had he been a man of pure morals himself, he might have been thought interested in protecting the innocence of my aunt; but those who knew him will not suspect him of any such virtue. Before he commenced whipping Aunt Hester, he took her into the kitchen, and stripped her from neck to waist, leaving her neck, shoulders, and back, entirely naked. He then told her to cross her hands, calling her at the same time a d——d b——h. After crossing her hands, he tied them with a strong rope, and led her to a stool under a large hook in the joist, put in for the purpose. He made her get upon the stool, and tied her hands to the hook. She now stood fair for his infernal purpose. Her arms were stretched up at their full length, so that she stood upon the ends of her toes. He then said to her, "Now, you d——d b——h, I'll learn you how to disobey my orders!" and after rolling up his sleeves, he commenced to lay on the heavy cowskin, and soon the warm, red blood (amid heart-rending shrieks from her, and horrid oaths from him) came dripping to the floor. I was so terrified and horror-stricken at the sight, that I hid myself in a closet, and dared not venture out till long after the bloody transaction was over. I expected it would be my turn next. It was all new to me. I have never seen any thing like it before. I had always lived with my grandmother on the outskirts of the plantation, where she was put to raise the children of the younger women. I had therefore been, until now, out of the way of the bloody scenes that often occurred on the plantation.

❖   ❖   ❖

CHAPTER VI

My new mistress proved to be all she appeared when I first met her at the door—a woman of the kindest heart and finest feelings. She had never had a slave under her control previously to myself, and prior to her marriage she had been dependent upon her own industry for a living. She was by trade a weaver; and by constant application to her business, she had been in a good degree preserved from the blighting and dehumanizing effects of slavery. I was utterly astonished at her goodness. I scarcely knew how to behave towards her. She was entirely unlike any other white woman I had ever seen. I could not approach her as I was accustomed to approach other white ladies. My early instruction was all out of place. The crouching servility, usually so acceptable a quality in a slave, did not answer when manifested toward her. Her favor was not gained by it; she seemed to be disturbed by it. She did not deem it impudent or unmannerly for a slave to look her in the face. The meanest slave was put fully at ease in her presence, and none left without feeling better for having seen her. Her face was made of heavenly smiles, and her voice of tranquil music.

But, alas! this kind heart had but a short time to remain such. The fatal poison of irresponsible power was already in her hands, and soon commenced its infernal work. That cheerful eye, under the influence of slavery, soon became red with rage; that voice, made all of sweet accord, changed to one of harsh and horrid discord; and that angelic face gave place to that of a demon.

Very soon after I went to live with Mr. and Mrs. Auld, she very kindly commenced to teach me the A, B, C. After I had learned this, she assisted me in learning to spell words of three or four letters. Just at this point of my progress, Mr. Auld found out what was going on, and at once forbade Mrs. Auld to instruct me further, telling her, among other things, that it was unlawful, as well as unsafe, to teach a slave to read. To use his own words, further he said, "If you give a nigger an inch, he will take an ell. A nigger should know nothing but to obey his master—to do as he is told to do. Learning would *spoil* the best nigger in the world." "Now," said he, "If you teach that nigger (speaking of myself) how to read, there would be no keeping him. It would forever unfit him to be a slave. He would at once become unmanageable, and of no value to his master. As to himself, it could do him no good, but a great deal of harm. It would make him discontented and unhappy." These words sank deep into my heart, stirred up sentiments within that lay slumbering, and called into existence an entirely new train of thought. It was a new and special revelation, explaining dark and mysterious things, with which my youthful understanding had struggled, but struggled in vain. I now understood what had been to me a most perplexing difficulty—to wit, the white man's power to enslave the black man. It was a grand achievement, and I prized it highly. From that moment, I understood the pathway from slavery to freedom. It was just what I wanted, and I got it at a time when I the least expected it. Whilst I was saddened by the thought of losing the aid of my kind mistress, I was gladdened by the invaluable instruction which, by the merest accident, I had gained from my master. Though conscious of the difficulty of learning without a teacher, I set out with high hope, and a fixed purpose, at whatever cost of trouble, to learn how to read. The very decided manner with which he spoke, and strove to impress his wife with the evil consequences of giving me instruction, served to convince me that he was deeply sensible of the truths he was uttering. It gave me the best assurance that I might rely with the utmost confidence on the results which, he said, would flow from teaching me to read. What he most dreaded, that I most desired. What he most loved, that I most hated. That which to him was a great evil, to be carefully shunned, was to me a great good, to be diligently sought; and the argument which he so warmly urged, against my learning to read, only served to inspire me with a desire and determination to learn. In learning to read, I owe almost as much to the bitter opposition of my master, as to the kindly aid of my mistress. I acknowledge the benefit of both.

I had resided but a short time in Baltimore before I observed a marked difference, in the treatment of slaves, from that which I had witnessed in the country. A city slave is almost a freeman, compared with a slave on the plantation. He is much better fed and clothed, and enjoys privileges altogether unknown to the slave on the plantation. There is a vestige of decency, a sense of shame, that does much to curb and check those outbreaks of atrocious cruelty so commonly enacted upon the plantation. He is a desperate slaveholder who will shock the humanity of his non-slaveholding neighbors with the cries of his lacerated slave. Few are willing to incur the odium attaching to the reputation of being a cruel master; and above all things, they would not be known as not giving a slave enough to eat. Every city slaveholder is anxious to have it known of him, that he feeds his slaves well; and it is due to them to say, that most of them do give their slaves enough to eat. There are, however, some painful exceptions to this rule. Directly opposite to us, on Philpot Street, lived Mr. Thomas Hamilton. He owned two slaves. Their names were Henrietta and Mary. Henrietta was about twenty-two years of age, Mary was about fourteen; and of all the mangled and emaciated creatures I ever looked upon, these two were the most so. His heart must be harder than stone, that could look upon these unmoved. The head, neck, and shoulders of Mary were literally cut to pieces. I have frequently felt her head, and found it nearly covered with festering sores, caused by the lash of her cruel mistress. I do not know that her master ever whipped her, but I have been an eye-witness to the cruelty of Mrs. Hamilton. I used to be in Mr. Hamilton's house nearly every day. Mrs. Hamilton used to sit in a large chair in the middle of the room, with a heavy cowskin always by her side, and scarce an hour passed during the day but was marked by the blood of one of these slaves. The girls seldom passed her without her saying, "Move faster, you *black gip!*" at the same time giving them a blow with the cowskin over the head or shoulders, often drawing the blood. She would then say, "Take that, you *black gip!*"—continuing, "if you don't move faster, I'll move you!" Added to the cruel lashings to which these slaves were subjected, they were kept nearly half-starved. They seldom knew what it was to eat a full meal. I have seen Mary contending with the pigs for the offal thrown into the street. So much was Mary kicked and cut to pieces, that she was oftener called "*pecked*" than by her name.

CHAPTER VII

I lived in Master Hugh's family about seven years. During this time, I succeeded in learning to read and write. In accomplishing this, I was compelled to resort to various stratagems. I had no regular teacher. My mistress, who had kindly commenced to instruct me, had, in compliance with the advice and direction of her husband, not only ceased to instruct, but had set her face against my being instructed by any one else. It is due, however, to my mistress to say of her, that she did not adopt this course of treatment immediately. She at first lacked the depravity indispensable to shutting me up in mental darkness. It was at least necessary for her to have some training in the exercise of irresponsible power, to make her equal to the task of treating me as though I were a brute.

My mistress was, as I have said, a kind and tender-hearted woman; and in the simplicity of her soul she commenced, when I first went to live with her, to treat me as she supposed one human being ought to treat another. In entering upon the duties of a slaveholder, she did not seem to perceive that I sustained to her the relation of a mere chattel, and that for her to treat me as a human being was not only wrong, but dangerously so. Slavery proved as injurious to her as it did to me. When I went there, she was a pious, warm, and tender-hearted woman. There was no sorrow or suffering for which she had not a tear. She had bread for the hungry, clothes for the naked, and comfort for every mourner that came within her reach. Slavery soon proved its ability to divest her of these heavenly qualities. Under its influence, the tender heart became stone, and the lamblike disposition gave way to one of tiger-like fierceness. The first step in her downward course was in her ceasing to instruct me. She now commenced to practice her husband's precepts. She finally became even more violent in her opposition than her husband himself. She was not satisfied with simply doing as well as he had commanded; she seemed anxious to do better. Nothing seemed to make her more angry than to see me with a newspaper. She seemed to think that here lay the danger. I have had her rush at me with a face made all up of fury, and snatch from me a newspaper, in a manner that fully revealed her apprehension. She was an apt woman; and a little experience soon demonstrated, to her satisfaction, that education and slavery were incompatible with each other.

From this time I was most narrowly watched. If I was in a separate room any considerable length of time, I was sure to be suspected of having a book, and was at once called to give an account of myself. All this, however, was too late. The first step had been taken. Mistress, in teaching me the alphabet, had given me the *inch*, and no precaution could prevent me from taking the *ell*.

The plan which I adopted, and the one by which I was most successful, was that of making friends of all the little white boys whom I met in the street. As many of these as I could, I converted into teachers. With their kindly aid, obtained at different times and in different places, I finally succeeded in learning to read. When I was sent on errands, I always took my book with me, and by doing one part of my errand quickly I found time to get a lesson before my return. I used also to carry bread with me, enough of which was always in the house, and to which I was always welcome; for I was much better off in this regard than many of the poor white children in our neighborhood. This bread I used to bestow upon the hungry little urchins, who, in return, would give me that more valuable bread of knowledge. I am strongly tempted to give the names of two or three of those little boys, as a testimonial of the gratitude and affection I bear them; but prudence forbids;—not that it would injure me, but it might embarrass them; for it is almost an unpardonable offence to teach slaves to read in this Christian country. It is enough to say of the dear little fellows, that they lived on Philpot Street, very near Durgin and Bailey's shipyard. I used to talk this matter of slavery over with them. I would sometimes say to them, I wished I could be as free as they would be when they got to be men. "You will be free as soon as you are twenty-one, *but I am a slave for life!* Have not I as good a right to be free as you have?" These words used to trouble them; they would express for me the liveliest sympathy, and console me with the hope that something would occur by which I might be free.

I was now about twelve years old, and the thought of being *a slave for life* began to bear heavily upon my heart. Just about this time, I got hold of a book entitled "The Columbian Orator." Every opportunity I got, I used to read this book. Among much of other interesting matter, I found in it a dialogue between a master and his slave. The slave was represented as having run away from his master three times. The dialogue represented the conversation which took place between them, when the slave was retaken the third time. In this dialogue, the whole argument in behalf of slavery was brought forward by the master, all of which was disposed of by the slave. The slave was made to say some very smart as well as impressive things in reply to his master—things which had the desired though unexpected effect; for the conversation resulted in the voluntary emancipation of the slave on the part of the master.

In the same book, I met with one of Sheridan's mighty speeches on and in behalf of Catholic emancipation. These were choice documents to me. I read them over and over again with unabated interest. They gave tongue to interesting thoughts of my own soul, which had frequently flashed through my mind, and died away for want of utterance. The moral which I gained from the dialogue was the power of truth over the conscience of even a slaveholder. What I got from Sheridan was a bold denunciation of slavery, and a powerful vindication of human rights. The reading of these documents enabled me to utter my thoughts, and to meet the arguments brought forward to sustain slavery; but while they relieved me of one difficulty, they brought on another even more painful than the one of which I was relieved. The more I read, the more I was led to abhor and detest my enslavers. I could regard them in no other light than a band of successful robbers, who had left their homes, and gone to Africa, and stolen us from our homes, and in a strange land reduced us to slavery. I loathed them as being the meanest as well as the most wicked of men. As I read and contemplated the subject, behold! that very discontentment which Master Hugh had pre-

dicted would follow my learning to read had already come, to torment
and sting my soul to unutterable anguish. As I writhed under it, I would
at times feel that learning to read had been a curse rather than a blessing.
It had given me a view of my wretched condition, without the remedy.
It opened my eyes to the horrible pit, but to no ladder upon which to
get out. In moments of agony, I envied my fellow-slaves for their stu-
pidity. I have often wished myself a beast. I preferred the condition of
the meanest reptile to my own. Any thing, no matter what, to get rid
of thinking! It was this everlasting thinking of my condition that tormented me. There was no getting rid of it. It was pressed upon me by
every object within sight of hearing, animate or inanimate. The silver
trump of freedom had roused my soul to eternal wakefulness. Freedom
now appeared, to disappear no more forever. It was heard in every sound,
and seen in every thing. It was ever present to torment me with a sense
of my wretched condition. I saw nothing without seeing it, I heard nothing without hearing it, and felt nothing without feeling it. It looked
from every star, it smiled in every calm, breathed in every wind, and
moved in every storm.

I often found myself regretting my own existence, and wishing
myself dead; and but for the hope of being free, I have no doubt but that
I should have killed myself, or done something for which I should have
been killed. While in this state of mind, I was eager to hear any one
speak of slavery. I was a ready listener. Every little while, I could hear
something about abolitionists. It was some time before I found what the
word meant. It was always used in such connections as to make it an
interesting word to me. If a slave ran away and succeeded in getting
clear, or if a slave killed his master, set fire to a barn, or did any thing
very wrong in the mind of a slaveholder, it was spoken of as the fruit
of *abolition*. Hearing the word in this connection very often, I set about
learning what it meant. The dictionary afforded me little or no help. I
found it was "the act of abolishing"; but then I did not know what was
to be abolished. Here I was perplexed. I did not dare to ask any one
about its meaning, for I was satisfied that it was something they wanted
me to know very little about. After a patient waiting, I got one of our
city papers, containing an account of the number of petitions from the
north, praying for the abolition of slavery in the District of Columbia,
and of the slave trade between the States. From this time I understood
the words *abolition* and *abolitionist*, and always drew near when that
word was spoken, expecting to hear something of importance to myself
and fellow-slaves. The light broke in upon me by degrees. I went one
day down on the wharf of Mr. Waters; and seenig two Irishmen unloading
a scow of stone, I went, unasked, and helped them. When we had finished,
one of them came to me and asked, "Are ye a slave for life?" I told him

that I was. The good Irishman seemed to be deeply affected by the statement. He said to the other that it was a pity so fine a little fellow as myself should be a slave for life. He said it was a shame to hold me. They both advised me to run away to the north; that I should find friends there, and that I should be free. I pretended not to be interested in what they said, and treated them as if I did not understand them; for I feared they might be treacherous. While men have been known to encourage slaves to escape, and then, to get the reward, catch them and return them to their masters. I was afraid that these seemingly good men might use me so; but I nevertheless remembered their advice, and from that time I resolved to run away. I looked forward to a time at which it would be safe for me to escape. I was too young to think of doing so immediately; besides, I wished to learn how to write, as I might have occasion to write my own pass. I consoled myself with the hope that I should one day find a good chance. Meanwhile, I would learn to write.

The idea as to how I might learn to write was suggested to me by being in Durgin and Bailey's ship-yard, and frequently seeing the ship carpenters, after hewing, and getting a piece of timber ready for use, write on the timber the name of that part of the ship for which it was intended. When a piece of timber was intended for the larboard side, it would be marked thus—"L." When a piece was for the starboard side, it would be marked thus—"S." A piece for the larboard side forward, would be marked thus—"L.F." When a piece was for starboard side forward, it would be marked thus—"S.F." For larboard aft, it would be marked thus—"L.A." For starboard aft, it would be marked thus— "S.A." I soon learned the names of these letters, and for what they were intended when placed upon a piece of timber in the ship-yard. I immediately commenced copying them, and in a short time was able to make the four letters named. After that, when I met with any boy who I knew could write, I would tell him I could write as well as he. The next word would be, "I don't believe you. Let me see you try it." I would then make the letters which I had been so fortunate as to learn, and ask him to beat that. In this way I got a good many lessons in writing, which it is quite possible I should never have gotten in any other way. During this time, my copy-book was the board fence, brick wall, and pavement; my pen and ink was a lump of chalk. With these, I learned mainly how to write. I then commenced and continued copying the Italics in Webster's Spelling Book, until I could make them all without looking on the book. By this time, my little Master Thomas had gone to school, and learned how to write, and had written over a number of copy-books. These had been brought home, and shown to some of our near neighbors, and then laid aside. My mistress used to go to class meeting at the Wilk Street meetinghouse every Monday afternoon, and leave me to take care of the house. When left thus, I used to spend this time writing in the spaces left in Master Thomas's copy-book, copying what he had written. I continued to do this until I could write a hand very similar to that of Master Thomas. Thus, after a long, tedious effort for years, I finally succeeded in learning how to write.

Dark Symphony

MELVIN B. TOLSON

I   ALLEGRO MODERATO

Black Crispus Attucks taught
            Us how to die
Before white Patrick Henry's bugle breath
Uttered the vertical
            Transmitting cry:
"Yea, give me liberty, or give me death."

And from that day to this
            Men black and strong
For Justice and Democracy have stood,
Steeled in the faith that Right
            Will conquer Wrong
And Time will usher in one brotherhood.

No Banquo's ghost can rise
            Against us now
And say we crushed men with a tyrant's boot
Or pressed the crown of thorns
            On Labor's brow,
Or ravaged lands and carted off the loot.

II   LENTO GRAVE

The centuries-old pathos in our voices
Saddens the great white world,
And the wizardy of our dusky rhythms
Conjures up shadow-shapes of ante-bellum years:

Black slaves singing *One More River to Cross*
In the torture tombs of slave ships,
Black slaves singing *Steal Away to Jesus*
In jungle swamps,
Black slaves singing *The Crucifixion*
In slave pens at midnight,
Black slaves singing *Swing Low, Sweet Chariot*
In cabins of death,
Black slaves singing *Go Down, Moses*
In the canebrakes of the Southern Pharaohs.

III   ANDANTE SOSTENUTO

They tell us to forget
The Golgotha we tread . . .
We who are scourged with hate,
A price upon our head.
They who have shackled us
Require of us a song,
They who have wasted us
Bid us o'erlook the wrong.

They tell us to forget
Democracy is spurned.
They tell us to forget
The Bill of Rights is burned.
Three hundred years we slaved,
We slave and suffer yet:
Though flesh and bone rebel,
They tell us to forget!

Oh, how can we forget
Our human rights denied?
Oh, how can we forget
Our manhood crucified?
When Justice is profaned
And plea with curse is met,
When Freedom's gates are barred,
Oh, how can we forget?

IV   TEMPO PRIMO

The New Negro strides upon the continent
In seven league boots . . .
The New Negro
Who sprang from the vigor-stout loins
Of Nat Turner, gallows-martyr for Freedom,
Of Joseph Cinquez, Black Moses of the Amistad Mutiny,
Of Frederick Douglass, oracle of the Catholic Man,
Of Sojourner Truth, eye and ear of Lincoln's legions,
Of Harriet Tubman, St. Bernard of the Underground Railroad.

V   LARGHETTO

None in the Land can say
To us black men Today:
You send the tractors on their bloody path,
And create Oakies for *The Grapes of Wrath.*
You breed the slum that breeds a *Native Son*
To damn the good earth Pilgrim Fathers won.

None in the Land can say
To us black men Today:
You dupe the poor with rags-to-riches tales,
And leave the workers empty dinner pails.
You stuff the ballot box, and honest men
Are muzzled by your demogogic din.

None in the Land can say
To us black men Today:
You smash stock markets with your coined blitzkriegs
And make a hundred million guinea pigs.
You counterfeit our Christianity,
And bring contempt upon Democracy.

None in the Land can say
To us black men Today:
You prowl when citizens are fast asleep,
And hatch Fifth Column plots to blast the deep
Foundations of the State and leave the Land
A vast Sahara with a Fascist brand.

None in the Land can say
To us black men Today:
You send flame-gutting tanks, like swarms of flies,
And pump a hell from dynamiting skies.
You fill machine-gunned towns with rotting dead—
A No Man's Land where children cry for bread.

VI   TEMPO DI MARCIA

Out of abysses of Illiteracy,
Through labyrinths of Lies,
Across wastelands of Disease . . .
We advance!

Out of dead-ends of Poverty,
Through wildernesses of Superstition,
Across barricades of Jim Crowism . . .
We advance!

With the Peoples of the World . . .
We advance!

For My People

MARGARET WALKER

For my people everywhere singing their slaves songs repeatedly; their
dirges and their ditties and their blues and jubilees, praying their
prayers nightly to an unknown god, bending their knees humbly
to an unseen power;
For my people lending their strength to the years: to the gone years
and the now years and the maybe years, washing ironing cooking
scrubbing sewing mending hoeing plowing digging planting pruning
patching dragging along never gaining never reaping never knowing
and never understanding;
For my playmates in the clay and dust and sand of Alabama backyards
playing baptizing and preaching, and doctor and jail and soldier and
school and mama and cooking and playhouse and concert and store
and Miss Choomby and hair and company;

For the cramped bewildered years we went to school to learn to know the reasons why and the answers to and the people who and the places where and the days when, in memory of the bitter hours when we discovered we were black and poor and small and different and nobody wondered and nobody understood;

For the boys and girls who grew in spite of these things to be Man and Woman, to laugh and dance and sing and play and drink their wine and religion and success, to marry their playmates and bear children and then die of consumption and anemia and lynching;

For my people thronging 47th Street in Chicago and Lenox Avenue in New York and Rampart Street in New Orleans, lost disinherited dispossessed and HAPPY people filling the cabarets and taverns and other people's pockets needing bread and shoes and milk and land and money and Something—Something all our own;

For my people walking blindly, spreading joy, losing time being lazy, sleeping when hungry, shouting when burdened, drinking when hopeless, tied and shackled and tangled among ourselves by the unseen creatures who tower over us omnisciently and laugh;

For my people blundering and groping and floundering in the dark of churches and schools and clubs and societies, associations and councils and committees and conventions, distressed and disturbed and deceived and devoured by money-hungry, glory-craving leeches, preyed on by facile force of state and fad and novelty by false prophet and holy believer;

For my people standing staring trying to fashion a better way from confusion from hypocrisy and misunderstanding, trying to fashion a world that will hold all the people all the faces all the adams and eves and their countless generations;

Let a new earth arise. Let another world be born. Let a bloody peace be written in the sky. Let a second generation full of courage issue forth, let a people loving freedom come to growth, let a beauty full of healing and a strength of final clenching be the pulsing in our spirits and our blood. Let the martial songs be written, let the dirges disappear. Let a race of men now rise and take control!

from **Black Boy**

RICHARD WRIGHT

I held a series of petty jobs for short periods, quitting some to work elsewhere, being driven off others because of my attitude, my speech, the look in my eyes. I was no nearer than ever to my goal of saving enough money to leave. At times I doubted if I could ever do it.

One jobless morning I went to my old classmate, Griggs, who worked for a Capitol Street jeweler. He was washing the windows of the store when I came upon him.

"Do you know where I can find a job?" I asked.

He looked at me with scorn.

"Yes, I know where you can find a job," he said, laughing.

"Where?"

"But I wonder if you can hold it," he said.

"What do you mean?" I asked. "Where's the job?"

"Take your time," he said. "You know, Dick, I know you. You've been trying to hold a job all summer, and you can't. Why? Because you're impatient. That's your big fault."

I said nothing, because he was repeating what I had already heard him say. He lit a cigarette and blew out smoke leisurely.

"Well," I said, egging him on to speak.

"I wish to hell I could talk to you," he said.

"I think I know what you want to tell me," I said.

He clapped me on the shoulder; his face was full of fear, hate, concern for me.

"Do you want to get killed?" he asked me.

"Hell, no!"

"Then, for God's sake, learn how to live in the South!"

"What do you mean?" I demanded. "Let white people tell me that. Why should you?"

"See?" he said, triumphantly, pointing his finger at me. "There it is, *now*! It's in your face. You won't let people tell you things. You rush too much. I'm trying to help you and you won't let me." He paused and looked about; the streets were filled with white people. He spoke to me in a low, full tone. "Dick, look, you're black, black, *black*, see? Can't you understand that?"

"Sure, I understand it," I said.

"You don't act a damn bit like it," he spat.

He then reeled off an account of my actions on every job I had held that summer.

"How did you know that?" I asked.

"White people make it their business to watch niggers," he explained. "And they pass the word around. Now, my boss is a Yankee and he tells me things. You're marked already."

Could I believe him? Was it true? How could I ever learn this strange world of white people?

"Then tell me how must I act?" I asked humbly. "I just want to make enough money to leave."

"Wait and I'll tell you," he said.

At that moment a woman and two men stepped from the jewelry store; I moved to one side to let them pass, my mind intent upon Griggs's words. Suddent Griggs reached for my arm and jerked me violently, sending me stumbling three or four feet across the pavement. I whirled.

"What's the matter with you?" I asked.

Griggs glared at me, then laughed.

"I'm teaching you how to get out of white people's way," he said.

I looked at the people who had come out of the store; yes, they were *white*, but I had not noticed it.

"Do you see what I mean?" he asked. "White people want you out of their way." He pronounced the words slowly so that they would sink into my mind.

"I know what you mean," I breathed.

"Dick, I'm treating you like a brother," he said. "You act around white people as if you didn't know that they were white. And they *see* it."

"Oh, Christ, I can't be a slave," I said hopelessly.

"But you've got to eat," he said.

"Yes, I got to eat."

"Then start acting like it," he hammered at me, pounding his fist in his palm. "When you're in front of white people, *think* before you act, *think* before you speak. Your way of doing things is all right among *our* people, but not for *white* people. They won't stand for it."

I stared bleakly into the morning sun. I was nearing my seventeenth birthday and I was wondering if I would ever be free of this plague. What Griggs was saying was true, but it was simply utterly impossible for me to calculate, to scheme, to act, to plot all the time. I would remember to dissemble for short periods, then I would forget and act straight and human again, not with the desire to harm anybody, but merely forgetting the artificial status of race and class. It was the same with whites as with blacks; it was my way with everybody. I sighed, looking at the glittering diamonds in the store windows, the rings and the neat rows of golden watches.

"I guess you're right," I said at last. "I've got to watch myself, break myself. . . ."

"No," he said quickly, feeling guilty now. Someone—a white man —went into the store and we paused in our talk. "You know, Dick, you may think I'm an Uncle Tom, but I'm not. I hate these white people, hate 'em with all my heart. But I can't show it; if I did, they'd kill me."

I laughed uneasily, looking at the white faces that passed me. But

Griggs when he laughed, covered his mouth with his hand and bent at the knees, a gesture which was unconsciously meant to conceal his excessive joy in the presence of whites.

"That's how I feel about 'em," he said proudly after he had finished his spasms of glee. He grew sober. "There's an optical company upstairs and the boss is a Yankee from Illinois. Now, he wants a boy to work all day in summer, mornings and evenings in winter. He wants to break a colored boy into the optical trade. You know algebra and you're just cut out for the work. I'll tell Mr. Crane about you and I'll get in touch with you."

"Do you suppose I could see him now?" I asked.

"For God's sake, take your *time!*" he thundered at me.

"Maybe that's what's wrong with Negroes," I said. "They take too much time."

I laughed, but he was disturbed. I thanked him and left. For a week I did not hear from him and I gave up hope. Then one afternoon Griggs came to my house.

"It looks like you've got a job," he said. "You're going to have a chance to learn a trade. But remember to keep your head. Remember you're black. You start tomorrow."

"What will I get?"

"Five dollars a week to start with; they'll raise you if they like you," he explained.

My hopes soared. Things were not quite so bad, after all. I would have a chance to learn a trade. And I need not give up school. I told him that I would take the job, that I would be humble.

"You'll be working for a Yankee and you ought to get along," he said.

The next morning I was outside the office of the optical company long before it opened. I was reminding myself that I must be polite, must think before I spoke, must think before I acted, must say "yes sir, no sir," that I must so conduct myself that white people would not think that I thought I was as good as they. Suddenly a white man came up to me.

"What do you want?" he asked me.

"I'm reporting for a job, sir," I said.

"O.K. Come on."

I followed him up a flight of steps and he unlocked the door of the office. I was a little tense, but the young white man's manner put me at ease and I sat and held my hat in my hand. A white girl came and began punching the typewriter. Soon another white man, thin and gray, entered and went into the rear room. Finally, a tall, red-faced white man arrived, shot me a quick glance and sat at his desk. His brisk manner branded him a Yankee.

"You're the new boy, eh?"

"Yes, sir."

"Let me get my mail out of the way and I'll talk with you," he said pleasantly.

"Yes, sir."

I even pitched my voice to a low plane, trying to rob it of any suggestions or overtones of aggressiveness.

Half an hour later Mr. Crane called me to his desk and questioned me closely about my schooling, about how much mathematics I had had. He seemed pleased when I told him I had had two years of algebra.

"How would you like to learn this trade?" he asked.

"I'd like it fine, sir. I'd like nothing better," I said.

He told me that he wanted to train a Negro boy in the optical trade; he wanted to help him, guide him. I tried to answer in a way that would let him know that I would try to be worthy of what he was doing. He took me to the stenographer and said:

"This is Richard. He's going to be with us."

He then led me into the rear room of the office, which turned out to be a tiny factory filled with many strange machines smeared with red dust.

"Reynolds," he said to a young white man, "this is Richard."

"What you saying there, boy!" Reynolds grinned and boomed at me.

Mr. Crane took me to the older man.

"Pease, this is Richard, who'll work with us."

Pease looked at me and nodded. Mr. Crane then held forth to the two white men about my duties; he told them to break me in gradually to the workings of the shop, to instruct me in the mechanics of grinding and polishing lenses. They nodded their assent.

"Now, boy, let's see how clean you can get this place," Mr. Crane said.

"Yes, sir."

I swept, mopped, dusted, and soon had the office and the shop clean. In the afternoons, when I had caught up with my work, I ran errands. In an idle moment I would stand and watch the two white men grinding lenses on the machines. They said nothing to me and I said nothing to them. The first day passed, the second, the third, a week passed and I received my five dollars. A month passed. But I was not learning anything and nobody had volunteered to help me. One afternoon I walked up to Reynolds and asked him to tell me about the work.

"What are you trying to do, get smart, nigger?" he asked me.

"No, sir," I said.

I was baffled. Perhaps he just did not want to help me. I went to

Pease, reminding him that the boss had said I was to be given a chance to learn the trade.

"Nigger, you think you're white, don't you?"

"No, sir."

"You're acting mighty like it," he said.

"I was only doing what the boss told me to do," I said.

Pease shook his fist in my face.

"This is a *white* man's work around here," he said.

From then on they changed toward me; they said good morning no more. When I was just a bit slow in performing some duty, I was called a lazy sonofabitch. I kept silent, striving to offer no excuse for worsening of relations. But one day Reynolds called me to his machine.

"Nigger, you think you'll ever amount to anything?" he asked in a slow, sadistic voice.

"I don't know, sir," I answered, turning my head away.

"What do niggers think about?" he asked.

"I don't know, sir," I said, my head still averted.

"If I was a nigger, I'd kill myself," he said.

I said nothing. I was angry.

"You know why?" he asked.

I still said nothing.

"But I don't reckon niggers mind being niggers," he said suddenly and laughed.

I ignored him. Mr. Pease was watching me closely; then I saw them exchange glances. My job was not leading to what Mr. Crane had said it would. I had been humble, and now I was reaping the wages of humility.

"Come here, boy," Pease said.

I walked to his bench.

"You didn't like what Reynolds just said, did you?" he asked.

"Oh, it's all right," I said smiling.

"You didn't like it. I could see it on your face," he said.

I stared at him and backed away.

"Did you ever get into any trouble?" he asked.

"No, sir."

"What would you do if you got into trouble?"

"I don't know, sir."

"Well, watch yourself and don't get into trouble," he warned.

I wanted to report these clashes to Mr. Crane, but the thought of what Pease or Reynolds would do to me if they learned that I had "snitched" stopped me. I worked through the days and tried to hide my resentment under a nervous, cryptic smile.

The climax came at noon one summer day. Pease called me to

his workbench; to get to him I had to go between two narrow benches and stand with my back against a wall.

"Richard, I want to ask you something," Pease began pleasantly, not looking up from his work.

"Yes, sir."

Reynolds came over and stood blocking the narrow passage between the benches; he folded his arms and stared at me solemnly. I looked from one to the other, sensing trouble. Pease looked up and spoke slowly, so there would be no possibility of my not understanding.

"Richard, Reynolds here tells me that you called me Pease," he said.

I stiffened. A void opened up in me. I knew that this was the showdown.

He meant that I had failed to call him Mr. Pease. I looked at Reynolds; he was gripping a steel bar in his hand. I opened my mouth to speak, to protest, to assure Pease that I had never called him simply *Pease*, and that I had never had any intention of doing so, when Reynolds grabbed me by the collar, ramming my head against a wall.

"Now, be careful, nigger," snarled Reynolds, baring his teeth. "I heard you call 'im *Pease*. And if you say you didn't you're calling me a liar, see?" He waved the steel bar threateningly.

If I had said: No, sir, Mr. Pease, I never called you *Pease*, I would by inference have been calling Reynolds a liar; and if I had said: Yes, sir, Mr. Pease, I called you *Pease*, I would have been pleading guilty to the worst insult that a Negro can offer to a southern white man. I stood trying to think of a neutral course that would resolve this quickly risen nightmare, but my tongue would not move.

"Richard, I asked you a question!" Pease said. Anger was creeping into his voice.

"I don't remember calling you *Pease*, Mr. Pease," I said cautiously. "And if I did, I sure didn't mean. . . ."

"You black sonofabitch! You called me *Pease*, then!" he spat, rising and slapping me till I bent sideways over a bench.

Reynolds was up on top of me demanding:

"Didn't you call him *Pease*? If you say you didn't, I'll rip your gut string loose with this f-k-g bar, you black granny dodger! You can't call a white man a liar and get away with it!"

I wilted. I begged them not to hit me. I knew what they wanted. They wanted me to leave the job.

"I'll leave," I promised. "I'll leave right now!"

They gave me a minute to get out of the factory, and warned me not to show up again or tell the boss. Reynolds loosened his hand on my collar and I ducked out of the room. I did not see Mr. Crane or the stenographer in the office. Pease and Reynolds had so timed it that Mr. Crane and the stenographer would be out when they turned on the terror. I went to the street and waited for the boss to return. I saw Griggs wiping glass shelves in the jewelry store and I beckoned to him. He came out and I told him what had happened.

"Then what are you standing there like a fool for?" he demanded. "Won't you ever learn? Get home! They might come down!"

I walked down Capitol Street feeling that the sidewalk was unreal, that I was unreal, that the people were unreal, yet expecting somebody to demand to know what right I had to be on the streets. My wound went deep; I felt that I had been slapped out of the human race. When I reached home, I did not tell the family what had happened; I merely told them that I had quit, that I was not making enough money, that I was seeking another job.

That night Griggs came to my house; we went for a walk.

"You got a goddam tough break," he said.

"Can you say it was my fault," I asked.

He shook his head.

"Well, what about your goddamn philosophy of meekness?" I asked him bitterly.

"These things just happen," he said, shrugging.

"They owe me money," I said.

"That's what I came about," he said. "Mr. Crane wants you to come in at ten in the morning. Ten sharp, now, mind you, because he'll be there and those guys won't gang up on you again."

The next morning at ten I crept up the stairs and peered into the office of the optical shop to make sure that Mr. Crane was in. He was at his desk. Pease and Reynolds were at their machines in the rear.

"Come in, Richard," Mr. Crane said.

I pulled off my hat and walked into the office; I stood before him.

"Sit down," he said.

I sat. He stared at me and shook his head.

"Tell me, what happened?"

An impulse to speak rose in me and died with the realization that I was facing a wall that I would never breech. I tried to speak several times and could make no sounds. I grew tense and tears burnt my cheeks.

"Now, just keep control of yourself," Mr. Crane said.

I clenched my fists and managed to talk.

"I tried to do my best here," I said.

"I believe you," he said. "But I want to know what happened. Which one bothered you?"

"Both of 'em," I said.

Reynolds came running to the door and I rose. Mr. Crane jumped to his feet.

"Get back in there," he told Reynolds.

"That nigger's lying!" Reynolds said. "I'll kill 'im if he lies on me!"

"Get back in there or get out," Mr. Crane said.

Reynolds backed away, keeping his eyes on me.

"Go ahead," Mr. Crane said. "Tell me what happened."

Then again I could not speak. What could I accomplish by telling him? I was black; I lived in the South. I would never learn to operate those machines as long as those two white men in there stood by them. Anger and fear welled in me as I felt what I had missed; I leaned forward and clapped my hands to my face.

"No, no, now," Mr. Crane said. "Keep control of yourself. No matter what happens, keep control. . . ."

"I know," I said in a voice not my own. "There's no use of my saying anything."

"Do you want to work here?" he asked me.

I looked at the white faces of Pease and Reynolds; I imagined their waylaying me, killing me. I was remembering what had happened to Ned's brother.

"No, sir," I breathed.

"Why?"

"I'm scared," I said. "They would kill me."

Mr. Crane turned and called Pease and Reynolds into the office.

"Now, tell me which one bothered you. Don't be afraid. Nobody's going to hurt you," Mr. Crane said.

I stared ahead of me and did not answer. He waved the men inside. The white stenographer looked at me with wide eyes and I felt drenched in shame, naked to my soul. The whole of my being felt violated, and I knew that my own fear had helped to violate it. I was breathing hard and struggling to master my feelings.

"Can I get my money, sir?" I asked at last.

"Just sit a minute and take hold of yourself," he said.

I waited and my roused senses grew slowly calm.

"I'm awfully sorry about this," he said.

"I had hoped for a lot from this job," I said. "I'd wanted to go to school, to college. . . ."

"I know," he said. "But what are you going to do now?"

My eyes traveled over the office, but I was not seeing.

"I'm going away," I said.

"What do you mean?"

"I'm going to get out of the South," I breathed.

"Maybe that's best," he said. "I'm from Illinois. Even for me, it's hard here. I can do just so much."

He handed me my money, more than I had earned for the week. I thanked him and rose to leave. He rose. I went into the hallway and he followed me. He reached out his hand.

"It's tough for you down here," he said.

I barely touched his hand. I walked swiftly down the hall, fighting against crying again. I ran down the steps, then paused and looked back up. He was standing at the head of the stairs, shaking his head. I went into the sunshine and walked home like a blind man.

from **A Raisin in the Sun**

LORRAINE HANSBERRY

ACT I
SCENE TWO

[*It is the following morning; a Saturday morning, and house cleaning is in progress at the* YOUNGERS. *Furniture has been shoved hither and yon and* MAMA *is giving the kitchen-area walls a washing down.* BENEATHA, *in dungarees, with a handkechief tied around her face, is spraying insecticide into the cracks in the walls. As they work, the radio is on and a Southside disk-jockey program is inappropriately filling the house with a rather exotic saxophone blues.* TRAVIS, *the sole idle one, is leaning on his arms, looking out of the window.*]

TRAVIS   Grandmama, that stuff Bennie is using smells awful. Can I go downstairs, please?

MAMA   Did you get all them chores done already? I ain't seen you doing much.

TRAVIS   Yes'm—finished early. Where did Mama go this morning?

MAMA   [*Looking at* BENEATHA] She had to go on a little errand.

TRAVIS   Where?

MAMA   To tend to her business.

TRAVIS   Can I go outside then?

MAMA   Oh, I guess so. You better stay right in front of the house, though and keep a good lookout for the postman.

TRAVIS   Yes'm. [*He starts out and decides to give his* AUNT BENEATHA *a good swat on the legs as he passes her*] Leave them poor little old cockroaches alone, they ain't bothering you none.

[*He runs as she swings the spray gun at him both viciously and playfully.* WALTER *enters from the bedroom and goes to the phone*]

MAMA   Look out there, girl, before you be spilling some of that stuff on that child!

TRAVIS   [*Teasing*] That's right—look out now!
[*He exits*]

BENEATHA   [*Drily*] I can't imagine that it would hurt him—it has never hurt the roaches.

MAMA   Well, little boys' hides ain't as tough as Southside roaches.

WALTER   [*Into phone*] Hello—Let me talk to Willy Harris.

MAMA   You better get over there behind the bureau. I seen one marching out of there like Napoleon yesterday.

WALTER   Hello, Willy? It ain't come yet. It'll be here in a few minutes. Did the lawyer give you the papers?

BENEATHA   There's really only one way to get rid of them, Mama—

MAMA   How?

BENEATHA   Set fire to this building.

WALTER   Good. Good. I'll be right over.

BENEATHA   Where did Ruth go, Walter?

WALTER   I don't know.
[*He exits abruptly*]

BENEATHA   Mama, where did Ruth go?

MAMA   [*Looking at her with meaning*]   To the doctor, I think.

BENEATHA   The doctor? What's the matter? [*They exchange glances*] You don't think—

MAMA   [*With her sense of drama*] Now I ain't saying what I think. But I ain't never been wrong 'bout a woman, either.
[*The phone rings*]

BENEATHA   [*At the phone*] Hay-lo . . . [*Pause, and a moment of recognition*] Well—when did you get back! . . . And how was it? . . . Of course I've missed you—in my way . . . This morning? No . . . house cleaning and all that and Mama hates it if I let people come over when the house is like this . . . You *have*? Well, that's different . . . What is it—Oh, what the hell, come on over . . . Right, see you then.
[*She hangs up*]

MAMA   [*Who has listened vigorously, as is her habit*] Who is that you inviting over here with this house looking like this? You ain't got the pride you was born with!

BENEATHA   Asagai doesn't care how houses look, Mama—he's an intellectual.

MAMA   *Who*?

BENEATHA   Asagai—Joseph Asagai. He's an African boy I met on campus. He's been studying in Canada all summer.

MAMA   What's his name?

BENEATHA   Asagai, Joseph. Ah-sah-guy . . . He's from Nigeria.

MAMA   Oh, that's the little country that was founded by slaves way back. . . .

BENEATHA   No, Mama—that's Liberia.

MAMA   I don't think I never met no African before.

BENEATHA   Well, do me a favor and don't ask him a whole lot of ignorant questions about Africans. I mean, do they wear clothes and all that—

MAMA   Well, now, I guess if you think we so ignorant 'round here maybe you shouldn't bring your friends here—

BENEATHA   It's just that people ask such crazy things. All anyone seems to know about them when it comes to Africa is Tarzan—

MAMA   [*Indignantly*] Why should I know anything about Africa?

BENEATHA   Why do you give money at church for the missionary work?

MAMA   Well, that's to help save people.

BENEATHA   You mean save them from *heathenism*—

MAMA   [*Innocently*] Yes.

BENEATHA   I'm afraid they need more salvation from the British and the French.

[RUTH *comes in forlornly and pulls off her coat with dejection. They both turn and look at her*]

RUTH   [*Dispiritedly*] Well, I guess from all the happy faces—everybody knows.

BENEATHA   You pregnant?

MAMA   Lord have mercy, I sure hope it's a little old girl. Travis ought to have a sister.

[BENEATHA *and* RUTH *give her a hopeless look for this grandmotherly enthusiasm*]

BENEATHA   How far along are you?

RUTH   Two months.

BENEATHA   Did you mean to? I mean did you plan it or was it an accident?

MAMA   What do you know about planning or not planning?

BENEATHA   Oh, Mama.

RUTH   [*Wearily*] She's twenty years old, Lena.

BENEATHA   Did you plan it, Ruth?

RUTH   Mind your own business.

BENEATHA   It is my business—where is he going to live, on the *roof*? [*There is silence following the remark as the three women react to the sense of it*] Gee—I didn't mean that, Ruth, honest. Gee, I don't feel like that at all. I—I think it is wonderful.

RUTH   [*Dully*] Wonderful.

BENEATHA   Yes—really.

MAMA   [*Looking at* RUTH, *worried*] Doctor say everything going to be all right?

RUTH   [*Far away*] Yes—she says everything is going to be fine. . . .

MAMA   [*Immediately suspicious*] "She"—What doctor you went to?

[RUTH *folds over, near hysteria*]

MAMA   [*Worriedly hovering over* RUTH] Ruth honey—what's the matter with you—you sick?

[RUTH *has her fists clenched on her thighs and is fighting hard to suppress a scream that seems to be rising in her*]

BENEATHA   What's the matter with her, Mama?

MAMA   [*Working her fingers in* RUTH's *shoulder to relax her*] She be all right. Women gets right depressed sometimes when they get her way. [*Speaking softly, expertly, rapidly*] Now you just relax. That's right . . . just lean back, don't think 'bout nothing at all . . . nothing at all—

RUTH   I'm all right. . . .

[*The glassy-eyed look melts and then she collapses into a fit of heavy sobbing. The bell rings*]

BENEATHA   Oh, my God—that must be Asagai.

MAMA   [*To* RUTH] Come on now, honey. You need to lie down and rest awhile . . . then have some nice hot food.

[*They exit,* RUTH's *weight on her mother-in-law.* BENEATHA, *herself profoundly disturbed, opens the door to admit a rather dramatic-looking young man with a large package*]

ASAGAI   Hello, Alaiyo—

BENEATHA   [*Holding the door open and regarding him with pleasure*] Hello . . . [*Long pause*] Well—come in. And please excuse everything. My mother was very upset about my letting anyone come here with the place like this.

ASAGAI   [*Coming into the room*] You look disturbed too. . . . Is something wrong?

BENEATHA   [*Still at the door, absently*] Yes . . . we've all got acute ghetto-itus. [*She smiles and comes toward him, finding a cigarette and sitting*] So—sit down! How was Canada.

ASAGAI   [*A sophisticate*] Canadian.

BENEATHA   [*Looking at him*] I'm very glad you are back.

ASAGAI   [*Looking back at her in turn*] Are you really?

BENEATHA   Yes—very.

ASAGAI   Why—you were quite glad when I went away. What happened?

BENEATHA   You went away.

ASAGAI   Ahhhhhhhh.

BENEATHA   Before—you wanted to be so serious before there was time.

ASAGAI   How much time must there be before one knows what one feels?

BENEATHA   [*Stalling this particular conversation. Her hands pressed together, in a deliberately childish gesture*] What did you bring me?

ASAGAI   [*Handing her the package*] Open it and see.

BENEATHA   [*Eagerly opening the package and drawing out some records and the colorful robes of a Nigerian woman*] Oh, Asagai! . . . You got them for me! . . . How beautiful . . . and the records too! [*She lifts out the robes and runs to the mirror with them and holds the drapery up in front of herself*]

ASAGAI   [*Coming to her at the mirror*] I shall have to teach you how to drape it correctly. [*He flings the material about her for the moment and stands back to look at her*] Ah—oh-pay-gay-day, oh-gbah-mu-shay. [*A Yoruba exclamation for admiration*] You wear it well . . . very well . . . mutilated hair and all.

BENEATHA   [*Turning suddenly*] My hair—what's wrong with my hair?

ASAGAI   [*Shrugging*] Were you born with it like that?

BENEATHA   [*Reaching up to touch it*] No . . . of course not. [*She looks back at the mirror, disturbed*]

ASAGAI   [*Smiling*] How then?

BENEATHA   You know perfectly well how . . . as crinkly as yours . . . that's how.

ASAGAI   And it is ugly to you that way?

BENEATHA   [*Quickly*] Oh, no—not ugly . . . [*More slowly, apologetically*] But it's so hard to manage when it's, well—raw.

ASAGAI   And so to accommodate that—you mutilate it every week?

BENEATHA   It's not mutilation!

ASAGAI   [*Laughing aloud at her seriousness*] Oh . . . please! I am only teasing you because you are so very serious about these things. [*He stands back from her and folds his arms across his chest as he watches her pulling at her hair and frowning in the mirror*] Do you remember the first time you met me at school? . . . [*He laughs*] You came up to me and you said—and I thought you were the most serious little thing I had ever seen—you said: [*He imitates her*] "Mr. Asagai—I want very much to talk with you. About Africa. You see, Mr. Asagai, I am looking for my *identity*!" [*He laughs*]

BENEATHA   [*Turning to him, not laughing*] Yes— [*Her face is quizzical, profoundly disturbed*]

ASAGAI   [*Still teasing and reaching out and taking her face in his hands and turning her profile to him*] Well . . . it is true that this is not so much a profile of a Hollywood queen as perhaps a queen of the Nile—[*A mock dismissal of the importance of the question*] But what does it matter? Assimilationism is so popular in your country.

BENEATHA   [*Wheeling, passionately, sharply*] I am not an assimilationist!

ASAGAI   [*The protest hangs in the room for a moment and* ASAGAI *studies her, his laughter fading*] Such a serious one. [*There is a pause*] So—you like the robes? You must take excellent care of them—they are from my sister's personal wardrobe.

BENEATHA   [*With incredulity*] You—you sent all the way home—for me?

ASAGAI—[*With charm*] For you—I would do much more. . . . Well, that is what I came for. I must go.

BENEATHA   Will you call me Monday?

ASAGAI   Yes. . . . We have a great deal to talk about. I mean about identity and time and all that.

BENEATHA   Time?

ASAGAI   Yes. About how much time one needs to know what one feels.

BENEATHA   You never understood that there is more than one kind of feeling which can exist between a man and a woman—or, at least, there should be.

ASAGAI   [*Shaking his head negatively but gently*] No. Between a man and a woman there need be only one kind of feeling. I have that for you. . . . Now even . . . right this moment. . . .

BENEATHA   I know—and by itself—it won't do. I can find that anywhere.

ASAGAI   For a woman it should be enough.

BENEATHA   I know—because that's what it says in all the novels that men write. But it isn't. Go ahead and laugh—but I'm not interested in being someone's little episode in America or—[*with feminine vengeance*]—one of them! [ASAGAI *has burst into laughter again*] That's funny as hell, huh!

ASAGAI   It's just that every American girl I have known has said that to me. White—black—in this you are all the same. And the same speech, too!

BENEATHA   [*Angrily*] Yuk, yuk, yuk!

ASAGAI   It's how you can be sure that the world's most liberated women are not liberated at all. You all talk about it too much!

[MAMA *enters and is immediately all social charm because of the presence of a guest*]

BENEATHA   Oh—Mama—this is Mr. Asagai.

MAMA   How do you do?

ASAGAI   [*Total politeness to an elder*] How do you do, Mrs. Younger. Please forgive me for coming at such an outrageous hour on a Saturday.

MAMA   Well, you are quite welcome. I just hope you understand that our house don't always look like this [*Chatterish*] You must come again. I would love to hear all about—[*Not sure of the name*]— your country. I think it's so sad the way our American Negroes don't know nothing about Africa 'cept Tarzan and all that. And all that money they pour into these churches when they ought to be helping you people over there drive out them French and Englishmen done taken away your land.

[*The mother flashes a slightly superior look at her daughter upon completion of the recitation*]

ASAGAI [*Taken aback by this sudden acutely unrelated expression of sympathy*] Yes . . . yes. . . .

MAMA [*Smiling at him suddenly and relaxing and looking him over*] How many miles is it from her to where you came from?

ASAGAI Many thousands.

MAMA [*Looking at him as she would* WALTER] I bet you don't half look after yourself, being away from your mama either. I spec you better come 'round here from time to time and get yourself some decent homecooked meals. . . .

ASAGAI [*Moved*] Thank you. Thank you very much. [*They are all quiet, then*—] Well . . . I must go. I will call you Monday, Alaiyo.

MAMA What's that he call you?

ASAGAI Oh—"Alaiyo." I hope you don't mind. It is what you would call a nickname, I think. It is a Yoruba word. I am a Yoruba.

MAMA [*Looking at* BENEATHA] I—I thought he was from—

ASAGAI [*Understanding*] Nigeria is my country. Yoruba is my tribal origin—

BENEATHA You didn't tell us what Alaiyo means . . . for all I know, you might be calling me Little Idiot or something. . . .

ASAGAI Well . . . let me see. . . . I do not know how just to explain it. . . . The sense of a thing can be so different when it changes languages.

BENEATHA You're evading.

ASAGAI No—really it is difficult. . . . [*Thinking*] It means . . . it means One for Whom Bread—Food—Is Not Enough. [*He looks at her*] Is that all right?

BENEATHA [*Understanding, softly*] Thank you.

MAMA [*Looking from one to the other and not understanding any of it*] Well . . . that's nice. . . . You must come see us again—Mr.—

ASAGAI Ah-sah-guy. . . .

MAMA Yes. . . . Do come again.

ASAGAI Good-bye.

[*He exits*]

MAMA [*After him*] Lord, that's a pretty thing just went out of here! [*Insinuatingly, to her daughter*] Yes, I guess I see why we done commence to get so interested in Africa 'round here. Missionaries my aunt Jenny!

[*She exits*]

BENEATHA Oh, Mama! . . .

[*She picks up the Nigerian dress, and holds it up to her in front of the mirror again. She sets the headdress on haphazardly and then notices her hair again and clutches at it and then replaces the headdress and frowns at herself. Then she starts to wriggle in front of the mirror as she thinks a Nigerian woman might.* TRAVIS *enters and regards her*]

TRAVIS   You cracking up?

BENEATHA   Shut up.

[*She pulls the headdress off and looks at herself in the mirror and clutches at her hair again and squinches her eyes as if trying to imagine something. Then, suddenly, she gets her raincoat and kerchief and hurriedly prepares for going out*]

from **Harlem Gallery**

MELVIN B. TOLSON

Black Boy,
beware of wine labels,
for the Republic does not guarantee
what the phrase "Château Bottled" means—
the estate, the proprietor, the quality.
This ignominy will baffle you, Black Boy,
because the white man's law
has raked your butt many a time
with fang and claw.
Beware of the waiter who wraps
a napkin around your Clos Saint Thierry,
if Chance takes you into high-hat places
open to all creeds and races
born to be or not to be.
Beware of the pop
of a champagne cork:
like the flatted fifth and octave jump in Bebop,
it is theatrical
in Vicksburg or New York.
Beware of the champagne cork
that does not swell up like your ma when she had you—*that*
comes out flat,
because the bottle of wine
is dead . . . dead
like Uncle Tom and the Jim Crow sign.
Beware . . . yet
your dreams in the Great White World
shall be unthrottled
by pigmented and unpigmented lionhearts,
for we know *without no*
every people, by and by, produces its "Château Bottled."

chapter 5

THE URBAN SLUM

There they are.
Thirty at the corner.
Black, raw, ready.
Sores in the city
That do not want to heal.

—Gwendolyn Brooks,
"As Seen by Disciplines"

The predicament of slum life, the thwarted dreams, and the feelings of despair are all reflected in the readings included in this section. The effects of ghetto life are pervasive for they attack at the very core—at the sense of self. The children of the slums often mask their feelings about self behind a hostile facade, which as the years go by is likely to harden into a societal hatred. If the children are black their problem is further complicated, for they very often are victims of racial as well as social-class prejudices. As the contradictions between democracy and racism become more apparent, many ghetto youths see no other outlet for their energies than to violate the codes of a system which they see as a huge hypocrisy. This is the story of Bigger Thomas.

The term "depressed area," as applied to the urban slum, carries with it a cluster of meanings, all of which suggest an emotional degeneration even more devastating than the physical squalor which spawns it. The atmosphere of the ghetto provides a fertile breeding ground for the social ills of drug addiction, alcoholism, and crime. The effect on the child is particularly devastating since he is provided, at a very young age, with a kind of in-service training on how to "beat the system." Denied access to the mainstream, the culture of the streets pushes him further away from a sense of self-respect, and he is caught up in a system which promises him—if nothing else—a feeling of being alive. In the act of murder Bigger Thomas, at least symbolically, announces his existence. "In all his life these two murders were the most meaningful things that had ever happened to him."[1]

From whatever perspective slums are viewed, the picture is a depressing one. Both the creative artist and the social scientist

---

[1] Richard Wright, *Native Son* (New York: Harper & Row, Publishers, 1966), p. 225.

may meticulously identify the conditions, but it is the former who breathes a special life into his material because he focuses on the feelings of individuals who live there and, if he is particularly skilled, he is able to capture the elusive tonal qualities of a slum area. Richard Wright and Lorraine Hansberry have successfully recreated in their own image the Southside section of Chicago. Though a work of art is a fiction, and as such can only be an illusion of reality, good literature can breathe life into a Beneatha Younger or a Bigger Thomas, and make them live.

I.   The readings in this chapter were selected for their relevance to the unit topic, *Conditions and Quality of Life in the Urban Slum.* Some of the subthemes developed in the selections are:

1.   The restrictions imposed by ghetto life
2.   Games and play-acting
3.   The physical setting
4.   Financial pressures

II.   The following readings are suggested as supplementary references for this thematic unit:

1.   Gwendolyn Brooks, *A Street in Bronzeville* (New York: Harper & Row, Publishers, 1945). (poetry)
2.   Gwendolyn Brooks, *In the Mecca* (New York: Harper & Row, Publishers, 1968). (poetry)
3.   Claude Brown, *Manchild in the Promised Land* (New York: Crowell-Collier and Macmillan, Inc., 1965). (autobiography)

QUESTIONS FOR DISCUSSION

1.   In the light of the readings in this unit, react to this quotation from *Nigger* by Dick Gregory:

"You didn't die a slave for nothing Momma. You and all the Negro mothers who gave their kids the strength to go on, to take that thimble to the well while the whites were taking buckets. Those of us who weren't destroyed got stronger, got calluses on our souls. And we're ready to change a system."

2.   What are the many ways in which Bigger Thomas handles his feelings of being an outsider?

3.   Do you feel that the characters in these selections have adopted a fatalistic view of life?

from **Native Son**

RICHARD WRIGHT

BOOK ONE
FEAR

Brrrrrrriiiiiiiiiiiiiiiiiiiinng!

An alarm clock clanged in the dark and silent room. A bedspring creaked. A woman's voice sang out impatiently:

"Bigger, shut that thing off!"

A surly grunt sounded above the tinny ring of metal. Naked feet swished dryly across the planks in the wooden floor and the clang ceased abruptly.

"Turn on the light, Bigger."

"Awright," came a sleepy mumble.

Light flooded the room and revealed a black boy standing in a narrow space between two iron beds, rubbing his eyes with the backs of his hands. From a bed to his right the woman spoke again:

"Buddy, get up from there! I got a big washing on my hand today and I want you-all out of here."

Another black boy rolled from bed and stoop up. The woman also rose and stood in her nightgown.

"Turn your heads so I can dress," she said.

The two boys averted their eyes and gazed into a far corner of the room. The woman rushed out of her nightgown and put on a pair of step-ins. She turned to the bed from which she had risen and called:

"Vera! Get up from there!"

"What time is it, Ma?" asked a muffled, adolescent voice from beneath a quilt.

"Get up from there, I say!"

"O.K., Ma."

A brown-skinned girl in a cotton gown got up and stretched her arms above her head and yawned. Sleepily, she sat on a chair and fumbled with her stockings. The two boys kept their faces averted while their mother and sister put on enough clothes to keep them from feeling ashamed; and the mother and sister did the same while the boys dressed. Abruptly, they all paused, holding their clothes in their hands, their attention caught by a light tapping in the thinly plastered walls of the room. They forgot their conspiracy against shame and their eyes strayed apprehensively over the floor.

"There he is again, Bigger!" the woman screamed, and the tiny one-room apartment galvanized into violent action. A chair toppled as the woman, half-dressed and in her stocking feet, scrambled breathlessly upon the bed. Her two sons, barefoot, stood tense and motionless, their eyes searching anxiously under the bed and chairs. The girl ran into a corner, half-stooped and gathered the hem of her slip into both of her hands and held it tightly over her knees.

"Oh! Oh!" she wailed.

"There he goes!"

The woman pointed a shaking finger. Her eyes were round with fascinated horror.

"Where?"

"I don't see 'im!"

"Bigger, he's behind the trunk!" the girl whimpered.

"Vera!" the woman screamed. "Get up here on the bed! Don't let that thing *bite* you!"

Frantically, Vera climbed upon the bed and the woman caught hold of her. With their arms entwined about each other, the black mother and the brown daughter gazed openmouthed at the trunk in the corner.

Bigger looked round the room wildly, then darted to a curtain and swept it aside and grabbed two heavy iron skillets from a wall above a gas stove. He whirled and called softly to his brother, his eyes glued to the trunk.

"Buddy!"

"Yeah?"

"Here; take this skillet."

"O.K."

"Now, get over by the door!"

"O.K."

Buddy crouched by the door and held the iron skillet by its handle, his arm flexed and poised. Save the quick, deep breathing of the four people, the room was quiet. Bigger crept on tiptoe toward the trunk with the skillet clutched stiffly in his hand, his eyes dancing and watching every inch of the wooden floor in front of him. He paused and, without moving an eye or muscle, called:

"Buddy!"

"Hunh?"

"Put that box in front of the hole so he can't get out!"

"O.K."

Buddy ran to a wooden box and shoved it quickly in front of a gaping hole in the molding and then backed again to the front door, holding the skillet ready. Bigger eased to the trunk and peered behind it cautiously. He saw nothing. Carefully, he stuck out his bare foot and pushed the trunk a few inches.

"There he is!" the mother screamed again.

A huge black rat squealed and leaped at Bigger's trouserleg and snagged it in his teeth, hanging on.

"Goddamn!" Bigger whispered fiercely, whirling and kicking out his leg with all the strength of his body. The force of his movement shook the rat loose and it sailed through the air and struck a wall. Instantly, it rolled over and leaped again. Bigger dodged and the rat landed against a table leg. With clenched teeth, Bigger held the skillet; he was afraid to hurl it, fearing that he might miss. The rat squeaked and turned and ran in a narrow circle, looking for a place to hide; it leaped again past Bigger and scurried on dry rasping feet to one side of the box and then to the other, searching for the hole. Then it turned and reared upon its hind legs.

"Hit 'im, Bigger!" Buddy shouted.

"Kill 'im!" the woman screamed.

The rat's belly pulsed with fear. Bigger advanced a step and the rat emitted a long thin song of defiance, its black beady eyes glittering. its tiny forefeet pawing the air restlessly. Bigger swung the skillet; it skidded over the floor, missing the rat, and clattered to a stop against a wall.

"Goddamn!"

The rat leaped. Bigger sprang to one side. The rat stopped under a chair and let out a furious screak. Bigger moved slowly backward toward the door.

"Gimme that skillet, Buddy," he asked quietly, not taking his eyes from the rat.

Buddy extended his hand. Bigger caught the skillet and lifted it high in the air. The rat scuttled across the floor and stopped again at the box and searched quickly for the hole; then it reared once more and bared long yellow fangs, piping shrilly, belly quivering.

Bigger aimed and let the skillet fly with a heavy grunt. There was a shattering of wood as the box caved in. The woman screamed and hid her face in her hands. Bigger tiptoed forward and peered.

"I got 'im," he muttered, his clenched teeth bared in a smile. "By God, I got 'im."

He kicked the splintered box out of the way and the flat black body of the rat lay exposed, its two long yellow tusks showing distinctly. Bigger took a shoe and pounded the rat's head, crushing it, cursing hysterically:

"You sonofa*bitch*!"

The woman on the bed sank to her knees and buried her face in the quilts and sobbed:

"Lord, Lord, have mercy. . . ."

"Aw, Mama," Vera whimpered, bending to her. "Don't cry. It's dead now."

The two brothers stood over the dead rat and spoke in tones of awed admiration.

"Gee, but he's a big bastard."

"That sonofabitch could cut your throat."

"He's over a foot long."

"How in hell do they get so big?"

"Eating garbage and anything else they can get."

"Look, Bigger, there's a three-inch rip in your pantleg."

"Yeah; he was after me, all right."

"Please, Bigger, take 'im out," Vera begged.

"Aw, don't be so scary," Buddy said.

The woman on the bed continued to sob. Bigger took a piece of newspaper and gingerly lifted the rat by its tail and held it out at arm's length.

"Bigger, take 'im out," Vera begged again.

Bigger laughed and approached the bed with the dangling rat, swinging it to and fro like a pendulum, enjoying his sister's fear.

"Bigger!" Vera gasped convulsively; she screamed and swayed and closed her eyes and fell headlong across her mother and rolled limply from the bed to the floor.

"Bigger, for God's sake!" the mother sobbed, rising and bending over Vera. "Don't do that! Throw that rat out!"

He laid the rat down and started to dress.

"Bigger, help me lift Vera to the bed," the mother said.

He paused and turned around.

"What's the matter?" he asked, feigning ignorance.

"Do what I asked you, will you, boy?"

He went to the bed and helped his mother lift Vera. Vera's eyes were closed. He turned away and finished dressing. He wrapped the rat in a newspaper and went out of the door and down the stairs and put it into a garbage can at the corner of an alley. When he returned to the room his mother was still bent over Vera, placing a wet towel upon her head. She straightened and faced him, her cheeks and eyes wet with tears and her lips tight with anger.

"Boy, sometimes I wonder what makes you act like you do."

"What I do now?" he demanded belligerently.

"Sometimes you act the biggest fool I ever saw."

"What you talking about?"

"You scared your sister with that rat and she *fainted*! Ain't you got no sense at *all*?"

"Aw, I didn't know she was that scary."

"Buddy!" the mother called.

"Yessum."

"Take a newspaper and spread it over that spot."

"Yessum."

Buddy opened out a newspaper and covered the smear of blood on the floor where the rat had been crushed. Bigger went to the window and stood looking out abstractedly into the street. His mother glared at his back.

"Bigger, sometimes I wonder why I birthed you," she said bitterly.

Bigger looked at her and turned away.

"Maybe you oughtn't't've. Maybe you ought to left me where I was."

"You shut your sassy mouth!"

"Aw, for chrissakes!" Bigger said, lighting a cigarette.

"Buddy, pick up them skillets and put 'em in the sink," the mother said.

"Yessum."

Bigger walked across the floor and sat on the bed. His mother's eyes followed him.

"We wouldn't have to live in this garbage dump if you had any manhood in you," she said.

"Aw, don't start that again."

"How you feel, Vera?" the mother asked.

Vera raised her head and looked about the room as though expecting to see another rat.

"Oh, Mama!"

"You poor thing!"

"I couldn't help it. Bigger scared me."

"Did you hurt yourself?"

"I bumped my head."

"Here, take it easy. You'll be all right."

"How come Bigger acts that way?" Vera asked, crying again.

"He's just crazy," the mother said. "Just plain dumb black crazy."

"I'll be late for my sewing class at the Y.W.C.A.," Vera said.

"Here, stretch out on the bed. You'll feel better in a little while," the mother said.

She left Vera on the bed and turned a pair of cold eyes upon Bigger.

"Suppose you wake up some morning and find your sister dead? What would you think then?" she asked. "Suppose those rats cut our veins at night when we sleep? Naw! Nothing like that ever bothers you! All you care about is your own pleasure! Even when the relief offers you a job you won't take it till they threaten to cut off your food and starve you! Bigger, honest, you the most no-countest man I ever seen in all my life!"

"You done told me that a thousand times," he said, not looking round.

"Well, I'm telling you again! And mark my word, some of these days you going to set down and *cry*. Some of these days you going to wish you had made something out of yourself, instead of just a tramp. But it'll be too late then."

"Stop prophesying about me," he said.

"I prophesy much as I please! And if you don't like it, you can get out. We can get along without you. We can live in one room just like we living now, even with you gone," she said.

"Aw, for chrissakes!" he said, his voice filled with nervous irritation.

"You'll regret how you living some day," she went on. "If you don't stop running with that gang of yours and do right you'll end up where you never thought you would. You think I don't know what you boys is doing, but I do. And the gallows is at the end of the road you traveling, boy. Just remember that." She turned and looked at Buddy. "Throw that box outside, Buddy."

"Yessum."

There was silence. Buddy took the box out. The mother went behind the curtain to the gas stove. Vera sat up in bed and swung her feet to the floor.

"Lay back down, Vera," the mother said.

"I feel all right now, Ma. I got to go to my sewing class."

"Well, if you feel like it, set the table," the mother said, going behind the curtain again. "Lord, I get so tired of this I don't know what to do," her voice floated plaintively from behind the curtain. "All I ever do is try to make a home for you children and you don't care."

"Aw, Ma," Vera protested. "Don't say that."

"Vera, sometimes I just want to lay down and quit."

"Ma, please don't say that."

"I can't last many more years, living like this."

"I'll be old enough to work soon, Ma."

"I reckon I'll be dead then. I reckon God'll call me home."

Vera went behind the curtain and Bigger heard her trying to comfort his mother. He shut their voices out of his mind. He hated his family because he knew that they were suffering and that he was powerless to help them. He knew that the moment he allowed himself to feel to its fullness how they lived, the shame and misery of their lives, he would be swept out of himself with fear and despair. So he held toward them an attitude of iron reserve; he lived with them, but behind a wall, a curtain. And toward himself he was even more exacting. He knew that the moment he allowed what his life meant to enter fully into his consciousness, he would either kill himself or someone else. So he denied himself and acted tough.

He got up and crushed his cigarette upon the window sill. Vera came into the room and placed knives and forks upon the table.

"Get ready to eat, you-all," the mother called.

He sat at the table. The odor of frying bacon and boiling coffee drifted to him from behind the curtain. His mother's voice floated to him in song.

> *Life is like a mountain railroad*
> *With an engineer that's brave*
> *We must make the run successful*
> *From the cradle to the grave. . . .*

The song irked him and he was glad when she stopped and came into the room with a pot of coffee and a plate of crinkled bacon. Vera brought the bread in and they sat down. His mother closed her eyes and lowered her head and mumbled.

"Lord, we thank Thee for the food You done placed before us for the nourishment of our bodies. Amen." She lifted her eyes and without changing her tone of voice, said, "You going to have to learn to get up earlier than this, Bigger, to hold a job."

He did not answer or look up.

"You want me to pour you some coffee?" Vera asked.

"Yeah."

"You going to take the job, ain't you, Bigger?" his mother asked.

He laid down his fork and stared at her.

"I told you last night I was going to take it. How many times you want to ask me?"

"Well, don't bite her head off," Vera said. "She only asked you a question."

"Pass the bread and stop being smart."

"You know you have to see Mr. Dalton at five-thirty," his mother said.

"You done said that ten times."

"I don't want you to forget, son."

"And you know how you can forget," Vera said.

"Aw, lay off Bigger," Buddy said. "He told you he was going to take the job."

"Don't tell 'em nothing," Bigger said.

"You shut your mouth, Buddy, or get up from this table," the mother said. "I'm not going to take any stinking sass from you. One fool in the family's enough."

"Lay off, Ma," Buddy said.

"Bigger's setting here like he ain't glad to get a job," she said.

"What you want me to do? Shout?" Bigger asked.

"Oh, Bigger!" his sister said.

"I wish you'd keep your big mouth out of this!" he told his sister.

"If you get that job," his mother said in a low, kind tone of voice, busy slicing a loaf of bread, "I can fix up a nice place for you children. You could be comfortable and not have to live like pigs."

"Bigger ain't decent enough to think of nothing like that," Vera said.

"God, I wish you-all would let me eat," Bigger said.

His mother talked on as though she had not heard him and he stopped listening.

"Ma's talking to you, Bigger," Vera said.

"So *what?*"

"Don't be that way, Bigger!"

He laid down his fork and his strong black fingers gripped the edge of the table; there was silence save for the tinkling of his brother's fork against a plate. He kept staring at his sister till her eyes fell.

"I wish you'd let me eat," he said again.

As he ate he felt that they were thinking of the job he was to get that evening and it made him angry; he felt that they had tricked him into a cheap surrender.

"I need some carfare," he said.

"Here's all I got," his mother said, pushing a quarter to the side of his plate.

He put the quarter in his pocket and drained his cup of coffee in one long swallow. He got his coat and cap and went to the door.

"You know, Bigger," his mother said, "if you don't take that job the relief'll cut us off. We won't have any food."

"I told you I'd take it!" he shouted and slammed the door.

He went down the steps into the vestibule and stood looking out into the street through the plate glass of the front door. Now and then a streetcar rattled past over steel tracks. He was sick of his life at home. Day in and day out there was nothing but shouts and bickering. But what could he do? Each time he asked himself that question his mind hit a blank wall and he stopped thinking. Across the street directly in front of him, he saw a truck pull to a stop at the curb and two white men in overalls got out with pails and brushes. Yes, he could take the job at Dalton's and be miserable, or he could refuse it and starve. It maddened him to think that he did not have a wider choice of action. Well, he could not stand here all day like this. What was he to do with himself? He tried to decide if he wanted to buy a ten-cent magazine, or go to a movie, or go to the poolroom and talk with the gang, or just loaf around. With his hands deep in his pockets, another cigarette slanting across his chin, he brooded and watched the men at work across the street. They were pasting a huge colored poster to a signboard. The poster showed a white face.

"That's Buckley!" He spoke softly to himself. "He's running for State's Attorney again." The men were slapping the poster with wet brushes. He looked at the round florid face and wagged his head. "I bet that sonofabitch rakes off a million bucks in graft a year. Boy, if I was in his shoes for just one day I'd *never* have to worry again."

When the men were through they gathered up their pails and brushes and got into the truck and drove off. He looked at the poster: the white face was fleshy but stern; one hand was uplifted and its index finger pointed straight out into the street at each passer-by. The poster showed one of those faces that looked straight at you when you looked at it and all the while you were walking and turning your head to look at it it kept looking unblinkingly back at you until you got so far from it you had to take your eyes away, and then it stopped, like a movie blackout. Above the top of the poster were tall red letters: IF YOU BREAK THE LAW, YOU CAN'T WIN!

He snuffed his cigarette and laughed silently. "You crook," he mumbled, shaking his head. "You let whoever pays *you* off win!" He opened the door and met the morning air. He went along the sidewalk with his head down, fingering his pockets; in his vest pocket he found a lone copper cent. That made a total of twenty-six cents, fourteen cents of which would have to be saved for carfare to Mr. Dalton's; that is, if he decided to take the job. In order to buy a magazine and go to the movies he would have to have at least twenty cents more. "Goddammit, I'm always broke!" he mumbled.

He stood on the corner in the sunshine, watching cars and people pass. He needed more money; if he did not get more than he had now he would not know what to do with himself for the rest of the day. He wanted to see a movie; his senses hungered for it. In a movie he could dream without effort; all he had to do was lean back in a seat and keep his eyes open.

He thought of Gus and G.H. and Jack. Should he go to the poolroom and talk with them? But there was no use in his going unless they were ready to do what they had been long planning to do. If they could, it would mean some sure and quick money. From three o'clock to four o'clock in the afternoon there was no policeman on duty in the block where Blum's Delicatessen was and it would be safe. One of them could hold a gun on Blum and keep him from yelling; one could watch the front door; one could watch the back; and one could get the money from the box under the counter. Then all four of them could lock Blum in the store and run out through the back and duck down the alley and meet an hour later, either at Doc's poolroom or at the South Side Boy's Club, and split the money.

Holding up Blum ought not take more than two minutes, at the most. And it would be their last job. But it would be the toughest one that they had ever pulled. All the other times they had raided newsstands, fruit stands, and apartments. And, too, they had never held up a white man before. They had always robbed Negroes. They felt that it was much easier and safer to rob their own people, for they knew that white policemen never really searched diligently for Negroes who committed crimes against other Negroes. For months they had talked of robbing Blum's, but had not been able to bring themselves to do it. They had the feeling that the robbing of Blum's would be a violation of ultimate taboo; it would be a trespassing into territory where the full wrath of an alien white world would be turned loose upon them; in short, it would be a symbolic challenge of the white world's rule over them; a challenge which they yearned to make, but were afraid to. Yes; if they could rob Blum's, it would be a real hold-up, in more senses than one. In comparison, all of their other jobs had been play.

"Good-bye, Bigger."

He looked up and saw Vera passing with a sewing kit dangling from her arm. She paused at the corner and came back to him.

"Now, what you want?"

"Bigger, please. . . . You're getting a good job now. Why don't you stay away from Jack and Gus and G.H. and keep out of trouble?"

"You keep your big mouth out of my business!"

"But, Bigger!"

"Go on to school, will you!"

She turned abruptly and walked on. He knew that his mother had been talking to Vera and Buddy about him, telling them that if he got into any more trouble he would be sent to prison and not just to the reform school, where they sent him last time. He did not mind what his mother said to Buddy about him. Buddy was all right. Tough, plenty. But Vera was a sappy girl; she did not have any more sense than to believe everything she was told.

He walked toward the poolroom. When he got to the door he saw Gus half a block away, coming toward him. He stopped and waited. It was Gus who had first thought of robbing Blum's.

"Hi, Bigger!"

"What you saying, Gus?"

"Nothing. Seen G.H. or Jack yet?"

"Naw. You?"

"Naw. Say, got a cigarette?"

"Yeah."

Bigger took out his pack and gave Gus a cigarette; he lit his and held the match for Gus. They leaned their backs against the red-brick wall of a building, smoking, their cigarettes slanting white across their black chins. To the east Bigger saw the sun burning a dazzling yellow. In the sky above him a few big white clouds drifted. He puffed silently, relaxed, his mind pleasantly vacant of purpose. Every slight movement in the street evoked a casual curiosity in him. Automatically, his eyes followed each car as it whirred over the smooth black asphalt. A woman came by and he watched the gentle sway of her body until she disappeared into a doorway. He sighed, scratched his chin and mumbled.

"Kinda warm today."

"Yeah," Gus said.

"You get more heat from this sun than from them old radiators at home."

"Yeah; them old white landlords sure don't give much heat."

"And they always knocking at your door for money."

"I'll be glad when summer comes."

"Me too," Bigger said.

He stretched his arms above his head and yawned; his eyes moistened. The sharp precision of the world of steel and stone dissolved into blurred waves. He blinked and the world grew hard again, mechanical, distinct. A weaving motion in the sky made him turn his eyes upward; he saw a slender streak of billowing white blooming against the deep blue. A plane was writing high up in the air.

"Look!" Bigger said.

"What?"

"That plane writing up there," Bigger said, pointing.

"Oh!"

They squinted at a tiny ribbon of unfolding vapor that spelled out the word: USE. . . . The plane was so far away that at times the strong glare of the sun blanked it from sight.

"You can hardly see it," Gus said.

"Looks like a little bird," Bigger breathed with childlike wonder.

"Them white boys sure can fly," Gus said.

"Yeah," Bigger said, wistfully. "They get a chance to do everything."

Noiselessly, the tiny plane looped and veered, vanishing and appearing, leaving behind it a long trail of white plumage, like coils of fluffy paste being squeezed from a tube; a plume-coil that grew and swelled and slowly began to fade into the air at the edges. The plane wrote another word: SPEED. . . .

"How high you reckon he is?" Bigger asked.

"I don't know. Maybe a hundred miles; maybe a thousand."

"I could fly one of them things if I had a chance." Bigger mumbled reflectively, as though talking to himself.

Gus pulled down the corners of his lips, stepped out from the wall, squared his shoulders, doffed his cap, bowed low and spoke with mock deference:

"Yessuh."

"You go to hell," Bigger said, smiling.

"Yessuh," Gus said again.

"I *could* fly a plane if I had a chance," Bigger said.

"If you wasn't black and if you had some money and if they'd let you go to that aviation school, you *could* fly a plane," Gus said.

For a moment Bigger contemplated all the "ifs" that Gus had mentioned. Then both boys broke into hard laughter, looking at each other through squinted eyes. When their laughter subsided, Bigger said in a voice that was half-question and half-statement:

"It's funny how the white folks treat us, ain't it?"

"It better be funny," Gus said.

"Maybe they right in not wanting us to fly," Bigger said. " 'Cause if I took a plane up I'd take a couple of bombs along and drop 'em as sure as hell. . . ."

They laughed again, still looking upward. The plane sailed and dipped and spread another word against the sky: GASOLINE. . . .

"Use Speed Gasoline," Bigger mused, rolling the words slowly from his lips. "God, I'd like to fly up there in that sky."

"God'll let you fly when He gives you your wings up in heaven," Gus said.

They laughed again, reclining against the wall, smoking, the lids of their eyes drooped softly against the sun. Cars whizzed past on rubber tires. Bigger's face was metallically black in the strong sunlight. There was in his eyes a pensive brooding amusement, as of a man who had been long confronted and tantalized by a riddle whose answer seemed always just on the verge of escaping him, but prodding him irresistibly on to seek its solution. The silence irked Bigger; he was anxious to do something to evade looking so squarely at this problem.

"Let's play 'white,' " Bigger said, referring to a game of play-acting in which he and his frends imitated the ways and manners of white folks.

"I don't feel like it," Gus said.

"General!" Bigger pronounced in a sonorous tone, looking at Gus expectantly.

"Aw, hell! I don't want to play," Gus whined.

"You'll be court-martialed," Bigger said, snapping out his words with military precision.

"Nigger, you nuts!" Gus laughed.

"General!" Bigger tried again, determinedly.

Gus looked wearily at Bigger, then straightened, saluted and answered:

"Yessuh."

"Send your men over the river at dawn and attack the enemy's left flank," Bigger ordered.

"Yessuh."

"Send the Fifth, Sixth, and Seventh Regiments," Bigger said, frowning. "And attack with tanks, gas, planes, and infantry."

"Yessuh!" Gus said again, saluting and clicking his heels.

For a moment they were silent, facing each other, their shoulders thrown back, their lips compressed to hold down the mounting impulse to laugh. Then they guffawed, partly at themselves and partly at the vast white world that sprawled and towered in the sun before them.

"Say, what's 'left flank'?" Gus asked.

"I don't know," Bigger said. "I heard it in the movies."

They laughed again. After a bit they relaxed and leaned against the wall, smoking. Bigger saw Gus cup his left hand to his ear, as though holding a telephone receiver; and cup his right hand to his mouth, as though talking into a transmitter.

"Hello," Gus said.

"Hello," Bigger said. "Who's this?"

"This is Mr. J. P. Morgan speaking," Gus said.

"Yessuh, Mr. Morgan," Bigger said; his eyes filled with mock adulation and respect.

"I want you to sell twenty thousand shares of U. S. Steel in the market this morning," Gus said.

"At what price, suh?" Bigger asked.

"Aw, just dump 'em at any price," Gus said with casual irritation. "We're holding too much."

"Yessuh," Bigger said.

"And call me at my club at two this afternoon and tell me if the President telephoned," Gus said.

"Yessuh, Mr. Morgan," Bigger said.

Both of them made gestures signifying that they were hanging up telephone receivers; then they bent double, laughing.

"I bet that's *just* the way they talk," Gus said.

"I wouldn't be surprised," Bigger said.

They were silent again. Presently, Bigger cupped his hand to his mouth and spoke through an imaginary telephone transmitter.

"Hello."

"Hello," Gus answered. "Who's this?"

"This is the President of the United States speaking," Bigger said.

"Oh, yessuh, Mr. President," Gus said.

"I'm calling a cabinet meeting this afternoon at four o'clock and you, as Secretary of State, *must* be there."

"Well, now, Mr. President," Gus said, "I'm pretty busy. They raising sand over there in Germany and I got to send 'em a note. . . ."

"But this is important," Bigger said.

"What you going to take up at this cabinet meeting?" Gus asked.

"Well, you see, the niggers is raising sand all over the country," Bigger said, struggling to keep back his laughter. "We've got to do something with these black folks. . . ."

"Oh, if it's about the niggers, I'll be right there, Mr. President," Gus said.

They hung up imaginary receivers and leaned against the wall and laughed. A street car rattled by. Bigger sighed and swore.

"Goddammit!"

"What's the matter?"

"They don't let us do *nothing*."

"Who?"

"The *white* folks."

"You talk like you just now finding that out," Gus said.

"Naw. But I just can't get used to it," Bigger said. "I swear to God I can't. I know I oughtn't think about it, but I can't help it. Every time I think about it I feel like somebody's poking a red-hot iron down my throat. Goddammit, look! We live here and they live there. We black and they white. They got things and we ain't. They do things and we can't. It's just like living in jail. Half the time I feel like I'm on the outside of the world peeping in through a knothole in the fence. . . ."

"Aw, ain't no use feeling that way about it. It don't help none," Gus said.

"You know one thing?" Bigger said.

"What?"

"Sometimes I feel like something awful's going to happen to me," Bigger spoke with a tinge of bitter pride in his voice.

"What you mean?" Gus asked, looking at him quickly. There was fear in Gus's eyes.

"I don't know. I just feel that way. Every time I get to thinking about me being black and they being white, me being here and they being there, I feel like something awful's going to happen to me. . . ."

"Aw, for chrissakes! There ain't nothing you can do about it. How come you want to worry yourself? You black and they make the laws. . . ."

"Why they make us live in one corner of the city? Why don't they let us fly planes and run ships. . . ."

Gus hunched Bigger with his elbow and mumbled good-naturedly, "Aw, nigger, quit thinking about it. You'll go nuts."

The plane was gone from the sky and the white plumes of floating smoke were thinly spread, vanishing. Because he was restless and had time on his hands, Bigger yawned again and hoisted his arms high above his head.

"Nothing ever happens," he complained.

"What you want to happen?"

"Anything," Bigger said with a wide sweep of his dingy palm, a sweep that included all the possible activities of the world.

Then their eyes were riveted; a slate-colored pigeon swooped down to the middle of the steel car tracks and began strutting to and fro with ruffled feathers, its fat neck bobbing with regal pride. A street car rumbled forward and the pigeon rose swiftly through the air on wings stretched so taut and sheer that Bigger could see the gold of the sun through their translucent tips. He tilted his head and watched the slate-colored bird flap and wheel out of sight over the edge of a high roof.

"Now, if I could only do that," Bigger said.

Gus laughed.

"Nigger, you nuts."

"I reckon we the only things in this city that can't go where we want to go and do what we want to do."

"Don't think about it," Gus said.

"I can't help it."

"That's why you feeling like something awful's going to happen to you," Gus said. "You think too much."

"What in hell can a man do?" Bigger asked, turning to Gus.

"Get drunk and sleep it off."

"I can't. I'm broke."

Bigger crushed his cigarette and took out another one and offered the package to Gus. They continued smoking. A huge truck swept past, lifting scraps of white paper into the sunshine; the bits settled down slowly.

"Gus?"

"Hunh?"

"You know where the white folks live?"

"Yeah," Gus said, pointing eastward. "Over across the 'line'; over there on Cottage Grove Avenue."

"Naw; they don't," Bigger said.

"What you mean?" Gus asked, puzzled. "Then, where do they live?"

Bigger doubled his fist and struck his solar plexus.

"Right down here in my stomach," he said.

Gus looked at Bigger searchingly, then away, as though ashamed.

"Yeah; I know what you mean," he whispered.

"Every time I think of 'em, I *feel* 'em," Bigger said.

"Yeah; and in your chest and throat, too," Gus said.

"It's like fire."

"And sometimes you can't hardly breathe. . . ."

Bigger's eyes were wide and placid, gazing into space.

"That's when I feel like something awful's going to happen to me. . . ." Bigger paused, narrowed his eyes. "Naw; it ain't like something going to happen to me. It's . . . It's like I was going to do something I can't help. . . ."

"Yeah!" Gus said with uneasy eagerness. His eyes were full of a look compounded of fear and admiration for Bigger. "Yeah; I know what you mean. It's like you going to fall and don't know where you going to land. . . ."

Gus's voice trailed off. The sun slid behind a big white cloud and the street was plunged in cool shadow; quickly the sun edged forth again and it was bright and warm once more. A long sleek black car, its fenders glinting like glass in the sun, shot past them at high speed and turned a corner a few blocks away. Bigger pursed his lips and sang:

"Zooooooooooom!"

"They got everything," Gus said.

"They own the world," Bigger said.

"Aw, what the hell," Gus said. "Let's go in the poolroom."

from **A Raisin in the Sun**

LORRAINE HANSBERRY

ACT I
SCENE ONE

[*The* YOUNGER *living room would be a comfortable and well-ordered room if it were not for a number of indestructible contradictions to this state of being. Its furnishings are typical and undistinguished and their primary feature now is that they have clearly had to accommodate the living of too many people for too many years—and they are tired. Still, we can see that at some time, a time probably no longer remembered by the family (except perhaps for* MAMA) *the furnishings of this room were actually selected with care and love and even hope—and brought to this apartment and arranged with taste and pride.*

[*That was a long time ago. Now the once loved pattern of the couch upholstery has to fight to show itself from under acres of crocheted doilies and couch covers which have themselves finally come to be more important than the upholstery. And here a table or a chair has been moved to disguise the worn places in the carpet; but the carpet has fought back by showing its weariness, with depressing uniformity, elsewhere on its surface.*

[*Weariness has, in fact, won in this room. Everything has been polished, washed, sat on, scrubbed too often. All pretenses but living itself have long since vanished from the very atmosphere of this room.*

[*Moreover, a section of this room, for it is not really a room unto itself, though the landlord's lease would make it seem so, slopes backward to provide a small kitchen area, where the family prepares the meals that are eaten in the living room proper, which must also serve as dining room. The single window that has been provided for these "two" rooms is located in this kitchen area. The sole natural light the family may enjoy in the course of the day is only that which fights its way through this little window.*

[*At left, a door leads to a bedroom which is shared by* MAMA *and her daughter,* BENEATHA. *At right, opposite, is a second room (which in the beginning of the life of this apartment was probably a breakfast room) which serves as a bedroom for* WALTER *and his wife,* RUTH.]

[*Time: Sometime between World War II and the present.*]

[*Place: Chicago's Southside.*]

[*At Rise: It is morning dark in the living room.* TRAVIS *is asleep on the make-down bed at center. An alarm clock sounds from within the bedroom at right, and presently* RUTH *enters from that room and closes the door behind her. She crosses sleepily toward the window. As she passes her sleeping son she reaches down and shakes him a little. At the window she raises the shade and a dusky Southside morning light comes in feebly. She fills a pot with water and puts it on to boil. She calls to the boy, between yawns, in a slightly muffled voice.*

[RUTH *is about thirty. We can see that she was a pretty girl, even exceptionally so, but now it is apparent that life has been little that she expected, and disappointment has already begun to hang in her face. In a few years, before thirty-five even, she will be known among her people as a "settled woman."*

[*She crosses to her son and gives him a good, final, rousing shake.*]

RUTH   Come on now, boy, it's seven thirty! [*Her son sits up at last, in a stupor of sleepiness*] I say hurry up, Travis! You ain't the only person in the world got to use a bathroom! [*The child, a sturdy, handsome little boy of ten or eleven, drags himself out of the bed and almost blindly takes his towels and "today's clothes" from drawers and a closet and goes out to the bathroom, which is in an outside hall and which is shared by another family or families on the same floor.* RUTH *crosses to the bedroom door at right and opens it and calls in to her husband*] Walter Lee! . . . It's after seven thirty! Lemme see you do some waking up in there now! [*She waits*] You better get up from there, man! It's after seven thirty I tell you. [*She waits again*] All right, you just go ahead and lay there and next thing you know Travis be finished and Mr. Johnson'll be in there and you'll be fussing and cussing round here like a mad man! And be late too! [*She waits, at the end of patience*] Walter Lee— it's time for you to get up!

[*She waits another second and then starts to go into the bedroom, but is apparently satisfied that her husband has begun to get up. She stops, pulls the door to, and returns to the kitchen area. She wipes her face with a moist cloth and runs her fingers through her sleep-disheveled hair in a vain effort and ties an apron around her housecoat. The bedroom door at right opens and her husband stands in the doorway in his pajamas, which are rumpled and mismated. He is a lean, intense young man in his middle thirties, inclined to quick nervous movements and erratic speech habits—and always in his voice there is a quality of indictment*]

WALTER   Is he out yet?

RUTH   What do you mean *out*? He ain't hardly got in there good yet.

WALTER   [*Wandering in, still more oriented to sleep than to a new day*] Well, what was you doing all that yelling for if I can't even get in there yet? [*Stopping and thinking*] Check coming today?

RUTH   They *said* Saturday and this is just Friday and I hopes to God you ain't going to get up here first thing this morning and start talking to me 'bout no money—'cause I 'bout don't want to hear it.

WALTER   Something the matter with you this morning?

RUTH   No—I'm just sleepy as the devil. What kind of eggs you want?

WALTER   Not scrambled. [RUTH *starts to scramble eggs*] Paper come? [RUTH *points impatiently to the rolled up Tribune on the table, and he gets it and spreads it out and vaguely reads the front page*] Set off another bomb yesterday.

RUTH   [*Maximum indifference*] Did they?

WALTER   [*Looking up*] What's the matter with you?

RUTH   Ain't nothing the matter with me. And don't keep asking me that this morning.

WALTER   Ain't nobody bothering you. [*Reading the news of the day absently again*] Say Colonel McCormick is sick.

RUTH [*Affecting tea-party interest*] Is he now? Poor thing.

WALTER [*Sighing and looking at his watch*] Oh, me. [*He waits*] Now what is that boy doing in that bathroom all this time? He just going to have to start getting up earlier. I can't be late to work on account of him fooling around in there.

RUTH [*Turning on him*] Oh, no, he ain't going to be getting up no earlier no such thing! It ain't his fault that he can't get to bed no earlier nights 'cause he got a bunch of crazy good-for-nothing clowns sitting up running their mouths in what is supposed to be his bedroom after ten o'clock at night. . . .

WALTER That's what you mad about, ain't it? The things I want to talk about with my friends just couldn't be important in your mind, could they?

[*He rises and finds a cigarette in her handbag on the table and crosses to the little window and looks out, smoking and deeply enjoying this first one*]

RUTH [*Almost matter of factly, a complaint too automatic to deserve emphasis*] Why you always got to smoke before you eat in the morning?

WALTER [*At the window*] Just look at 'em down there. . . . Running and racing to work. . . . [*He turns and faces his wife and watches her a moment at the stove, and then, suddenly*] You look young this morning, baby.

RUTH [*Indifferently*] Yeah?

WALTER Just for a second—stirring them eggs. It's gone now—just for a second it was—you looked real young again. [*Then, drily*] It's gone now—you look like yourself again.

RUTH Man, if you don't shut up and leave me alone.

WALTER [*Looking out to the street again*] First thing a man ought to learn in life is not to make love to no colored woman first thing in the morning. You all some evil people at eight o'clock in the morning.

[TRAVIS *appears in the hall doorway, almost fully dressed and quite wide awake now, his towels and pajamas across his shoulders. He opens the door and signals for his father to make the bathroom in a hurry*]

TRAVIS [*Watching the bathroom*] Daddy, come on! [WALTER *gets his bathroom utensils and flies out to the bathroom*]

RUTH Sit down and have your breakfast, Travis.

TRAVIS Mama, this is Friday. [*Gleefully*] Check coming tomorrow, huh?

RUTH You get your mind off money and eat your breakfast.

TRAVIS [*Eating*] This is the morning we supposed to bring the fifty cents to school.

RUTH Well, I ain't got no fifty cents this morning.

TRAVIS   Teacher say we have to.

RUTH   I don't care what teacher say, I ain't got it. Eat your breakfast, Travis.

TRAVIS   I *am* eating.

RUTH   Hush up now and just eat!

[*The boy gives her an exasperated look for her lack of understanding, and eats grudgingly*]

TRAVIS   You think Grandmama would have it?

RUTH   No! And I want you to stop asking your grandmother for money, you hear me?

TRAVIS   [*Outraged*] Gaaaleee! I don't ask her, she just gimme it sometimes!

RUTH   Travis Willard Younger—I got too much on me this morning to be—

TRAVIS   Maybe Daddy—

RUTH   *Travis!!*

[*The boy hushes abruptly. They are both quiet and tense for several seconds*]

TRAVIS   [*Presently*] Could I maybe go carry some groceries in front of the supermarket for a little while after school then?

RUTH   Just hush, I said. [TRAVIS *jabs his spoon into his cereal bowl viciously, and rests his head in anger upon his fists*] If you through eating, you can get over there and make up your bed.

[*The boy obeys stiffly and crosses the room, almost mechanically, to the bed and more or less carefully folds the covering. He carries the bedding into his mother's room and returns with his books and cap*]

TRAVIS   [*Sulking and standing apart from her unnaturally*] I'm gone.

RUTH   [*Looking up from the stove to inspect him automatically*] Come here. [*He crosses to her and she studies his head*] If you don't take this comb and fix this here head, you better! [TRAVIS *puts down his books with a great sigh of oppression, and crosses to the mirror. [His mother mutters under her breath about his "stubborness"*] 'Bout to march out of here with that head looking just like chickens slept in it! I just don't know where you get your stubborn ways. . . . And get your jacket, too. Looks chilly out this morning.

TRAVIS   [*With conspicuously brushed hair and jacket*] I'm gone.

RUTH   Get carfare and milk money—[*Waving one finger*]—and not a single penny for no caps, you hear me?

TRAVIS   [*With sullen politeness*] Yes'm.

[*He turns in outrage to leave. His mother watches after him as in frustration he approaches the door almost comically. When she speaks to him, her voice has become a very gentle tease*]

RUTH   [*Mocking; as she thinks he would say it*] Oh, Mama makes me so mad sometimes, I don't know what to do! [*She waits and continues to his back as he stands stockstill in front of the door*] I wouldn't kiss that woman good-bye for nothing in this world this morning! [*The boy finally turns around and rolls his eyes at her, knowing the mood has changed and he is vindicated; he does not, however, move toward her yet*] Not for nothing in this world! [*She finally laughs aloud at him and holds out her arms to him and we see that it is a way between them, very old and practiced. He crosses to her and allows her to embrace him warmly but keeps his face fixed with masculine rigidity. She holds him back from her presently and looks at him and runs her fingers over the features of his face. With utter gentleness*] Now—whose little old angry man are you?

TRAVIS   [*The masculinity and gruffness start to fade at last*] Aw gaalee —Mama. . . .

RUTH   [*Mimicking*] Aw—gaaaaalleeeee, Mama! [*She pushes him, with rough playfulness and finality, toward the door*] Get on out of here or you going to be late.

TRAVIS   [*In the face of love, new aggressiveness*] Mama, could I *please* go carry groceries?

RUTH   Honey, it's starting to get so cold evenings.

WALTER   [*Coming in from the bathroom and drawing a make-believe gun from a make-believe holster and shooting at his son*] What is it he wants to do?

RUTH   Go carry groceries after school at the supermarket.

WALTER   Well, let him go. . . .

TRAVIS   [*Quickly, to the ally*] I *have* to—she won't gimme the fifty cents. . . .

WALTER   [*To his wife only*] Why not?

RUTH   [*Simply, and with flavor*] 'Cause we don't have it.

WALTER   [*To RUTH only*] What you tell the boy things like that for? [*Reaching down into his pants with a rather important gesture*] Here, son—

[*He hands the boy the coin, but his eyes are directed to his wife's.* TRAVIS *takes the money happily*]

TRAVIS   Thanks, Daddy.

[*He starts out.* RUTH *watches both of them with murder in her eyes.* WALTER *stands and stares back at her with defiance, and suddenly reaches into his pocket again on an afterthought*]

WALTER   [*Without even looking at his son, still staring hard at his wife*] In fact, here's another fifty cents. . . . Buy yourself some fruit today —or take a taxicab to school or something!

TRAVIS   Whoopee—

[*He leaps up and clasps his father around the middle with his legs, and they face each other in mutual appreciation; slowly* WALTER LEE *peeks around the boy to catch the violent rays from his wife's eyes and draws his head back as if shot*]

WALTER   You better get down now—and get to school, man.

TRAVIS   [*At the door*] O.K. Good-bye.

    [*he exits*]

chapter 6

SOCIAL
FACTORS OF INFLUENCE

It is a terrible, an inexorable, law that one cannot deny the humanity
of another without diminishing one's own: in the face of one's victim,
one sees oneself. Walk through the streets of Harlem and see what we,
this nation, have become.

—James Baldwin,
Nobody Knows My Name

The writer who studies Negro life cannot help but explore American society itself. For the black man in the United States is a
tangible production of that culture. More than anything else, Negro
writers are telling us about the quality of American life. They
are focusing on the values of the society, the political power plays,
the social class structures, and the prevailing customs and mores.
The importance of the Negro artist's vision is twofold. As a writer,
he articulates the interior life and, as a black man, he examines
societal behavior from the perspective of a member of a minority
group. The influences of religion, the color-caste system, regional
attitudes, and segregation, to mention only a few, offer the writer
a multidimensional matrix upon which he may pattern his story.

The reader who approaches the selections in this unit in a
chronological order may detect a trend in the thinking of the
Negro writers who are represented. He may, along with the artist,
embark upon a journey which seems to be a climb in an upward
direction. For the analysis of Negro literature can be compared to
Mama's plant from *A Raisin in the Sun*: both are traveling from
the gloomy ghetto window sill to the lighted, sunny room.

Early writers, like Frederick Douglass, may only identify the
darkness in terms of the boundaries which it establishes, but more
modern writers, farther along the road to freedom, direct attention
to the social factors of change. Richard Wright's characters relentlessly rebel against the "shadowy region" of their existence, and
Ralph Ellison's invisible man is working his way upward from the
moment he leaves his underground cave. Both these writers and
certainly many younger, contemporary artists have concluded that

the hibernation of the Negro is at an end, the eclipse has passed, and the black man will emerge as an active participant in American society.

Negro writers who seek to interpret their world find that it is pregnant with ambiguities. For as Bone observes, "The Negro must still structure his life in terms of a culture to which he is denied full access. He is at once a part of and apart from the wider community in which he lives."[1] On the one hand, the Negro wants to believe the "American Dream" of the 1970s, yet black writers so frequently tell us that this same Negro experiences the world of 1800. The black man, the victim of what W. E. B. DuBois speaks of as a "double-consciousness," is plagued by his own ambivalent feelings and often translates this frustration into "blue vein" societies, hostility for his own people, and a rejection of his own heritage. Obviously, this is not always the situation; many black men cry out against this betrayal and seek to establish cultural forms with which the Negro can identify.

The excerpts in this thematic unit articulate the hypocrisy and contradictions of American society as felt by the Negro artist. Segregated housing, as represented by Mr. Lindner when he says, "The overwhelming majority of our people out there feel that people get along better, take more of a common interest in the life of the community, when they share a common background,"[2] is antithetical to the principles of equality. And in the words of Trueblood, from *Invisible Man*: "That's what I don't understand. I done the worse things a man could ever do in his family and instead of chasin' me out of the county, they gimme more help than they ever give any other colored man, no matter how good a nigguh he was."[3] Or even a mulatto son's reprimand to his white father, "what father's duty have you ever performed for me? Did you give me your name, or even your protection?"[4]

As the Negro artist writes so that he may increase his own consciousness of certain cultural imperatives, he frequently focuses on the black bourgeoisie. One has to wonder whether or not the artist sees himself as a member of this group and is seeking to understand his own social position through the catharsis of written

---

[1] Robert A. Bone, *The Negro Novel in America* (New Haven, Conn.: Yale University Press, 1965), p. 3.

[2] Lorraine Hansberry, *A Raisin in the Sun* (New York: New American Library, 1958), p. 97.

[3] Ralph Ellison, *Invisible Man* (New York: New American Library of World Literature, Inc., 1952), pp. 64–65.

[4] Charles Chesnutt, "The Sheriff's Children," *The Wife of His Youth* (Ann Arbor: University of Michigan Press, 1968), p. 85.

expression or is it more likely that the artist cannot so easily be categorized? The Negro artist, in particular, is atypical and gains an objective perspective because he is somehow beyond classification. Furthermore, it is not the group itself that the writer attacks with such passion, but the values that its members seem to espouse. Modeled after white middle-class society, it is the prototype, in reality, that is under fire. Charles Chesnutt condemns its artificial social standards, Richard Wright criticizes its patronizing stance, and Ralph Ellison launches out against the philanthropic mask behind which the group may hide.

The black middle class is accused of sloughing-off its blackness, and having a vested interest in denying Negro culture. Dr. Bledsoe, the president of a southern Negro college, is invented by Ellison to do this very thing. Edward Margolies notes that, "Despite his abject and humble exterior, (Bledsoe) is one of the most powerful men in the South, who sustains a vested interest in keeping the Negro 'invisible.' "[5] Charles Chesnutt is accusatory in this regard, for he would like to see the black middle class exemplifying the values of honor and a sense of justice.

E. Franklin Frazier makes the point that the Negro middle class often lives in a make-believe world and seeks compensations in material things.[6] Nor is it difficult to appreciate the roots of this fantasy life, for many Negroes see themselves as Americans, not Africans, and feel dispossessed by the prevailing culture. In Ellison's language, they are "invisible"; in Wright's metaphors they are "underground men," and in Cullen's words, they are "tortured" souls. Struggling for status and recognition, some Negroes have sought refuge in what they believe is "white" philosophy or even a bleached physiognomy, when this is possible. It takes the Negro artist to identify subtly the implications of intermarriage, "passing," and the social stratifications of the Negro color-caste system. As one gives himself over to the Negro writer's perception of the black man's cultural dilemma, one senses a unanimity of feeling. For though each writer focuses on a different aspect of Negro reality, what emerges in clamorous tones is the cry for the black man to come to terms with his own identity in order that he may live in a world that is not an illusion.

This chapter attempts to identify the social factors that influence the America Negro's interpretation in relation to his world.

---

[5] Edward Margolies, *Native Sons: A Critical Study* (Philadelphia: J. B. Lippincott, 1969), p. 138.

[6] R. Franklin Frazier, *Black Bourgeoisie* (New York: The Free Press, 1957), p. 148.

It is the subject of the next chapter to illustrate how individual black men react to and interpret the societal climate.

I.   The readings in this chapter were selected for their relevance to the unit topic *Social Factors of Influence*. Some of the sub-themes which are developed in the selections are:

1.   The color-caste system within the black culture
2.   The black bourgeoisie
3.   Societal pressures
4.   Democracy and racism
5.   Discrimination in housing
6.   The "white liberal"
7.   The ambiguities of Negro life

II.   The following readings are suggested as supplementary references for this thematic unit:

1.   James Woldon Johnson, *God's Trombones* (New York: Viking Press, 1955). (poetry)
2.   LeRoi Jones, *The Dutchman* (New York: William Morrow and Company, 1964). (play)
3.   William Melvin Kelley, "The Only Man on Liberty Street," *The Best Short Stories by Negro Writers*, Langston Hughes, ed. (Boston: Little, Brown and Company, 1967). (short story)
4.   Anne Moody, *Coming of Age in Mississippi: An Auto-biography* (New York: Dial Press, 1968). (autobiography)
5.   Carl T. Rowan, *South of Freedom* (New York: Alfred A. Knopf, 1952). (social commentary)
6.   Jean Toomer, *Cane* (New York: Harper & Row, Publishers, 1969). (novel)
7.   Richard Wright, "Between the World and Me," *Black Voices*, Abraham Chapman, ed. (New York: Mentor, 1968). (poetry)

QUESTIONS FOR DISCUSSION

1.   What tone does Charles Chesnutt adopt toward the Blue Vein Society?

2.   "The Sheriff's Children" has been called a parable for today's racial crisis. Do you see its relevance?

3.   Blindness is used as a metaphor in many of the readings. In *Native Son*, what is the nature of Mary's and Jan's blindness? Does the main character, Bigger Thomas, suffer from an inability to see?

4.   What illusions and ambiguities about American society is Ellison seeking to expose?

5.   What paradoxes does the character of Simple highlight?

"What to the Slave Is the Fourth of July?"

FREDERICK DOUGLASS

From a speech given in Rochester, New York, on July 4, 1852.

Fellow citizens: Pardon me, and allow me to ask, why am I called upon to speak here today? What have I or those I represent to do with your national independence? Are the great principles of political freedom and of natural justice, embodied in that Declaration of Independence, extended to us? And am I, therefore, called upon to bring our humble offering to the national altar, and to confess the benefits, and express devout gratitude for the blessings resulting from your independence to us?

Would to God, both for your sakes and ours, that an affirmative answer could be truthfully returned to these questions. Then would my task be light, and my burden easy and delightful. For who is there so cold that a nation's sympathy could not warm him? Who so obdurate and dead to the claims of gratitude, that would not thankfully acknowledge such priceless benefits? Who so stolid and selfish that would not give his voice to swell the haleluiahs of a nation's jubilee, when the chains of servitude had been torn from his limbs? I am not that man.

. . . I say it with a sad sense of disparity between us. I am not included within the pale of this glorious anniversary! Your high independence only reveals the immeasurable distance between us. The blessings in which you this day rejoice are not enjoyed in common. The rich inheritance of justice, liberty, prosperity, and independence bequeathed by your fathers is shared by you, not by me. The sunlight that brought life and healing to you has brought stripes and death to me. This Fourth of July is *yours*, not *mine*. *You* may rejoice, *I* must mourn. To drag a man in fetters into the grand illuminated temple of liberty, and call upon him to join you in joyous anthems, were inhuman mockery and sacrilegious irony. Do you mean, citizens, to mock me, by asking me to speak today? If so, there is a parallel to your conduct. And let me warn you, that it is dangerous to copy the example of a nation whose crimes, towering up to heaven, were thrown down by the breath of the Almighty, burying that nation in irrecoverable ruin. I can today take up the lament of a peeled and woe-smitten people.

"By the rivers of Babylon, there we sat down. Yes! We wept when we remembered Zion. We hanged our harps upon the willows in the midst thereof. For there they that carried us away captive, required of us a song; and they who wasted us, required of us mirth, saying, Sing us one of the songs of Zion. How can we sing the Lord's song in a strange land? If I forget thee, O Jerusalem, let my right hand forget her cunning. If I do not remember thee, let my tongue cleave to the roof of my mouth."

Fellow citizens, above your national, tumultuous joy, I hear the mournful wail of millions, whose chains, heavy and grievous yesterday, are today rendered more intolerable by the jubilant shouts that reach them. If I do forget, if I do not remember those bleeding children of sorrow this day, "may my right hand forget her cunning, and may my tongue cleave to the roof of my mouth!" To forget them, to pass lightly over their wrongs, and to chime in with the popular theme, would be treason most scandalous and shocking, and would make me a reproach before God and the world. My subject, then, fellow citizens, is "American Slavery." I shall see this day and its popular characteristics from the slave's point of view. Standing here, identified with the American bond-man, making his wrongs mine, I do not hesitate to declare, with all my soul, that the character and conduct of this nation never looked blacker to me than on this Fourth of July. Whether we turn to the declaration of the past, or to the professions of the present, the conduct of the nation seems equally hideous and revolting. America is false to the past, false to the present, and solemnly binds herself to be false to the future. Standing with God and the crushed and bleeding slave on this occasion, I will, in the name of humanity, which is outraged, in the name of liberty, which is fettered, in the name of the Constitution and the Bible, which are disregarded and trampled upon, dare to call in question and to denounce, with all the emphasis I can command, everything that serves to perpetuate slavery—the great sin and shame of America! "I will not equivocate; I will not excuse"; I will use the severest language I can command, and yet not one word shall escape me that any man, whose judgment is not blinded by prejudice, or who is not at heart a slave-holder, shall not confess to be right and just.

But I fancy I hear some of my audience say it is just in this circumstance that you and your brother Abolitionists fail to make a favorable impression on the public mind. Would you argue more and denounce less, would you persuade more and rebuke less, your cause would be much more likely to succeed. But, I submit, where all is plain there is nothing to be argued. What point in the anti-slavery creed would you have me argue? On what branch of the subject do the people of this country need light? Must I undertake to prove that the slave is a man? That point is conceded already. Nobody doubts it. The slave-holders themselves acknowledge it in the enactment of laws for their government. They acknowledge it when they punish disobedience on the part of the slave. There are seventy-two crimes in the State of Virginia, which, if committed by a black man (no matter how ignorant he be), subject him to the punishment of death; while only two of these same crimes will subject a white man to like punishment. What is this but the acknowledgement that the slave is a moral, intellectual, and responsible being? The manhood of the slave is conceded. It is admitted in the fact that Southern statute-books are covered with enactments, forbidding under severe fines and penalties, the teaching of the slave to read and write. When you can point to any such laws in reference to the beasts of the field, then I may consent to argue the manhood of the slave. When the dogs in your streets, when the fowls of the air, when the cattle on your hills, when the fish of the sea, and the reptiles that crawl, shall be unable to distinguish the slave from a brute, then I will argue with you that the slave is a man!

For the present it is enough to affirm the equal manhood of the Negro race. Is it not astonishing that, while we are plowing, planting, and reaping, using all kinds of mechanical tools, erecting houses, constructing bridges, building ships, working in metals of brass, iron, copper, silver, and gold; that while we are reading, writing, and cyphering, acting as clerks, merchants, and secretaries, having among us lawyers, doctors, ministers, poets, authors, editors, orators, and teachers; that while we are engaged in all the enterprises common to other men— digging gold in California, capturing the whale in the Pacific, feeding sheep and cattle on the hillside, living, moving, acting, thinking, planning, living in families as husbands, wives, and children, and above all, confessing and worshipping the Christian God, and looking hopefully for life and immortality beyond the grave—we are called upon to prove that we are men?

Would you have me argue that man is entitled to Liberty? That he is the rightful owner of his own body? You have already declared it. Must I argue the wrongfulness of slavery? Is that a question for Republicans? Is it to be settled by the rules of logic and argumentation, as a matter beset with great difficulty, involving a doubtful application of the principle of justice, hard to understand? How should I look today in the presence of Americans, dividing and subdividing a discourse, to show that men have a natural right to freedom, speaking of it relatively and positively, negatively and affirmatively? To do so would be to make myself ridiculous, and to offer an insult to your understanding. There is not a man beneath the canopy of heaven who does not know that slavery is wrong *for him*.

What! Am I to argue that it is wrong to make men brutes, to rob them of their liberty, to work them without wages, to keep them ignorant of their relations to their fellow men, to beat them with sticks, to flay their flesh with the lash, to load their limbs with irons, to hunt them with dogs, to sell them at auction, to sunder their families, to knock out their teeth, to burn their flesh, to starve them into obedience and sub-mission to their masters? Must I argue that a system thus marked with blood and stained with pollution is wrong? No; I will not. I have better employment for my time and strength than such arguments would imply.

What, then, remains to be argued? Is it that slavery is not divine; that God did not establish it; that our doctors of divinity are mis-taken? There is blasphemy in the thought. That which is inhuman can-not be divine. Who can reason on such a proposition? They that can, may; I cannot. The time for such argument is past.

At a time like this, scorching irony, not convincing argument, is needed. Oh! had I the ability, and could I reach the nation's ear, I would today pour out a fiery stream of biting ridicule, blasting reproach, withering sarcasm, and stern rebuke. For it is not light that is needed, but fire; it is not the gentle shower, but thunder. We need the storm, the whirlwind, and the earthquake. The feeling of the nation must be quickened; the conscience of the nation must be roused; the propriety of the nation must be startled; the hypocrisy of the nation must be ex-posed; and its crimes against God and man must be denounced.

What to the American slave is your Fourth of July? I answer, a day that reveals to him more than all other days of the year, the gross in-justice and cruelty to which he is the constant victim. To him your celebration is a sham; your boasted liberty and unholy license; your national greatness, swelling vanity; your sounds of rejoicing are empty and heartless; your denunciation of tyrants, brass-fronted impudence; your shouts of liberty and equality, hollow mockery; your prayers and hymns, your sermons and thanksgivings, with all your religious parade and solemnity, are to him mere bombast, fraud, deception, impiety, and hypocrisy—a thin veil to cover up crimes which would disgrace a nation of savages. . . .

The Wife of His Youth

CHARLES W. CHESNUTT

I

Mr. Ryder was going to give a ball. There were several reasons why this was an opportune time for such an event.

Mr. Ryder might aptly be called the dean of the Blue Veins. The original Blue Veins were a little society of colored persons organized in a certain Northern city shortly after the war. Its purpose was to establish and maintain correct social standards among a people whose social condition presented almost unlimited room for improvement. By accident, combined perhaps with some natural affinity, the society consisted of individuals who were, generally speaking, more white than black. Some envious outsider made the suggestion that no one was eligible for membership who was not white enough to show blue veins. The suggestion was readily adopted by those who were not of the favored few, and since that time the society, though possessing a longer and more pretentious name, had been known far and wide as the "Blue Vein Society," and its members as the "Blue Veins."

The Blue Veins did not allow that any such requirement existed for admission to their circle, but, on the contrary, declared that character and culture were the only things considered; and that if most of their members were light-colored, it was because such persons, as a rule, had had better opportunities to qualify themselves for membership. Opinions differed, too, as to the usefulness of the society. There were those who had been known to assail it violently as a glaring example of the very prejudice from which the colored race had suffered most; and later, when such critics had succeeded in getting on the inside, they had been heard to maintain with zeal and earnestness that the society was a lifeboat, an anchor, a bulwark and a shield,—a pillar of cloud by day and of fire by night, to guide their people through the social wilderness. Another alleged prerequisite for Blue Vein membership was that of free birth; and while there was really no such requirement, it is doubtless true that very few of the members would have been unable to meet it if there had been. If there were one or two of the older members who had come up from the South and from slavery, their history presented enough romantic circumstances to rob their servile origin of its grosser aspects.

While there were no such tests of eligibility, it is true that the Blue Veins had their notions on these subjects, and that not all of them were equally liberal in regard to the things they collectively disclaimed. Mr. Ryder was one of the most conservative. Though he had not been among the founders of the society, but had come in some years later, his genius for social leadership was such that he had speedily become its recognized adviser and head, the custodian of its standards, and the preserver of its traditions. He shaped its social policy, was active in providing for its entertainment, and when the interest fell off, as it sometimes did, he fanned the embers until they burst again into a cheerful flame.

There were still other reasons for his popularity. While he was not as white as some of the Blue Veins, his appearance was such as to confer distinction upon them. His features were of a refined type, his hair was almost straight; he was always neatly dressed; his manners were irreproachable, and his morals above suspicion. He had come to Groveland a young man, and, obtaining employment in the office of a railroad company as messenger, had in time worked himself up to the position of stationery clerk, having charge of the distribution of the office supplies for the whole company. Although the lack of early training had hindered the orderly development of a naturally fine mind, it had not prevented him from doing a great deal of reading or from forming decidedly literary tastes. Poetry was his passion. He could repeat whole pages of the great English poets; and if his pronunciation was sometimes faulty, his eye, his voice, his gestures, would respond to the changing sentiment with a precision that revealed a poetic soul and disarmed criticism. He was economical, and had saved money; he owned and occupied a very comfortable house on a respectable street. His residence was handsomely furnished, containing among other things a good library, especially rich in poetry, a piano, and some choice engravings. He generally shared his house with some young couple, who looked after his wants and were company for him; for Mr. Ryder was a single man. In the early days of his connection with the Blue Veins he had been regarded as quite a catch, and young ladies and their mothers had manoeuvred with much ingenuity to capture him. Not, however, until Mrs. Molly Dixon visited Groveland had any woman ever made him wish to change his condition to that of a married man.

Mrs. Dixon had come to Groveland from Washington in the spring, and before the summer was over she had won Mr. Ryder's heart. She possessed many attractive qualities. She was much younger than he; in fact, he was old enough to have been her father, though no one knew exactly how old he was. She was whiter than he, and better educated. She had moved in the best colored society of the country at Washington, and had taught in the schools of that city. Such a superior person had been eagerly welcomed to the Blue Vein Society, and had taken a leading part in its activities. Mr. Ryder had at first been attracted by her charms of person, for she was very good looking and not over twenty-five; then by her refined manners and the vivacity of her wit. Her husband had been a government clerk, and at his death had left a considerable life insurance. She was visiting friends in Groveland, and, finding the town and the people to her liking, had prolonged her stay indefinitely. She had not seemed displeased at Mr. Ryder's attentions, but on the contrary had given him every proper encouragement; indeed, a younger and less cautious man would long since have spoken. But he had made up his mind, and had only to determine the time when he would ask her to be his wife. He decided to give a ball in her honor, and at some time during the evening of the ball to offer her his heart and hand. He had no special fears about the outcome, but, with a little touch of romance, he wanted the surroundings to be in harmony with his own feelings when he should have received the answer he expected.

Mr. Ryder resolved that this ball should mark an epoch in the social history of Groveland. He knew, of course—no one could know better —the entertainments that had taken place in past years, and what must be done to surpass them. His ball must be worthy of the lady in whose honor it was to be given, and must, by the quality of its guests, set an example for the future. He had observed of late a growing liberality, almost a laxity, in social matters, even among members of his own set, and had several times been forced to meet in a social way persons whose complexions and callings in life were hardly up to the standard which he considered proper for the society to maintain. He had a theory of his own.

"I have no race prejudice," he would say, "but we people of mixed blood are ground between the upper and the nether millstone. Our fate lies between absorption by the white race and extinction in the black. The one doesn't want us yet, but may take us in time. The other would welcome us, but it would be for us a backward step. 'With malice toward none, with charity for all,' we must do the best we can for ourselves and those who are to follow us. Self-preservation is the first law of nature."

His ball would serve by its exclusiveness to counteract leveling tendencies, and his marriage with Mrs. Dixon would help to further the upward process of absorption he had been wishing and waiting for.

II

The ball was to take place on Friday night. The house had been put in order, the carpets covered with canvas, the halls and stairs decorated with palms and potted plants; and in the afternoon Mr. Ryder sat on his front porch, which the shade of a vine running up over a wire netting made a cool and pleasant lounging place. He expected to respond to the toast "The Ladies" at the supper, and from a volume of Tennyson —his favorite poet—was fortifying himself with apt quotations. The volume was open at "A Dream of Fair Women." His eyes fell on these lines, and he read them aloud to judge better of their effect:—

> "At length I saw a lady within call,
>   Stiller than chisell'd marble, standing there;
> A daughter of the gods, divinely tall,
>   And most divinely fair."

He marked the verse, and turning the page read the stanza beginning,—

> "O sweet pale Margaret,
> O rare pale Margaret."

He weighed the passage a moment, and decided that it would not do. Mrs. Dixon was the palest lady he expected at the ball, and she was of a rather ruddy complexion, and of lively disposition and buxom build. So he ran over the leaves until his eye rested on the description of Queen Guinevere:—

> "She seem'd a part of joyous Spring:
> A gown of grass-green silk she wore,
> Buckled with golden clasps before;
> A light-green tuft of plumes she bore
> Closed in a golden ring.
> "She look'd so lovely, as she sway'd
> The rein with dainty finger-tips,
> A man had given all other bliss,
> And all his worldly worth for this,
> To waste his whole heart in one kiss
> Upon her perfect lips."

As Mr. Ryder murmured these words audibly, with an appreciative thrill, he heard the latch of his gate click, and a light footfall sounding on the steps. He turned his head, and saw a woman standing before his door.

She was a little woman, not five feet tall, and proportioned to her height. Although she stood erect, and looked around her with very bright and restless eyes, she seemed quite old; for her face was crossed and recrossed with a hundred wrinkles, and around the edges of her bonnet could be seen protruding here and there a tuft of short gray wool. She wore a blue calico gown of ancient cut, a little red shawl fastened around her shoulders with an old-fashioned brass brooch, and a large bonnet profusely ornamented with faded red and yellow artificial flowers. And she was very black—so black that her toothless gums, revealed when she opened her mouth to speak, were not red, but blue. She looked like a bit of the old plantation life, summoned up from the past by the wave of a magician's wand, as the poet's fancy had called into being the gracious shapes of which Mr. Ryder had just been reading.

He rose from his chair and came over to where she stood.

"Good-afternoon, madam," he said.

"Good-evenin', suh," she answered, ducking suddenly with a quaint curtsy. Her voice was shrill and piping, but softened somewhat by age.

"Is dis yere whar Mistuh Ryduh lib, suh?" she asked, looking around her doubtfully, and glancing into the open windows, through which some of the preparations for the evening were visible.

"Yes," he replied, with an air of kindly patronage, unconsciously flattered by her manner, "I am Mr. Ryder. Did you want to see me?"

"Yas, suh, ef I ain't 'sturbin' of you too much."

"Not at all. Have a seat over here behind the vine, where it is cool. What can I do for you?"

" 'Scuse me, suh," she continued, when she had sat down on the edge of a chair, " 'scuse me, suh, I's lookin' for my husban'. I heered you wuz a big man an' had libbed heah a long time, an' I 'lowed you wouldn't min' ef I'd come roun' an' ax you ef you'd ever heerd of a merlatter man by de name er Sam Taylor 'quirin' roun' in de chu'ches ermongs' de people fer his wife 'Liza Jane?"

Mr. Ryder seemed to think for a moment.

"There used to be many such cases right after the war," he said, "but it has been so long that I have forgotten them. There are very few now. But tell me your story, and it may refresh my memory."

She sat back farther in her chair so as to be more comfortable, and folded her withered hands in her lap.

"My name's 'Liza," she began, " 'Liza Jane. W'en I wuz young I us'ter b'long ter Marse Bob Smif, down in ole Missoura. I wuz bawn down dere. W'en I wuz a gal I wuz married ter a man named Jim. But Jim died, an' after dat I married a merlatter man named Sam Taylor. Sam wuz free-bawn, but his mammy and daddy died, an' de w'ite folks 'prenticed him ter my marster fer ter work fer 'im 'tel he wuz growed up. Sam worked in de fiel', an' I wuz de cook. One day Ma'y Ann, ole miss's maid, came rushin' out ter de kitchen, an' says she, 'Liza Jane, ole marse gwine sell yo' Sam down de ribber.'

" 'Go way f'm yere,' says I; 'my husban' 's free!'

" 'Don' make no diff'ence. I heerd ole marse tell ole miss he wuz gwine take yo' Sam 'way wid 'im ter-morrow, fer he needed money, an' he knowed whar he could git a t'ousan' dollars fer Sam an' no questions axed.'

"W'en Sam come home f'm de fiel' dat night, I tole him 'bout ole marse gwine steal 'im, an' Sam run erway. His time wuz mos' up, an' he swo' dat w'en he wuz twenty-one he would come back an' he'p me run erway, er else save up de money ter buy my freedom. An' I know he'd 'a' done it, fer he thought a heap er me, Sam did. But w'en he come back he didn' fin' me, fer I wuzn' dere. Ole marse had heerd dat I warned Sam, so he had me whip' an' sol' down de ribber.

"Den de wah broke out, an' w'en it wuz ober de cullud folks wuz scattered. I went back ter de ole home; but Sam wuzn't dere, an' I couldn' l'arn nuffin' 'bout 'im. But I knowed he'd be'n dere to look fer me an' hadn' foun' me, an' had gone erway ter hunt fer me.

"I's be'n lookin' fer 'em eber sence," she added simply, as though twenty-five years were but a couple of weeks, "an' I knows he's be'n lookin' fer me. Fer he sot a heap er sto' by me, Sam did, an' I know he's be'n huntin' fer me all dese years,—'less'n he's be'n sick er sump'n, so he couldn' work, er out'n his head, so he couldn' 'member his promise. I went back down de ribber, fer I 'lowed he'd gone down dere lookin' fer me. I's be'n ter Noo Orleans, an' Atlanty, an' Charleston, an' Richmon'; an' w'en I'd be'n all ober de Souf I come ter de Norf. Fer I knows I'll fin' 'im some er dese days," she added softly, "er he'll fin' me, an' den we'll bofe be as happy in freedom as we wuz in de ole days befo' de wah." A smile stole over her withered countenance as she paused a moment, and her bright eyes softened into a faraway look.

This was the substance of the old woman's story. She had wandered a little here and there. Mr. Ryder was looking at her curiously when she finished.

"How have you lived all these years?" he asked.

"Cookin', suh. I's a good cook. Does you know anybody w'at needs a good cook, suh? I's stoppin' wid a cullud fam'ly roun' de corner yonder 'tel I kin git a place."

"Do you really expect to find your husband? He may be dead long ago."

She shook her head emphatically. "Oh no, he ain' dead. De signs an' de tokens tells me. I dremp three nights runnin' on'y dis las' week dat I foun' him."

"He may have married another woman. Your slave marriage would not have prevented him, for you never lived with him after the war, and without that your marriage doesn't count."

"Wouldn' make no diff'ence wid Sam. He wouldn' marry no yuther 'ooman 'tel he foun' out 'bout me. I knows it," she added. "Sump'n's be'n tellin' me all dese years dat I's gwine fin' Sam 'fo' I dies."

"Perhaps he's outgrown you, and climbed up in the world where he wouldn't care to have you find him."

"No, indeed, suh," she replied, "Sam ain' dat kin' er man. He wuz good ter me, Sam wuz, but he wuzn' much good ter nobody e'se, fer he wuz one er de triflin'es' han's on de plantation. I 'spec's ter haf ter suppo't 'im w'en I fin' 'im, fer he nebber would work 'less'n he had ter. But den he wuz free, an' he didn' git no pay fer his work, an' I don' blame 'im much. Mebbe he's done better sence he run erway, but I ain' 'spectin' much."

"You may have passed him on the street a hundred times during the twenty-five years, and not have known him; time works great changes."

She smiled incredulously. "I'd know 'im 'mongs' a hund'ed men. Fer dey wuzn' no yuther merlatter man like my man Sam, an' I couldn' be mistook. I's toted his picture roun' wid me twenty-five years."

"May I see it?" asked Mr. Ryder. "It might help me to remember whether I have seen the original."

As she drew a small parcel from her bosom he saw that it was fastened to a string that went around her neck. Removing several wrappers, she brought to light an old-fashioned daguerreotype in a black case. He looked long and intently at the portrait. It was faded with time, but the features were still distinct, and it was easy to see what manner of man it had represented.

He closed the case, and with a slow movement handed it back to her.

"I don't know of any man in town who goes by that name," he said, "nor have I heard of any one making such inquiries. But if you will leave me your address, I will give the matter some attention, and if I find out anything I will let you know."

She gave him the number of a house in the neighborhood, and went away, after thanking him warmly.

He wrote the address on the fly-leaf of the volume of Tennyson, and, when she had gone, rose to his feet and stood looking after her curiously. As she walked down the street with mincing step, he saw several persons whom she passed turn and look back at her with a smile of kindly amusement. When she had turned the corner, he went upstairs to his bedroom, and stood for a long time before the mirror of his dressing-case, gazing thoughtfully at the reflection of his own face.

III

At eight o'clock the ballroom was a blaze of light and the guests had begun to assemble; for there was a literary programme and some routine business of the society to be gone through with before the dancing. A black servant in evening dress waited at the door and directed the guests to the dressing-rooms.

The occasion was long memorable among the colored people of the city; not alone for the dress and display, but for the high average of intelligence and culture that distinguished the gathering as a whole. There were a number of school-teachers, several young doctors, three or four lawyers, some professional singers, an editor, a lieutenant in the United States Army spending his furlough in the city, and others in various polite callings; these were colored, though most of them would not have attracted even a casual glance because of any marked difference from white people. Most of the ladies were in evening costume, and dress coats and dancing pumps were the rule among the men. A band of string music, stationed in an alcove behind a row of palms, played popular airs while the guests were gathering.

The dancing began at half past nine. At eleven o'clock supper was served. Mr. Ryder had left the ballroom some little time before the intermission, but reappeared at the supper-table. The spread was worthy of the occasion, and the guests did full justice to it. When the coffee had been served, the toast-master, Mr. Solomon Sadler, rapped for order. He made a brief introductory speech, complimenting host and guests, and then presented in their order the toasts of the evening. They were responded to with a very fair display of after-dinner wit.

"The last toast," said the toast-master, when he reached the end of the list, "is one which must appeal to us all. There is no one of us of the sterner sex who is not at some time dependent upon woman—in infancy for protection, in manhood for companionship, in old age for care and comforting. Our good host has been trying to live alone, but the fair faces I see around me to-night prove that he too is largely dependent upon the gentler sex for most that makes life worth living—the society and love of friends—and rumor is at fault if he does not soon yield entire subjection to one of them. Mr. Ryder will now respond to the toast—The Ladies."

There was a pensive look in Mr. Ryder's eyes as he took the floor and adjusted his eye-glasses. He began by speaking of a woman as the gift of Heaven to man, and after some general observations on the relations of the sexes he said: "But perhaps the quality which most distinguishes woman is her fidelity and devotion to those she loves. History is full of examples, but has recorded none more striking than one which only to-day came under my notice."

He then related, simply but effectively, the story told by his visitor of the afternoon. He gave it in the same soft dialect, which came readily to his lips, while the company listened attentively and sympathetically. For the story had awakened a responsive thrill in many hearts. There were some present who had seen, and others who had heard their fathers and grandfathers tell, the wrongs and sufferings of this past generation, and all of them still felt, in their darker moments, the shadow hanging over them. Mr. Ryder went on:—

"Such devotion and confidence are rare even among women. There are many who would have searched a year, some who would have waited five years, a few who might have hoped for ten years; but for twenty-five years this woman has retained her affection for and her faith in a man she has not seen or heard from in all that time.

"She came to me to-day in the hope that I might be able to help her find this long-lost husband. And when she was gone I gave my fancy rein, and imagined a case I will put to you.

"Suppose that this husband, soon after his escape, had learned that his wife had been sold away, and that such inquiries as he could make brought no information of her whereabouts. Suppose that he was young, and she much older than he; that he was light, and she was black; that their marriage was a slave marriage, and legally binding only if they chose to make it so after the war. Suppose, too, that he made his way to the North, as some of us have done, and there, where he had larger opportunities, had improved them, and had in the course of all these years grown to be as different from the ignorant boy who ran away from fear of slavery as the day is from the night. Suppose, even, that he had qualified himself, by industry, by thrift, and by study, to win the friendship and be considered worthy of the society of such people as these I see around me to-night, gracing my board and filling my heart with gladness; for I am old enough to remember the day when such a gathering would not have been possible in this land. Suppose, too, that, as the years went by, this man's memory of the past grew more and more indistinct, until at last it was rarely, except in his dreams, that any image of this bygone period rose before his mind. And then suppose that accident should bring to his knowledge the fact that the wife of his youth, the wife he had left behind him—not one who had walked by his side and kept pace with him in his upward struggle, but one upon whom advancing years and a laborious life had set their mark— was alive and seeking him, but that he was absolutely safe from recognition or discovery, unless he chose to reveal himself. My friends, what would the man do? I will presume that he was one who loved honor, and tried to deal justly with all men. I will even carry the case further, and suppose that perhaps he had set his heart upon another, whom he had hoped to call his own. What would he do, or rather what ought he to do, in such a crisis of a lifetime?

"It seemed to me that he might hesitate, and I imagined that I was an old friend, a near friend, and that he had come to me for advice; and I argued the case with him. I tried to discuss it impartially. After we had looked upon the matter from every point of view, I said to him, in words that we all know:—

> 'This above all: to thine own self be true,
> And it must follow, as the night the day,
> Thou canst not then be false to any man.'

Then, finally, I put the question to him, 'Shall you acknowledge her?'

"And now, ladies and gentlemen, friends and companions, I ask you, what should he have done?"

There was something in Mr. Ryder's voice that stirred the hearts of those who sat around him. It suggested more than mere sympathy with an imaginary situation; it seemed rather in the nature of a personal appeal. It was observed, too, that his look rested more especially upon Mrs. Dixon, with a mingled expression of renunciation and inquiry.

She had listened, with parted lips and streaming eyes. She was the first to speak: "He should have acknowledged her."

"My friends and companions," responded Mr. Ryder, "I thank you, one and all. It is the answer I expected, for I knew your hearts."

He turned and walked toward the closed door of an adjoining room, while every eye followed him in wondering curiosity. He came back in a moment, leading by the hand his visitor of the afternoon, who stood startled and trembling at the sudden plunge into this scene of brilliant gayety. She was neatly dressed in gray, and wore the white cap of an elderly woman.

"Ladies and gentlemen," he said, "this is the woman, and I am the man, whose story I have told you. Permit me to introduce to you the wife of my youth."

The Sheriff's Children

CHARLES W. CHESNUTT

[*The first pages of this story describe the village of Troy, county seat of Branson County, North Carolina.*]

A murder was a rare event in Branson County. Every well-informed citizen could tell the number of homicides committed in the county for fifty years back, and whether the slayer, in any given circumstance, had escaped, either by flight or acquittal, or had suffered the penalty of the law. So, when it became known in Troy early one Friday morning in summer, about ten years after the war, that old Captain Walker, who had served in Mexico under Scott, and had left an arm on the field of Gettysburg, had been foully murdered during the night, there was intense excitement in the village. Business was practically suspended, and the citizens gathered in little groups to discuss the murder, and speculate upon the identity of the murderer. It transpired from testimony at the cornorer's inquest, held during the morning, that a strange mulatto had been seen going in the direction of Captain Walker's house the night before, and had been met going away from Troy early Friday morning, by a farmer on his way to town. Other circumstances seemed to connect the stranger with the crime. The sheriff organized a posse to search for him, and early in the evening, when most of the citizens of Troy were at supper, the suspected man was brought in and lodged in the county jail.

By the following morning the news of the capture had spread to the farthest limits of the county. A much larger number of people than usual came to town that Saturday,—bearded men in straw hats and blue homespun shirts, and butternut trousers of great amplitude of material and vagueness of outline; women in homespun frocks and slat-bonnets, with faces as expressionless as the dreary sand-hills which gave them a meagre sustenance.

The murder was almost the sole topic of conversation. A steady stream of curious observers visited the house of mourning, and gazed upon the rugged face of the old veteran, now stiff and cold in death; and more than one eye dropped a tear at the remembrance of the cheery smile, and the joke—sometimes superannuated, generally feeble, but always good-natured—with which the captain had been wont to greet his acquaintances. There was a growing sentiment of anger among these stern men, toward the murderer who had thus cut down their friend, and a strong feeling that ordinary justice was too slight a punishment for such a crime.

Toward noon there was an informal gathering of citizens in Dan Tyson's store.

"I hear it 'lowed that Square Kyahtah's too sick ter hol' co'te this evenin'," said one, "an' that the purlim'nary hearin' 'll haf ter go over 'tel nex' week."

A look of disappointment went round the crowd.

"Hit's the durndes', meanes' murder ever committed in this caounty," said another, with moody emphasis.

"I s'pose the nigger 'lowed the Cap'n had some greenbacks," observed a third speaker.

"The Cap'n," said another, with an air of superior information, "has left two bairls of Confedrit money, which he 'spected 'ud be good some day er nuther."

This statement gave rise to a discussion of the speculative value of Confederate money; but in a little while the conversation returned to the murder.

"Hangin' air too good fer the murderer," said one; "he oughter be burnt, stidier bein' hung."

There was an impressive pause at this point, during which a jug of moonlight whiskey went the round of the crowd.

"Well," said a round-shouldered farmer, who, in spite of his peaceable expression and faded gray eye, was known to have been one of the most daring followers of a rebel guerrilla chieftain, "what air yer gwine ter do about it? Ef you fellers air gwine ter set down an' let a wuthless nigger kill the bes' white man in Branson, an' not say nuthin' ner do nuthin', *I'll* move outen the caounty."

This speech gave tone and direction to the rest of the conversation. Whether the fear of losing the round-shouldered farmer operated to bring about the result or not is immaterial to this narrative; but, at all events, the crowd decided to lynch the negro. They agreed that this was the least that could be done to avenge the death of their murdered friend, and that it was a becoming way in which to honor his memory. They had some vague notions of the majesty of the law and the rights of the citizen, but in the passion of the moment these sunk into oblivion; a white man had been killed by a negro.

"The Cap'n was an ole sodger," said one of his friends solemnly. "He'll sleep better when he knows that a co'te-martial has be'n hilt an' jestice done."

By agreement the lynchers were to meet at Tyson's store at five o'clock in the afternoon, and proceed thence to the jail, which was situated down the Lumberton Dirt Road (as the old turnpike antedating the plank-road was called), about half a mile south of the court-house. When the preliminaries of the lynching had been arranged, and a committee appointed to manage the affair, the crowd dispersed, some to go to their dinners, and some to secure recruits for the lynching party.

It was twenty minutes to five o'clock, when an excited negro, panting and perspiring, rushed up to the back door of Sheriff Campbell's dwelling, which stood at a little distance from the jail and somewhat farther than the latter building from the court-house. A turbaned colored woman came to the door in response to the negro's knock.

"Hoddy, Sis' Nance."

"Hoddy, Brer Sam."

"Is de shurff in," inquired the negro.

"Yas, Brer Sam, he's eatin' his dinner," was the answer.

"Will yer ax 'im ter step ter de do' a minute, Sis' Nance?"

The woman went into the dining-room, and a moment later the

sheriff came to the door. He was a tall, muscular man, of a ruddier complexion than is usual among Southerners. A pair of keen, deep-set gray eyes looked out from under bushy eyebrows, and about his mouth was a masterful expression, which a full beard, once sandy in color, but now profusely sprinkled with gray, could not entirely conceal. The day was hot; the sheriff had discarded his coat and vest, and had his white shirt open at the throat.

"What do you want, Sam?" he inquired of the negro, who stood hat in hand, wiping the moisture from his face with a ragged shirt-sleeve.

"Shurff, dey gwine ter hang de pris'ner w'at's lock' up in de jail. Dey're comin' dis a-way now. I wuz layin' down on a sack er corn down at de sto', behine a pile er flour-bairls, w'en I hearn Doc' Cain en Kunnel Wright talkin' erbout it. I slip' outen de back so', en run here as fas' as I could. I hearn you say down ter de sto' once't dat you wouldn't let nobody take a pris'ner 'way fum you widout walkin' over yo' dead body, en I thought I'd let you know 'fo' dey come, so yer could pertec' de pris'ner."

The sheriff listened calmly, but his face grew firmer, and a determined gleam lit up his gray eyes. His frame grew more erect, and he unconsciously assumed the attitude of a soldier who momentarily expects to meet the enemy face to face.

"Much obliged, Sam," he answered. "I'll protect the prisoner. Who's coming?"

"I dunno who-all *is* comin'," replied the negro. "Dere's a Mistah Mc-Swayne, en Doc' Cain, en Maje' McDonal' en Kunnel Wright, en a heap er yuthers. I wuz so skeered I done furgot mo'd'n half un 'em. I spec' dey mus' be mos' here by dis time, so I'll git outen de way, fer I don't want nobody fer ter think I wuz mix' up in dis business." The negro glanced nervously down the road toward the town, and made a movement as if to go away.

"Won't you have some dinner first?" asked the sheriff.

The negro looked longingly in at the open door, and sniffed the appetizing odor of boiled pork and collards.

"I ain't got no time fer ter tarry, Shurff," he said, "but Sis' Nance mought gin me sump'n I could kyar in my han' en eat on de way."

A moment later Nancy brought him a huge sandwich of split corn-pone, with a thick slice of fat bacon inserted between the halves, and a couple of baked yams. The negro hastily replaced his ragged hat on his head, dropped the yams in the pocket of his capacious trousers, and, taking the sandwich in his hand, hurried across the road and disappeared in the woods beyond.

The sheriff reëntered the house, and put on his coat and hat. He then took down a double-barreled shotgun and loaded it with buck-shot. Filling the chambers of a revolver with fresh cartridges, he slipped it into the pocket of the sack-coat which he wore.

A comely young women in a calico dress watched these proceedings with anxious surprise.

"Where are you going, father?" she asked. She had not heard the conversation with the negro.

"I am goin' over to the jail," responded the sheriff. "There's a mob comin' this way to lynch the nigger we've got locked up. But they won't do it," he added, with emphasis.

"Oh, father! don't go!" pleaded the girl, clinging to his arm; "they'll shoot you if you don't give him up."

"You never mind me, Polly," said her father reassuringly, as he gently unclasped her hands from his arm. "I'll take care of myself and the prisoner, too. There ain't a man in Branson County that would shoot me. Besides, I have faced fire too often to be scared away from my duty. You keep close in the house," he continued, "and if any one disturbs you just use the old horse-pistol in the top bureau drawer. It's a little old-fashioned, but it did good work a few years ago."

The young girl shuddered at this sanguinary allusion, but made no further objection to her father's departure.

The sheriff of Branson was a man far above the average of the community in wealth, education, and social position. His had been one of the few families in the county that before the war had owned large estates and numerous slaves. He had graduated at the State University at Chapel Hill, and had kept up some acquaintance with current literature and advanced thought. He had traveled some in his youth, and was looked up to in the county as an authority on all subjects connected with the outer world. At first an ardent supporter of the Union, he had opposed the secession movement in his native State as long as opposition availed to stem the tide of public opinion. Yielding at last to the force of circumstances, he had entered the Confederate service rather late in the war, and served with distinction through several campaigns, rising in time to the rank of colonel. After the war he had taken the oath of allegiance, and had been chosen by the people as the most available candidate for the office of sheriff, to which he had been elected without opposition. He had filled the office for several terms, and was universally popular with his constituents.

Colonel or Sheriff Campbell, as he was indifferently called, as the military or civil title happened to be most important in the opinion of the person addressing him, had a high sense of the responsibility attaching to his office. He had sworn to do his duty faithfully, and he knew what his duty was, as sheriff, perhaps more clearly than he had apprehended it in other passages of his life. It was, therefore, with no uncertainty in regard to his course that he prepared his weapons and went over to the jail. He had no fears for Polly's safety.

The sheriff had just locked the heavy front door of the jail behind him when a half-dozen horsemen, followed by a crowd of men on foot, came round a bend in the road and drew near the jail. They halted in front of the picket fence that surrounded the building, while several of the committee of arrangements rode on a few rods farther to the sheriff's house. One of them dismounted and rapped on the door with his riding-whip.

"Is the sheriff at home?" he inquired.

"No, he has just gone out," replied Polly, who had come to the door.

"We want the jail keys," he continued.

"They are not here," said Polly. "The sheriff has them himself." Then she added, with assumed indifference, "He is at the jail now."

The man turned away, and Polly went into the front room, from which she peered anxiously between the slats of the green blinds of a window that looked toward the jail. Meanwhile the messenger returned to his companions and announced his discovery. It looked as though the sheriff had learned of their design and was preparing to resist it.

One of them stepped forward and rapped on the jail door.

"Well, what is it?" said the sheriff, from within.

"We want to talk to you, Sheriff," replied the spokesman.

There was a little wicket in the door; this the sheriff opened, and answered through it.

"All right, boys, talk away. You are all strangers to me, and I don't know what business you can have." The sheriff did not think it necessary to recognize anybody in particular on such an occasion; the question of identity sometimes comes up in the investigation of these extra-judicial executions.

"We're a committee of citizens and we want to get into the jail."

"What for? It ain't much trouble to get into jail. Most people want to keep out."

The mob was in no humor to appreciate a joke, and the sheriff's witticism fell dead upon an unresponsive audience.

"We want to have a talk with the nigger that killed Cap'n Walker."

"You can talk to that nigger in the court-house, when he's brought out for trial. Court will be in session here next week. I know what you fellows want, but you can't get my prisoner to-day. Do you want to take the bread out of a poor man's mouth? I get seventy-five cents a day for keeping this prisoner, and he's the only one in jail. I can't have my family suffer just to please you fellows."

One or two young men in the crowd laughed at the idea of Sheriff

Campbell's suffering for want of seventy-five cents a day; but they were frowned into silence by those who stood near them.

"Ef yer don't let us in," cried a voice, "we'll bus' the do' open."

"Bust away," answered the sheriff, raising his voice so that all could hear. "But I give you fair warning. The first man that tries it will be filled with buckshot. I'm sheriff of this county; I know my duty, and I mean to do it."

"What's the use of kicking, Sheriff?" argued one of the leaders of the mob. "The nigger is sure to hang anyhow; he richly deserves it; and we've got to do something to teach the niggers their places, or white people won't be able to live in the county."

"There's no use talking, boys," responded the sheriff. "I'm a white man outside, but in this jail I'm sheriff; and if this nigger's to be hung in this county, I propose to do the hanging. So you fellows might as well right-about-face, and march back to Troy. You've had a pleasant trip, and the exercise will be good for you. You know *me*. I've got powder and ball, and I've faced fire before now, with nothing between me and the enemy, and I don't mean to surrender this jail while I'm able to shoot." Having thus announced his determination, the sheriff closed and fastened the wicket, and looked around for the best position from which to defend the building.

The crowd drew off a little, and the leaders conversed together in low tones.

The Branson County jail was a small, two-story brick building, strongly constructed, with no attempt at architectural ornamentation. Each story was divided into two large cells by a passage running from front to rear. A grated iron door gave entrance from the passage to each of the four cells. The jail seldom had many prisoners in it, and the lower windows had been boarded up. When the sheriff had closed the wicket, he ascended the steep wooden stairs to the upper floor. There was no window at the front of the upper passage, and the most available position from which to watch the movements of the crowd below was the front window of the cell occupied by the solitary prisoner.

The sheriff unlocked the door and entered the cell. The prisoner was crouched in a corner, his yellow face, blanched with terror, looking ghastly in the semi-darkness of the room. A cold perspiration had gathered on his forehead, and his teeth were chattering with affright.

"For God's sake, Sheriff," he murmured hoarsely, "don't let 'em lynch me; I didn't kill the old man."

The sheriff glanced at the cowering wretch with a look of mingled contempt and loathing.

"Get up," he said sharply. "You will probably be hung sooner or later, but it shall not be to-day, if I can help it. I'll unlock your fetters, and if I can't hold the jail, you'll have to make the best fight you can. If I'm shot, I'll consider my responsibility at an end."

There were iron fetters on the prisoner's ankles, and handcuffs on his wrists. These the sheriff unlocked, and they fell clanking to the floor.

"Keep back from the window," said the sheriff. "They might shoot if they saw you."

The sheriff drew toward the window a pine bench which formed a part of the scanty furniture of the cell, and laid his revolver upon it. Then he took his gun in hand, and took his stand at the side of the window where he could, with least exposure of himself, watch the movement of the crowd below.

The lynchers had not anticipated any determined resistance. Of course they had looked for a formal protest, and perhaps a sufficient show of opposition to excuse the sheriff in the eye of any stickler for legal formalities. They had not however come prepared to fight a battle, and no one of them seemed willing to lead an attack upon the jail. The leaders of the party conferred together with a good deal of animated gesticulation, which was visible to the sheriff from his outlook, though the distance was too great for him to hear what was said. At length one of them broke away from the group, and rode back to the main body of the lynchers, who were restlessly awaiting orders.

"Well, boys," said the messenger, "we'll have to let it go for the present. The sheriff says he'll shoot, and he's got the drop on us this time. There ain't any of us that want to follow Cap'n Walker jest yet. Besides, the sheriff is a good fellow, and we don't want to hurt 'im. But," he added, as if to reassure the crowd, which began to show signs of disappointment, "the nigger might as well say his prayers, for he ain't got long to live."

There was a murmur of dissent from the mob, and several voices insisted that an attack be made on the jail. But pacific counsels finally prevailed, and the mob sullenly withdrew.

The sheriff stood at the window until they had disappeared around the bend in the road. He did not relax his watchfulness when the last one was out of sight. Their withdrawal might be a mere feint, to be followed by a further attempt. So closely, indeed, was his attention drawn to the outside, that he neither saw nor heard the prisoner creep stealthily across the floor, reach out his hand and secure the revolver which lay on the bench behind the sheriff, and creep as noiselessly back to his place in the corner of the room.

A moment after the last of the lynching party had disappeared there was a shot fired from the woods across the road; a bullet whistled by the window and buried itself in the wooden casing a few inches from where the sheriff was standing. Quick as thought, with the instinct born of a semi-guerrilla army experience, he raised his gun and fired twice at the point from which a faint puff of smoke showed the hostile bullet to have been sent. He stood a moment watching, and then rested his gun against the window, and reached behind him mechanically for the other weapon. It was not on the bench. As the sheriff realized this fact, he turned his head and looked into the muzzle of the revolver.

"Stay where you are, Sheriff," said the prisoner, his eyes glistening, his face almost ruddy with excitement.

The sheriff mentally cursed his own carelessness for allowing him to be caught in such a predicament. He had not expected anything of the kind. He had relied on the negro's cowardice and subordination in the presence of an armed white man as a matter of course. The sheriff was a brave man, but realized that the prisoner had him at an immense disadvantage. The two men stood thus for a moment, fighting a harmless duel with their eyes.

"Well, what do you mean to do?" asked the sheriff with apparent calmness.

"To get away, of course," said the prisoner, in a tone which caused the sheriff to look at him more closely, and with an involuntary feeling of apprehension; if the man was not mad, he was in a state of mind akin to madness, and quite as dangerous. The sheriff felt that he must speak the prisoner fair, and watch for a chance to turn the tables on him. The keen-eyed, desperate man before him was a different being altogether from the groveling wretch who had begged so piteously for life a few minutes before.

At length the sheriff spoke:—

"Is this your gratitude to me for saving your life at the risk of my own? If I had not done so, you would now be swinging from the limb of some neighboring tree."

"True," said the prisoner, "you saved my life, but for how long? When you came in, you said Court would sit next week. When the crowd went away they said I had not long to live. It is merely a choice of two ropes."

"While there's life there's hope," replied the sheriff. He uttered this commonplace mechanically, while his brain was busy in trying to think out some way of escape. "If you are innocent you can prove it."

The mulatto kept his eye upon the sheriff. "I didn't kill the old man," he replied, "but I shall never be able to clear myself. I was at his house at nine o'clock. I stole from it the coat that was on my back when I was taken. I would be convicted, even with a fair trial, unless the real murderer were discovered beforehand."

The sheriff knew this only too well. While he was thinking what argument next to use, the prisoner continued:—

"Throw me the keys—no, unlock the door."

The sheriff stood a moment irresolute. The mulatto's eye glittered ominously. The sheriff crossed the room and unlocked the door leading into the passage.

"Now go down and unlock the outside door."

The heart of the sheriff leaped within him. Perhaps he might make a dash for liberty, and gain the outside. He descended the narrow stairs, the prisoner keeping close behind him.

The sheriff inserted the huge iron key into the lock. The rusty bolt yielded slowly. It still remained for him to pull the door open.

"Stop!" thundered the mulatto, who seemed to divine the sheriff's purpose. "Move a muscle, and I'll blow your brains out."

The sheriff obeyed; he realized that his chance had not yet come.

"Now keep on that side of the passage, and go back upstairs."

Keeping the sheriff under cover of the revolver, the mulatto followed him up the stairs. The sheriff expected the prisoner to lock him into the cell and make his own escape. He had about come to the conclusion that the best thing he could do under the circumstances was to submit quietly, and take his chances of recapturing the prisoner after the alarm had been given. The sheriff had faced death more than once upon the battlefield. A few minutes before, well armed, and with a brick wall between him and them he had dared a hundred men to fight; but he felt instinctively that the desperate man confronting him was not to be trifled with, and he was too prudent a man to risk his life against such heavy odds. He had Polly to look after, and there was a limit beyond which devotion to duty would be quixotic and even foolish.

"I want to get away," said the prisoner, "and I don't want to be captured; for if I am I know I will be hung on the spot. I am afraid," he added somewhat reflectively, "that in order to save myself I shall have to kill you."

"Good God!" exclaimed the sheriff in involuntary terror; "you would not kill the man to whom you owe your own life."

"You speak more truly than you know," replied the mulatto. "I indeed owe my life to you."

The sheriff started. He was capable of surprise, even in that moment of extreme peril. "Who are you?" he asked in amazement.

"Tom, Cicely's son," returned the other. He had closed the door and stood talking to the sheriff through the grated opening. "Don't you remember Cicely—Cicely whom you sold, with her child, to the speculator on his way to Alabama?"

The sheriff did remember. He had been sorry for it many times since. It had been the old story of debts, mortgages, and bad crops. He had quarreled with the mother. The price offered for her and her child had been unusually large, and he had yielded to the combination of anger and pecuniary stress.

"Good God!" he gasped, "you would not murder your own father?"

"My father?" replied the mulatto. "It were well enough for me to claim the relationship, but it comes with poor grace from you to ask anything by reason of it. What father's duty have you ever performed for me? Did you give me your name, or even your protection? Other white men gave their colored sons freedom and money, and sent them to the free States. *You* sold *me* to the rice swamps."

"I at least gave you the life you cling to," murmured the sheriff.

"Life?" said the prisoner, with a sarcastic laugh. "What kind of a life? You gave me your own blood, your own features—no man need look at us together twice to see that—and you gave me a black mother. Poor wretch! She died under the lash, because she had enough womanhood to call her soul her own. You gave me a white man's spirit, and you made me a slave, and crushed it out."

"But you are free now," said the sheriff. He had not doubted, could not doubt, the mulatto's words. He knew whose passions coursed beneath that swarthy skin and burned in the black eyes opposite his own. He saw in this mulatto what he himself might have become had not the safeguards of parental restraint and public opinion been thrown around him.

"Free to do what?" replied the mulatto. "Free in name, but despised and scorned and set aside by the people to whose race I belong far more than to my mother's."

"There are schools," said the sheriff. "You have been to school." He had noticed that the mulatto spoke more eloquently and used better language than most Branson County people.

"I have been to school, and dreamed when I went that it would work some marvelous change in my condition. But what did I learn? I learned to feel that no degree of learning or wisdom will change the color of my skin and that I shall always wear what in my own country is a badge of degradation. When I think about it seriously I do not care particularly for such a life. It is the animal in me, not the man, that flees the gallows. I owe you nothing," he went on, "and expect nothing of you; and it would be no more than justice if I should avenge upon you my mother's wrongs and my own. But still I hate to shoot you; I have never yet taken human life—for I did *not* kill the old captain. Will you promise to give no alarm and make no attempt to capture me until morning, if I do not shoot?"

So absorbed were the two men in their colloquy and their own tumultuous thoughts that neither of them had heard the door below move upon its hinges. Neither of them had heard a light step come stealthily up the stairs, nor seen a slender form creep along the darkening passage toward the mulatto.

The sheriff hesitated. The struggle between his love of life and his sense of duty was a terrific one. It may seem strange that a man who could sell his own child into slavery should hesitate at such a moment, when his life was trembling in the balance. But the baleful influence of human slavery poisoned the very fountains of life, and created new standards of right. The sheriff was conscientious; his conscience had merely been warped by his environment. Let no one ask what his answer would have been; he was spared the necessity of a decision.

"Stop," said the mulatto, "you need not promise. I could not trust you if you did. It is your life for mine; there is but one safe way for me; you must die."

He raised his arm to fire, when there was a flash—a report from the passage behind him. His arm fell heavily at his side, and the pistol dropped at his feet.

The sheriff recovered first from his surprise, and throwing open the door secured the fallen weapon. Then seizing the prisoner he thrust him into the cell and locked the door upon him; after which he turned to Polly, who leaned half-fainting against the wall, her hands clasped over her heart.

"Oh, father, I was just in time!" she cried hysterically, and, wildly sobbing, threw herself into her father's arms.

"I watched until they all went away," she said. "I heard the shot from the woods and I saw you shoot. Then when you did not come out I feared something had happened, that perhaps you had been wounded. I got out the other pistol and ran over here. When I found the door open, I knew something was wrong, and when I heard voices I crept upstairs, and reached the top just in time to hear him say he would kill you. Oh, it was a narrow escape!"

When she had grown somewhat calmer, the sheriff left her standing there and went back into the cell. The prisoner's arm was bleeding from a flesh wound. His bravado had given place to a stony apathy. There was no sign in his face of fear or disappointment or feeling of any kind. The sheriff sent Polly to the house for cloth, and bound up the prisoner's wound with a rude skill acquired during his army life.

"I'll have a doctor come and dress the wound in the morning," he said to the prisoner. "It will do very well until then, if you will keep quiet. If the doctor asks you how the wound was caused, you can say that you were struck by the bullet fired from the woods. It would do you no good to have it known that you were shot while attempting to escape."

The prisoner uttered no word of thanks or apology, but sat in sullen silence. When the wounded arm had been bandaged, Polly and her father returned to the house.

The sheriff was in an unusually thoughtful mood that evening. He put salt in his coffee at supper, and poured vinegar over his pancakes. To many of Polly's questions he returned random answers. When he had gone to bed he lay awake for several hours.

In the silent watches of the night, when he was alone with God, there came into his mind a flood of unaccustomed thoughts. An hour or two before, standing face to face with death, he had experienced a sensation similar to that which drowning men are said to feel—a kind of clarifying of the moral faculty, in which the veil of the flesh, with its obscuring passions and prejudices, is pushed aside for a moment, and all the acts of one's life stand out, in the clear light of truth, in their correct proportions and relations,—a state of mind in which one sees himself as God may be supposed to see him. In the reaction following his rescue, this feeling had given place for a time to far different emotions. But now, in the silence of midnight, something of this clearness of spirit returned to the sheriff. He saw that he had owed some duty to this son of his,—that neither law nor custom could destroy a responsibility inherent in the nature of mankind. He could not thus, in the eyes of God at least, shake off the consequences of his sin. Had he never sinned, this wayward spirit would never have come back from the vanished past to haunt him. As these thoughts came, his anger against the mulatto died away, and in its place there sprang up a great pity. The hand of parental authority might have restrained the passions he had seen burning in the prisoner's eyes when the desperate man spoke the words which had seemed to doom his father to death. The sheriff felt that he might have saved this fiery spirit from the slough of slavery; that he might have sent him to the free North, and given him there, or in some other land, an opportunity to turn to usefulness and honorable pursuits the talents that had run to crime, perhaps to madness; he might, still less, have given this son of his the poor simulacrum of liberty which men of his caste could possess in a slave-holding community; or least of all, but still something, he might have kept the boy on the plantation, where the burdens of slavery would have fallen lightly upon him.

The sheriff recalled his own youth. He had inherited an honored name to keep untarnished; he had had a future to make; the picture of a fair young bride had beckoned him on to happiness. The poor wretch now stretched upon a pallet of straw between the brick walls of the jail had had none of these things,—no name, no father, no mother —in the true meaning of motherhood,—and until the past few years no possible future, and then one vague and shadowy in its outline, and dependent for form and substance upon the slow solution of a problem in which there were many unknown quantities.

From what he might have done to what he might yet do was an easy transition for the awakened conscience of the sheriff. It occurred to him, purely as a hypothesis, that he might permit his prisoner to escape; but his oath of office, his duty as sheriff, stood in the way of such a course, and the sheriff dismissed the idea from his mind. He could, however, investigate the circumstances of the murder, and move Heaven and earth to discover the real criminal, for he no longer doubted the prisoner's innocence; he could employ counsel for the accused, and perhaps influence public opinion in his favor. An acquittal once secured, some plan could be devised by which the sheriff might in some degree atone for his crime against this son of his—against society—against God.

When the sheriff had reached this conclusion he fell into an unquiet slumber, from which he awoke late the next morning.

He went over to the jail before breakfast and found the prisoner lying on his pallet, his face turned to the wall; he did not move when the sheriff rattled the door.

"Good-morning," said the latter, in a tone intended to waken the prisoner.

There was no response. The sheriff looked more keenly at the recumbent figure; there was an unnatural rigidity about its attitude.

He hastily unlocked the door and, entering the cell, bent over the prostrate form. There was no sound of breathing; he turned the body over—it was cold and stiff. The prisoner had torn the bandage from his wound and bled to death during the night. He had evidently been dead several hours.

Yet Do I Marvel

COUNTEE CULLEN

I doubt not God is good, well-meaning, kind,
And did He stoop to quibble could tell why
The little buried mole continues blind,
Why flesh that mirrors Him must someday die,
Make plain the reason tortured Tantalus
Is baited by the fickle fruit, declare
If merely brute caprice dooms Sisyphus
To struggle up a never-ending stair.
Inscrutable His ways are, and immune
To catechism by a mind too strewn
With petty cares to slightly understand

What awful brain compels His awful hand.
Yet do I marvel at this curious thing:
To make a poet black, and bid him sing!

from **Native Son**

RICHARD WRIGHT

Outside his window he saw the sun dying over the rooftops in the western sky and watched the first shade of dusk fall. Now and then a street car ran past. The rusty radiator hissed at the far end of the room. All day long it had been springlike; but now dark clouds were slowly swallowing the sun. All at once the street lamps came on and the sky was black and close to the house-tops.

Inside his shirt he felt the cold metal of the gun resting against his naked skin; he ought to put it back between the mattresses. No! He would keep it. He would take it with him to the Dalton place. He felt that he would be safer if he took it. He was not planning to use it and there was nothing in particular that he was afraid of, but there was in him an uneasiness and distrust that made him feel that he ought to have it along. He was going among white people, so he would take his knife and his gun; it would make him feel that he was the equal of them, give him a sense of completeness. Then he thought of a good reason why he should take it; in order to get to the Dalton place, he had to go through a white neighborhood. He had not heard of any Negroes being molested recently, but he felt that it was always possible.

Far away a clock boomed five times. He sighed and got up and yawned and stretched his arms high above his head to loosen the muscles of his body. He got his overcoat, for it was growing cold outdoors; then got his cap. He tiptoed to the door, wanting to slip out without his mother hearing him. Just as he was about to open it, she called.

"Bigger!"

He stopped and frowned.

"Yeah, Ma."

"You going to see about that job?"

"Yeah."

"Ain't you going to eat?"

"I ain't got time now."

She came to the door, wiping her soapy hands upon an apron.

"Here; take this quarter and buy you something."

"O.K."

"And be careful, son."

He went out and walked south to Forty-sixth Street, then eastward. Well, he would see in a few moments if the Daltons for whom he was to work were like the people he had seen and heard in the movie. But while walking through this quiet and spacious white neighborhood, he did not feel the pull and mystery of the thing as strongly as he had in the movie. The houses he passed were huge; lights glowed softly in windows. The streets were empty, save for an occasional car that zoomed past on swift rubber tires. This was a cold and distant world; a world of white secrets carefully guarded. He could feel a pride, a certainty, and a confidence in these streets and houses. He came to Drexel Boulevard and began to look for 4605. When he came to it, he stopped and stood before a high, black, iron picket fence, feeling constricted inside. All he had felt in the movie was gone; only fear and emptiness filled him now.

Would they expect him to come in the front way or back? It was queer that he had not thought of that. Goddamn! He walked the length of the picket fence in front of the house, seeking for a walk leading to the rear. But there was none. Other than the front gate, there was only a driveway, the entrance to which was securely locked. Suppose a policeman saw him wandering in a white neighborhood like this? It would be thought that he was trying to rob or rape somebody. He grew angry. Why had he come to take this goddamn job? He could have stayed among his own people and escaped feeling this fear and hate. This was not his world; he had been foolish in thinking that he would have liked it. He stood in the middle of the sidewalk with his jaws clamped tight; he wanted to strike something with his fist. Well . . . Goddamn! There was nothing to do but go in the front way. If he were doing wrong, they could not kill him, at least; all they could do was to tell him that he could not get the job.

Timidly, he lifted the latch on the gate and walked to the steps. He paused, waiting for someone to challenge him. Nothing happened. Maybe nobody was home? He went to the door and saw a dim light burning in a shaded niche above a doorbell. He pushed it and was startled to hear a soft gong sound within. Maybe he had pushed it too hard? Aw, what the hell! He had to do better than this; he relaxed his taut muscles and stood at ease, waiting. The doorknob turned. The door opened. He saw a white face. It was a woman.

"Hello!"

"Yessum," he said.

"You want to see somebody?"

"Er ... Er ... I want to see Mr. Dalton."

"Are you the Thomas boy?"

"Yessum."

"Come in."

He edged through the door slowly, then stopped halfway. The woman was so close to him that he could see a tiny mole at the corner of her mouth. He held his breath. It seemed that there was not room enough for him to pass without actually touching her.

"Come in," the woman said.

"Yessum," he whispered.

He squeezed through and stood uncertainly in a softly lighted hallway.

"Follow me," she said.

With cap in hand and shoulders sloped, he followed, walking over a rug so soft and deep that it seemed he was going to fall at each step he took. He went into a dimly lit room.

"Take a seat," she said. "I'll tell Mr. Dalton that you're here and he'll be out in a moment."

"Yessum."

He sat and looked up at the woman; she was staring at him and he looked away in confusion. He was glad when she left. That old bastard! What's so damn funny about me? I'm just like she is. . . . He felt that the position in which he was sitting was too awkward and found that he was on the very edge of the chair. He rose slightly to sit farther back; but when he sat he sank down so suddenly and deeply that he thought the chair had collapsed under him. He bounded halfway up, in fear; then, realizing what had happened, he sank distrustfully down again. He looked round the room; it was lit by dim lights glowing from a hidden source. He tried to find them by roving his eyes, but could not. He had not expected anything like this; he had not thought that this world would be so utterly different from his own that it would intimidate him. On the smooth walls were several paintings whose nature he tried to make out, but failed. He would have liked to examine them, but dared not. Then he listened; a faint sound of piano music floated to him from somewhere. He was sitting in a white home; dim lights burned round him; strange objects challenged him; and he was feeling angry and uncomfortable.

"All right. Come this way."

He started at the sound of a man's voice.

"Suh?"

"Come this way."

Misjudging how far back he was sitting in the chair, his first attempt to rise failed and he slipped back, resting on his side. Grabbing the arms of the chair, he pulled himself upright and found a tall, lean, white-haired man holding a piece of paper in his hand. The man was gazing at him with an amused smile that made him conscious of every square inch of skin on his black body.

"Thomas?" the man asked. "Bigger Thomas?"

"Yessuh," he whispered; not speaking, really; but hearing his words issue voluntarily from his lips, as of a force of their own.

"Come this way."

"Yessuh."

He followed the man out of the room and down a hall. The man stopped abruptly. Bigger paused, bewildered; then he saw coming slowly toward him a tall, thin, white woman, walking silently, her hands lifted delicately in the air and touching the walls to either side of her. Bigger stepped back to let her pass. Her face and hair were completely white; she seemed to him like a ghost. The man took her arm gently and held her for a moment. Bigger saw that she was old and her gray eyes looked stony.

"Are you all right?" the man asked.

"Yes," she answered.

"Where's Peggy?"

"She's preparing dinner. I'm quite all right, Henry."

"You shouldn't be alone this way. When is Mrs. Patterson coming back?" the man asked.

"She'll be back Monday. But Mary's here. I'm all right; don't worry about me. Is someone with you?"

"Oh, yes. This is the boy the relief sent."

"The relief people were very anxious for you to work for us," the woman said; she did not move her body or face as she talked, but she spoke in a tone of voice that indicated that she was speaking to Bigger. "I hope you'll like it here."

"Yessum," Bigger whispered faintly, wondering as he did so if he ought to say anything at all.

"How far did you go in school?"

"To the eighth grade, mam."

"Don't you think it would be a wise procedure to inject him into his new environment at once, so he could get the feel of things?" the woman asked, addressing herself by the tone of her voice to the man now.

"Well, tomorrow'll be time enough," the man said hesitantly.

"I think it's important emotionally that he feels free to trust his environment," the woman said. "Using the analysis contained in the case record the relief sent us, I think we should evoke an immediate feeling of confidence. . . ."

"But that's too abrupt," the man said.

Bigger listened, blinking and bewildered. The long strange words they used made no sense to him; it was another language. He felt from the tone of their voices that they were having a difference of opinion about him, but he could not determine what it was about. It made him uneasy, tense, as though there were influences and presences about him which he could feel but not see. He felt strangely blind.

"Well, let's try it," the woman said.

"Oh, all right. We'll see. We'll see," the man said.

The man let go of the woman and she walked on slowly, the long white fingers of her hands just barely touching the walls. Behind the woman, following at the hem of her dress, was a big white cat, pacing without sound. She's blind! Bigger thought in amazement.

"Come on; this way," the man said.

"Yessuh."

"That was Mrs. Dalton," the man said. "She's blind."

"Yessuh."

"She has a very deep interest in colored people."

"Yessuh." Bigger whispered. He was conscious of the effort to breathe; he licked his lips and fumbled nervously with his cap.

"Well, I'm Mr. Dalton."

"Yessuh."

"Do you think you'd like driving a car?"

"Oh, yessuh."

"Did you bring the paper?"

"Suh?"

"Didn't the relief give you a note to me?"

"Oh, yessuh!"

He had completely forgotten about the paper. He stood to reach into his vest pocket and, in doing so, dropped his cap. For a moment his impulses were deadlocked; he did not know if he should pick up his cap and then find the paper, or find the paper and then pick up his cap. He decided to pick up his cap.

"Put your cap here," said Mr. Dalton, indicating a place on his desk.

"Yessuh."

Then he was stone-still; the white cat bounded past him and leaped upon the desk; it sat looking at him with large placid eyes and mewed plaintively.

"What's the matter, Kate?" Mr. Dalton asked, stroking the cat's fur and smiling. Mr. Dalton turned back to Bigger. "Did you find it?"

"Nawsuh. But I got it here, somewhere."

He hated himself at that moment. Why was he acting and feeling this way? He wanted to wave his hand and blot out the white man who was making him feel like this. If not that, he wanted to blot himself out. He had not raised his eyes to the level of Mr. Dalton's face once since he had been in the house. He stood with his knees slightly bent, his lips partly open, his shoulders stooped; and his eyes held a look that went only to the surface of things. There was an organic conviction in him that this was the way white folks wanted him to be when in their presence; none ever told him that in so many words, but their manner had made him feel that they did. He laid the cap down, noticing that Mr. Dalton was watching him closely. Maybe he was not acting right? Goddamn! Clumsily, he searched for the paper. He could not find it at first and he felt called upon to say something for taking so long.

"I had it right here in my vest pocket," he mumbled.

"Take your time."

"Oh, here it is."

He drew the paper forth. It was crumpled and soiled. Nervously, he straightened it out and handed it to Mr. Dalton, holding it by its very tip end.

"All right, now," said Mr. Dalton. "Let's see what you've got here. You live at 3721 Indiana Avenue?"

"Yessuh."

Mr. Dalton paused, frowned, and looked up at the ceiling.

"What kind of a building is that over there?"

"You mean where I live, suh?"

"Yes."

"Oh, it's just an old building."

"Where do you pay rent?"

"Down on Thirty-first Street."

"To the South Side Real Estate Company?"

"Yessuh."

Bigger wondered what all these questions could mean; he had heard that Mr. Dalton owned the South Side Real Estate Company, but he was not sure.

"How much rent do you pay?"

"Eight dollars a week."

"For how many rooms?"

"We just got one, suh."

"I see. . . . Now, Bigger, tell me, how old are you?"

"I'm twenty, suh."

"Married?"

"Nawsuh."

"Sit down. You needn't stand. And I won't be long."

"Yessuh."

❖   ❖   ❖

"How far did you say you went in school, Bigger?"

"To the eighth grade, mam."

"Did you ever think of going back?"

"Well, I gotta work now, mam."

"Suppose you had the chance to go back?"

"Well, I don't know, mam."

"The last man who worked here went to night school and got an education."

"Yessum."

"What would you want to be if you had an education?"

"I don't know, mam."

"Did you ever think about it?"

"No'm."

"You would rather work?"

"I reckon I would, mam."

"Well, we'll talk about that some other time. I think you'd better get the car for Miss Dalton now."

"Yessum."

He left her standing in the middle of the kitchen floor, exactly as he had found her. He did not know just how to take her; she made him feel that she would judge all he did harshly but kindly. He had a feeling toward her that was akin to that which he held toward his mother. The difference in his feelings toward Mrs. Dalton and his mother was that he felt that his mother wanted him to do the things *she* wanted him to do, and he felt that Mrs. Dalton wanted him to do the things he felt that *he* should have wanted to do. But he did not want to go to night school. Night school was all right; but he had other plans. Well, he didn't know just what they were right now, but he was working them out.

The night air had grown warmer. A wind had risen. He lit a cigarette and unlocked the garage; the door swung in and again he was surprised and pleased to see the lights spring on automatically. These people's got everything, he mused. He examined the car; it was a dark blue Buick, with steel spoke wheels and of a new make. He stepped back from it and looked it over; then he opened the door and looked at the dashboard. He was a little disappointed that the car was not so expensive as he had hoped, but what it lacked in price was more than made up for in color and style. "It's all right," he said half-aloud. He got in and backed it into the driveway and turned it around and pulled it up to the side door.

"Is that you, Bigger?"

The girl stood on the steps.

"Yessum."

He got out and held the rear door open for her.

"Thank you."

He touched his cap and wondered if it were the right thing to do.

"Is it that university-school out there on the Midway, mam?"

Through the rear mirror above him he saw her hesitate before answering.

"Yes; that's the one."

He pulled the car into the street and headed south, driving about thirty-five miles an hour. He handled the car expertly, picking up speed at the beginning of each block and slowing slightly as he approached each street intersection.

"You drive well," she said.

"Yessum," he said proudly.

He watched her through the rear mirror as he drove; she was kind of pretty, but very little. She looked like a doll in a show window: black eyes, white face, red lips. And she was not acting at all now as she had acted when he first saw her. In fact, she had a remote look in her eyes. He stopped the car at Forty-seventh Street for a red light; he did not have to stop again until he reached Fifty-first Street where a long line of cars formed in front of him and a long line in back. He held the steering wheel lightly, waiting for the line to move forward. He had a keen sense of power when driving; the feel of a car added something to him. He loved to press his foot against a pedal and sail along, watching others stand still, seeing the asphalt road unwind under him. The lights flashed from red to green and he nosed the car forward.

"Bigger!"

"Yessum."

"Turn at this corner and pull up on a side street."

"Here, mam?"

"Yes; here."

Now, what on earth did this mean? He pulled the car off Cottage Grove Avenue and drew to a curb. He turned to look at her and was startled to see that she was sitting on the sheer edge of the back seat, her face some six inches from his.

"I scare you?" she asked softly, smiling.

"Oh, no'm," he mumbled, bewildered.

He watched her through the mirror. Her tiny white hands dangled over the back of the front seat and her eyes looked out vacantly.

"I don't know how to say what I'm going to say," she said.

He said nothing. There was a long silence. What in all hell did this girl want? A street car rumbled by. Behind him, reflected in the rear mirror, he saw the traffic lights flash from green to red, and back again. Well, whatever she was going to say, he wished she would say it and get it over. This girl was strange. She did the unexpected every minute. He waited for her to speak. She took her hands from the back of the front seat and fumbled in her purse.

"Gotta match?"

"Yessum."

He dug a match from his vest pocket.

"Strike it," she said.

He blinked. He struck the match and held the flame for her. She smoked a while in silence.

"You're not a tattletale, are you?" she asked with a smile.

He opened his mouth to reply, but no words came. What she had asked and the tone of voice in which she had asked it made him feel that he ought to have answered in some way; but what?

"I'm not going to the University," she said at last. "But you can forget that. I want you to drive me to the Loop. But if anyone should ask you, then I went to the University, see, Bigger?"

"Yessum, it's all right with me," he mumbled.

"I think I can trust you."

"Yessum."

"After all, I'm on your side."

Now, what did *that* mean? She was on *his* side. What side was he on? Did she mean that she liked colored people? Well, he had heard that about her whole family. Was she really crazy? How much did her folks know of how she acted? But if she were really crazy, why did Mr. Dalton let him drive her out?

"I'm going to meet a friend of mine who's also a friend of yours," she said.

"Friend of mine!" he could not help exclaiming.

"Oh, you don't know him yet," she said laughing.

"Oh."

"Go to the Outer Drive and then to 16 Lake Street."

"Yessum."

Maybe she was talking about the *reds*? *That* was it. But none of his friends were reds. What was all this? If Mr. Dalton should ask him if he had taken her to the University, he would have to say yes and depend upon her to back him up. But suppose Mr. Dalton had someone watching, someone who would tell where he had really taken her? He had heard that many rich people had detectives working for them. If only he knew what this was all about he would feel much better. And she had said that she was going to meet someone who was a friend of his. He didn't want to meet any Communists. They didn't have any money. He felt that it was all right for a man to go to jail for robbery, but to go to jail for fooling around with reds was bunk. Well, he would drive her; that was what he had been hired for. But he was going to watch his step in this business. The only thing he hoped was that she would not make him lose his job. He pulled the car off the Outer Drive at Seventh Street, drove north on Michigan Boulevard to Lake Street, then headed west for two blocks, looking for number 16.

"It's right here, Bigger."

"Yessum."

He pulled to a stop in front of a dark building.

"Wait," she said, getting out of the car.

He saw her smiling broadly at him, almost laughing. He felt that she knew every feeling and thought he had at that moment and he turned his head away in confusion. Goddamn that woman!

"I won't be long," she said.

She started off, then turned back.

"Take it easy, Bigger. You'll understand it better bye and bye."

"Yessum," he said, trying to smile; but couldn't.

"Isn't there a song like that, a song your people sing?"

"Like what, mam?"

"We'll understand it better bye and bye?"

"Oh, yessum."

She was an odd girl, all right. He felt something in her over and above the fear she inspired in him. She responded to him as if he were human, as if he lived in the same world as she. And he had never felt that before in a white person. But why? Was this some kind of game? The guarded feeling of freedom he had while listening to her was tangled with the hard fact that she was white and rich, a part of the world of people who told him what he could and could not do.

He looked at the building into which she had gone; it was old and unpainted; there were no lights in the windows or doorway. Maybe she was meeting her sweetheart? If that was all, then things would straighten out. But if she had gone to meet those Communists? And what were Communists like, anyway? Was *she* one? What made people Communists? He remembered seeing many cartoons of Communists in newspapers and always they had flaming torches in their hands and wore beards and were trying to commit murder or set things on fire. People who acted that way were crazy. All he could recall having heard about Communists was associated in his mind with darkness, old houses, people speaking in whispers, and trade unions on strike. And this was something like it.

He stiffened; the door into which she had gone opened. She came out, followed by a young white man. They walked to the car; but, instead of getting into the back seat, they came to the side of the car and stood, facing him.

"Oh, Bigger, this is Jan. And Jan, this is Bigger Thomas."

Jan smiled broadly, then extended an open palm toward him. Bigger's entire body tightened with suspense and dread.

"How are you, Bigger?"

Bigger's right hand gripped the steering wheel and he wondered if he ought to shake hands with this white man.

"I'm fine," he mumbled.

Jan's hand was still extended. Bigger's right hand raised itself about three inches, then stopped in mid-air.

"Come on and shake," Jan said.

Bigger extended a limp palm, his mouth open in astonishment. He felt Jan's fingers tighten about his own. He tried to pull his hand away, ever so gently, but Jan held on, firmly, smiling.

"We may as well get to know each other," Jan said. "I'm a friend of Mary's."

"Yessuh," he mumbled.

"First of all," Jan continued, putting his foot upon the running-board, "Don't say *sir* to me. I'll call you Bigger and you'll call me Jan. That's the way it'll be between us. How's that?"

Bigger did not answer. Mary was smiling. Jan still gripped his hand and Bigger held his head at an oblique angle, so that he could, by merely shifting his eyes, look at Jan and then out onto the street whenever he did not wish to meet Jan's gaze. He heard Mary laughing softly.

"It's all right, Bigger," she said. "Jan *means* it."

He flushed warm with anger. Goddam her soul to hell! Was she laughing at him? Were they making fun of him? What was it that they wanted? Why didn't they leave him alone? He was not bothering them. Yes, anything could happen with people like them. Yes, anything could happen with people like these. His entire mind and body were painfully concentrated into a single sharp point of attention. He was trying desperately to understand. He felt foolish sitting behind the steering wheel like this and letting a white man hold his hand. What would people passing along the street think? He was very conscious of his black skin and there was in him a prodding conviction that Jan and men like him had made it so that he would be conscious of that black skin. Did not white people despise a black skin? Then why was Jan doing this? Why was Mary standing there so eagerly, with shining eyes? What could they get out of this? Maybe they did not despise him? But they made him feel his black skin by just standing there looking at him, one holding his hand and the other smiling. He felt he had no physical existence at all right then; he was something he hated, the badge of shame which he knew was attached to a black skin. It was a shadowy region, a No Man's Land, the ground that separated the white world from the black that he stood upon. He felt naked, transparent; he felt that this white man, having helped to put him down, having helped to deform him, held him up now to look at him and be amused. At that moment he felt toward Mary and Jan a dumb, cold, and inarticulate hate.

"Let me drive awhile," Jan said, letting go of his hand and opening the door.

Bigger looked at Mary. She came forward and touched his arm.

"It's all right, Bigger," she said.

He turned in the seat to get out, but Jan stopped him.

"No; stay in and move over."

He slid over and Jan took his place at the wheel. He was still feeling his hand strangely; it seemed that the pressure of Jan's fingers had left an indelible imprint. Mary was getting into the front seat, too.

"Move over, Bigger," she said.

He moved closer to Jan. Mary pushed herself in, wedging tightly between him and the outer door of the car. There were white people to either side of him; he was sitting between two vast white looming walls. Never in his life had he been so close to a white woman. He smelt the odor of her hair and felt the soft pressure of her thigh against his own. Jan headed the car back to the Outer Drive, weaving in and out of the line of traffic. Soon they were speeding along the lake front, past a huge flat sheet of dully gleaming water. The sky was heavy with snow clouds and the wind was blowing strong.

"Isn't it glorious tonight?" she said.

"God, yes!" Jan said.

Bigger listened to the tone of their voices, to their strange accents, to the exuberant phrases that flowed so freely from their lips.

"That sky!"

"And that water!"

"It's so beautiful it makes you ache just to look at it," said Mary.

"This is a beautiful world, Bigger," Jan said, turning to him. "Look at that skyline!"

Bigger looked without turning his head; he just rolled his eyes. Stretching to one side of him was a vast sweep of tall buildings flecked with tiny squares of yellow light.

"We'll own all that some day, Bigger," Jan said with a wave of his hand. "After the revolution it'll be ours. But we'll have to fight for it. What a world to win, Bigger! And when that day comes, things'll be different. There'll be no white and no black; there'll be no rich and no poor."

Bigger said nothing. The car whirred along.

"We seem strange to you, don't we, Bigger?" Mary asked.

"Oh, no'm," he breathed softly, knowing that she did not believe him, but finding it impossible to answer her in any other way.

His arms and legs were aching from being cramped into so small a space, but he dared not move. He knew that they would not have cared if he had made himself more comfortable, but his moving would have called attention to himself and his black body. And he did not want to do that. These people made him feel things he did not want to feel. If he were white, if he were like them, it would have been different. But he was black. So he sat still, his arms and legs aching.

"Say, Bigger," asked Jan, "where can we get a good meal on the South Side?"

"Well," Bigger said, reflectively.

"We want to go to a *real* place," Mary said, turning to him gayly.

"You want to go to a night club?" Bigger asked in a tone that indicated that he was simply mentioning names and not recommending places to go.

"No; we want to eat."

"Look, Bigger. We want one of those places where colored people eat, not one of those show places."

What *did* these people want? When he answered his voice was neutral and toneless.

"Well, there's Ernie's Kitchen Shack. . . ."

"That sounds good!"

"Let's go there, Jan," Mary said.

"O.K.," Jan said. "Where is it?"

"It's at Forty-seventh Street and Indiana," Bigger told them.

Jan swung the car off the Outer Drive at Thirty-first Street and drove westward to Indiana Avenue. Bigger wanted Jan to drive faster, so that they could reach Ernie's Kitchen Shack in the shortest possible time. That would allow him a chance to sit in the car and stretch out his cramped and aching legs while they ate. Jan turned onto Indiana Avenue and headed South. Bigger wondered what Jack and Gus and G.H. would say if they saw him sitting between two white people in a car like this. They would tease him about such a thing as long as they could remember it. He felt Mary turn in her seat. She placed her hand on his arm.

"You know, Bigger, I've long wanted to go into those houses," she said, pointing to the tall, dark apartment buildings looming to either side of them, "and just *see* how your people live. You know what I mean? I've been to England, France and Mexico, but I don't know how people live ten blocks from me. We know so *little* about each other. I just want to *see*. I want to *know* these people. Never in my life have

I been inside of a Negro home. Yet they *must* live like we live. They're *human*. . . . There are twelve million of them. . . . They live in our country. . . . In the same city with us. . . ." Her voice trailed off wistfully.

There was silence. The car sped through the Black Belt, past tall buildings holding black life. Bigger knew that they were thinking of his life and the life of his people. Suddenly he wanted to seize some heavy object in his hand and grip it with all the strength of his body and in some strange way rise up and stand in naked space above the speeding car and with one final blow blot it out—with himself and them in it. His heart was beating fast and he struggled to control his breath. This thing was getting the better of him; he felt that he should not give way to his feelings like this. But he could not help it. Why didn't they leave him alone? What had he done to them? What good could they get out of sitting here making him feel so miserable?

"Tell me where it is, Bigger," Jan said.

"Yessuh."

Bigger looked out and saw that they were at Forty-sixth Street.

"It's at the end of the next block, suh."

"Can I park along here somewhere?"

"Oh; yessuh."

"Bigger, *please!* Don't say *sir* to me. . . . I don't *like* it. You're a man just like I am; I'm no better than you. Maybe other white men like it. But I don't. Look, Bigger. . . ."

"Yes. . . ." Bigger paused, swallowed, and looked down at his black hands. "O.K.," he mumbled, hoping that they did not hear the choke in his voice.

"You see, Bigger. . . ." Jan began.

Mary reached her hand round back of Bigger and touched Jan's shoulder.

"Let's get out," she said hurriedly.

Jan pulled the car to the curb and opened the door and stepped out. Bigger slipped behind the steering wheel again, glad to have room at last for his arms and legs. Mary got out of the other door. Now, he could get some rest. So intensely taken up was he with his own immediate sensations, that he did not look up until he felt something strange in the long silence. When he did look he saw, in a split second of time, Mary turn her eyes away from his face. She was looking at Jan and Jan was looking at her. There was no mistaking the meaning of the look in their eyes. To Bigger it was plainly a bewildered and questioning look, a look that asked: What on earth is wrong with him? Bigger's teeth clamped tight and he stared straight before him.

"Aren't you coming with us, Bigger?" Mary asked in a sweet tone that made him want to leap at her.

The people in Ernie's Kitchen Shack knew him and he did not want them to see him with these white people. He knew that if he went in they would ask one another: Who're them white folks Bigger's hanging around with?

"I—I . . . I don't want to go in. . . ." he whispered breathlessly.

"Aren't you hungry?" Jan asked.

"Naw; I ain't hungry."

Jan and Mary came close to the car.

"Come and sit with us anyhow," Jan said.

"I . . . I . . ." Bigger stammered.

"It'll be all right," Mary said.

"I can stay here. Somebody has to watch the car," he said.

"Oh, to hell with the car!" Mary said. "Come on in."

"I don't want to eat," Bigger said stubbornly.

"Well," Jan sighed. "If that's the way you feel about it, we won't go in."

Bigger felt trapped. Oh, goddamn! He saw in a flash that he could have made all of this very easy if he had simply acted from the beginning as if they were doing nothing unusual. But he did not understand them; he distrusted them, really hated them. He was puzzled as to why they were treating him this way. But, after all, this was his job and it was just as painful to sit here and let them stare at him as it was to go in.

"O.K.," he mumbled angrily.

He got out and slammed the door. Mary came close to him and caught his arm. He stared at her in a long silence; it was the first time he had ever looked directly at her, and he was able to do so only because he was angry.

"Bigger," she said, "you don't have to come in unless you really want to. Please, don't think . . . Oh, Bigger . . . We're not trying to make you feel badly. . . ."

Her voice stopped. In the dim light of the street lamp Bigger saw her eyes cloud and her lips tremble. She swayed against the car. He stepped backward, as though she were contaminated with an invisible contagion. Jan slipped his arm about her waist, supporting her. Bigger heard her sob softly. Good God! He had a wild impulse to turn around and walk away. He felt ensnared in a tangle of deep shadows, shadows as black as the night that stretched above his head. The way he had acted had made her cry, and yet the way she had acted had made him feel that he had to act as he had toward her. In his relations with her he felt that he was riding a seesaw; never were they on a common level; either he or she was up in the air. Mary dried her eyes and Jan whispered something to her. Bigger wondered what he could say to his mother, or the relief, or Mr. Dalton, if he left them. They would be sure to ask why he had walked off his job, and he would not be able to tell.

"I'm all right now, Jan," he heard Mary say. "I'm sorry. I'm just a fool, I suppose. . . . I acted a ninny." She lifted her eyes to Bigger. "Don't mind me, Bigger. I'm just silly, I guess. . . ."

He said nothing.

"Come on, Bigger," Jan said in a voice that sought to cover up everything. "Let's eat."

Jan caught his arm and tried to pull him forward, but Bigger hung back. Jan and Mary walked toward the entrance of the café and Bigger followed, confused and resentful. Jan went to a small table near a wall.

"Sit down, Bigger."

Bigger sat. Jan and Mary sat in front of him.

"You like fried chicken?" Jan asked.

"Yessuh," he whispered.

He scratched his head. How on earth could he learn not to say *yessuh* and *yessum* to white people in one night when he had been saying it all his life long? He looked before him in such a way that his eyes would not meet theirs. The waitress came and Jan ordered three beers and three portions of fried chicken.

"Hi, Bigger!"

He turned and saw Jack waving at him, but staring at Jan and Mary. He waved a stiff palm in return. Goddamn! Jack walked away hurriedly. Cautiously, Bigger looked around; the waitresses and several people at other tables were staring at him. They all knew him and he knew that they were wondering as he would have wondered if he had been in their places. Mary touched his arm.

"Have you ever been here before, Bigger?"

He groped for neutral words, words that would convey information but not indicate any shade of his own feelings.

"A few times."

"It's very nice," Mary said.

Somebody put a nickel in an automatic phonograph and they listened to the music. Then Bigger felt a hand grab his shoulder.

"Hi, Bigger! Where you been?"

He looked up and saw Bessie laughing in his face.

"Hi," he said gruffly.

"Oh, 'scuse me. I didn't know you had company," she said, walking away with her eyes upon Jan and Mary.

"Tell her to come over, Bigger," Mary said.

Bessie had gone to a far table and was sitting with another girl.

"She's over there now," Bigger said.

The waitress brought the beer and chicken.

"This is simply grand!" Mary exclaimed.

"You got something there," Jan said, looking at Bigger. "Did I say that right, Bigger?"

Bigger hesitated.

"That's the way they say it," he spoke flatly.

from **Invisible Man**

RALPH ELLISON

CHAPTER ONE

It goes a long way back, some twenty years. All my life I had been looking for something, and everywhere I turned someone tried to tell me what it was. I accepted their answers too, though they were often in contradiction and even self-contradictory. I was naïve. I was looking for myself and asking everyone except myself questions which I, and only I, could answer. It took me a long time and much painful boomeranging of my expectations to achieve a realization everyone else appears to have been born with: That I am nobody but myself. But first I had to discover that I am an invisible man!

And yet I am no freak of nature, nor of history. I was in the cards, other things having been equal (or unequal) eighty-five years ago. I am not ashamed of my grandparents for having been slaves. I am only ashamed of myself for having at one time been ashamed. About eighty-five years ago they were told that they were free, united with others of our country in everything pertaining to the common good, and, in everything social, separate like the fingers of the hand. And they believed it. They exulted in it. They stayed in their place, worked hard, and brought up my father to do the same. But my grandfather is the one. He was an odd old guy, my grandfather, and I am told I take after him. It was he who caused the trouble. On his deathbed he called my father to him and said, "Son, after I'm gone I want you to keep up the good fight. I never told you, but our life is a war and I have been a traitor all my born days, a spy in the enemy's country ever since I give up my gun back in the Reconstruction. Live with your head in the lion's mouth. I want you to overcome 'em with yeses, undermine 'em with grins, agree 'em to death and destruction, let 'em swoller you till they vomit or bust wide open." They thought the old man had gone out of his mind. He had been the meekest of men. The younger children were rushed from the room, the shades drawn and the flame of the lamp turned so low that it sputtered on the wick like the old man's breathing. "Learn it to the younguns," he whispered fiercely; then he died.

But my folks were more alarmed over his last words than over his dying. It was as though he had not died at all, his words caused so much anxiety. I was warned emphatically to forget what he had said and, indeed, this is the first time it has been mentioned outside the family circle. It had a tremendous effect upon me, however. I could never be sure of what he meant. Grandfather had been a quiet old man who never made any trouble, yet on his deathbed he had called himself a traitor and a spy, and he had spoken of his meekness as a dangerous activity. It became a constant puzzle which lay unanswered in the back of my mind. And whenever things went well for me I remembered my grandfather and felt guilty and uncomfortable. It was as though I was carrying out his advice in spite of myself. And to make it worse, everyone loved me for it. I was praised by the most lily-white men of the town. I was considered an example of desirable conduct just as my grandfather had been. And what puzzled me was that the old man defined it as *treachery*. When I was praised for my conduct I felt a guilt that in some way I was doing something that was really against the wishes of the white folks, that if they had understood they would have desired me to act just the opposite, that I should have been sulky and mean, and that that really would have been what they wanted, even though they were fooled and thought they wanted me to act as I did. It made me afraid that some day they would look upon me as a traitor and I would be lost. Still I was more afraid to act any other way because they didn't like that at all. The old man's words were like a curse. On my graduation day I delivered an oration in which I showed that humility was the secret, indeed, the very essence of progress.

(Not that I believed this—how could I, remembering my grandfather?—I only believed that it worked.) It was a great success. Everyone praised me and I was invited to give a speech at a gathering of the town's leading white citizens. It was a triumph for our whole community.

It was in the main ballroom of the leading hotel. When I got there I discovered that it was on the occasion of a smoker, and I was told that since I was to be there anyway, I might as well take part in the battle royal to be fought by some of my schoolmates as part of the entertainment. The battle royal came first.

All of the town's big shots were there in their tuxedos, wolfing down the buffet foods, drinking beer and whiskey and smoking black cigars. It was a large room with a high ceiling. Chairs were arranged in neat rows around three sides of a portable boxing ring. The fourth side was

clear, revealing a gleaming space of polished floor. I had some mis-
givings over the battle royal, by the way. Not from a distaste for fighting,
but because I didn't care too much for the other fellows who were to
take part. They were tough guys who seemed to have no grandfather's
curse worrying their minds. No one could mistake their toughness. And
besides, I suspected that fighting a battle royal might detract from
the dignity of my speech. In those pre-invisible days I visualized myself
as a potential Booker T. Washington. But the other fellows didn't care
too much for me either, and there were nine of them. I felt superior
to them in my way, and I didn't like the manner in which we were all
crowded together into the servants' elevator. Nor did they like my being
there. In fact, as the warmly lighted floors flashed past the elevator
we had words over the fact that I, by taking part in the fight, had
knocked one of their friends out of a night's work.

We were led out of the elevator through a rococo hall into an
anteroom and told to get into our fighting togs. Each of us was issued
a pair of boxing gloves and ushered out into the big mirrored hall,
which we entered looking cautiously about us and whispering, lest
we might accidentally be heard above the noise of the room. It was
foggy with cigar smoke. And already the whiskey was taking effect. I
was shocked to see some of the most important men of the town quite
tipsy. They were all there—bankers, lawyers, judges, doctors, fire
chiefs, teachers, merchants. Even one of the more fashionable pastors.
Something we could not see was going on up front. A clarinet was
vibrating sensuously and the men were standing up and moving eagerly
forward. We were a small tight group, clustered together, our bare
upper bodies touching and shining with anticipatory sweat; while up
front the big shots were becoming increasingly excited over something
we still could not see. Suddenly I heard the school superintendent,
who had told me to come, yell; "Bring up the shines, gentlemen! Bring
up the little shines!"

We were rushed up to the front of the ballroom, where it smelled
even more strongly of tobacco and whiskey. Then we were pushed into
place. I almost wet my pants. A sea of faces, some hostile, some
amused, ringed around us, and in the center, facing us, stood a magnificent blonde—stark naked. There was dead silence. I felt a blast of
cold air chill me. I tried to back away, but they were behind me, and
around me. Some of the boys stood with lowered heads, trembling. I
felt a wave of irrational guilt and fear. My teeth chattered, my skin
turned to goose flesh, my knees knocked. Yet I was strongly attracted
and looked in spite of myself. Had the price of looking been blindness,
I would have looked. The hair was yellow like that of a circus kewpie
doll, the face heavily powdered and rouged, as though to form an

abstract mask, the eyes hollow and smeared a cold blue, the color of a baboon's butt. I felt a desire to spit upon her as my eyes brushed slowly over her body. Her breasts were firm and round as the domes of East Indian temples, and I stood so close as to see the fine skin texture and beads of pearly perspiration glistening like dew around the pink and erected buds of her nipples. I wanted at one and the same time to run from the room, to sink through the floor, or go to her and cover her from my eyes and the eyes of the others with my body; to feel the soft thighs, to caress her and destroy her, to love her and murder her, to hide from her, and yet to stroke where below the small American flag tattooed upon her belly her thighs formed a capital V. I had a notion that of all in the room she saw only me with her impersonal eyes.

And then she began to dance, a slow sensuous movement; the smoke of a hundred cigars clinging to her like the thinnest of veils. She seemed like a fair bird-girl girdled in veils calling to me from the angry surface of some gray and threatening sea. I was transported. Then I became aware of the clarinet playing and the big shots yelling at us. Some threatened us if we looked and others if we did not. On my right I saw one boy faint. And now a man grabbed a silver pitcher from a table and stepped close as he dashed ice water upon him and stood him up and forced two of us to support him as his head hung and moans issued from his thick bluish lips. Another boy began to plead to go home. He was the largest of the group, wearing dark red fighting trunks much too small to conceal the erection which projected from him as though in answer to the insinuating low-registered moaning of the clarinet. He tried to hide himself with his boxing gloves.

And all the while the blonde continued dancing, smiling faintly at the big shots who watched her with fascination, and faintly smiling at our fear. I noticed a certain merchant who followed her hungrily, his lips loose and drooling. He was a large man who wore diamond studs in a shirtfront which swelled with the ample paunch underneath, and each time the blonde swayed her undulating hips he ran his hand through the thin hair of his bald head and, with his arms upheld, his posture clumsy like that of an intoxicated panda, wound his belly in a slow and obscene grind. This creature was completely hypnotized. The music had quickened. As the dancer flung herself about with a detached expression on her face, the men began reaching out to touch her. I could see their beefy fingers sink into the soft flesh. Some of the others tried to stop them and she began to move around the floor in graceful circles, as they gave chase, slipping and sliding over the polished floor. It was mad. Chairs went crashing, drinks were spilt, as they ran laughing and howling after her. They caught her just as she reached a door, raised her from the floor, and tossed her as college boys are tossed at a hazing, and above her red, fixed-smiling lips I saw the terror and disgust in her eyes, almost like my own terror and that which I saw in some of the other boys. As I watched, they tossed her twice and her soft breasts seemed to flatten against the air and her legs flung wildly as she spun. Some of the more sober ones helped her to escape. And I started off the floor, heading for the anteroom with the rest of the boys.

Some were still crying and in hysteria. But as we tried to leave we were stopped and ordered to get into the ring. There was nothing to do but what we were told. All ten of us climbed under the ropes and allowed ourselves to be blindfolded with broad bands of white cloth. One of the men seemed to feel a bit sympathetic and tried to cheer us up as we stood with our backs against the ropes. Some of us tried to grin. "See that boy over there?" one of the men said. "I want you to run across at the bell and give it to him right in the belly. If you don't get him, I'm going to get you. I don't like his looks." Each of us was told the same. The blindfolds were put on. Yet even then I had been going over my speech. In my mind each word was as bright as a flame. I felt the cloth pressed into place, and frowned so that it would be loosened when I relaxed.

But now I felt a sudden fit of blind terror. I was unused to darkness. It was as though I had suddenly found myself in a dark room filled with poisonous cottonmouths. I could hear the bleary voices yelling insistently for the battle royal to begin.

"Get going in there!"

"Let me at that big nigger!"

I strained to pick up the school superintendent's voice, as though to squeeze some security out of that slightly more familiar sound.

"Let me at those black sonsabitches!" someone yelled.

"No, Jackson, no!" another voice yelled. "Here, somebody, help me hold Jack."

"I want to get at that ginger-colored nigger. Tear him limb from limb," the first voice yelled.

I stood against the ropes trembling. For in those days I was what they called ginger-colored, and he sounded as though he might crunch me between his teeth like a crisp ginger cookie.

Quite a struggle was going on. Chairs were being kicked about and I could hear voices grunting as with a terrific effort. I wanted to see, to see more desperately than ever before. But the blindfold was as tight as a thick skin-puckering scab and when I raised my gloved hands to push the layers of white aside a voice yelled, "Oh, no you don't, black bastard! Leave that alone!"

"Ring the bell before Jackson kills him a coon!" someone boomed in the sudden silence. And I heard the bell clang and the sound of the feet scuffling forward.

A glove smacked against my head. I pivoted, striking out stiffly as someone went past, and felt the jar ripple along the length of my arm to my shoulder. Then it seemed as though all nine of the boys had turned upon me at once. Blows pounded me from all sides while I struck out as best I could. So many blows landed upon me that I wondered if I were not the only blindfolded fighter in the ring, or if the man called Jackson hadn't succeeded in getting me after all.

Blindfolded, I could no longer control my emotions. I had no dignity. I stumbled about like a baby or a drunken man. The smoke had become thicker and with each new blow it seemed to sear and further restrict my lungs. My saliva became like hot bitter glue. A glove connected with my head, filling my mouth with warm blood. It was everywhere. I could not tell if the moisture I felt upon my body was sweat or blood. A blow landed hard against the nape of my neck. I felt myself going over, my head hitting the floor. Streaks of blue light filled the black world behind the blindfold. I lay prone, pretending that I was knocked out, but felt myself seized by hands and yanked to my feet. "Get going, black boy! Mix it up!" My arms were like lead, my head smarting from blows. I managed to feel my way to the ropes and held on, trying to catch my breath. A glove landed in my mid-section and I went over again, feeling as though the smoke had become a knife jabbed into my guts. Pushed this way and that by the legs milling around me, I finally pulled erect and discovered that I could see the black, sweat-washed forms weaving in the smoky-blue atmosphere like drunken dancers weaving to the rapid drum-like thuds of blows.

Everyone fought hysterically. It was complete anarchy. Everybody fought everybody else. No group fought together for long. Two, three, four, fought one, then turned to fight each other, were themselves attacked. Blows landed below the belt and in the kidney, with the gloves open as well as closed, and with my eye partly opened now there was not so much terror. I moved carefully, avoiding blows, although not too many to attract attention, fighting from group to group. The boys groped about like blind, cautious crabs crouching to protect their mid-sections, their heads pulled in short against their shoulders, their arms stretched nervously before them, with their fists testing the smoke-filled air like the knobbed feelers of hyper-sensitive snails. In one corner I glimpsed a boy violently punching the air and heard him scream in pain as he smashed his hand against a ring post. For a second I saw him bent over holding his hand, then going down as a blow caught his unprotected head. I played one group against the other, slipping in and throwing a punch then stepping out of range while pushing the others into the melee to take the blows blindly aimed at me. The smoke was agonizing and there were no rounds, no bells at three-minute intervals to relieve our exhaustion. The room spun round me, a swirl of lights, smoke, sweating bodies surrounded by tense white faces. I bled from both nose and mouth, the blood spattering upon my chest.

The men kept yelling, "Slug him, black boy! Knock his guts out!"

"Uppercut him! Kill him! Kill that big boy!"

Taking a fake fall, I saw a boy going down heavily beside me as though we were felled by a single blow, saw a sneaker-clad foot shoot into his groin as the two who had knocked him down stumbled upon him. I rolled out of range, feeling a twinge of nausea.

The harder we fought the more threatening the men became. And yet, I had begun to worry about my speech again. How would it go? Would they recognize my ability? What would they give me?

I was fighting automatically when suddenly I noticed that one after another of the boys was leaving the ring. I was surprised, filled with panic, as though I had been left alone with an unknown danger. Then I understood. The boys had arranged it among themselves. It was the custom for the two men left in the ring to slug it out for the winner's prize. I discovered this too late. When the bell sounded two men in tuxedos leaped into the ring and removed the blindfold. I found myself facing Tatlock, the biggest of the gang. I felt sick at my stomach. Hardly had the bell stopped ringing in my ears than it clanged again and I saw him moving swiftly toward me. Thinking of nothing else to do I hit him smash on the nose. He kept coming, bringing the rank sharp violence of stale sweat. His face was a black blank of a face, only his eyes alive —with hate of me and aglow with a feverish terror from what had happened to us all. I became anxious. I wanted to deliver my speech and he came at me as though he meant to beat it out of me. I smashed him again and again, taking his blows as they came. Then on a sudden impulse I struck him lightly and as we clinched, I whispered, "Fake like I knocked you out, you can have the prize."

"I'll break your behind," he whispered hoarsely.

"For *them*?"

"For *me*, sonofabitch!"

They were yelling for us to break it up and Tatlock spun me half around with a blow, and as a joggled camera sweeps in a reeling scene, I saw the howling red faces crouching tense beneath the cloud of blue-gray smoke. For a moment the world wavered, unraveled, flowed, then my head cleared and Tatlock bounced before me. That fluttering shadow before my eyes was his jabbing left hand. Then falling forward, my head against his damp shoulder, I whispered,

"I'll make it five dollars more."

"Go to hell!"

But his muscles relaxed a trifle beneath my pressure and I breathed, "Seven?"

"Give it to your ma," he said, ripping me beneath the heart.

And while I still held him, I butted him and moved away. I felt myself bombarded with punches. I fought back with hopeless desperation. I wanted to deliver my speech more than anything else in the world, because I felt that only these men could judge truly my ability, and now this stupid clown was ruining my chances. I began fighting carefully now, moving in to punch him and out again with my greater speed. A lucky blow to his chin and I had him going too—until I heard a loud voice yell, "I got my money on the big boy!"

Hearing this, I almost dropped my guard. I was confused: Should I try to win against the voice out there? Would not this go against my speech, and was not this a moment for humility, for nonresistance? A blow to my head as I danced about sent my right eye popping like a jack-in-the-box and settled my dilemma. The room went red as I fell. It was a dream fall, my body languid and fastidious as to where to land, until the floor became impatient and smashed up to meet me. A moment later I came to. An hypnotic voice said FIVE emphatically. And I lay there, hazily watching a dark red spot of my own shaping itself into a butterfly, glistening and soaking into the solid gray world of the canvas.

When the voice drawled TEN I was lifted up and dragged to a chair. I sat dazed. My eye pained and swelled with each throb of my pounding heart and I wondered if now I would be allowed to speak. I was wringing wet, my mouth still bleeding. We were grouped along the wall now. The other boys ignored me as they congratulated Tatlock and speculated as to how much they would be paid. One boy whimpered over his smashed hand. Looking up front, I saw attendants in white jackets rolling the portable ring away and placing a small square rug in the vacant space surrounded by chairs. Perhaps, I thought, I will stand on the rug to deliver my speech.

Then the M.C. called to us, "Come on up here boys and get your money."

We ran forward to where the men laughed and talked in their chairs, waiting. Everyone seemed friendly now.

"There it is on the rug," the man said. I saw the rug covered with coins of all dimensions and a few crumpled bills. But what excited me, scattered here and there, were the gold pieces.

"Boys, it's all yours," the man said. "You get all you grab."

"That's right, Sambo," a blond man said, winking at me confidentially.

I trembled with excitement, forgetting my pain. I would get the gold and the bills, I thought. I would use both hands. I would throw my body against the boys nearest me to block them from the gold.

"Get down around the rug now," the man commanded, "and don't anyone touch it until I give the signal."

"This ought to be good," I heard.

As told, we got around the square rug on our knees. Slowly the man raised his freckled hand as we followed it upward with our eyes.

I heard, "These niggers look like they're about to pray!"

Then, "Ready," the man said. "Go!"

I lunged for a yellow coin lying on the blue design of the carpet, touching it and sending a surprised shriek to join those rising around me. I tried frantically to remove my hand but could not let go. A hot, violent force tore through my body, shaking me like a wet rat. The rug was electrified. The hair bristled up on my head as I shook myself free. My muscles jumped, my nerves jangled, writhed. But I saw that this was not stopping the other boys. Laughing in fear and embarrassment, some were holding back and scooping up the coins knocked off by the painful contortions of the others. The men roared above us as we struggled.

"Pick it up, goddammit, pick it up!" someone called like a bass-voiced parrot. "Go on, get it!"

I crawled rapidly around the floor, picking up the coins, trying to avoid the coppers and to get greenbacks and the gold. Ignoring the shock by laughing, as I brushed the coins off quickly, I discover that I could contain the electricity—a contradiction, but it works. Then the men began to push us onto the rug. Laughing embarrassedly, we struggled out of their hands and kept after the coins. We were all wet and slippery and hard to hold. Suddenly I saw a boy lifted into the air, glistening with sweat like a circus seal, and dropped, his wet back landing flush upon the charged rug, heard him yell and saw him literally dance upon his back, his elbows beating a frenzied tattoo upon the floor, his muscles twitching like the flesh of a horse stung by many flies. When he finally rolled off, his face was gray and no one stopped him when he ran from the floor amid booming laughter.

"Get the money," the M.C. called. "That's good hard American cash!"

And we snatched and grabbed, snatched and grabbed. I was careful not to come too close to the rug now, and when I felt the hot whiskey breath descend upon me like a cloud of foul air I reached out and grabbed the leg of a chair. It was occupied and I held on desperately.

"Leggo, nigger! Leggo!"

The huge face wavered down to mine as he tried to push me free. But my body was slippery and he was too drunk. It was Mr. Colcord, who owned a chain of movie houses and "entertainment palaces." Each time he grabbed me I slipped out of his hands. It became a real struggle. I feared the rug more than I did the drunk, so I held on, surprising myself for a moment by trying to topple *him* upon the rug. It was such an enormous idea that I found myself actually carrying it out. I tried not to be obvious, yet when I grabbed his leg, trying to tumble him

out of the chair, he raised up roaring with laughter, and, looking at
me with soberness dead in the eye, kicked me viciously in the chest.
The chair leg flew out of my hand and I felt myself going and rolled.
It was as though I had rolled through a bed of hot coals. It seemed a
whole century would pass before I would roll free, a century in which
I was seared through the deepest levels of my body to the fearful breath
within me and the breath seared and heated to the point of explosion.
It'll all be over in a flash, I thought as I rolled clear. I'll be over in a flash.

But not yet, the men on the other side were waiting, red faces
swollen as though from apoplexy as they bent forward in their chairs.
Seeing their fingers coming toward me I rolled away as a fumbled
football rolls off the receiver's fingertips, back into the coals. That time
I luckily sent the rug sliding out of place and heard the coins ringing
against the floor and the boys scuffling to pick them up and the M.C.
calling, "All right, boys, that's all. Go get dressed and get your money."

I was limp as a dish rag. My back felt as though it had been beaten
with wires.

When we had dressed the M.C. came in and gave us each five dollars,
except Tatlock, who got ten for being last in the ring. Then he told us
to leave. I was not to get a chance to deliver my speech, I thought. I
going out into the dim alley in despair when I was stopped and told
to go back. I returned to the ballroom, where the men were pushing back
their chairs and gathering in groups to talk.

The M.C. knocked on a table for quiet. "Gentlemen," he said, "we
almost forgot an important part of the program. A most serious part,
glentlemen. This boy was brought here to deliver a speech which he
made at his graduation yesterday. . . ."

"Bravo!"

"I'm told that he is the smartest boy we've got out there in Green-
wood. I'm told that he knows more big words than a pocket-sized dictionary."

Much applause and laughter.

"So now, gentlemen, I want you to give him your attention."

There was still laughter as I faced them, my mouth dry, my eye
throbbing. I began slowly, but evidently my throat was tense, because
they began shouting, "Louder! Louder!"

"We of the younger generation extol the wisdom of that great
leader and educator," I shouted, "who first spoke these flaming words
of wisdom: 'A ship lost at sea for many days suddenly sighted a friendly
vessel. From the mast of the unfortunate vessel was seen a signal:
"Water, water; we die of thirst!" The answer from the friendly vessel
came back: "Cast down your bucket where you are." The captain of
the distressed vessel, at last heeding the injunction, cast down his

bucket, and it came up full of fresh, sparkling water from the mouth of the Amazon River.' And like him I say, and in his words, 'To those of my race who depend upon bettering their condition in a foreign land, or who underestimate the importance of cultivating friendly relations with the Southern white man, who is his next-door neighbor, I would say: "Cast down your bucket where you are"—cast it down in making friends in every manly way of the people of all races by whom we are surrounded. . . .' "

I spoke automatically and with such fervor that I did not realize that the men were still talking and laughing until my dry mouth, filling up with blood from the cut, almost strangled me. I coughed, wanting to stop and go to one of the tall brass, sand-filled spittoons to relieve myself, but a few of the men, especially the superintendent, were listening and I was afraid. So I gulped it down, blood, saliva and all, and continued. (What powers of endurance I had during those days! What enthusiasm! What a belief in the rightness of things!) I spoke even louder in spite of the pain. But still they talked and still they laughed, as though deaf with cotton in dirty ears. So I spoke with greater emotional emphasis. I closed my ears and swallowed blood until I was nauseated. The speech seemed a hundred times as long as before, but I could not leave out a single word. All had to be said, each memorized nuance considered, rendered. Nor was that all. Whenever I uttered a word of three or more syllables a group of voices would yell for me to repeat it. I used the phrase "social responsibility" and they yelled:

"What's that word you say, boy?"

"Social responsibility," I said.

"What?"

"Social . . ."

"Louder."

". . . responsibility."

"More!"

"Respon—"

"Repeat!"

"—sibility."

The room filled with the uproar of laughter until, no doubt, distracted by having to gulp down my blood, I made a mistake and yelled a phrase I had often seen denounced in newspaper editorials, heard debated in private.

"Social . . ."

"What?" they yelled.

". . . equality—"

The laughter hung smokelike in the sudden stillness. I opened my eyes, puzzled. Sounds of displeasure filled the room. The M.C. rushed forward. They shouted hostile phrases at me. But I did not understand.

A small, dry, mustached man in the front row blared out, "Say that slowly, son!"

"What, sir?"

"What you just said!"

"Social responsibility, sir," I said.

"You weren't being smart, were you, boy?" he said, not unkindly.

"No, sir!"

"You sure that about 'equality' was a mistake?"

"Oh, yes, sir," I said. "I was swallowing blood."

"Well, you had better speak more slowly so we can understand. We mean to do right by you, but you've got to know your place at all times. All right, now, go on with your speech."

I was afraid. I wanted to leave but I wanted also to speak and I was afraid they'd snatch me down.

"Thank you, sir," I said, beginning where I had left off, and having them ignore me as before.

Yet when I finished there was a thunderous applause. I was surprised to see the superintendent come forth with a package wrapped in white tissue paper, and, gesturing for quiet, address the men.

"Gentlemen, you see that I did not overpraise this boy. He makes a good speech and some day he'll lead his people in the proper paths. And I don't have to tell you that that is important in these days and times. This is a good, smart boy, and so to encourage him in the right direction, in the name of the Board of Education I wish to present him a prize in the form of this . . ."

He paused, removing the tissue paper and revealing a gleaming calfskin briefcase.

". . . in the form of this first-class article from Shad Whitmore's shop."

"Boy," he said, addressing me, "take this prize and keep it well. Consider it a badge of office. Prize it. Keep developing as you are and some day it will be filled with important papers that will help shape the destiny of your people."

I was so moved that I could hardly express my thanks. A rope of bloody saliva forming a shape like an undiscovered continent drooled upon the leather and I wiped it quickly away. I felt an importance that I had never dreamed.

"Open it and see what's inside," I was told.

My fingers a-tremble, I complied, smelling the fresh leather and finding an official-looking document inside. It was a scholarship to the state college for Negroes. My eyes filled with tears and I ran awkwardly off the floor.

I was overjoyed; I did not even mind when I discovered that the gold pieces I had scrambled for were brass pocket tokens advertising a certain make of automobile.

When I reached home everyone was excited. Next day the neighbors came to congratulate me. I even felt safe from grandfather, whose deathbed curse usually spoiled my triumphs. I stood beneath his photograph with my briefcase in hand and smiled triumphantly into his stolid black peasant's face. It was a face that fascinated me. The eyes seemed to follow everywhere I went.

That night I dreamed I was at a circus with him and that he refused to laugh at the clowns no matter what they did. Then later he told me to open my brief case and read what was inside and I did, finding an official envelope stamped with the state seal: and inside the envelope I found another and another, endlessly, and I thought I would fall of weariness. "Them's years," he said. "Now open that one." And I did and in it I found an engraved document containing a short message in letters of gold. "Read it," my grandfather said. "Out loud."

"To Whom It May Concern," I intoned. "Keep this Nigger-Boy Running."

I awoke with the old man's laughter ringing in my ears.

(It was a dream I was to remember and dream again for many years after. But at that time I had no insight into its meaning. First I had to attend college.)

❉   ❉   ❉

CHAPTER TEN

The plant was in Long Island, and I crossed a bridge in the fog to get there and came down in a stream of workers. Ahead of me a huge electric sign announced its message through the drifting strands of fog:

KEEP AMERICA PURE

WITH

LIBERTY PAINTS

Flags were fluttering in the breeze from each of a maze of buildings below the sign, and for a moment it was like watching some vast patriotic ceremony from a distance. But no shots were fired and no bugles sounded. I hurried ahead with the others through the fog.

I was worried, since I had used Emerson's name without his permission, but when I found my way to the personnel office it worked like magic. I was interviewed by a little droopy-eyed man named Mr. MacDuffy and sent to work for a Mr. Kimbro. An office boy came along to direct me.

"If Kimbro needs him," MacDuffy told the boy, "come back and have his name entered on the shipping department's payroll."

"It's tremendous," I said as we left the building. "It looks like a small city."

"It's big all right," he said. "We're one of the biggest outfits in the business. Make a lot of paint for the government."

We entered one of the buildings now and started down a pure white hall.

"You better leave your things in the locker room," he said, opening a door through which I saw a room with low wooden benches and rows of green lockers. There were keys in several of the locks, and he selected one for me. "Put your stuff in there and take the key," he said. Dressing, I felt nervous. He sprawled with one foot on a bench, watching me closely as he chewed on a match stem. Did he suspect that Emerson hadn't sent me?"

"They have a new racket around here," he said, twirling the match between his finger and thumb. There was a note of insinuation in his voice, and I looked up from tying my shoe, breathing with conscious evenness.

"What kind of racket?" I said.

"Oh, you know. The wise guys firing the regular guys and putting on you colored college boys. Pretty smart," he said. "That way they don't have to pay union wages."

"How did you know I went to college?" I said.

"Oh, there're about six of you guys out here already. Some up in the testing lab. Everybody knows about that."

"But I had no idea that was why I was hired," I said.

"Forget it, Mac," he said. "It's not your fault. You new guys don't know the score. Just like the union says, it's the wise guys in the office. They're the ones who make scabs out of you—Hey! we better hurry."

We entered a long, shed-like room in which I saw a series of overhead doors along one side and a row of small offices on the other. I followed the boy down an aisle between endless cans, buckets and drums labeled with the company's trademark, a screaming eagle. The paint was stacked in neatly pyramided lots along the concrete floor. Then, starting into one of the offices, the boy stopped short and grinned.

"Listen to that!"

Someone inside the office was swearing violently over a telephone.

"Who's that?" I asked.

He grinned. "Your boss, the terrible Mr. Kimbro. We call him 'Colonel,' but don't let him catch you."

I didn't like it. The voice was raving about some failure of the laboratory and I felt a swift uneasiness. I didn't like the idea of starting to work for a man who was in such a nasty mood. Perhaps he was angry at one of the men from the school, and that wouldn't make him feel too friendly toward me.

"Let's go in," the boy said. "I've got to get back."

As we entered, the man slammed down the phone and picked up some papers.

"Mr. MacDuffy wants to know if you can use this new man," the boy said.

"You damn right I can use him and . . ." the voice trailed off, the eyes above the stiff military mustache going hard.

"Well, can you use him?" the boy said. "I got to go make out his card."

"Okay," the man said finally. "I can use him. I gotta. What's his name?"

The boy read my name off a card.

"All right," he said, "you go right to work. And you," he said to the boy, "get the hell out of here before I give you a chance to earn some of the money wasted on you every payday!"

"Aw, gwan, you slave driver," the boy said, dashing from the room.

Reddening, Kimbro turned to me, "Come along, let's get going."

I followed him into the long room where the lots of paint were stacked along the floor beneath numbered markers that hung from the ceiling. Toward the rear I could see two men unloading heavy buckets from a truck, stacking them neatly on a low loading platform.

"Now get this straight," Kimbro said gruffly. "This is a busy department and I don't have time to repeat things. You have to follow instructions and you're going to be doing things you don't understand, so get your orders the first time and get them right! I won't have time to stop and explain everything. You have to catch on by doing exactly what I tell you. You got that?"

I nodded, noting that his voice became louder when the men across the floor stopped to listen.

"All right," he said, picking up several tools. "Now come over here."

"He's Kimbro," one of the men said.

I watched him kneel and open one of the buckets, stirring a milky brown substance. A nauseating stench arose. I wanted to step away. But he stirred it vigorously until it became glossy white, holding the spatula like a delicate instrument and studying the paint as it laced off the blade, back into the bucket. Kimbro frowned.

"Damn those laboratory blubberheads to hell! There's got to be dope put in every single sonofabitching bucket. And that's what you're going to do, *and* it's got to be put in so it can be trucked out of here before 11:30." He handed me a white enamel graduate and what looked like a battery hydrometer.

"The idea is to open each bucket and put in ten drops of this stuff," he said. "Then you stir it 'til it disappears. After it's mixed you take this brush and paint out a sample on one of these." He produced a number of small rectangular boards and a small brush from his jacket pocket. "You understand?"

"Yes, sir." But when I looked into the white graduate I hesitated; the liquid inside was dead black. Was he trying to kid me?

"What's wrong?"

"I don't know, sir . . . I mean. Well, I don't want to start by asking a lot of stupid questions, but do you know what's in this graduate?"

His eyes snapped. "You damn right I know," he said. "You just do what you're told!"

"I just wanted to make sure, sir," I said.

"Look," he said, drawing in his breath and with an exaggerated show of patience. "Take the dropper and fill it full. . . . Go on, do it!"

I filled it.

"Now measure ten drops into the paint. . . . There, that's it, not too goddam fast. Now. You want no more than ten, and no less."

Slowly, I measured the glistening black drops, seeing them settle upon the surface and become blacker still, spreading suddenly out to the edges.

"That's it. That's all you have to do," he said. "Never mind how it looks. That's my worry. You just do what you're told and don't try to think about it. When you've done five or six buckets, come back and see if the samples are dry. . . . And hurry, we've got to get this batch back off to Washington by 11:30. . . ."

I worked fast but carefully. With a man like this Kimbro the least thing done incorrectly would cause trouble. So I wasn't supposed to think! To hell with him. Just a flunkey, a northern redneck, a Yankee cracker! I mixed the paint thoroughly, then brushed it smoothly on one of the pieces of board, careful that the brush strokes were uniform.

Struggling to remove an especially difficult cover, I wondered if the same Liberty paint was used on the campus, or if this "Optic White" was something made exclusively for the government. Perhaps it was of a better quality, a special mix. And in my mind I could see the brightly trimmed and freshly decorated campus buildings as they appeared on spring mornings—after the fall painting and the light winter snows, with a cloud riding over and a daring bird above—framed by the trees and encircling vines. The buildings had always seemed more impressive because they were the only buildings to receive regular paintings; usually, the nearby houses and cabins were left untouched to become the dull grained gray of weathered wood. And I remembered how the splinters in some of the boards were raised from the grain by the wind, the sun and the rain until the clapboards shone with a satiny, silvery, silver-fish sheen. Like Trueblood's cabin, or the Golden Day. . . . The Golden Day had once been painted white; now its paint was flaking away with the years, the scratch of a finger being enough to send it showering down. Damn that Golden Day! But it was strange how life connected up; because I had carried Mr. Norton to the old rundown building with rotting paint, I was here. If, I thought, one could slow down his heartbeats and memory to the tempo of the black drops falling so slowly into the bucket yet reacting so swiftly, it would seem like a sequence in a feverish dream. . . . I was so deep in reverie that I failed to hear Kimbro approach.

"How's it coming?" he said, standing with hands on hips.

"All right, sir."

"Let's see," he said, selecting a sample and running his thumb across the board. "That's it, as white as George Washington's Sunday-go-to-meetin' wig and as sound as the all-mighty dollar! That's paint!" he said proudly. "That's paint that'll cover just about everything!"

He looked as though I had expressed a doubt and I hurried to say, "It's certainly white all right."

"White! It's the purest white that can be found. Nobody makes a paint any whiter. This batch right here is heading for a national monument!"

"I see," I said, quite impressed.

He looked at his watch. "Just keep it up," he said. "If I don't hurry I'll be late for that production conference! Say, you're nearly out of dope: you'd better go in the tank room and refill it. . . . And don't waste any time! I've got to go."

He shot away without telling me where the tank room was. It was easy to find, but I wasn't prepared for so many tanks. There were seven; each with a puzzling code stenciled on it. It's just like Kimbro not to tell me, I thought. You can't trust any of them. Well, it doesn't matter. I'll pick the tank from the contents of the drip cans hanging from the spigots.

But while the first five tanks contained clear liquids that smelled like turpentine, the last two contained something black like the dope, but with different codes. So I had to make a choice. Selecting the tank with the drip can that smelled most like the dope, I filled the graduate, congratulating myself for not having to waste time until Kimbro returned.

The work went faster now, the mixing easier. The pigment and heavy oils came free of the bottom much quicker, and when Kimbro returned I was going at top speed. "How many have you finished?" he asked.

"About seventy-five, I think, sir. I lost count."

"That's pretty good, but not fast enough. They've been putting pressure on me to get the stuff out. Here, I'll give you a hand."

They must have given him hell, I thought, as he got grunting to his knees and began removing covers from the buckets. But he had hardly started when he was called away.

When he left I took a look at the last bunch of samples and got a shock! Instead of the smooth, hard surface of the first, they were covered with a sticky goo through which I could see the grain of the wood. What on earth had happened? The paint was not as white and glossy as before; it had a gray tinge. I stirred it vigorously then grabbed a rag, wiping each of the boards clean, then made a new sample of each bucket. I grew panicky lest Kimbro return before I finished. Working feverishly, I made it, but since the paint required a few minutes to dry I picked up two finished buckets and started lugging them over to the loading platform. I dropped them with a thump as the voice rang out behind me. It was Kimbro.

"What the hell!" he yelled, smearing his finger over one of the samples. "This stuff's still wet!"

I didn't know what to say. He snatched up several of the later samples, smearing them, and letting out a groan. "Of all the things to happen to me. First they take all my good men and then they send me you. What'd you do to it?"

"Nothing, sir. I followed your directions," I said defensively.

I watched him peer into the graduate, lifting the dropper and sniffling it, his face glowing with exasperation.

"Who the hell gave you this?"

"No one. . . ."

"Then where'd you get it?"

"From the tank room."

Suddenly he dashed for the tank room, sloshing the liquid as he ran. I thought, Oh, hell, and before I could follow, he burst out the door in a frenzy.

"You took the wrong tank," he shouted. "What the hell, you trying to sabotage the company? That stuff wouldn't work in a million years. It's remover, *concentrated* remover! Don't you know the difference?"

"No, sir, I don't. It looked the same to me. I didn't know what I was using and you didn't tell me. I was trying to save time and took what I thought was right."

"But why this one?"

"Because it smelled the same—" I began.

"*Smelled!*" he roared. "Goddamit, don't you know you can't smell shit around all those fumes? Come on to my office."

I was torn between protesting and pleading for fairness. It was not all my fault and I didn't want the blame, but I did wish to finish out the day. Throbbing with anger I followed, listening as he called personnel.

"Hello? Mac? Mac, this is Kimbro. It's about this fellow you sent me this morning. I'm sending him in to pick up his pay. . . . What did he do? He doesn't satisfy me, that's what. I don't like his work. . . . So the old man has to have a report, so what? Make him one. Tell him goddamit this fellow ruined a batch of government stuff—Hey! No, don't tell him that. . . . Listen, Mac, you got anyone else out there? . . . Okay, forget it."

He crashed down the phone and swung toward me. "I swear I don't know why they hire you fellows. You just don't belong in a paint plant. Come on."

Bewildered, I followed him into the tank room, yearning to quit and tell him to go to hell. But I needed the money, and even though this was the North I wasn't ready to fight unless I had to. Here I'd be one against how many?

I watched him empty the graduate back in the tank and noted carefully when he went to another marked SKA-3-69-T-Y and refilled it. Next time I would know.

"Now, for God's sake," he said, handing me the graduate, "be careful and try to do the job right. And if you don't know what to do, ask somebody. I'll be in my office."

I returned to the buckets, my emotions whirling. Kimbro had forgotten to say what was to be done with the spoiled paint. Seeing it there I was suddenly seized by an angry impulse, and, filling the dropper with fresh dope, I stirred ten drops into each bucket and pressed home the covers. Let the government worry about that, I thought, and started to work on the unopened buckets. I stirred until my arm ached and painted the samples as smoothly as I could, becoming more skillful as I went along.

When Kimbro came down the floor and watched I glanced up silently and continued stirring.

"How is it?" he said, frowning.

"I don't know," I said, picking up a sample and hesitating.

"Well?"

"It's nothing . . . a speck of dirt," I said, standing and holding out the sample, a tightness growing within me.

Holding it close to his face, he ran his fingers over the surface and squinted at the texture. "That's more like it," he said. "That's the way it oughta be."

I watched with a sense of unbelief as he rubbed his thumb over the sample, handed it back and left without a further word.

I looked at the painted slab. It appeared the same: a gray tinge glowed through the whiteness, and Kimbro had failed to detect it. I stared for about a minute, wondering if I were seeing things, inspected another and another. All were the same, a brilliant white diffused with gray, I closed my eyes for a moment and looked again and still no change. Well, I thought, as long as he's satisfied. . . .

But I had a feeling that something had gone wrong, something far more important than the paint; that either I had played a trick on Kimbro or he, like the trustees and Bledsoe, was playing one on me. . . .

When the truck backed up to the platform I was pressing the cover on the last bucket—and there stood Kimbro above me.

"Let's see your samples," he said.

I reached, trying to select the whitest, as the blue-shirted truck-men climbed through the loading door.

"How about it, Kimbro," one of them said, "can we get started?"

"Just a minute, now," he said, studying the sample, "just a minute. . . ."

I watched him nervously, waiting for him to throw a fit over the gray tinge and hating myself for feeling nervous and afraid. What would I say? But now he was turning to the truckmen.

"All right, boys, get the hell out of here."

"And you," he said to me, "go see MacDuffy; you're through."

I stood there, staring at the back of his head, at the pink neck beneath the cloth cap and the iron-gray hair. So he'd let me stay only to finish the mixing. I turned away, there was nothing that I could do. I cursed him all the way to the personnel office. Should I write the owners about what had happened? Perhaps they didn't know that Kimbro was having so much to do with the quality of the paint. But upon reaching the office I changed my mind. Perhaps that is how things are done here, I thought, perhaps the real quality of the paint is *always* determined by the man who ships it rather than by those who mix it. To hell with the whole thing . . . I'll find another job.

But I wasn't fired. MacDuffy sent me to the basement of Building No. 2 on a new assignment.

"When you get down there just tell Brockway that Mr. Sparland insists that he have an assistant. You do whatever he tells you."

"What is that name again, sir?" I said.

"Lucius *Brockway*," he said. "He's in charge."

from **A Raisin in the Sun**

LORRAINE HANSBERRY

ACT III
SCENE THREE

[*Time: Saturday, moving day, one week later.*

[*Before the curtain rises,* RUTH's *voice, a strident, dramatic church alto, cuts through the silence.*

[*It is, in the darkness, a triumphant surge, a penetrating statement of expectation:* "Oh, Lord, I don't feel no ways tired! Children, oh, glory hallelujah!"

[*As the curtain rises we see that* RUTH *is alone in the living room, finishing up the family's packing. It is moving day. She is nailing crates and tying cartons.* BENEATHA *enters, carrying a guitar case, and watches her exuberant sister-in-law.*]

RUTH   Hey!

BENEATHA   [*Putting away the case*] Hi.

RUTH   [*Pointing at a package*] Honey—look in that package there and see what I found on sale this morning at the South Center. [RUTH *gets up and moves to the package and draws out some curtains*] Lookahere—hand-turned hems!

BENEATHA   How do you know the window size out there?

RUTH   [*Who hadn't thought of that*] Oh— Well, they bound to fit something in the whole house. Anyhow, they was too good a bargain to pass up. [RUTH *slaps her head, suddenly remembering something*] Oh, Bennie—I meant to put a special note on that carton over there. That's your mama's good china and she wants 'em to be very careful with it.

BENEATHA   I'll do it.

[BENEATHA *finds a piece of paper and starts to draw large letters on it*]

RUTH   You know what I'm going to do soon as I get in that new house?

BENEATHA   What?

RUTH   Honey—I'm going to run me a tub of water up to here. . . .

[*With her fingers practically up to her nostrils*] And I'm going to get in it—and I am going to sit . . . and sit . . . and sit in that hot water and the first person who knocks to tell *me* to hurry up and come out—

BENEATHA   Gets shot at sunrise.

RUTH   [*Laughing happily*] You said it, sister! [*Noticing how large* BENEATHA *is absent-mindedly making the note*] Honey, they ain't going to read that from no airplane.

BENEATHA   [*Laughing herself*] I guess I always think things have more emphasis if they are big, somehow.

RUTH   [*Looking up at her and smiling*] You and your brother seem to have that as a philosophy of life. Lord, that man—done changed so 'round here. You know—you know what we did last night? Me and Walter Lee?

BENEATHA   What?

RUTH   [*Smiling to herself*] We went to the movies. [*Looking at* BENEATHA *to see if she understands*] We went to the movies. You know the last time me and Walter went to the movies together?

BENEATHA   No.

RUTH   Me neither. That's how long it been. [*Smiling again*] But we went last night. The picture wasn't much good, but that didn't seem to matter. We went—and we held hands.

BENEATHA   Oh, Lord!

RUTH   We held hands—and you know what?

BENEATHA   What?

RUTH   When we come out of the show it was late and dark and all the stores and things was closed up . . . and it was kind of chilly and there wasn't many people on the streets . . . and we was still holding hands, me and Walter.

BENEATHA   You're killing me.

[WALTER *enters with a large package. His happiness is deep in him; he cannot keep still with his new-found exuberance. He is singing and wiggling and snapping his fingers. He puts his package in a corner and puts a phonograph record, which he has brought in with him, on the record player. As the music comes up he dances over to* RUTH *and tries to get her to dance with him. She gives in at last to his raunchiness and in a fit of giggling allows herself to be drawn into his mood and together they deliberately burlesque an old social dance of their youth*]

BENEATHA   [*Regarding them a long time as they dance, then drawing in her breath for a deeply exaggerated comment which she does not particularly mean*] Talk about—olddddddddddd-fashioneddddddd—Negroes!

WALTER   [*Stopping momentarily*] What kind of Negroes? [*He says this in fun. He is not angry with her today, nor with anyone. He starts to dance with his wife again*]

BENEATHA   Old-fashioned.

WALTER   [*As he dances with* RUTH] You know, when these *New Negroes* have their convention—(Pointing at his sister)—that is going to be the chairman of the Committee on Unending Agitation. [*He goes on dancing, then stops*] Race, race, race! . . . Girl, I do believe you are the first person in the history of the entire human race to successfully brainwash yourself. [BENEATHA *breaks up and he goes on dancing. He stops again, enjoying his tease*] Damn, even the N double A C P takes a holiday sometimes! [BENEATHA *and* RUTH *laugh. He dances with* RUTH *some more and starts to laugh and stops and pantomimes someone over an operating table*] I can just see that chick someday looking down at some poor cat on an operating table before she starts to slice him, saying . . . [*Pulling his sleeves back maliciously*] "By the way, what are your views on civil rights down there? . . ."

BENEATHA   Sticks and stones may break my bones but . . . words will never hurt me!

[BENEATHA *goes to the door and opens it as* WALTER *and* RUTH *go on wtih the clowning.* BENEATHA *is somewhat surprised to see a quiet-looking middle-aged white man in a business suit, holding his hat and a briefcase in his hand and consulting a small piece of paper*]

MAN   Uh—how do you do, miss. I am looking for a Mrs.—[*He looks at the slip of paper*] Mrs. Lena Younger?

BENEATHA   [*Smoothing her hair with slight embarrassment*] Oh—yes, that's my mother. Excuse me. [*She closes the door and turns to quiet the other two*] Ruth! Brother! Somebody's here. [*Then she opens the door. The* MAN *casts a curious quick glance at all of them*] Uh—come in please.

MAN   [*Coming in*] Thank you.

BENEATHA   My mother isn't here just now. Is it business?

MAN   Yes . . . well, of a sort.

WALTER   [*Freely, the Man of the House*] Have a seat. I'm Mrs. Younger's son. I look after most of her business matters.

[RUTH *and* BENEATHA *exchange amused glances*]

MAN   [*Regarding* WALTER, *and sitting*] Well—my name is Karl Lindner. . . .

WALTER   [*Stretching out his hand*] Walter Younger. This is my wife—[RUTH *nods politely*]—and my sister.

LINDNER   How do you do.

WALTER   [*Amiably, as he sits himself easily on a chair, leaning with interest forward on his knees and looking expectantly into the newcomer's face*] What can we do for you, Mr. Lindner!

LINDNER [*Some minor shuffling of the hat and briefcase on his knees*]
Well—I am a representative of the Clybourne Park Improvement
Association—

WALTER [*Pointing*] Why don't you sit your things on the floor?

LINDNER Oh—yes. Thank you. [*He slides the briefcase and hat under
the chair*] And as I was saying—I am from the Clybourne Park
Improvement Association and we have had it brought to our attention at the last meeting that you people—or at least your mother—
has bought a piece of residential property at—[*He digs for the
slip of paper again*]—four o six Clybourne Street. . . .

WALTER That's right. Care for something to drink? Ruth, get Mr. Lindner
a beer.

LINDNER [*Upset for some reason*] Oh—no, really. I mean thank you
very much, but no thank you.

RUTH [*Innocently*] Some coffee?

LINDNER Thank you, nothing at all.
   [BENEATHA *is watching the man carefully*]

LINDNER Well, I don't know how much you folks know about our organization. [*He is a gentle man; thoughtful and somewhat labored
in his manner*] It is one of these community organizations set up
to look after—oh, you know, things like block upkeep and special
projects and we also have what we call our New Neighbors Orientation Committee. . . .

BENEATHA [*Drily*] Yes—and what do they do?

LINDNER [*Turning a little to her and then returning the main force to
WALTER*] Well—it's what you might call a sort of welcoming committee, I guess. I mean they, we, I'm the chairman of the committee
—go around and see the new people who move into the neighborhood and sort of give them the lowdown on the way we do things
out in Clybourne Park.

BENEATHA [*With appreciation of the two meanings, which escape* RUTH
and WALTER] Un-huh.

LINDNER And we also have the category of what the association calls—
[*He looks elsewhere*]—uh—special community problems. . . .

BENEATHA Yes—and what are some of those?

WALTER Girl, let the man talk.

LINDNER [*With understated relief*] Thank you. I would sort of like to
explain this thing in my own way. I mean I want to explain to you
in a certain way.

WALTER Go ahead.

LINDNER Yes. Well. I'm going to try to get right to the point. I'm
sure we'll appreciate that in the long run.

BENEATHA Yes.

WALTER Be still now!

LINDNER   Well—

RUTH   [*Still innocently*] Would you like another chair—you don't look comfortable.

LINDNER   [*More frustrated than annoyed*] No, thank you very much. Please. Well—to get right to the point I—[*A great breath, and and he is off at last*] I am sure you people must be aware of some of the incidents which have happened in various parts of the city when colored people have moved into certain areas—[BENEATHA *exhales heavily and starts tossing a piece of fruit up and down in the air*] Well—because we have what I think is going to be a unique type of organization in American community life—not only do we deplore that kind of thing—but we are trying to do something about it. [BENEATHA *stops tossing and turns with a new and quizzical interest to the man*] We feel—[*gaining confidence in his mission because of the interest in the faces of the people he is talking to*]—we feel that most of the trouble in this world, when you come right down to it—[*He hits his knee for emphasis*]—most of the trouble exists because people just don't sit down and talk to each other.

RUTH   [*Nodding as she might in church, pleased with the remark*] You can say that again, mister.

LINDNER   [*More encouraged by such affirmation*] That we don't try hard enough in this world to understand the other fellow's problem. The other guy's point of view.

RUTH   Now that's right.

[BENEATHA *and* WALTER *merely watch and listen with genuine interest*]

LINDNER   Yes—that's the way we feel out in Clybourne Park. And that's why I was elected to come here this afternoon and talk to you people. Friendly like, you know, the way people should talk to each other and see if we couldn't find some way to work this thing out. As I say, the whole business is a matter of *caring* about the other fellow. Anybody can see that you are a nice family of folks, hard working and honest I'm sure. [BENEATHA *frowns slightly, quizzically, her head tilted regarding him*] Today everybody knows what it means to be on the outside of *something*. And of course, there is always somebody who is out to take advantage of people who don't always understand.

WALTER   What do you mean?

LINDNER   Well—you see our community is made up of people who've worked hard as the dickens for years to build up that little community. They're not rich and fancy people; just hard-working, honest people who don't really have much but those little homes and a dream of the kind of community they want to raise their children in. Now, I don't say we are perfect and there is a lot wrong in some of the things they want. But you've got to admit that a man, right or wrong, has the right to want to have the neighborhood he lives in a certain kind of way. And at the moment the overwhelming majority of our people out there feel that people get along better, take more of a common interest in the life of the community, when they share a common background. I want you to believe me when I tell you that race prejudice simply doesn't enter into it. It is a matter of the people of Clybourne Park believing, rightly or wrongly, as I say, that for the happiness of all concerned that our Negro families are happier when they live in their *own* communities.

BENEATHA [*With a grand and bitter gesture*] This, friends, is the Welcoming Committee!

WALTER [*Dumfounded, looking at* LINDNER] Is this what you came marching all the way over here to tell us?

LINDNER Well, now we've been having a fine conversation. I hope you'll hear me all the way through.

WALTER [*Tightly*] Go ahead, man.

LINDNER You see—in the face of all the things I have said, we are prepared to make your family a very generous offer. . .

BENEATHA Thirty pieces and not a coin less!

WALTER Yeah?

LINDNER [*Putting on his glasses and drawing a form out of the brief-case*] Our association is prepared, through the collective effort of our people, to buy the house from you at a financial gain to your family.

RUTH Lord have mercy, ain't this the living gall!

WALTER All right, you through?

LINDNER Well, I want to give you the exact terms of the financial arrangement—

WALTER We don't want to hear no exact terms of no arrangements. I want to know if you got any more to tell us 'bout getting together?

LINDNER [*Taking off his glasses*] Well—I don't suppose that you feel. . .

WALTER Never mind how I feel—you got any more to say 'bout how people ought to sit down and talk to each other? . . . Get out of my house, man.

[*He turns his back and walks to the door*]

LINDNER [*Looking around at the hostile faces and reaching and assembling his hat and briefcase*] Well—I don't understand why you people are reacting this way. What do you think you are going to gain by moving into a neighborhood where you just aren't wanted and where some elements—well—people can get awful worked up when they feel that their whole way of life and everything they've ever worked for is threatened.

WALTER   Get out.

LINDNER   [*At the door, holding a small card*] Well—I'm sorry it went like this.

WALTER   Get out.

LINDNER   [*Almost sadly regarding* WALTER] You just can't force people to change their hearts, son.

[*He turns and puts his card on a table and exits.* WALTER *pushes the door to with stinging hatred, and stands looking at it.* RUTH *just sits and* BENEATHA *just stands. They say nothing.* MAMA *and* TRAVIS *enter*]

from Simple's Uncle Sam

LANGSTON HUGHES

CENSUS

"I have had so many hardships in this life," said Simple, "that it is a wonder I'll live until I die. I was born young, black, voteless, poor, and hungry, in a state where white folks did not even put Negroes on the census. My daddy said he were never counted in his life by the United States government. And nobody could find a birth certificate for me nowhere. It were not until I came to Harlem that one day a census taker dropped around to my house and asked me where were I born and why, also my age and if I was still living. I said, 'Yes, I am here, in spite of all.'

" 'All of what?' asked the census taker. 'Give me the data.'

" 'All my corns and bunions, for one,' I said. 'I were borned with corns. Most colored peoples get corns so young, they must be inherited. As for bunions, they seem to come natural, we stands on our feet so much. These feet of mine have stood in everything from soup lines to the draft board. They have supported everything from a packing trunk to a hongry woman. My feet have walked ten thousand miles running errands for white folks and another ten thousand trying to keep up with colored. My feet have stood before altars, at crap tables, bars, graves, kitchen doors, welfare windows, and social security railings. Be sure and include my feet on that census you are taking,' I told that man.

"Then I went on to tell him how my feet have helped to keep the American shoe industry going, due to the money I have spent on my feet. 'Have wore out seven hundred pairs of shoes, eight-nine tennis shoes, forty-four summer sandals, and two hundred and two loafers. The razor blades I have used cutting away my corns could pay for a razor plant. Oh, my feet have helped to make America rich, and I am still standing on them.

" 'I stepped on a rusty nail once, and mighty near had lockjaw. And from my feet up, so many other things have happened to me, since, it is a wonder I made it through this world. In my time, I have been cut, stabbed, run over, hit by a car, tromped by a horse, robbed, fooled, deceived, double-crossed, dealt seconds, and mighty near blackmailed—but I am still here! I have been laid off, fired and not rehired, Jim Crowed, segregated, insulted, eliminated, locked in, locked out, locked up, left holding the bag, and denied relief. I have been caught in the rain, caught in jails, caught short with my rent, and caught with the wrong woman—but I am still here!

" 'My mama should have named me Job instead of Jesse B. Simple. I have been underfed, underpaid, undernourished, and everything but undertaken—yet I am still here. The only thing I am afraid of now —is that I will die before my time. So man, put me on your census now this year, because I may not be here when the next census comes around.'

"The census man said, 'What do you expect to die of—complaining?'

" 'No,' I said, 'I expect to ugly away.' At which I thought the man would laugh. Instead you know he nodded his head, and wrote it down. He were white and did not know I was making a joke. Do you reckon that man really thought I am homely?"

from **Tales of Simple**

LANGSTON HUGHES

COFFEE BREAK

"My boss is white," said Simple.

"Most bosses are," I said.

"And being white and curious, my boss keeps asking me just what does THE Negro want. Yesterday he tackled me during the coffee break, talking about THE Negro. He always says 'THE Negro,' as if there was not 50–11 different kinds of Negroes in the U.S.A.," complained Simple. "My boss says, 'Now that you-all have got the Civil Rights Bill and the Supreme Court, Adam Powell in Congress, Ralph Bunche in the United Nations, and Leontyne Price singing in the Metropolitan Opera, plus Dr. Martin Luther King getting the Nobel Prize, what more do you want? I am asking you, just what does THE Negro want?' "

" 'I am not THE Negro,' I says, 'I am *me.*'

" 'Well,' says my boss, 'you represent THE Negro.'

" 'I do not,' I says. 'I represent my own self.'

" 'Ralph Bunche represents you, then,' says my boss, and Thurgood Marshall and Martin Luther King. Do they not?'

" 'I am proud to be represented by such men, if you say they represent me,' I said. 'But all them men you name are *way* up there, and they do not drink beer in my bar. I have never seen a single one of them mens on Lenox Avenue in my natural life. So far as I know, they do not even live in Harlem. I cannot find them in the telephone book. They all got private numbers. But since you say they represent THE Negro, why do you not ask them what THE Negro wants?'

" 'I cannot get to them,' says my boss.

" 'Neither can I,' I says, 'so we both is in the same boat.'

" 'Well then, to come nearer home,' says my boss, 'Roy Wilkins fights your battles, also James Farmer.'

" 'They do not drink in my bar, neither,' I said.

" 'Don't Wilkins and Farmer live in Harlem?' he asked.

" 'Not to my knowledge,' I said. 'And I bet they have not been to the Apollo since Jackie Mabley cracked the first joke.'

" 'I do not know him,' said my boss, 'but I see Nipsey Russell and Bill Cosby on TV.'

" 'Jackie Mabley is no *him,*' I said. She is a *she*—better known as Moms.'

" 'Oh,' said my boss.

" 'And Moms Mabley has a story on one of her records about Little Cindy Ella and the magic slippers going to the Junior Prom at Ole Miss which tells all about what THE Negro wants.'

" 'What's its conclusion?' asked my boss.

" 'When the clock strikes midnight, Little Cindy Ella is dancing with the President of the Ku Klux Klan, says Moms, but at the stroke of twelve, Cindy Ella turns back to her natural self, black, and her blonde wig turns to a stocking cap—and her trial comes up next week.'

" 'A symbolic tale,' says my boss, 'meaning, I take it, that THE Negro is in jail. But you are not in jail.'

" 'That's what you think,' I said.

" 'Anyhow, you claim you are not THE Negro,' said my boss.

" 'I am not,' I said. 'I am *this* Negro.'

" 'Then what do *you* want?' asked my boss.

" 'To get out of jail,' I said.

" 'What jail?'

" 'The jail you got me in.'

" 'Me?' yells my boss. 'I have not got you in jail. Why, boy, I like you. I am a liberal. I voted for Kennedy. And this time for Johnson. I believe in integration. Now that you got it, though, what more do you want?'

" 'Reintegration,' I said.

" 'Meaning by that, what?'

" 'That you be integrated with *me*, not me with you.'

" 'Do you mean that I come and live in Harlem?' asked my boss. 'Never!'

" 'I live in Harlem,' I said.

" 'You are adjusted to it,' said my boss. 'But there is so much crime in Harlem.'

" 'There are no two-hundred-thousand dollar bank robberies, though,' I said, 'of which there was three lately *elsewhere*—all done by white folks, and nary one in Harlem. The biggest and best crime is outside of Harlem. We never has no half-million-dollar jewelry robberies, no missing star sapphires. You better come uptown with me and reintegrate.'

" 'Negroes are the ones who want to be integrated,' said my boss.

" 'And white folks are the ones who do *not* want to be,' I said.

" 'Up to a point, we do,' said my boss.

" 'That is what THE Negro wants,' I said, to remove that *point*.'

" 'The coffee break is over,' said my boss."

chapter 7

PSYCHOLOGICAL RESPONSES

As the end of the term approaches, I ask myself, "Can I really still hate so much?" Is all of the hate still there just waiting to be awakened by some kind of white backlash? Do I hate as an act of self-defense because I know that I'm hated? Or do I hate because I'm evil too? Will I ever be entirely free of this hatred, or has it grown in me for so long that it *is* me, now and inseparable? I'll find out soon. Yes, real soon. But as of now, I don't know. I just don't know.

—Thedford Slaughter,
"Up from Hate"

Any human being will soon discover that if he defines himself too exclusively, in terms of another's perceptions, he will have to wear many hats. Though the responses of others do provide the individual with cumulative clues of societal values, there must also be a point at which the mature adult embraces and respects his own judgment. However, for the Negro American, this matter of self-judgment is particularly difficult. For if self-consciousness is the product of an outsider's perception, then the black man experiences what W. E. B. DuBois describes as a kind of "two-ness." Furthermore, the stigma of color and the contradictions that become apparent as the Negro encounters the American reality serve to further complicate self-perception. The dominant culture has its impact: "It is still the white man's society," Kenneth Clark notes, "that governs the Negro's image of himself."[1]

The individual, defined by another, summons up a variety of defenses and behavioral adjustments to secure for himself some sense of identity. Hereditary factors, individual differences, family backgrounds, and social experiences all mitigate against defining "The Negro." Therefore, it becomes increasingly difficult to speak of "the Negro Experience," "the Black Psyche," or "Negro Identity." Robert Penn Warren devotes an entire book to the question of *Who Speaks for the Negro?* and finds many voices—not always in chorus. There are many Negro experiences, several million Negro

---

[1] Kenneth B. Clark, *Dark Ghetto: Dilemmas of Social Power* (New York: Harper & Row, Publishers, 1965), p. 64.

183

psyches, and more than one Negro identity. The responses of the Negro, like those of all groups, are diverse, disparate, and elude categorization. But to the extent that the black man in America has been exposed to social and personal injustices, his behavioral patterns can be grouped under the umbrella of responses to the white majority. In most cases, if not individually, then certainly as a group, Negroes have experienced rejection, hatred, segregation, and prejudice. As early as 1923 Charles S. Johnson discussed the consequences of these attitudes for Negro personality:

> From the beginning they are saturated in a tradition of their own incompetence. . . . They become race conscious. Opinions and feelings on general questions must always be filtered through this narrow screen that separates them from their neighbors. Their opinions are, therefore, largely a negative product, either disparagement of difficulties or protest.[2]

Articulate leaders characterize the blacks as "the outnumbered," "the outsiders" or "the marginal men." Literary artists write of the Negro's "facelessness," his "invisibility," or his "speechlessness." How does the Negro come to terms with what seem to be preconditions for living? How does he write off his wounded psyche? How does he cope with the frustrations that accompany feelings of inferiority? Exclusion and rejection are not desired or voluntary states, yet to some extent the victims of this oppression can be made to accommodate to this status.[3]

Each Negro, in a different way, will work out the problems of his relationship to a society that shuns him. The selections in this unit suggest a few of the many reactions to rejection. Very frequently, the by-product of this rejection is hatred; an emotion that is often disguised.

Masking has become a defensive response of many Negroes. This disguise of feelings provides a kind of protective armor, not only against the outside world, but against one's own inner longings. The toll exacted for this patronage has far-reaching implications for the development of a sense of identity. One poet writes:

> We smile, but, O great Christ, our cries
> To Thee from tortured souls arise.

---

[2] Charles S. Johnson, as quoted in *Anger, and Beyond: The Negro Writer in the United States,* Herbert Hill, ed. (New York: Harper & Row, Publishers, 1968), p. 17.

[3] Clark, p. 63.

> We sing, but oh, the clay is vile
> Beneath our feet, and long the mile:
> But let the world dream otherwise,
> We wear the mask.[4]

Masking is translated into behavioral terms when authors like Richard Wright describe "the ethics of living Jim Crow." Though the overt responses may be condescension and self-negation, they frequently disguise hostile, manipulative motives:

> I was very careful to pronounce my *sirs* distinctly, in order that he might know that I was polite, that I knew where I was, and that I knew he was a *white* man. I wanted that job badly.[5]

But in the new idiom LeRoi Jones writes,

> black man, quit stuttering and shuffling, look up,
> black man, quit whining and stooping, for all of him,
> Great Malcolm a prince of the earth, let nothing in us rest
> until we avenge ourselves for his death."[6]

Many authors describe themselves as marginal men creating symbols and images of men who live off the "underbelly" of the world. The characters in Negro literature live in racial jails, caves, or sewers; half the time they feel like they are "on the outside of the world peeping in through a knot-hole in the fence. . . ."[7] In Tolson's symbolic language, they are "inside," and "sometimes the shark swallows the sea turtle whole."[8] For those who cannot, who do not have the inner strength to "gnaw" their way to the outside, for the breath of fresh air, underground living becomes a way of life, as in Richard Wright's novella, "The Man Who Lived Underground." After an initial period of adjustment, the narrator begins to accept the confinement of the sewer, and adapt to the peculiar logic of the underground. Safe beneath the surface of things, he has the opportunity to mock the "aboveground" values and, at least in this solitary world, to feel and sense his own consciousness.

[4] Paul Laurence Dunbar, "We Wear the Mask," *Complete Poems of Paul Laurence Dunbar* (New York: Dodd, Mead & Co., Inc., 1965), p. 112.

[5] Richard Wright, "The Ethics of Living Jim Crow," *Dark Symphony: Negro Literature in America*, James A. Emanuel and Theodore L. Gross, eds. (New York: The Free Press, 1968), p. 240.

[6] LeRoi Jones, "A Poem for Black Hearts," *Dark Symphony: Negro Literature in America* (New York: The Free Press, 1968), p. 516.

[7] Richard Wright, *Native Son* (New York: Harper & Row, Publishers, 1966), p. 23.

[8] M. B. Tolson, *Harlem Gallery* (New York: Twayne Publishers, 1965), p. 140.

Unfortunately, others like John Grimes (the name is symbolic), internalize society's rejection and come to see themselves as something dirty, evil, and contaminated. After a while, the pain of this feeling is translated into a shield of numbness:

John thought with shame and horror, yet in angry hardness of heart: *He who is filthy, let him be filthy still. . . .* He moved to the table and sat down, feeling the most bewildering panic of his life, a need to touch things, the table and chairs and the walls of the room, to make certain that the room existed and that he was in the room.[9]

Feelings of rejection are not always turned inward. In the selected readings, Claude McKay, Eldridge Cleaver, and LeRoi Jones lash out in open hostility against a society that refuses to respect them. The symbols of the prevailing power structure are desecrated. From a slightly different perspective, Richard Wright identifies the relationship between frustration and lawlessness. Bigger Thomas feels beyond the bounds of legal restrictions, as does the narrator in "The Man Who Lived Underground." Many of the selections that follow provide ample evidence that the reaction to hatred is a still greater hate. Claude McKay writes,

Oh, I must search for wisdom every hour,
Deep in my wrathful bosom sore and raw,
And find in it the superhuman power
To hold me in the letter of your law!
Oh, I must keep my heart inviolate
Against the potent poison of your hate.[10]

The great drive for a Negro identity has led to militancy, both violent and nonviolent. A by-product of this movement is the development of objectives and a framework for behavior. The black artist sees himself as playing a key role in the generation of goals. In the readings that follow, the authors implore the black man to develop a sense of dignity. More than one writer extols Malcolm X as a symbol of hope, and, to many black men, the eulogy delivered by Ossie Davis expresses their own feelings:

. . . every last, black glory-hugging one of them knew that Malcolm
—whatever else he was or was not—*Malcolm was a man!* White

---

[9] James Baldwin, *Go Tell It on the Mountain* (New York: Dell Publishing Company, 1968), p. 22.

[10] Claude McKay, "The White House," *Selected Poems of Claude McKay* (New York: Bookman Associates, 1953), p. 78.

folks do not need anybody to remind them that they are men.
We do! . . .[11]

Eldridge Cleaver reiterates: "Malcolm was our manhood, our living, black manhood!", and "We shall have our manhood. We shall
have it or the earth will be leveled by our attempts to gain it."[12]

Along with Cleaver, Jones, Wright, and Tolson, many black
writers have taken unto themselves the liberation of the Negro.
They clearly identify their roles as image-makers and strive to en-
able the black man to see with his own eyes and hear with his
own ears in order that he may summon forth a true black identity.

The handwriting is on the wall; the message is clear. Literary
artists, often in the vanguard of society, are articulately describing
the feelings of the black man, and these outcries, no doubt have
led and will lead to considerable soul-searching on the part of
white readers. Young blacks, however, are demanding an immediate
place in the sun, and the resulting societal clashes are termed, by
some, a revolution. To paraphrase Milton Mayer, one thing is clear:
we have run out of time. It is this generation which must bring
light to the world, and what is wanted is unanswerable intelligence, for men cannot shoot, or burn, or brawl their way to dignity.
Whoever speaks for man speaks for one world or none, and must
refuse to let any man be segregated by anybody—even by himself.[13]

I.   The readings in this chapter have been selected for their
relevance to the unit topic, *Psychological Responses*. Some of
the subthemes developed in the selections are:

1.   Masking
2.   The need for dignity
3.   The alienated Negro
4.   Hostility and lawlessness
5.   The search for identity
6.   The meaning of Malcolm X

II.   The following readings are suggested as supplementary
references for this thematic unit:

---

[11] Ossie Davis, "On Malcolm X," *The Autobiography of Malcolm X* (New York:
Grove Press, Inc., 1966), p. 457.

[12] Eldridge Cleaver, *Soul on Ice* (New York: McGraw-Hill, Inc., 1968), pp.
60–61.

[13] Milton Mayer, "There Used To Be Negroes," *The Gadfly*, 19, Fall 1969
(Chicago: The Great Books Foundation).

1.   William Attaway, *Blood on the Forge* (New York: Doubleday & Company, Inc., 1941). (novel)
2.   James Baldwin, "Exodus," *American Negro Short Stories,* James Henrik Clarke, ed. (New York: Hill & Wang Inc. 1966), pp. 197–204. (short story)
3.   William Demby, *Beetlecreek* (New York: Holt, Rinehart and Winston, Inc., 1950). (novel)
4.   Langston Hughes, "Cross," *The Poetry of the Negro, 1746–1959,* Langston Hughes and Arna Bontemps, eds. (New York: Doubleday & Company, Inc., 1949), p. 103. (poem)
5.   Langston Hughes, "Mother to Son," *American Negro Poetry,* Arna Bontemps, ed. (New York: Hill & Wang, Inc., 1968), p. 67. (poem)
6.   James Weldon Johnson, *The Autobiography of an Ex-Colored Man* (New York: Sherman, French and Company, 1912). (novel)

QUESTIONS FOR DISCUSSION

1.   How do the selections identify factors that build suspicion?
2.   It has been said that Cleaver's writings will make you either cheer or flinch. How did you feel?
3.   In "The Man Who Lived Underground," what is the nature of the narrator's rebellion? What are the symbols of his revolt?
4.   Claude McKay and Melvin Tolson have chosen to utilize animalistic language in their poetry. Can you account for this?
5.   How is the intent of the symbolic meaning of the name Grimes developed throughout the selection from *Go Tell It on the Mountain*?
6.   In the readings in this unit, how is the personal sense of self controlled by the internal or external forces in life which encourage masking?

We Wear the Mask

PAUL LAURENCE DUNBAR

We wear the mask that grins and lies,
It hides our cheeks and shades our eyes,
This debt we pay to human guile;
With torn and bleeding hearts we smile,
And mouth with myriad subtleties.

Why should the world be overwise,
In counting all our tears and sighs?
Nay, let them only see us, while
   We wear the mask.

We smile, but, O great Christ, our cries
To Thee from tortured souls arise.
We sing, but oh, the clay is vile
Beneath our feet, and long the mile;
But let the world dream otherwise,
   We wear the mask.

The White House

CLAUDE McKAY

Your door is shut against my tightened face,
And I am sharp as steel with discontent;
But I possess the courage and the grace
To bear my anger proudly and unbent.
The pavement slabs burn loose beneath my feet,
A chafing savage, down the decent street;
And passion rends my vitals as I pass,
Where boldly shines your shuttered door of glass.
Oh, I must search for wisdom every hour,

Deep in my wrathful bosom sore and raw,
And find in it the superhuman power
To hold me to the letter of your law!
Oh, I must keep my heart inviolate
Against the potent poison of your hate.

If We Must Die

CLAUDE McKAY

If we must die—let it not be like hogs
Hunted and penned in an inglorious spot,
While round us bark the mad and hungry dogs,
Making their mock at our accursed lot.
If we must die—oh, let us nobly die.
So that our precious blood may not be shed
In vain; then even the monsters we defy
Shall be constrained to honor us though dead!
Oh, Kinsmen! We must meet the common foe;
Though far outnumbered, let us show us brave,
And for their thousand blows deal one deathblow!
What though before us lies the open grave?
Like men we'll face the murderous, cowardly pack,
Pressed to the wall, dying, but fighting back!

The Man Who Lived Underground

RICHARD WRIGHT

I've got to hide, he told himself. His chest heaved as he waited, crouching in a dark corner of the vestibule. He was tired of running and dodging. Either he had to find a place to hide, or he had to surrender. A police car swished by through the rain, its siren rising sharply. They're looking for me all over. . . . He crept to the door and squinted through the fogged plate glass. He stiffened as the siren rose and died in the distance. Yes, he had to hide, but where? He gritted his teeth. Then a sudden movement in the street caught his attention. A throng of tiny columns of water snaked into the air from the perforations of a manhole cover. The column stopped abruptly, as though the perforations had become clogged; a gray spout of sewer water jutted up from under ground and lifted the circular metal cover, juggled it for a moment, then let it fall with a clang.

He hatched a tentative plan: he would wait until the siren sounded far off, then he would go out. He smoked and waited, tense. At last the siren gave him his signal; it wailed, dying, going away from him. He stepped to the sidewalk, then paused and looked curiously at the open manhole, half expecting the cover to leap up again. He went to the center of the street and stooped and peered into the hole, but could see nothing. Water rustled in the black depths.

He started with terror; the siren sounded so near that he had the idea that he had been dreaming and had awakened to find the car upon him. He dropped instinctively to his knees and his hands grasped the rim of the manhole. The siren seemed to hoot directly above him and with a wild gasp of exertion he snatched the cover far enough off to admit his body. He swung his legs over the opening and lowered himself into watery darkness. He hung for an eternal moment to the rim by his finger tips, then he felt rough metal prongs and at once he knew that sewer workmen used these ridges to lower themselves into manholes. Fist over fist, he let his body sink until he could feel no more prongs. He swayed in dank space; the siren seemed to howl at the very rim of the manhole. He dropped and was washed violently into an ocean of warm, leaping water. His head was battered against a wall and he wondered if this were death. Frenziedly his fingers clawed and sank into a crevice. He steadied himself and measured the strength of the current with his own muscular tension. He stood slowly in water that dashed past his knees with fearful velocity.

He heard a prolonged scream of brakes and the siren broke off. Oh, God! They had found him! Looming above his head in the rain a white face hovered over the hole. "How did this damn thing get off?" he heard a policeman ask. He saw the steel cover move slowly until the hole looked like a quarter moon turned black. "Give me a hand here," someone called. The cover clanged into place, muffling the sights and sounds of the upper world. Knee-deep in the pulsing current, he breathed with aching chest, filling his lungs with the hot stench of the yeasty rot.

From the perforations of the manhole cover, delicate lances of hazy violet sifted down and wove a mottled pattern upon the surface of the streaking current. His lips parted as a car swept past along the wet pavement overhead, its heavy rumble soon dying out, like the hum of a plane speeding through a dense cloud. He had never thought that cars could sound like that; everything seemed strange and unreal under here. He stood in darkness for a long time, knee-deep in rustling water, musing.

The odor of rot had become so general that he no longer smelled it. He got his cigarettes, but discovered that his matches were wet. He searched and found a dry folder in the pocket of his shirt and managed to strike one; it flared weirdly in the wet gloom, glowing greenishly, turning red, orange, then yellow. He lit a crumpled cigarette; then, by the flickering light of the match, he looked for support so that he would not have to keep his muscles flexed against the pouring water. His pupils narrowed and he saw to either side of him two steaming walls that rose and curved inward some six feet above his head to form a dripping, mouse-colored dome. The bottom of the sewer was a sloping V-trough. To the left, the sewer vanished in ashen fog. To the right was a steep down-curve into which water plunged.

He saw now that had he not regained his feet in time, he would have been swept to death, or had he entered any other manhole he would have probably drowned. Above the rush of the current he heard sharp juttings of water; tiny streams were spewing into the sewer from smaller conduits. The match died; he struck another and saw a mass of debris sweep past him and clog the throat of the down-curve. At once the water began rising rapidly. Could he climb out before he drowned? A long hiss sounded and the debris was sucked from sight; the current lowered. He understood now what had made the water toss the manhole cover; the down-curve had become temporarily obstructed and the perforations had become clogged.

He was in danger; he might slide into a down-curve; he might wander with a lighted match into a pocket of gas and blow himself up; or he might contract some horrible disease. . . . Though he wanted to leave, an irrational impulse held him rooted. To the left, the convex ceiling swooped to a height of less than five feet. With cigarette slanting from pursed lips, he waded with taut muscles, his feet sloshing over the slimy bottom, his shoes sinking into spongy slop, the slate-colored water cracking in creamy foam against his knees. Pressing his flat left palm against the lowered ceiling, he struck another match and saw a metal pole nestling in a niche of the wall. Yes, some sewer workman had left it. He reached for it, then jerked his head away as a whisper of scurrying life whisked past and was still. He held the match close and saw a huge rat, wet with slime, blinking beady eyes and baring tiny fangs. The light blinded the rat and the frizzled head moved aimlessly. He grabbed the pole and let it fly agaisnt the rat's soft body; there was shrill piping and the grizzly body splashed into the dun-colored water and was snatched out of sight, spinning in the scuttling stream.

He swallowed and pushed on, following the curve of the misty cavern, sounding the water with the pole. By the faint light of another manhole cover he saw, amid loose wet brick, a hole with walls of damp earth leading into blackness. Gingerly he poked the pole into it; it was hollow and went beyond the length of the pole. He shoved the pole before him, hoisted himself upward, got to his hands and knees, and crawled. After a few yards he paused, struck to wonderment by the silence; it seemed that he had traveled a million miles away from the world. As he inched forward again he could sense the bottom of the dirt tunnel becoming dry and lowering slightly. Slowly he rose and to his astonishment he stood erect. He could not hear the rustling of the water now and he felt confoundingly alone, yet lured by the darkness and silence.

He crept a long way, then stopped, curious, afraid. He put his right foot forward and it dangled in space; he drew back in fear. He thrust the pole outward and it swung in emptiness. He trembled, imagining the earth crumbling and burying him alive. He scratched a match and saw that the dirt floor sheered away steeply and widened into a sort of cave some five feet below him. An old sewer, he muttered. He cocked his head, hearing a feathery cadence which he could not identify. The match ceased to burn.

Using the pole as a kind of ladder, he slid down and stood in darkness. The air was a little fresher and he could still hear vague noises. Where was he? He felt suddenly that someone was standing near him and he turned sharply, but there was only darkness. He poked cautiously and felt a brick wall; he followed it and the strange sounds grew louder. He ought to get out of here. This was crazy. He could not remain here for any length of time; there was no food and no place to sleep. But the faint sounds tantalized him; they were strange but familiar. Was it a motor? A baby crying? Music? A siren? He groped on, and the sounds came so clearly that he could feel the pitch and timbre of human voices. Yes, singing! That was it! He listened with open mouth. It was a church service. Enchanted, he groped toward the waves of melody.

> *Jesus, take me to your home above*
> *And fold me in the bosom of Thy love . . .*

The singing was on the other side of a brick wall. Excited, he wanted to watch the service without being seen. Whose church was it? He knew most of the churches in this area above ground, but the singing sounded too strange and detached for him to guess. He looked to the left, to the right, down to the black dirt, then upward and was startled to see a bright sliver of light slicing the darkness like the blade of a razor. He struck one of his two remaining matches and saw rusty pipes running along an old concrete ceiling. Photographically he located the exact position of the pipes in his mind. The match flame sank and he sprang upward; his hands clutched a pipe. He swung his legs and tossed his body onto the bed of pipes and they creaked, swaying up and down; he thought that the tier was about to crash, but nothing happened. He edged to the crevice and saw a segment of black men and women, dressed in white robes, singing, holding tattered songbooks in their black palms. His first impulse was to laugh, but he checked himself.

What was he doing? He was crushed with a sense of guilt. Would God strike him dead for that? The singing swept on and he shook his head, disagreeing in spite of himself. They oughtn't to do that, he thought. But he could think of no reason *why* they should not do it. Just singing with the air of the sewer blowing in on them. . . . He felt that he was gazing upon something abysmally obscene, yet he could not bring himself to leave.

After a long time he grew numb and dropped to the dirt. Pains throbbed in his legs and a deeper pain, induced by the sight of those black people groveling and begging for something they could never get, churned in him. A vague conviction made him feel that these people should stand unrepentant and yield no quarter in singing and praying, yet *he* had run away from the police, had pleaded with them to believe in *his* innocence. He shook his head, bewildered.

How long had he been down here? He did not know. This was a new kind of living for him; the intensity of feelings he had experienced when looking at the church people sing made him certain that he had been down here a long time, but his mind told him that the time must have been short. In this darkness the only notion he had of time was when a match flared and measured time by its fleeting light. He groped back through the hole toward the sewer and the waves of song subsided and finally he could not hear them at all. He came to where the earth hole ended and he heard the noise of the current and time lived again for him, measuring the moments by the wash of water.

The rain must have slackened, for the flow of water had lessened and came only to his ankles. Ought he to go up into the streets and take his chances on hiding somewhere else? But they would surely catch him. The mere thought of dodging and running again from the police made him tense. No, he would stay and plot how to elude them. But what could he do down here? He walked forward into the sewer and came to another manhole cover; he stood beneath it, debating. Fine pencils of gold spilled suddenly from the little circles in the manhole cover and trembled on the surface of the current. Yes, street lamps. . . . It must be night. . . .

He went forward for about a quarter of an hour, wading aimlessly, poking the pole carefully before him. Then he stopped, his eyes fixed and intent. What's that? A strangely familiar image attracted and repelled him. Lit by the yellow stems from another manhole cover was a tiny nude body of a baby snagged by debris and half-submerged in water. Thinking that the baby was alive, he moved impulsively to save it, but his roused feelings told him that it was dead, cold, nothing, the same nothingness he had felt while watching the men and women singing in the church. Water blossomed about the tiny legs, the tiny arms, the tiny head, and rushed onward. The eyes were closed, as though in sleep; the fists were clenched, as though in protest; and the mouth gaped black in a soundless cry.

He straightened and drew in his breath, feeling that he had been staring for all eternity at the ripples of veined water skimming impersonally over the shriveled limbs. He felt as condemned as when the policemen accused him. Involuntarily he lifted his hand to brush the vision away, but his arm fell listlessly to his side. Then he acted; he closed his eyes and reached forward slowly with the soggy shoe of his right foot and shoved the dead baby from where it had been lodged. He kept his eyes closed, seeing the little body twisting in the current as it floated from sight. He opened his eyes, shivered, placed his knuckles in the sockets, hearing the water speed in the somber shadows.

He tramped on, sensing at times a sudden quickening in the current as he passed some conduit whose waters were swelling the stream that slid by his feet. A few minutes later he was standing under another manhole cover, listening to the faint rumble of noises above ground. Streetcars and trucks, he mused. He looked down and saw a stagnant pool of gray-green sludge; at intervals, a balloon pocket rose from the scum, glistening a bluish-purple, and burst. Then another. He turned, shook his head, and tramped back to the dirt cave by the church, his lips quivering.

Back in the cave, he sat and leaned his back against a dirt wall. His body was trembling slightly. Finally his senses quieted and he slept. When he awakened he felt stiff and cold. He had to leave this foul place, but leaving meant facing those policemen who had wrongly accused him. No, he could not go back aboveground. He remembered the beating they had given him and how he had signed his name to a confession, a confession which he had not even read. He had been too tired when they had shouted at him, demanding that he sign his name; he had signed it to end his pain.

He stood and groped about in the darkness. The church singing had stopped. How long had he slept? He did not know. But he felt refreshed and hungry. He doubled his fist nervously, realizing that he could not make a decision. As he walked about he stumbled over an old rusty iron pipe. He picked it up and felt a jagged edge. Yes, there was a brick wall and he could dig into it. What would he find? Smiling, he groped to the brick wall, sat, and began digging idly into damp cement. I can't make any noise, he cautioned himself. As time passed he grew thirsty, but there was no water. He had to kill time or go aboveground. The cement came out of the wall easily; he extracted four bricks and felt a soft draft blowing into his face. He stopped, afraid. What was beyond? He waited a long time and nothing happened; then he began digging again, soundlessly, slowly; he enlarged the hole and crawled through into a dark room and collided with another wall. He felt his way to the right; the wall ended and his fingers toyed in space, like the antennae of an insect.

He fumbled on and his feet struck something hollow, like wood. What's this? He felt with his fingers. Steps. . . . He stooped and pulled off his shoes and mounted the stairs and saw a yellow chink of light shining and heard a low voice speaking. He placed his eye to a keyhole and saw the nude waxen figure of a man stretched out upon a white table. The voice, low-pitched and vibrant, mumbled indistinguishable words, neither rising nor falling. He craned his neck and squinted to see the man who was talking, but he could not locate him. Above the naked figure was suspended a huge glass container filled with a blood-red liquid from which a white rubber tube dangled. He crouched closer to the door and saw the tip end of a black object lined with pink satin. A coffin, he breathed. This is an undertaker's establishment. . . . A fine-spun lace of ice covered his body and he shuddered. A throaty chuckle sounded in the depths of the yellow room.

He turned to leave. Three steps down it occurred to him that a light switch should be nearby; he felt along the wall, found an electric button, pressed it, and a blinding glare smote his pupils so hard that he was sightless, defenseless. His pupils contracted and he wrinkled his nostrils at a peculiar odor. At once he knew that he had been dimly aware of this odor in the darkness, but the light had brought it sharply to his attention. Some kind of stuff they use to embalm, he thought. He went down the steps and saw piles of lumber, coffins, and a long workbench. In one corner was a tool chest. Yes, he could use tools, could tunnel through walls with them. He lifted the lid of the chest and saw nails, a hammer, a crowbar, a screwdriver, a light bulb, a long length of electric wire. Good! He would lug these back to his cave.

He was about to hoist the chest to his shoulders when he discovered a door behind the furnace. Where did it lead? He tried to open it and found it securely bolted. Using the crowbar so as to make no sound, he pried the door open; it swung on creaking hinges, outward. Fresh air came to his face and he caught the faint roar of faraway sound. Easy now, he told himself. He widened the door and a lump of coal rattled toward him. A coalbin. . . . Evidently the door led to another basement. The roaring noise was louder now, but he could not identify it. Where was he? He groped slowly over the coal pile, then ranged in a darkness over a gritty floor. The roaring noise seemed to come from above him, then below. His fingers followed a wall until he touched a wooden ridge. A door, he breathed.

The noise died to a low pitch; he felt his skin prickle. It seemed that he was playing a game with an unseen person whose intelligence outstripped his. He put his ear to the flat surface of the door. Yes, voices. . . . Was this a prize-fight stadium? The sound of the voices came near and sharp, but he could not tell if they were joyous or despairing. He twisted the knob until he heard a soft click and felt the springy weight of the door swinging toward him. He was afraid to open it, yet captured by curiosity and wonder. He jerked the door wide and saw on the far side of the basement a furnace glowing red. Ten feet away was still another door, half ajar. He crossed and peered through the door into an empty, high-ceilinged corridor that terminated in a dark complex of shadow. The belling voices rolled about him and his eagerness mounted. He stepped into the corridor and the voices swelled louder. He crept on and came to a narrow stairway leading circularly upward; there was no question but that he was going to ascend those stairs.

Mounting the spiraled staircase, he heard the voices roll in a steady wave, then leap to crescendo, only to die way, but always remaining audible. Ahead of him glowed red letters: E-X-I-T. At the top of the steps he paused in front of a black curtain that fluttered uncertainly. He parted the folds and looked into a convex depth that gleamed with clusters of shimmering lights. Sprawling below him was a stretch of human faces, tilted upward, chanting, whistling, screaming, laughing. Dangling before the faces, high upon a screen of silver, were jerking shadows. A movie, he said with slow laughter breaking from his lips.

He stood in a box in the reserved section of a movie house and the impulse he had had to tell the people in the church to stop their singing seized him. These people were laughing at their lives, he thought with amazement. They were shouting and yelling at the animated shadows of themselves. His compassion fired his imagination and he stepped out of the box, walked out upon thin air, walked on down to the audience; and, hovering in the air just above them, he stretched out his hand to touch them. . . . His tension snapped and he found himself back in the box, looking down into the sea of faces. No; it could not be done; he could not awaken them. He sighed. Yes, these people were children, sleeping in their living, awake in their dying.

He turned away, parted the black curtain, and looked out. He saw no one. He started down the white stone steps and when he reached the bottom he saw a man in trim blue uniform coming toward him. So used had he become to being underground that he thought that he could walk past the man, as though he were a ghost. But the man stopped. And he stopped.

"Looking for the men's room, sir?" the man asked, and, without waiting for an answer, he turned and pointed. "This way, sir. The first door to your right."

He watched the man turn and walk up the steps and go out of sight. Then he laughed. What a funny fellow! He went back to the basement and stood in the red darkness, watching the glowing embers in the furnace. He went to the sink and turned the faucet and the water flowed in a smooth silent stream that looked like a spout of blood. He brushed the mad image from his mind and began to wash his hands leisurely, looking about for the usual bar of soap. He found one and rubbed it in his palms until a rich lather bloomed in his cupped fingers, like a scarlet sponge. He scrubbed and rinsed his hands meticulously, then hunted for a towel; there was none. He shut off the water, pulled off his shirt, dried his hands on it; when he put it on again he was grateful for the cool dampness that came to his skin.

Yes, he was thirsty; he turned on the faucet again, bowled his fingers and when the water bubbled over the brim of his cupped palms, he drank in long, slow swallows. His bladder grew tight; he shut off the water, faced the wall, bent his head, and watched a red stream strike the floor. His nostrils wrinkled against acrid wisps of vapor; though he had tramped in the waters of the sewer, he stepped back from the wall so that his shoes, wet with sewer slime, would not touch his urine.

He heard footsteps and crawled quickly into the coalbin. Lumps rattled noisily. The footsteps came into the basement and stopped. Who was it? Had someone heard him and come down to investigate? He waited, crouching, sweating. For a long time there was silence, then he heard the clang of metal and a brighter glow lit the room. Somebody's tending the furnace, he thought. Footsteps came closer and he stiffened. Looming before him was a white face lined with coal dust, the face of an old man with watery blue eyes. Highlights spotted his gaunt cheekbones, and he held a huge shovel. There was a screechy scrape of metal against stone, and the old man lifted a shovelful of coal and went from sight.

The room dimmed momentarily, then a yellow glare came as coal flared at the furnace door. Six times the old man came to the bin and went to the furnace with shovels of coal, but not once did he lift his eyes. Finally he dropped the shovel, mopped his face with a dirty handkerchief, and sighed: "Wheeew!" He turned slowly and trudged out of the basement, his footsteps dying away.

He stood, and lumps of coal clattered down the pile. He stepped from the bin and was startled to see the shadowy outline of an electric bulb hanging above his head. Why had not the old man turned it on? Oh, yes. . . . He understood. The old man had worked here for so long that he had no need for light; he had learned a way of seeing in his dark world, like those sightless worms that inch along underground by a sense of touch.

His eyes fell upon a lunch pail and he was afraid to hope that it was full. He picked it up; it was heavy. He opened it. *Sandwiches!* He looked guiltily around; he was alone. He searched farther and found a folder of matches and a half-empty tin of tobacco; he put them eagerly into his pocket and clicked off the light. With the lunch pail under his arm, he went through the door, groped over the pile of coal, and stood again in the lighted basement of the undertaking establishment. I've got to get those tools, he told himself. And turn off that light. He tiptoed back up the steps and switched off the light; the invisible voice still droned on behind the door. He crept down and, seeing with his fingers, opened the lunch pail and tore off a piece of paper bag and brought out the tin and spilled grains of tobacco into the makeshift concave. He rolled it and wet it with spittle, then inserted one end into his mouth and lit it: he sucked smoke that bit his lungs. The nicotine reached his brain, went out along his arms to his fingertips, down to his stomach, and over all the tired nerves of his body.

He carted the tools to the hole he had made in the wall. Would the noise of the falling chest betray him? But he would have to take a chance; he had to have those tools. He lifted the chest and shoved it; it hit the dirt on the other side of the wall with a loud clatter. He waited, listening; nothing happened. Head first, he slithered through and stood in the cave. He grinned, filled with a cunning idea. Yes, he would now go back into the basement of the undertaking establishment and crouch behind the coal pile and dig another hole. Sure! Fumbling, he opened the tool chest and extracted a crowbar, a screwdriver, and a hammer; he fastened them securely about his person.

With another lumpish cigarette in his flexed lips, he crawled back through the hole and over the coal pile, and sat, facing the brick wall. He jabbed with the crowbar and the cement sheered away; quicker than he thought, a brick came loose. He worked an hour; the other bricks did not come easily. He sighed, weak from effort. I ought to rest a little, he thought. I'm hungry. He felt his way back to the cave and stumbled along the wall till he came to the tool chest. He sat upon it, opened the lunch pail, and took out two thick sandwiches. He smelled them. Pork chops. . . . His mouth watered. He closed his eyes and devoured a sandwich, savoring the smooth rye bread and juicy meat. He ate rapidly, gulping down lumpy mouthfuls that made him long for water. He ate the other sandwich and found an apple and gobbled that up too, sucking the core till that last trace of flavor was drained from it. Then, like a dog, he ground the meat bones with his teeth, enjoying the salty, tangy marrow. He finished and stretched out full length on the ground and went to sleep. . . .

. . . His body was washed by cold water that gradually turned warm and he was buoyed upon a stream and swept out to sea where waves rolled gently and suddenly he found himself walking upon the water how strange and delightful to walk upon the water and he came upon a nude woman holding a nude baby in her arms and the woman was sinking into the water holding the baby above her head and screaming *help* and he ran over the water to the woman and he reached her just before she went down and he took the baby from her hands and stood watching the breaking bubbles where the woman sank and he called *lady* and still no answer yes dive down there and rescue that woman but he could not take this baby with him and he stopped and laid the baby tenderly upon the surface of the water expecting it to sink but it floated and he leaped into the water and held his breath and strained his eyes to see through the gloomy volume of water but there was no woman and he opened his mouth and called *lady* and the water bubbled and his chest ached and his arms were tired but he could not see the woman and he called again *lady lady* and his feet touched sand at the bottom of the sea and his chest felt as though it would burst and he bent his knees and propelled himself upward and the water rushed past him and his head bobbed out and he breathed deeply and looked around where was the baby the baby was gone and he rushed over the water looking for the baby calling *where is it* and the empty sky and sea threw back his voice *where is it* and he began to doubt that he could stand upon the water and then he was sinking and as he struggled the water rushed him downward spinning dizzily and he opened his mouth to call for help and water surged into his lungs and he choked. . . .

He groaned and leaped erect in the dark, his eyes wide. The images of terror that thronged his brain would not let him sleep. He rose, made sure that the tools were hitched to his belt, and groped his way to the coal pile and found the rectangular gap from which he had taken the bricks. He took out the crowbar and hacked. Then dread paralyzed him. How long had he slept? Was it day or night now? He had to be careful. Someone might hear him if it were day. He hewed softly for hours at the cement, working silently. Faintly quivering in the air above him was the dim sound of yelling voices. Crazy people, he muttered. They're still there in that movie. . . .

Having rested, he found the digging much easier. He soon had a dozen bricks out. His spirits rose. He took out another brick and his fingers fluttered in space. Good! What lay ahead of him? Another basement? He made the hole larger, climbed through, walked over an uneven floor and felt a metal surface. He lighted a match and saw that he was standing behind a furnace in a basement; before him, on the far side of the room, was a door. He crossed and opened it; it was full of odds and ends. Daylight spilled from a window above his head.

Then he was aware of a soft, continuous tapping, What was it? A clock? No, it was louder than a clock and more irregular. He placed an old empty box beneath the window, stood upon it, and looked into an areaway. He eased the window up and crawled through; the sound of the tapping came clearly now. He glanced about; he was alone. Then he looked upward at a series of window ledges. The tapping identified itself. That's a typewriter, he said to himself. It seemed to be coming from just above. He grasped the ridges of a rain pipe and lifted himself upward; through a half-inch opening of window he saw a doorknob about three feet away. No, it was not a doorknob; it was a small circular disk made of stainless steel with many fine markings upon it. He held his breath: an eerie white hand, seemingly detached from its arm, touched the metal knob and whirled it, first to the left, then to the right. It's a safe! . . . Suddenly he could see the dial no more; a huge metal door swung slowly toward him and he was looking into a safe filled with green wads of paper money, rows of coins wrapped in brown paper, and glass jars and boxes of various sizes. His heart quickened. Good Lord! The white hand went in and out of the safe, taking wads of bills and cylinders of coins. The hand vanished and he heard the muffled click of the big door as it closed. Only the steel dial was visible now. The typewriter still tapped in his ears, but he could not see it. He blinked, wondering if what he had seen was real. There was more money in that safe than he had seen in all his life.

As he clung to the rain pipe, a daring idea came to him and he pulled the screwdriver from his belt. If the white hand twirled that dial again, he would be able to see how far to the left and right it spun and he would have the combination! His blood tingled. I can scratch the numbers right here, he thought. Holding the pipe with one hand, he made the sharp edge of the screwdriver bite into the brick wall. Yes, he could do it. Now, he was set. Now, he had a reason for staying here in the underground. He waited for a long time, but the white hand did not return. Goddamn! Had he been more alert, he would have counted the twirls and he would have had the combination. He got down and stood in the areaway, sunk in reflection.

How could he get into that room? He climbed back into the basement and saw wooden steps leading upward. Was that the room where the safe stood? Fearing that the dial was now being twirled, he clambered through the window, hoisted himself up the rain pipe, and peered; he saw only the naked gleam of the steel dial. He got down and doubled his fists. Well, he would explore the basement. He returned to the basement room and mounted the steps to the door and squinted through the keyhole; all was dark, but the tapping was still somewhere near, still faint and directionless. He pushed the door in; along one wall of a room was a table piled with radios and electrical equipment. A radio shop, he muttered.

Well, he could rig up a radio in his cave. He found a sack, slid the radio into it, and slung it across his back. Closing the door, he went down the steps and stood again in the basement, disappointed. He had not solved the problem of the steel dial and he was irked. He set the radio on the floor and again hoisted himself through the window and up the rain pipe and squinted; the metal door was swinging shut. Goddamn! He's worked the combination again. If I had been patient, I'd have had it! How could he get into that room? He *had* to get into it. He could jimmy the window, but it would be much better if he could get in without any traces. To the right of him, he calculated, should be the basement of the building that held the safe; therefore, if he dug a hole right *here*, he ought to reach his goal.

He began a quiet scraping; it was hard work, for the bricks were not damp. He eventually got one out and lowered it softly to the floor. He had to be careful; perhaps people were beyond this wall. He extracted a second layer of brick and found still another. He gritted his teeth, ready to quit. I'll dig one more, he resolved. When the next brick came out he felt air blowing into his face. He waited to be challenged, but nothing happened.

He enlarged the hole and pulled himself through and stood in quiet darkness. He scratched a match to flame and saw steps; he mounted and peered through a keyhole: Darkness. . . . He strained to hear the typewriter, but there was only silence. Maybe the office had closed? He twisted the knob and swung the door in; a frigid blast made him shiver. In the shadows before him were halves and quarters of hogs and lambs and steers hanging from metal hooks on the low ceiling, red meat encased in folds of cold white fat. Fronting him was frost-coated glass from behind which came indistinguishable sounds. The odor of fresh raw meat sickened him and he backed away. A meat market, he whispered.

He ducked his head, suddenly blinded by light. He narrowed his eyes; the red-white rows of meat were drenched in yellow glare. A man wearing a crimson-spotted jacket came in and took down a bloody meat cleaver. He eased the door to, holding it ajar just enough to watch the man, hoping that the darkness in which he stood would keep him from being seen. The man took down a hunk of steer and place it upon a bloody wooden block and bent forward and whacked with the cleaver. The man's face was hard, square, grim; a jet of mustache smudged his upper lip and a glistening cowlick of hair fell over his left eye. Each time he lifted the cleaver and brought it down upon the meat, he let out a short, deep-chested grunt. After he had cut the meat, he wiped blood off the wooden block with a sticky wad of gunny sack and hung the cleaver upon a hook. His face was proud as he placed the chunk of meat in the crook of his elbow and left.

The door slammed and the light went off; once more he stood in shadow. His tension ebbed. From behind the frosted glass he heard the man's voice: "Forty-eight cents a pound, ma'am." He shuddered, feeling that there was something he had to do. But what? He stared fixedly at the cleaver, then he sneezed and was terrified for fear that the man had heard him. But the door did not open. He took down the cleaver and examined the sharp edge smeared with cold blood. Behind the ice-coated glass a cash register rang with a vibrating, musical tinkle.

Absentmindedly holding the meat cleaver, he rubbed the glass with his thumb and cleared a spot that enabled him to see into the front of the store. The shop was empty, save for the man who was now putting on his hat and coat. Beyond the front window a wan sun shone in the streets; people passed and now and then a fragment of laughter or the whir of a speeding auto came to him. He peered closer and saw on the right counter of the shop a mosquito netting covering pears, grapes, lemons, oranges, bananas, peaches, and plums. His stomach contracted.

The man clicked out the light and he gritted his teeth, muttering, Don't lock the icebox door. . . . The man went through the door of the shop and locked it from the outside. Thank God! Now, he would eat some more! He waited, trembling. The sun died and its rays lingered on in the sky, turning the streets to dusk. He opened the door and stepped inside the shop. In reverse letters across the front window was: NICK'S FRUITS AND MEATS. He laughed, picked up a soft ripe yellow pear and bit into it; juice squirted; his mouth ached as his saliva glands reacted to the acid of the fruit. He ate three pears, gobbled six bananas, and made away with several oranges, taking a bite out of their tops and holding them to his lips and squeezing them as he hungrily sucked the juice.

He found a faucet, turned it on, laid the cleaver aside, pursed his lips under the stream until his stomach felt about to burst. He straightened and belched, feeling satisfied for the first time since he had been underground. He sat upon the floor, rolled and lit a cigarette, his bloodshot eyes squinting against the film of drifting smoke. He watched a patch of sky turn red, then purple; night fell and he lit another cigarette, brooding. Some part of him was trying to remember the world he had left, and another part of him did not want to remember it. Sprawling before him in his mind was his wife, Mrs. Wooten for whom he worked, the three policemen who had picked him up. . . . He possessed them now more completely than he had ever possessed them when he had lived aboveground. How this had come about he could not say, but he had no desire to go back to them. He laughed, crushed the cigarette, and stood up.

He went to the front door and gazed out. Emotionally he hovered between the world aboveground and the world underground. He longed to go out, but sober judgment urged him to remain here. Then impulsively he pried the lock loose with one swift twist of the crowbar; the door swung outward. Through the twilight he saw a white man and a white woman coming toward him. He held himself tense, waiting for them to pass; but they came directly to the door and confronted him.

"I want to buy a pound of grapes," the woman said.

Terrified, he stepped back into the store. The white man stood to one side and the woman entered.

"Give me a pound of dark ones," the woman said.

The white man came slowly forward, blinking his eyes.

"Where's Nick?" the man asked.

"Were you just closing?" the woman asked.

"Yes, ma'am," he mumbled. For a second he did not breathe, then he mumbled again: "Yes, ma'am."

"I'm sorry," the woman said.

The street lamps came on, lighting the store somewhat. Ought he run? But that would raise an alarm. He moved slowly, dreamily, to a counter and lifted up a bunch of grapes and showed them to the woman.

"Fine," the woman said. "But isn't that more than a pound?"

He did not answer. The man was staring at him intently.

"Put them in a bag for me," the woman said, fumbling with her purse.

"Yes, ma'am."

He saw a pile of paper bags under a narrow ledge; he opened one and put the grapes in.

"Thanks," the woman said, taking the bag and placing a dime in his dark palm.

"Where's Nick?" the man asked again. "At supper?"

"Sir? Yes, sir," he breathed.

They left the store and he stood trembling in the doorway. When they were out of sight, he burst out laughing and crying. A trolley car rolled noisily past and he controlled himself quickly. He flung the dime to the pavement with a gesture of contempt and stepped into the warm light air. A few shy stars trembled above him. The look of things was beautiful, yet he felt a lurking threat. He went to an unattended newsstand and looked at a stack of papers. He saw a headline: HUNT NEGRO FOR MURDER.

He felt that someone had slipped up on him from behind and was stripping off his clothes; he looked about wildly, went quickly back into the store, picked up the meat cleaver where he had left it near the sink, then made his way through the icebox to the basement. He stood for a long time, breathing heavily. They know I didn't do anything, he muttered. But how could he prove it? He had signed a confession. Though innocent, he felt guilty, condemned. He struck a match and held it near the steel blade, fascinated and repelled by the dried blotches of blood. Then his fingers gripped the handle of the cleaver with all the strength of his body, he wanted to fling the cleaver from him, but he could not. The match flame wavered and fled; he struggled through the hole and put the cleaver in the sack with the radio. He was determined to keep it, for what purpose he did not know.

He was about to leave when he remembered the safe. Where was it? He wanted to give up, but felt that he ought to make one more try. Opposite the last hole he had dug he tunneled again, plying the crowbar. Once he was so exhausted that he lay on the concrete floor and panted. Finally he made another hole. He wriggled through and his nostrils filled with the fresh smell of coal. He struck a match; yes, the usual steps led upward. He tiptoed to a door and eased it open. A fair-haired white girl stood in front of a steel cabinet, her blue eyes wide upon him. She turned chalky and gave a high-pitched scream. He bounded down the steps and raced to his hole and clambered through, replacing the bricks with nervous haste. He paused, hearing loud voices.

"What's the matter, Alice?"

"A man. . . ."

"What man? Where?"

"A man was at that door. . . ."

"Oh nonsense!"

"He was looking at me through the door!"

"Aw, you're dreaming."

"I *did* see a man!"

The girl was crying now.

"There's nobody here."

Another man's voice sounded.

"What is it, Bob?"

"Alice says she saw a man in here, in that door!"

"Let's take a look."

He waited, poised for flight. Footsteps descended the stairs.

"There's nobody down here."

"The window's locked."

"And there's no door."

"You ought to fire that dame."

"Oh, I don't know. Women are that way."

"She's too hysterical."

The men laughed. Footsteps sounded again on the stairs. A door slammed. He sighed, relieved that he had escaped. But he had not done what he had set out to do; his glimpse of the room had been too brief to determine if the safe was there. He had to know. Boldly he groped through the hole once more; he reached the steps and pulled off his shoes and tiptoed up and peered through the keyhole. His head accidentally touched the door and it swung silently in a fraction of an inch, he saw the girl bent over the cabinet, her back to him. Beyond her was the safe. He crept back down the steps, thinking exultingly: I found it!

Now he had to get the combination. Even if the window in the areaway was locked and bolted, he could gain entrance when the office closed. He scoured through the hole he had dug and stood again in the basement where he had left the radio and the cleaver. Again he crawled out of the window and lifted himself up the rain pipe and peered. The steel dial showed lonely and bright, reflecting the yellow glow of an unseen light. Resigned to a long wait, he sat and leaned against a wall. From far off came the faint sounds of life aboveground; once he looked with a baffled expression at the dark sky. Frequently he rose and climbed the pipe to see the white hand spin the dial, but nothing happened. He bit his lip with impatience. It was not the money that was luring him, but the mere fact that he could get it with impunity. Was the hand now twirling the dial? He rose and looked, but the white hand was not in sight.

Perhaps it would be better to watch continuously? Yes; he clung to the pipe and watched the dial until his eyes thickened with tears.

Exhausted, he stood again in the areaway. He heard a door being shut and he clawed up the pipe and looked. He jerked tense as a vague figure passed in front of him. He stared unblinkingly, hugging the pipe with one hand and holding the screwdriver with the other, ready to etch the combination upon the wall. His ears caught: *Dong . . . Dong . . . Dong . . . Dong . . . Dong . . . Dong . . . Dong. . . .* Seven o'clock, he whispered. Maybe they were closing now? What kind of a store would be open as late as this? he wondered. Did anyone live in the rear? Was there a night watchman? Perhaps the safe was *already* locked for the night! Goddamn! While he had been eating in that shop, they had locked up everything. . . . Then, just as he was about to give up, the white hand touched the dial and turned it once to the right and stopped at six. With quivering fingers, he etched 1-R-6 upon the brick wall with the tip of the screwdriver. The hand twirled the dial twice to the left and stopped at two, and he engraved 2-L-2 upon the wall. The dial was spun four times to the right and stopped at six again; he wrote 4-R-6. The dial rotated three times to the left and was centered straight up and down; he wrote 3-L-0. The door swung open and again he saw the piles of green money and the rows of wrapped coins. I got it, he said grimly.

Then he was stone still, astonished. There were two hands now. A right hand lifted a wad of green bills and deftly slipped it up the sleeve of a left arm. The hands trembled; again the right hand slipped a packet of bills up the left sleeve. He's stealing, he said to himself. He grew indignant, as if the money belonged to him. Though *he* had planned to steal the money, he despised and pitied the man. He felt that his stealing the money and the man's stealing were two entirely different things. He wanted to steal the money merely for the sensation involved in getting it, and he had no intention whatever of spending a penny of it; but he knew that the man who was now stealing it was going to spend it, perhaps for pleasure. The huge steel door closed with a soft click.

Though angry, he was somewhat satisfied. The office would close soon. I'll clean the place out, he mused. He imagined the entire office staff cringing with fear; the police would question everyone for a crime they had not committed, just as they had questioned him. And they would have no idea of how the money had been stolen until they discovered the holes he had tunneled in the walls of the basements. He lowered himself and laughed mischievously, with the abandoned glee of an adolescent.

He flattened himself against the wall as the window above him closed with rasping sound. He looked; somebody was bolting the window securely with a metal screen. That won't help you, he snickered to himself. He clung to the rain pipe until the yellow light in the office went out. He went back into the basement, picked up the sack containing the radio and cleaver, and crawled through the two holes he had dug and groped his way into the basement of the building that held the safe. He moved in slow motion, breathing softly. Be careful now, he told himself. There might be a night watchman. . . . In his memory was the combination written in bold white characters as upon a blackboard. Eel-like he squeezed through the last hole and crept up the steps and put his hand on the knob and pushed the door in about three inches. Then his courage ebbed; his imagination wove dangers for him.

Perhaps the night watchman was waiting in there, ready to shoot. He dangled his cap on a forefinger and poked it past the jamb of the door. If anyone fired, they would hit his cap; but nothing happened. He widened the door, holding the crowbar high above his head, ready to beat off an assailant. He stood like that for five minutes; the rumble of a streetcar brought him to himself. He entered the room. Moonlight floated in from a wide window. He confronted the safe, then checked himself. Better take a look around first. . . . He stepped about and found a closed door. Was the night watchman in there? He opened it and saw a washbowl, a faucet, and a commode. To the left was still another door that opened into a huge dark room that seemed empty; on the far side of that room he made out the shadow of still another door. Nobody's here, he told himself.

He turned back to the safe and fingered the dial; it spun with ease. He laughed and twirled it just for fun. Get to work, he told himself. He turned the dial to the figures he saw on the blackboard of his memory; it was so easy that he felt that the safe had not been locked at all. The heavy door eased loose and he caught hold of the handle and pulled hard, but the door swung open with a slow momentum of its own. Breathless, he gaped at wads of green bills, rows of wrapped coins, curious glass jars full of white pellets, and many oblong green metal boxes. He glanced guiltily over his shoulder; it seemed impossible that someone should not call to him to stop.

They'll be surprised in the morning, he thought. He opened the top of the sack and lifted a wad of compactly tied bills; the money was crisp and new. He admired the smooth, clean-cut edges. The fellows in Washington sure know how to make this stuff, he mused. He rubbed the money with his fingers, as though expecting it to reveal hidden qualities. He lifted the wad to his nose and smelled the fresh odor of ink. Just like any other paper, he mumbled. He dropped the wad into the sack and picked up another. Holding the bag, he thought and laughed.

There was in him no sense of possessiveness; he was intrigued with the form and color of the money, with the manifold reactions which he knew that men aboveground held toward it. The sack was one-third full when it occurred to him to examine the denominations of the bills; without realizing it, he had put many wads of one-dollar bills into the sack. Aw, nuts, he said in disgust. Take the big ones. . . . He dumped the one-dollar bills onto the floor and swept all the hundred-dollar bills he could find into the sack, then he raked in rolls of coins with crooked fingers.

He walked to a desk upon which sat a typewriter, the same machine which the blond girl had used. He was fascinated by it; never in his life had he used one of them. It was a queer instrument of business, something beyond the rim of his life. Whenever he had been in an office where a girl was typing, he had almost always spoken in whispers. Remembering vaguely what he had seen others do, he inserted a sheet of paper into the machine; it went in lopsided and he did not know how to straighten it. Spelling in a soft diffident voice, he pecked out his name on the keys: *freddaniels.* He looked at it and laughed. He would learn to type correctly one of these days.

Yes, he would take the typewriter too. He lifted the machine and placed it atop the bulk of money in the sack. He did not feel that he was stealing, for the cleaver, the radio, the money, and the typewriter were all on the same level of value, all meant the same thing to him. They were the serious toys of the men who lived in the dead world of sunshine and rain he had left, the world that had condemned him, branded him guilty.

But what kind of a place is this? he wondered. What was in that dark room to his rear? He felt for his matches and found that he had only one left. He leaned the sack against the safe and groped forward into the room, encountering smooth, metallic objects that felt like machines. Baffled, he touched a wall and tried vainly to locate an electric switch. Well, he *had* to strike his last match. He knelt and struck it, cupping the flame near the floor with his palms. The place seemed to be a factory, with benches and tables. There were bulbs with green shades spaced about the tables; he turned on a light and twisted it low so that the glare was limited. There were stools at the benches and he concluded that men worked here at some trade. He wandered and found a few half-used folders of matches. If only he could find more cigarettes! But there were none.

But what kind of a place was this? On a bench he saw a pad of paper captioned: PEER'S—MANUFACTURING JEWELERS. His lips formed an "O," then he snapped off the light and ran back to the safe and lifted one of the glass jars and stared at the tiny white pellets. Gingerly he picked up one and found that it was wrapped in tissue paper. He peeled the paper and saw a glittering stone that looked like glass, glinting white and blue sparks. Diamonds, he breathed.

Roughly he tore the paper from the pellets and soon his palm quivered with precious fire. Trembling, he took all four glass jars from the safe and put them into the sack. He grabbed one of the metal boxes, shook it, and heard a tinny rattle. He pried off the lid with the screwdriver. Rings! Hundreds of them. . . . Were they worth anything? He scooped up a handful and jets of fire shot fitfully from the stones. These are diamonds too, he said. He pried open another box. Watches! A chorus of soft, metallic ticking filled his ears. For a moment he could not move, then he dumped all the boxes into the sack.

He shut the safe door, then stood looking around, anxious not to overlook anything. Oh! He had seen a door in the room where the machines were. What was in there? More valuables? He re-entered the room, crossed the floor, and stood undecided before the door. He finally caught hold of the knob and pushed the door in; the room beyond was dark. He advanced cautiously inside and ran his fingers along the wall for the usual switch, then he was stark still. *Something had moved in the room!* What was it? Ought he to creep out, taking the rings and diamonds and money? Why risk what he already had? He waited and the ensuing silence gave him confidence to explore further. Dare he strike a match? Would not a match flame make him a good target? He tensed again as he heard a faint sigh; he was now convinced that there was something alive near him, something that lived and breathed. On tiptoe he felt slowly along the wall, hoping that he would not collide with anything. Luck was with him; he found the light switch.

No; don't turn the light on. . . . Then suddenly he realized that he did not know in what direction the door was. Goddamn! He had to turn the light on or strike a match. He fingered the switch for a long time, then thought of an idea. He knelt upon the floor, reached his arm up to the switch and flicked the button, hoping that if anyone shot, the bullet would go above his head. The moment the light came on he narrowed his eyes to see quickly. He sucked in his breath and his body gave a violent twitch and was still. In front of him, so close that it made him want to bound up and scream, was a human face.

He was afraid to move lest he touch the man. If the man had opened his eyes at that moment, there was no telling what he might have done. The man—long and rawboned—was stretched out on his back upon a little cot, sleeping in his clothes, his head cushioned by a dirty pillow; his face, clouded by a dark stubble of beard, looked straight up to the ceiling. The man sighed, and he grew tense to defend himself; the man mumbled and turned his face away from the light. I've got to turn off that light, he thought. Just as he was about to rise, he saw a gun and cartridge belt on the floor at the man's side. Yes, he would take the gun and cartridge belt, not to use them, but just to keep them, as one takes a memento from a country fair. He picked them up and was about to click off the light when his eyes fell upon a photograph perched upon a chair near the man's head; it was the picture of a woman, smiling, shown against a background of open fields; at the woman's side were two young children, a boy and a girl. He smiled indulgently; he could never send a bullet into that man's brain and time would be over for him. . . .

He clicked off the light and crept silently back into the room where the safe stood; he fastened the cartridge belt about him and adjusted the holster at his right hip. He strutted about the room on tiptoe, lolling his head nonchalantly, then paused abruptly, pulled the gun, and pointed it with grim face toward an imaginary foe. "Boom!" he whispered fiercely. Then he bent forward with silent laughter. That's just like they do it in the movies, he said.

He contemplated his loot for a long time, then got a towel from the washroom and tied the sack securely. When he looked up he was momentarily frightened by his shadow looming on the wall before him. He lifted the sack, dragged it down the basement steps, lugged it across the basement, gasping for breath. After he had struggled through the hole, he clumsily replaced the bricks, then tussled with the sack until he got it to the cave. He stood in the dark, wet with sweat, brooding about the diamonds, the rings, the watches, the money; he remembered the singing in the church, the people yelling in the movie, the dead baby, the nude man stretched out upon the white table. . . . He saw these items hovering before his eyes and felt that some dim meaning linked them together, that some magical relationship made them kin. He stared with vacant eyes, convinced that all of these images, with their tongueless reality, were striving to tell him something. . . .

Later, seeing with his fingers, he untied the sack and set each item neatly upon the dirt floor. Exploring, he took the bulb, the socket, and the wire out of the tool chest; he was elated to find a double socket at one end of the wire. He crammed the stuff into his pockets and hoisted himself upon the rusty pipes and squinted into the church; it was dim and empty. Somewhere in this wall were live electric wires; but where? He lowered himself, groped and tapped the wall with the butt of the screwdriver, listening vainly for hollow sounds. I'll just take a chance and dig, he said.

For an hour he tried to dislodge a brick, and when he struck a match, he found that he had dug a depth of only an inch! No use in digging here, he sighed. By the flickering light of a match, he looked upward, then lowered his eyes, only to glance up again, startled. Directly above his head, beyond the pipes, was a wealth of electric wiring. I'll be damned, he snickered.

He got an old dull knife from the chest and, seeing again with his fingers, separated the two strands of wire and cut away the insulation. Twice he received a slight shock. He scraped the wiring clean and managed to join the two twin ends, then screwed in the bulb. The sudden illumination blinded him and he shut his lids to kill the pain in his eyeballs. I've got that much done, he thought jubilantly.

He placed the bulb on the dirt floor and the light cast a blatant glare on the bleak clay walls. Next he plugged one end of the wire that dangled from the radio into the light socket and bent down and switched on the button; almost at once there was the harsh sound of static, but no words or music. Why won't it work? he wondered. Had he damaged the mechanism in any way? Maybe it needed grounding? Yes. . . . He rummaged in the tool chest and found another length of wire, fastened it to the ground of the radio, and then tied the opposite end to a pipe. Rising and growing distinct, a slow strain of music entranced him with its measured sound. He sat upon the chest, deliriously happy.

Later he searched again in the chest and found a half-gallon can of glue; he opened it and smelled the sharp odor. Then he recalled that he had not even looked at the money. He took a wad of green bills and weighed it in his palm, then broke the seal and held one of the bills up to the light and studied it closely. *The United States of America will pay to the bearer on demand one hundred dollars*, he read in slow speech; then: *This note is legal tender for all debts, public and private*. . . . He broke into a musing laugh, feeling that he was reading of the doings of people who lived on some far-off planet. He turned the bill over and saw on the other side of it a delicately beautiful building gleaming with paint and set amidst green grass. He had no desire whatever to count the money; it was what it stood for—the various currents of life swirling aboveground—that captivated him. Next he opened the rolls of coins and let them slide from their paper wrappings to the ground; the bright, new gleaming pennies and nickels and dimes piled high at his feet, a glowing mound of shimmering copper and silver. He sifted them through his fingers, listening to their tinkle as they struck the conical heap.

Oh, yes! He had forgotten. He would now write his name on the typewriter. He inserted a piece of paper and poised his fingers to write. But what was his name? He stared, trying to remember. He stood and glared about the dirt cave, his name on the tip of his lips. But it would not come to him. Why was he here? Yes, he had been running away from the police. But why? His mind was blank. He bit his lips and sat again, feeling a vague terror. But why worry? He laughed, then pecked slowly: *itwasalonghotday*. He was determined to type the sentence without making any mistakes. How did one make capital letters? He experimented and luckily discovered how to lock the machine for capital letters and then shift it back to lower case. Next he discovered how to make spaces, then he wrote neatly and correctly: *It was a long hot day.* Just why he selected that sentence he did not know; it was merely the ritual of performing the thing that appealed to him. He took the sheet out of the machine and looked around with stiff neck and hard eyes and spoke to an imaginary person:

"Yes, I'll have the contracts ready tomorrow."

He laughed. That's just the way they talked, he said. He grew weary of the game and pushed the machine aside. His eyes fell upon the can of glue, and a mischievous idea bloomed in him, filling him with nervous eagerness. He leaped up and opened the can of glue, then broke the seals on all the wads of money. I'm going to have some wallpaper, he said with a luxurious, physical laugh that made him bend at the knees. He took the towel with which he had tied the sack and balled it into a swab and dipped it into the can of glue and dabbed glue onto the wall; then he pasted one green bill by the side of another. He stepped back and cocked his head. Jesus! That's funny. . . . He slapped his thighs and guffawed. He had triumphed over the world aboveground! He was free! If only people could see this! He wanted to run from this cave and yell his discovery to the world.

He swabbed all the dirt walls of the cave and pasted them with green bills; when he had finished the walls blazed with a yellow-green fire. Yes, this room would be his hideout; between him and the world that had branded him guilty would stand this mocking symbol. He had not stolen the money; he had simply picked it up, just as a man would pick up firewood in a forest. And that was how the world aboveground now seemed to him, a wild forest filled with death.

The walls of money finally palled on him and he looked about for new interests to feed his emotions. The cleaver! He drove a nail into the wall and hung the bloody cleaver upon it. Still another idea welled up. He pried open the metal boxes and lined them side by side on the dirt floor. He grinned at the gold and fire. From one box he lifted up a fistful of ticking gold watches and dangled them by their gleaming chains. He stared with an idle smile, then began to wind them up; he did not attempt to set them at any given hour, for there was no time for him now. He took a fistful of nails and drove them into the papered walls and hung the watches upon them, letting them swing down by their glittering chains, trembling and ticking busily against the backdrop of green with the lemon sheen of the electric light shining upon the metal watch casings, converting the golden disks into blobs of liquid yellow. Hardly had he hung up the last watch than the idea extended itself; he took more nails from the chest and drove them into the green paper and took the boxes of rings and went from nail to nail and hung up the golden bands. The blue and white sparks from the stones filled the cave with brittle laughter, as though enjoying his hilarious secret. People certainly can do some funny things, he said to himself.

He sat upon the tool chest, alternately laughing and shaking his head soberly. Hours later he became conscious of the gun sagging at his hip and he pulled it from the holster. He had seen men fire guns in movies, but somehow his life had never led him into contact with firearms. A desire to feel the sensation others felt in firing came over him. But someone might hear. . . . Well, what if they did? They would not know where the shot had come from. Not in their wildest notions would they think that it had come from under the streets! He tightened his finger on the trigger; there was a deafening report and it seemed that the entire underground had caved in upon his eardrums; and in the same instant there flashed an orange-blue spurt of flame that died quickly but lingered as a vivid afterimage. He smelled the acrid stench of burnt powder filling his lungs and he dropped the gun abruptly.

The intensity of his feelings died and he hung the gun and cartridge belt upon the wall. Next he lifted the jars of diamonds and turned them bottom upward, dumping the white pellets upon the ground. One by one he picked them up and peeled the tissue paper from them and piled them in a neat heap. He wiped his sweaty hand on his trousers, lit a cigarette, and commenced playing another game. He imagined that he was a rich man who lived aboveground in the obscene sunshine and he was strolling through a park of a summer morning, smiling, nodding to his neighbors, sucking an after-breakfast cigar. Many times he crossed the floor of the cave, avoiding the diamonds with his feet, yet subtly gauging his footsteps so that his shoes, wet with sewer slime, would strike the diamonds at some undetermined moment. After twenty minutes of sauntering, his right foot smashed into the heap and diamonds lay scattered in all directions, glinting with a million tiny chuckles of icy laughter. Oh, shucks, he mumbled in mock regret, intrigued by the damage he had wrought. He continued walking, ignoring the brittle fire. He felt that he had a glorious victory locked in his heart.

He stooped and flung the diamonds more evenly over the floor and they showered rich sparks, collaborating with him. He went over the floor and tramped the stones just deep enough for them to be faintly visible, as though they were set delicately in the prongs of a thousand rings. A ghostly light bathed the cave. He sat on the chest and frowned. Maybe *any*thing's right, he mumbled. Yes, if the world as men had made it was right, then anything else was right, any act a man took to satisfy himself, murder, theft, torture.

He straightened with a start. What was happening to him? He was drawn to these crazy thoughts, yet they made him feel vaguely guilty. He would stretch out upon the ground, then get up; he would want to crawl again through the holes he had dug, but would restrain himself; he would think of going again up into the streets, but fear would hold him still. He stood in the middle of the cave, surrounded by green walls and a laughing floor, trembling. He was going to do something, but what? Yes, he was afraid of himself, afraid of doing some nameless thing.

To control himself, he turned on the radio. A melancholy piece of music rose. Brooding over the diamonds on the floor was like looking up into a sky full of restless stars; then the illusion turned into its opposite; he was high up in the air looking down at the twinkling lights of a sprawling city. The music ended and a man recited news events. In the same attitude in which he had contemplated the city, so now, as he heard the cultivated tone, he looked down upon land and sea as men fought, as cities were razed, as planes scattered death upon open towns, as long lines of trenches wavered and broke. He heard the names of generals and the names of mountains and the names of countries and the names and numbers of divisions that were in action on different battle fronts. He saw black smoke billowing from the stacks of warships as they neared each other over wastes of water and he heard their huge guns thunder as red-hot shells screamed across the surface of night seas. He saw hundreds of planes wheeling and droning in the sky and heard the clatter of machine guns as they fought each other and he saw planes falling in plumes of smoke and blaze of fire. He saw steel tanks rumbling across fields of ripe wheat to meet other tanks and there was a loud clang of steel as numberless tanks collided. He saw troops with fixed bayonets charging in waves against other troops who held fixed bayonets and men groaned as steel ripped into their bodies and they went down to die. . . . The voice of the radio faded and he was staring at the diamonds on the floor at his feet.

He shut off the radio, fighting an irrational compulsion to act. He walked aimlessly about the cave, touching the walls with his finger tips. Suddenly he stood still. *What was the matter with him?* Yes, he knew. . . . It was these walls; these crazy walls were filling him with a wild urge to climb out into the dark sunshine aboveground. Quickly he doused the light to banish the shouting walls, then sat again upon the tool chest. Yes, he was trapped. His muscles were flexed taut and sweat ran down his face. He knew now that he could not stay here and he could not go out. He lit a cigarette with shaking fingers; the match flame revealed the green-papered walls with militant distinctness; the purple on the gun barrel glinted like a threat; the meat cleaver brooded with its eloquent splotches of blood; the mound of silver and copper smoldered angrily; the diamonds winked at him from the floor; and the gold watches ticked and trembled, crowning time the king of consciousness, defining the limits of living. . . . The match blaze died and he bolted from where he stood and collided brutally with the nails upon the walls. The spell was broken. He shuddered, feeling that, in spite of his fear, sooner or later he would go up into that dead sunshine and somehow say something to somebody about all this.

He sat again upon the tool chest. Fatigue weighed upon his forehead and eyes. Minutes passed and he relaxed. He dozed, but his imagination was alert. He saw himself rising, wading again in the sweeping water of the sewer; he came to a manhole and climbed out and was amazed to discover that he had hoisted himself into a room filled with armed policemen who were watching him intently. He jumped awake in the dark; he had not moved. He sighed, closed his eyes, and slept again; this time his imagination designed a scheme of protection for him. His dreaming made him feel that he was standing in a room watching over his own nude body lying stiff and cold upon a white table. At the far end of the room he saw a crowd of people huddled in a corner, afraid of his body. Though lying dead upon the table, he was standing in some mysterious way at his side, warding off the people, guarding his body, and laughing to himself as he observed the situation. They're scared of me, he thought.

He awakened with a start, leaped to his feet, and stood in the center of the black cave. It was a full minute before he moved again. He hovered between sleeping and waking, unprotected, a prey of wild fears. He could neither see nor hear. One part of him was asleep; his blood coursed slowly and his flesh was numb. On the other hand he was roused to a strange, high pitch of tension. He lifted his fingers to his face, as though about to weep. Gradually his hands lowered and he struck a match, looking about, expecting to see a door through which he could walk to safety; but there was no door, only the green walls and the moving floor. The match flame died and it was dark again.

Five minutes later he was still standing when the thought came to him that he had been asleep. Yes. . . . But he was not yet fully awake; he was still queerly blind and deaf. How long had he slept? Where was he? Then suddenly he recalled the green-papered walls of the cave and in the same instant he heard loud singing coming from the church beyond the wall. Yes, they woke me up, he muttered. He hoisted himself and lay atop the bed of pipes and brought his face to the narrow slit. Men and women stood here and there between pews. A song ended and a young black girl tossed back her head and closed her eyes and broke plaintively into another hymn.

Glad, glad, glad, oh, so glad
I got Jesus in my soul . . .

Those few words were all she sang, but what her words did not say, her emotions said as she repeated the lines, varying the mood and tempo, making her tone express meanings which her conscious mind did not know. Another woman melted her voice with the girl's, and then an old man's voice merged with that of the two women. Soon the entire congregation was singing:

> Glad, glad, glad, oh, so glad
> I got Jesus in my soul . . .

They're wrong, he whispered in the lyric darkness. He felt that their search for a happiness they could never find made them feel that they had committed some dreadful offense which they could not remember or understand. He was now in possession of the feeling that had gripped him when he had first come into the underground. It came to him in a series of questions: Why was this sense of guilt so seemingly innate, so easy to come by, to think, to feel, so verily physical? It seemed that when one felt this guilt one was retracing in one's feeling a faint pattern designed long before; it seemed that one was always trying to remember a gigantic shock that had left a haunting impression upon one's body which one could not forget or shake off, but which had been forgotten by the conscious mind, creating in one's life a state of eternal anxiety.

He had to tear himself away from this; he got down from the pipes. His nerves were so taut that he seemed to feel his brain pushing through his skull. He felt that he had to do something, but he could not figure out what it was. Yet he knew that if he stood here until he made up his mind, he would never move. He crawled through the hole he had made in the brick wall and the exertion afforded him respite from tension. When he entered the basement of the radio store, he stopped in fear, hearing loud voices.

"Come on boy! Tell us what you did with the radio!"

"Mister, I didn't steal the radio! I swear!"

He heard a dull thumping sound and he imagined a boy being struck violently.

"Please, mister!"

"Did you take it to a pawn shop?"

"No, sir! I didn't steal the radio! I got a radio at home," the boy's voice pleaded hysterically. "Go to my home and look!"

There came to his ears the sound of another blow. It was so funny that he had to clap his hand over his mouth to keep from laughing out loud. They're beating some poor boy, he whispered to himself, shaking his head. He felt a sort of distant pity for the boy and wondered if he ought to bring back the radio and leave it in the basement. No.

Perhaps it was a good thing that they were beating the boy; perhaps the beating would bring to the boy's attention, for the first time in his life, the secret of his existence, the guilt that he could never get rid of.

Smiling, he scampered over a coal pile and stood again in the basement of the building where he had stolen the money and jewelry. He lifted himself into the areaway, climbed the rain pipe, and squinted through a two-inch opening of window. The guilty familiarity of what he saw made his muscles tighten. Framed before him in a bright tableau of daylight was the night watchman sitting upon the edge of a chair, stripped to the waist, his head sagging forward, his eyes red and puffy. The watchman's face and shoulders were stippled with red and black welts. Back of the watchman stood the safe, the steel door wide open showing the empty vault. Yes, they think he did it, he mused.

Footsteps sounded in the room and a man in a blue suit passed in front of him, then another, then still another. Policemen, he breathed. Yes, they were trying to make the watchman confess, just as they had once made him confess to a crime he had not done. He stared into the room, trying to recall something. Oh. . . . Those were the same policemen who had beaten him, had made him sign that paper when he had been too tired and sick to care. Now, they were doing the same thing to the watchman. His heart pounded as he saw one of the policemen shake a finger into the watchman's face.

"Why don't you admit it's an inside job, Thompson?" the policeman said.

"I've told you all I know," the watchman mumbled through swollen lips.

"But nobody was here but you!" the policeman shouted.

"I was sleeping," the watchman said. "It was wrong, but I was sleeping all that night!"

"Stop telling us that lie!"

"It's the truth!"

"When did you get the combination?"

"I don't know how to open the safe," the watchman said.

He clung to the rain pipe, tense; he wanted to laugh, but he controlled himself. He felt a great sense of power; yes, he could go back to the cave, rip the money off the walls, pick up the diamonds and rings, and bring them here and write a note, telling them where to look for their foolish toys. No. . . . What good would that do? It was not worth the effort. The watchman was guilty; although he was not guilty of the crime of which he had been accused, he was guilty, had always been guilty. The only thing that worried him was that the man who had been really stealing was not being accused. But he consoled himself: they'll catch him sometime during his life.

He saw one of the policeman slap the watchman across the mouth.
"Come clean, you bastard!"

"I've told you all I know," the watchman mumbled like a child.

One of the police went to the rear of the watchman's chair and
jerked it from under him; the watchman pitched forward upon his face.

"Get up!" a policeman said.

Trembling, the watchman pulled himself up and sat limply again
in the chair.

"Now, are you going to talk?"

"I've told you all I know," the watchman gasped.

"Where did you hide the stuff?"

"I didn't take it!"

"Thompson, your brains are in your feet," one of the policemen
said. "We're going to string you up and get them back into your skull."

He watched the policemen clamp handcuffs on the watchman's
wrists and ankles; then they lifted the watchman and swung him
upside-down and hoisted his feet to the edge of a door. The watchman
hung, head down, his eyes bulging. They're crazy, he whispered to
himself as he clung to the ridges of the pipe.

"You going to talk?" a policeman shouted into the watchman's ear.

He heard the watchman groan.

"We'll let you hang there till you talk, see?"

He saw the watchman close his eyes.

"Let's take 'im down. He passed out," a policeman said.

He grinned as he watched them take the body down and dump it
carelessly upon the floor. The policeman took off the handcuffs.

"Let 'im come to. Let's get a smoke," a policeman said.

The three policemen left the scope of his vision. A door slammed.
He had an impulse to yell to the watchman that he could escape
through the hole in the basement and live with him in the cave. But
he wouldn't understand that, he told himself. After a moment he saw
the watchman rise and stand swaying from weakness. He stumbled
across the room to a desk, opened a drawer, and took out a gun. He's
going to kill himself, he thought, intent, eager, detached, yearning to
see the end of the man's actions. As the watchman stared vaguely about
he lifted the gun to his temple; he stood like that for some minutes,
biting his lips until a line of blood etched its way down a corner of
his chin. No, he oughtn't do that, he said to himself in a mood of pity.

"Don't!" he half whispered and half yelled.

The watchman looked wildly about; he had heard him. But it did
not help; there was a loud report and the watchman's head jerked
violently and he fell like a log and lay prone, the gun clattering over
the floor.

The three policemen came running into the room with drawn guns. One of the policemen knelt and rolled the watchman's body over and stared at a ragged, scarlet hole in the temple.

"Our hunch was right," the kneeling policeman said. "He was guilty, all right."

"Well, this ends the case," another policeman said.

"He knew he was licked," the third one said with grim satisfaction.

He eased down the rain pipe, crawled back through the holes he had made, and went back into his cave. A fever burned in his bones. He had to act, yet he was afraid. His eyes stared in the darkness as though propped open by invisible hands, as though they had become lidless. His muscles were rigid and he stood for what seemed to him a thousand years.

When he moved again his actions were informed with precision, his muscular system reinforced from a reservoir of energy. He crawled through the hole of earth, dropped into the gray sewer current, and sloshed ahead. When his right foot went forward at a street intersection, he fell backward and shot down into water. In a spasm of terror his right hand grabbed the concrete ledge of a down-curve and he felt the streaking water tugging violently at his body. The current reached his neck and for a moment he was still. He knew that if he moved clumsily he would be sucked under. He held onto the ledge with both hands and slowly pulled himself up. He sighed, standing once more in the sweeping water, thankful that he had missed death.

He waded on through sludge, moving with care, until he came to a web of light sifting down from a manhole cover. He saw steel hooks running up the side of the sewer wall; he caught hold and lifted himself and put his shoulder to the cover and moved it an inch. A crash of sound came to him as he looked into a hot glare of sunshine through which blurred shapes moved. Fear scalded him and he dropped back into the pallid current and stood paralyzed in the shadows. A heavy car rumbled past overhead, jarring the pavement, warning him to stay in his world of dark light, knocking the cover back into place with an imperious clang.

He did not know how much fear he felt, for fear claimed him completely; yet it was not a fear of the police or of people, but a cold dread at the thought of the actions he knew he would perform if he went out into that cruel sunshine. His mind said no; his body said yes; and his mind could not understand his feelings. A low whine broke from him and he was in the act of uncoiling. He climbed upward and heard the faint honking of auto horns. Like a frantic cat clutching a rag, he clung to the steel prongs and heaved his shoulder against the cover and pushed it off halfway. For a split second his eyes were drowned in the terror of yellow light and he was in a deeper darkness than he had ever known in the underground.

Partly out of the hole, he blinked, regaining enough sight to make out meaningful forms. An odd thing was happening: No one was rushing forward to challenge him. He had imagined the moment of his emergence as a desperate tussle with men who wanted to cart him off to be killed; instead, life froze about him as the traffic stopped. He pushed the cover aside, stood, swaying in a world so fragile that he expected it to collapse and drop him into some deep void. But nobody seemed to pay him heed. The cars were now swerving to shun him and the gaping hole.

"Why in hell don't you put up a red light, dummy?" a raucous voice yelled.

He understood; they thought that he was a sewer workman. He walked toward the sidewalk, weaving unsteadily through the moving traffic.

"Look where you're going, nigger!"

"That's right! Stay there and get killed!"

"You blind, you bastard?"

"Go home and sleep your drunk off!"

A policeman stood at the curb, looking in the opposite direction. When he passed the policeman, he feared that he would be grabbed, but nothing happened. Where was he? Was this real? He wanted to look about to get his bearings, but felt that something awful would happen to him if he did. He wandered into a spacious doorway of a store that sold men's clothing and saw his reflection in a long mirror: his cheekbones protruded from a hairy black face; his greasy cap was perched askew upon his head and his eyes were red and glassy. His shirt and trousers were caked with mud and hung loosely. His hands were gummed with a black stickiness. He threw back his head and laughed so loudly that passersby stopped and stared.

He ambled on down the sidewalk, not having the merest notion of where he was going. Yet, sleeping within him, was the drive to go somewhere and say something to somebody. Half an hour later his ears caught the sound of spirited singing.

> *The Lamb, the Lamb, the Lamb*
> *I hear thy voice a-calling*
> *The Lamb, the Lamb, the Lamb*
> *I feel thy grace a-falling*

A church! he exclaimed. He broke into a run and came to brick steps leading downward to a subbasement. This is it! The church into which he had peered. Yes, he was going in and tell them. What? He did not know; but, once face to face with them, he would think of what to say. Must be Sunday, he mused. He ran down the steps and jerked the door open; the church was crowded and a deluge of song swept over him.

The Lamb, the Lamb, the Lamb
Tell me again your story
The Lamb, the Lamb, the Lamb
Flood my soul with your glory

He stared at the singing faces with a trembling smile.
"Say!" he shouted.
Many turned to look at him, but the song rolled on. His arm was jerked violently.
"I'm sorry, Brother, but you can't do that in here," a man said.
"But, mister!"
"You can't act rowdy in God's house," the man said.
"He's filthy," another man said.
"But I want to tell 'em," he said loudly.
"He stinks," someone muttered.
The song had stopped, but at once another one began.

Oh, wondrous sight upon the cross
Vision sweet and divine
Oh, wondrous sight upon the cross
Full of such love sublime

He attempted to twist away, but other hands grabbed him and rushed him into the doorway.
"Let me alone!" he screamed, struggling.
"Get out!"
"He's drunk," somebody said. "He ought to be ashamed!"
"He acts crazy!"
He felt that he was failing and he grew frantic.
"But, mister, let me tell—"
"Get away from this door, or I'll call the police!"
He stared, his trembling smile fading in a sense of wonderment.
"The police," he repeated vacantly.
"Now, get!"
He was pushed toward the brick steps and the door banged shut. The waves of song came.

Oh, wondrous sight, wondrous sight
Lift my heavy heart above

Oh, wondrous sight, wondrous sight
Fill my weary soul with love

He was smiling again now. Yes, the police. . . . That was it! Why had he not thought of it before? The idea had been deep down in him, and only now did it assume supreme importance. He looked up and saw a street sign: COURT STREET—HARTSDALE AVENUE. He turned and walked northward, his mind filled with the image of the police station. Yes, that was where they had beaten him, accused him, and had made him sign a confession of his guilt. He would go there and clear up everything, make a statement. What statement? He did not know. He was the statement, and since it was all so clear to him, surely he would be able to make it clear to others.

He came to the corner of Hartsdale Avenue and turned westward. Yeah, there's the station. . . . A policeman came down the steps and walked past him without a glance. He mounted the stone steps and went through the door, paused; he was in a hallway where several policemen were standing, talking, smoking. One turned to him.

"What do you want, boy?"

He looked at the policeman and laughed.

"What in hell are you laughing about?" the policeman asked.

He stopped laughing and stared. His whole being was full of what he wanted to say to them, but he could not say it.

"Are you looking for the Desk Sergeant?"

"Yes, sir," he said quickly; then: "Oh, no, sir."

"Well, make up your mind, now."

Four policemen grouped themselves around him.

"I'm looking for the men," he said.

"What men?"

Peculiarly, at that moment he could not remember the names of the policemen; he recalled their beating him, the confession he had signed, and how he had run away from them. He saw the cave next to the church, the money on the walls, the guns, the rings, the cleaver, the watches, and the diamonds on the floor.

"They brought me here," he began.

"When?"

His mind flew back over the blur of the time lived in the underground blackness. He had no idea of how much time had elapsed, but the intensity of what had happened to him told him that it could not have transpired in a short space of time, yet his mind told him that time must have been brief.

"It was a long time ago." He spoke like a child relating a dimly remembered dream. "It was a long time," he repeated, following the promptings of his emotions. "They beat me . . . I was scared . . . I ran away."

A policeman raised a finger to his temple and made a derisive circle. "Nuts," the policeman said.

"Do you know what place this is, boy?"

"Yes, sir. The police station," he answered sturdily, almost proudly.

"Well, who do you want to see?"

"The men," he said again, feeling that surely they knew the men. "You know the men," he said in a hurt tone.

"What's your name?"

He opened his lips to answer but no words came. He had forgotten. But what did it matter if he had? It was not important.

"Where do you live?"

Where did he live? It had been so long since he had lived up here in this strange world that he felt it was foolish even to try to remember. Then for a moment the old mood that had dominated him in the underground surged back. He leaned forward and spoke eagerly.

"They said I killed the woman."

"What woman?" a policeman asked.

"And I signed a paper that said I was guilty," he went on, ignoring their questions. "Then I ran off. . . ."

"Did you run off from an institution?"

"No, sir," he said, blinking and shaking his head. "I came from under the ground. I pushed off the manhole cover and climbed out. . . ."

"All right, now," a policeman said, placing an arm about his shoulder. "We'll send you to the psycho and you'll be taken care of."

"Maybe he's a Fifth Columnist!" a policeman shouted.

There was laughter and, despite his anxiety, he joined in. But the laughter lasted so long that it irked him.

"I got to find those men," he protested mildly.

"Say, boy, what have you been drinking?"

"Water," he said. "I got some water in a basement."

"Were the men you ran away from dressed in white, boy?"

"No, sir," he said brightly. "They were men like you."

An elderly policeman caught hold of his arm.

"Try and think hard. Where did they pick you up?"

He knitted his brows in an effort to remember, but he was blank inside. The policeman stood before him demanding logical answers and he could no longer think with his mind; he thought with his feelings and no words came.

"I was guilty," he said. "Oh, no, sir. I wasn't then, I mean, mister!"

"Aw, talk sense. Now, where did they pick you up?"

He felt challenged and his mind began reconstructing events in reverse; his feelings ranged back over the long hours and he saw the cave, the sewer, the bloody room where it was said that a woman had been killed.

"Oh, yes, sir," he said, smiling. "I was coming from Mrs. Wooten's."

"Who is she?"

"I work for her."

"Where does she live?"

"Next door to Mrs. Peabody, the woman who was killed."

The policemen were very quiet now, looking at him intently.

"What do you know about Mrs. Peabody's death, boy?"

"Nothing, sir. But they said I killed her. But it doesn't make any difference. I'm guilty!"

"What are you talking about, boy?"

His smile faded and he was possessed with memories of the underground; he saw the cave next to the church and his lips moved to speak. But how could he say it? The distance between what he felt and what these men meant was vast. Something told him, as he stood there looking into their faces, that he would never be able to tell them, that they would never believe him even if he told them.

"All the people I saw was guilty," he began slowly.

"Aw, nuts," a policeman muttered.

"Say," another policeman said, "that Peabody woman was killed over on Winewood. That's Number Ten's beat."

"Where's Number Ten?" a policeman asked.

"Upstairs in the swing room," someone answered.

"Take this boy up, Sam," a policeman ordered.

"O.K. Come along, boy."

An elderly policeman caught hold of his arm and led him up a flight of wooden stairs, down a long hall, and to a door.

"Squad Ten!" the policeman called through the door.

"What?" a gruff voice answered.

"Someone to see you!"

"About what?"

The old policeman pushed the door in and then shoved him into the room.

He stared, his lips open, his heart barely beating. Before him were the three policemen who had picked him up and had beaten him to extract the confession. They were seated about a small table, playing cards. The air was blue with smoke and sunshine poured through a high window, lighting up fantastic smoke shapes. He saw one of the policemen look up; the policeman's face was tired and a cigarette drooped limply from one corner of his mouth and both of his fat, puffy eyes were squinting and his hands gripped his cards.

"Lawson!" the man exclaimed.

The moment the man's name sounded he remembered the names of all of them: Lawson, Murphy, and Johnson. How simple it was. He waited, smiling, wondering how they would react when they knew that he had come back.

"Looking for me?" the man who had been called Lawson mumbled, sorting his cards. "For what?"

So far only Murphy, the red-headed one, had recognized him.

"Don't you-all remember me?" he blurted, running to the table.

All three of the policemen were looking at him now. Lawson, who seemed the leader, jumped to his feet.

"Where in hell have you been?"

"Do you know 'im, Lawson?" the old policeman asked.

"Huh?" Lawson frowned. "Oh, yes. I'll handle 'im." The old policeman left the room and Lawson crossed to the door and turned the key in the lock. "Come here, boy," he ordered in a cold tone.

He did not move: he looked from face to face. Yes, he would tell them about his cave.

"He looks batty to me," Johnson said, the one who had not spoken before.

"Why in hell did you come back here?" Lawson said.

"I—I just didn't want to run away no more," he said. "I'm all right, now." He paused; the men's attitude puzzled him.

"You've been hiding, huh?" Lawson asked in a tone that denoted that he had not heard his previous words. "You told us you were sick, and when we left you in the room, you jumped out of the window and ran away."

Panic filled him. Yes, they were indifferent to what he would say! They were waiting for him to speak and they would laugh at him. He had to rescue himself from this bog; he had to force the reality of himself upon them.

"Mister, I took a sackful of money and pasted it on the walls. . . ." he began.

"I'll be damned," Lawson said.

"Listen," said Murphy, "let me tell you something for your own good. We don't want you, see? You're free, free as air. Now go home and forget it. It was all a mistake. We caught the guy who did the Peabody job. He wasn't colored at all. He was an Eyetalian."

"Shut up!" Lawson yelled. "Have you no sense!"

"But I want to tell 'im," Murphy said.

"We can't let this crazy fool go," Lawson exploded. "He acts nuts, but this may be a stunt. . . ."

"I was down in the basement," he began in a childlike tone as though repeating a lesson learned by heart; "and I went into a movie.

. . ." His voice failed. He was getting ahead of his story. First, he ought to tell them about the singing in the church, but what words could he use? He looked at them appealingly. "I went into a shop and took a sackful of money and diamonds and watches and rings. . . . I didn't steal 'em; I'll give 'em all back. I just took 'em to play with. . . ." He paused, stunned by their disbelieving eyes.

Lawson lit a cigarette and looked at him coldly.

"What did you do with the money?" he asked in a quiet, waiting voice.

"I pasted the hundred-dollar bills on the walls."

"What walls?" Lawson asked.

"The walls of the dirt room," he said, smiling, "the room next to the church. I hung up the rings and the watches and I stamped the diamonds into the dirt. . . ." He saw that they were not understanding what he was saying. He grew frantic to make them believe, his voice tumbled on eagerly. "I saw a dead baby and a dead man. . . ."

"Aw, you're nuts," Lawson snarled, shoving him into a chair.

"But, mister. . . ."

"Johnson, where's the paper he signed?" Lawson asked.

"What paper?"

"The confession, fool!"

Johnson pulled out his billfold and extracted a crumpled piece of paper.

"Yes, sir, mister," he said, stretching forth his hand. "That's the paper I signed. . . ."

Lawson slapped him and he would have toppled had his chair not struck a wall behind him. Lawson scratched a match and held the paper over the flame; the confession burned down to Lawson's fingertips.

He stared, thunderstruck; the sun of the underground was fleeing and the terrible darkness of the day stood before him. They did not believe him, but he *had* to make them believe him!

"But, mister. . . ."

"It's going to be all right, boy," Lawson said with a quiet, soothing laugh. "I've burned your confession, see? You didn't sign anything." Lawson came close to him with the black ashes cupped in his palm. "You don't remember a thing about this, do you?"

"Don't you-all be scared of me," he pleaded, sensing their uneasiness. "I'll sign another paper, if you want me to. I'll show you the cave."

"What's your game, boy?" Lawson asked suddenly.

"What are you trying to find out?" Johnson asked.

"Who sent you here?" Murphy demanded.

"Nobody sent me, mister," he said. "I just want to show you the room. . . ."

"Aw, he's plumb bats," Murphy said. "Let's ship 'im to the psycho."

"No," Lawson said. "He's playing a game and I wish to God I knew what it was."

There flashed through his mind a definite way to make them believe him; he rose from the chair with nervous excitement.

"Mister, I saw the night watchman blow his brains out because you accused him of stealing," he told them. "But he didn't steal the money and diamonds. I took 'em."

Tigerishly Lawson grabbed his collar and lifted him bodily.

"*Who told you about that?*"

"Don't get excited, Lawson," Johnson said. "He read about it in the papers."

Lawson flung him away.

"He couldn't have," Lawson said, pulling papers from his pocket. "I haven't turned in the reports yet."

"Then how *did* he find out?" Murphy asked.

"Let's get out of here," Lawson said with quick resolution. "Listen, boy, we're going to take you to a nice, quiet place, see?"

"Yes, sir," he said. "And I'll show you the underground."

"Goddamn," Lawson muttered, fastening the gun at his hip. He narrowed his eyes at Johnson and Murphy. "Listen," he spoke above a whisper, "say nothing about this, you hear?"

"O.K.," Johnson said.

"Sure," Murphy said.

Lawson unlocked the door and Johnson and Murphy led him down the stairs. The hallway was crowded with policemen.

"What have you got there, Lawson?"

"What did he do, Lawson?"

"He's psycho, ain't he, Lawson?"

Lawson did not answer; Johnson and Murphy led him to the car parked at the curb, pushed him into the back seat. Lawson got behind the steering wheel and the car rolled forward.

"What's up, Lawson?" Murphy asked.

"Listen," Lawson began slowly, "we tell the papers that he spilled about the Peabody job, then he escapes. The Wop is caught and we tell the papers that we steered them wrong to trap the real guy, see? Now this dope shows up and acts nuts. If we let him go, he'll squeal that we framed him, see?"

"I'm all right, mister," he said, feeling Murphy's and Johnson's arms locked rigidly into his. "I'm guilty . . . I'll show you everything in the underground. I laughed and laughed. . . ."

"Shut that fool up!" Lawson ordered.

Johnson tapped him across the head with a blackjack and he fell back against the seat cushion, dazed.

"Yes, sir," he mumbled. "I'm all right."

The car sped along Hartsdale Avenue, then swung into Pine Street and rolled to State Street, then turned south. It slowed to a stop, turned in the middle of a block, and headed north again.

"You're going around in circles, Lawson," Murphy said.

Lawson did not answer; he was hunched over the steering wheel. Finally he pulled the car to a stop at the curb.

"Say, boy, tell us the truth," Lawson asked quietly. "Where did you hide?"

"I didn't hide, mister."

The three policemen were staring at him now; he felt that for the first time they were willing to understand him.

"Then what happened?"

"Mister, when I poked through all of those holes and saw how people were living, I loved 'em. . . ."

"Cut out that crazy talk!" Lawson snapped. "Who sent you back here?"

"Nobody, mister."

"Maybe he's talking straight," Johnson ventured.

"All right," Lawson said. "Nobody hid you. Now, tell us *where* you hid."

"I went underground. . . ."

"What goddamn underground do you keep talking about?"

"I just went. . . ." He paused and looked into the street, then pointed to a manhole cover. "I went down in there and stayed."

"In the *sewer*?"

"Yes, sir."

The policemen burst into a sudden laugh and ended quickly. Lawson swung the car around and drove to Woodside Avenue; he brought the car to a stop in front of a tall apartment building.

"What're we going to do, Lawson?" Murphy asked.

"I'm taking him up to my place," Lawson said. "We've got to wait until night. There's nothing we can do now."

They took him out of the car and led him into a vestibule.

"Take the steps," Lawson muttered.

They led him up four flights of stairs and into the living room of a small apartment. Johnson and Murphy let go of his arms and he stood uncertainly in the middle of the room.

"Now, listen, boy," Lawson began, "forget those wild lies you've been telling us. Where did you hide?"

"I just went underground, like I told you."

The room rocked with laughter. Lawson went to a cabinet and got a bottle of whisky; he placed glasses for Johnson and Murphy. The three of them drank.

He felt that he could not explain himself to them. He tried to muster all the sprawling images that floated in him; the images stood out sharply in his mind, but he could not make them have the meaning for others that they had for him. He felt so helpless that he began to cry.

"He's nuts, all right," Johnson said. "All nuts cry like that."

Murphy crossed the room and slapped him.

"Stop that raving!"

A sense of excitement flooded him; he ran to Murphy and grabbed his arm.

"Let me show you the cave," he said. "Come on, and you'll see!"

Before he knew it a sharp blow had clipped him on the chin; darkness covered his eyes. He dimly felt himself being lifted and laid out on the sofa. He heard low voices and struggled to rise, but hard hands held him down. His brain was clearing now. He pulled to a sitting position and stared with glazed eyes. It had grown dark. How long had he been out?

"Say, boy," Lawson said soothingly, "will you show us the underground?"

His eyes shone and his heart swelled with gratitude. Lawson believed him! He rose, glad; he grabbed Lawson's arm, making the policeman spill whisky from the glass to his shirt.

"Take it easy, goddammit," Lawson said.

"Yes, sir."

"O.K. We'll take you down. But you'd better be telling us the truth, you hear?"

He clapped his hands in wild joy.

"I'll show you everything!"

He had triumphed at last! He would now do what he had felt was compelling him all along. At last he would be free of his burden.

"Take 'im down," Lawson ordered.

They led him down to the vestibule; when he reached the sidewalk he saw that it was night and a fine rain was falling.

"It's just like when I went down," he told them.

"What?" Lawson asked.

"The rain," he said, sweeping his arm in a wide arc. "It was raining when I went down. The rain made the water rise and lift the cover off."

"Cut it out," Lawson snapped.

They did not believe him now, but they would. A mood of high selflessness throbbed in him. He could barely contain his rising spirits. They would see what he had seen; they would feel what he had felt. He would lead them through all the holes he had dug and. . . . He wanted to make a hymn, prance about in physical ecstasy, throw his arms about the policemen in fellowship.

"Get into the car," Lawson ordered.

He climbed in and Johnson and Murphy sat at either side of him; Lawson slid behind the steering wheel and started the motor.

"Now, tell us where to go," Lawson said.

"It's right around the corner from where the lady was killed," he said.

The car rolled slowly and he closed his eyes, remembering the song he had heard in the church, the song that had wrought him to such a high pitch of terror and pity. He sang softly, lolling his head:

> Glad, glad, glad, oh, so glad
> I got Jesus in my soul . . .

"Mister," he said, stopping his song, "you ought to see how funny the rings look on the wall." He giggled. "I fired a pistol, too. Just once, to see how it felt."

"What do you suppose he's suffering from?" Johnson asked.

"Delusions of grandeur, maybe," Murphy said.

"Maybe it's because he lives in a white man's world," Lawson said.

"Say, boy, what did you eat down there?" Murphy asked, prodding Johnson anticipatorily with his elbow.

"Pears, oranges, bananas, and pork chops," he said.

The car filled with laughter.

"You didn't eat any watermelon?" Lawson asked, smiling.

"No, sir," he answered calmly. "I didn't see any."

The three policemen roared harder and louder.

"Boy, you're sure some case," Murphy said, shaking his head in wonder.

The car pulled to a curb.

"All right, boy," Lawson said. "Tell us where to go."

He peered through the rain and saw where he had gone down. The streets, save for a few dim lamps glowing softly through the rain, were dark and empty.

"Right there, mister," he said, pointing.

"Come on; let's take a look," Lawson said.

"Well, suppose he did hide down there," Johnson said, "what is that supposed to prove?"

"I don't believe he hid down there," Murphy said.

"It won't hurt to take a look," Lawson said. "Leave things to me."

Lawson got out of the car and looked up and down the street.

He was eager to show them the cave now. If he could show them what he had seen, then they would feel what he had felt and they in turn would show it to others and those others would feel as they had felt, and soon everybody would be governed by the same impulse of pity.

"Take 'im out," Lawson ordered.

Johnson and Murphy opened the door and pushed him out; he stood trembling in the rain, smiling. Again Lawson looked up and down the street; no one was in sight. The rain came down hard, slanting like black wires across the windswept air.

"All right," Lawson said. "Show us."

He walked to the center of the street, stopped and inserted a finger in one of the tiny holes of the cover and tugged, but he was too weak to budge it.

"Did you really go down in there, boy?" Lawson asked; there was a doubt in his voice.

"Yes, sir. Just a minute, I'll show you."

"Help 'im get that damn thing off," Lawson said.

Johnson stepped forward and lifted the cover; it clanged against the wet pavement. The hole gaped round and black.

"I went down in there," he announced with pride.

Lawson gazed at him for a long time without speaking then he reached his right hand to his holster and drew his gun.

"Mister, I got a gun just like that down there," he said, laughing and looking into Lawson's face. "I fired it once then hung it on the wall. I'll show you."

"Show us how you went down," Lawson said quietly.

"I'll go down first, mister, and then you-all can come after me, hear?" He spoke like a little boy playing a game.

"Sure, sure," Lawson said soothingly. "Go ahead. We'll come."

He looked brightly at the policemen; he was bursting with happiness. He bent down and placed his hands on the rim of the hole and sat on the edge, his feet dangling into watery darkness. He heard the familiar drone of the gray current. He lowered his body and hung for a moment by his fingers, then he went downward on the steel prongs, hand over hand, until he reached the last rung. He dropped and his feet hit the water and he felt the stiff current trying to suck him away. He balanced himself quickly and looked back upward at the policemen.

"Come on, you-all!" he yelled, casting his voice above the rustling at his feet.

The vague forms that towered above him in the rain did not move. He laughed, feeling that they doubted him. But, once they saw the things he had done, they would never doubt again.

"Come on! The cave isn't far!" he yelled. "But be careful when your feet hit the water, because the current's pretty rough down here!"

Lawson still held the gun. Murphy and Johnson looked at Lawson quizzically.

"What are we going to do, Lawson?" Murphy asked.

"We are not going to follow that crazy nigger down into that sewer, are we?" Johnson asked.

"Come on, you-all!" he begged in a shout.

He saw Lawson raise the gun and point it directly at him. Lawson's face twitched, as though he were hesitating.

Then there was a tremendous report and a streak of fire ripped through his chest. He was hurled into the water, flat on his back. He looked in amazement at the blurred white faces looming above him. They shot me, he said to himself. The water flowed past him, blossoming in foam about his arms, his legs, and his head. His jaw sagged and his mouth gaped soundless. A vast pain gripped his head and gradually squeezed out consciousness. As from a great distance he heard hollow voices.

"What did you shoot him for, Lawson?"

"I had to."

"Why?"

"You've got to shoot his kind. They'd wreck things."

As though in a deep dream, he heard a metallic clank; they had replaced the manhole cover, shutting out forever the sound of wind and rain. From overhead came the muffled roar of a powerful motor and the swish of a speeding car. He felt the strong tide pushing him slowly into the middle of the sewer, turning him about. For a split second there hovered before his eyes the glittering cave, the shouting walls, and the laughing floor. . . . Then his mouth was full of thick, bitter water. The current spun him around. He sighed and closed his eyes, a whirling object rushing alone in the darkness, veering, tossing, lost in the heart of the earth.

from Lenox Avenue Mural

LANGSTON HUGHES

HARLEM

What happens to a dream deferred?
    Does it dry up
    like a raisin in the sun?
    Or fester like a sore—
    And then run?

Does it stink like rotten meat?
Or crust and sugar over—
Like a syrupy sweet?

Maybe it just sags
like a heavy load.

Or does it explode?

GOOD MORNING

Good morning, daddy!
I was born here, he said,
watched Harlem grow
until colored folks spread
from river to river
across the middle of Manhattan
out of Penn Station
dark tenth of a nation,
planes from Puerto Rico,
and holds of boats, chico,
up from Cuba Haiti Jamaica,
in busses marked New York
from Georgia Florida Louisiana
to Harlem Brooklyn the Bronx
but most of all to Harlem
dusky sash across Manhattan
I've seen them come dark
        wondering
        wide-eyed
        dreaming
out of Penn Station—
but the trains are late.
The gates open—
but there's bars
at each gate.
        What happens
        to a dream deferred?
Daddy, ain't you heard?

SAME IN BLUES

I said to my baby,
Baby, take it slow.

I can't, she said, I can't!
I got to go!
  There's a certain
  amount of traveling
  in a dream deferred.
Lulu said to Leonard,
I want a diamond ring.
Leonard said to Lulu,
You won't get a goddamn thing!
  A certain
  amount of nothing
  in a dream deferred.
Daddy, daddy, daddy,
All I want is you.
You can have me, baby—
but my lovin' days is through.
  A certain
  amount of impotence
  in a dream deferred.
Three parties
On my party line—
But that third party,
Lord, ain't mine!
  There's liable
  to be confusion
  in a dream deferred.
From river to river
Uptown and down,
There's liable to be confusion
when a dream gets kicked around.
  You talk like
  they don't kick
  dreams around
  Downtown.
I expect they do—
But I'm talking about
Harlem to you!

from **Go Tell It on the Mountain**

JAMES BALDWIN

Everyone had always said that John would be a preacher when he grew up, just like his father. It had been said so often that John, without ever thinking about it, had come to believe it himself. Not until the morning of his fourteenth birthday did he really begin to think about it, and by then it was already too late.

His earliest memories—which were in a way, his only memories —were of the hurry and brightness of Sunday mornings. They all rose together on that day; his father, who did not have to go to work, and led them in prayer before breakfast; his mother, who dressed up on that day, and looked almost young, with her hair straightened, and on her head the close-fitting white cap that was the uniform of holy women; his younger brother, Roy, who was silent that day because his father was home. Sarah, who wore a red ribbon in her hair that day, and was fondled by her father. And the baby, Ruth, who was dressed in pink and white, and rode in her mother's arms to church.

The church was not very far away, four blocks up Lenox Avenue, on a corner not far from the hospital. It was to this hospital that his mother had gone when Roy, and Sarah, and Ruth were born. John did not remember very clearly the first time she had gone, to have Roy; folks said that he had cried and carried on the whole time his mother was away; he remembered only enough to be afraid every time her belly began to swell, knowing that each time the swelling began it would not end until she was taken from him, to come back with a stranger. Each time this happened she became a little more of a stranger herself. She would soon be going away again, Roy said—he knew much more about such things than John. John had observed his mother closely, seeing no swelling yet, but his father had prayed one morning for the "little voyager soon to be among them," and so John knew that Roy spoke the truth.

Every Sunday morning, then, since John could remember, they had taken to the streets, the Grimes family on their way to church. Sinners along the avenue watched them—men still wearing their Saturday-night clothes, wrinkled and dusty now, muddy-eyed and muddy-faced; and women with harsh voices and tight, bright dresses, cigarettes between their fingers or held tightly in the corners of their mouths. They talked, and laughed, and fought together, and the women fought like the men. John and Roy, passing these men and women, looked at one another briefly, John embarrassed and Roy amused. Roy would be like them when he grew up, if the Lord did not change his heart. These men and women they passed on Sunday mornings had spent the night in bars, or in cat houses, or on the streets, or on rooftops, or under the stairs. They had been drinking. They had gone from cursing to laughter, to anger, to lust. Once he and Roy had watched a man and woman in the basement of a condemned house. They did it standing up. The woman had wanted fifty cents, and the man had flashed a razor.

John had never watched again; he had been afraid. But Roy had watched them many times, and he told John he had done it with some girls down the block.

And his mother and father, who went to church on Sundays, they did it too, and sometimes John heard them in the bedroom behind him, over the sound of rats' feet, and rat screams, and the music and cursing from the harlot's house downstairs.

Their church was called the Temple of the Fire Baptized. It was not the biggest church in Harlem, nor yet the smallest, but John had been brought up to believe it was the holiest and best. His father was head deacon in this church—there were only two, the other a round, black man named Deacon Braithwaite—and he took up the collection, and sometimes he preached. The pastor, Father James, was a genial, well-fed man with a face like a darker moon. It was he who preached on Pentecost Sundays, and led revivals in the summertime, and anointed and healed the sick.

On Sunday mornings and Sunday nights the church was always full; on special Sundays it was full all day. The Grimes family arrived in a body, always a little late, usually in the middle of Sunday school, which began at nine o'clock. This lateness was always their mother's fault— at least in the eyes of their father; she could not seem to get herself and the children ready on time, ever, and sometimes she actually remained behind, not to appear until the morning service. When they all arrived together, they separated upon entering the doors, father and mother going to sit in the Adult Class, which was taught by Sister McCandless, Sarah going to the Infant's Class, John and Roy sitting in the Intermediate, which was taught by Brother Elisha.

When he was young, John had paid no attention in Sunday school, and always forgot the golden text, which earned him the wrath of his father. Around the time of his fourteenth birthday, with all the pressures of church and home uniting to drive him to the altar, he strove to appear more serious and therefore less conspicuous. But he was distracted by his new teacher, Elisha, who was the pastor's nephew and who had but lately arrived from Georgia. He was not much older than John, only seventeen, and he was already saved and was a preacher. John stared at Elisha all during the lesson, admiring the timbre of Elisha's voice, much deeper and manlier than his own, admiring the leanness, and grace, and strength, and darkness of Elisha in his Sunday suit, wondering if he would ever be holy as Elisha was holy. But he did not follow the lesson, and when, sometimes, Elisha paused to ask John a question, John was ashamed and confused, feeling the palms of his hands become wet and his heart pound like a hammer. Elisha would smile and reprimand him gently, and the lesson would go on.

Roy never knew his Sunday school lesson either, but it was different with Roy—no one really expected of Roy what was expected of John. Everyone was always praying that the Lord would change Roy's heart, but it was John who was expected to be good, to be a good example.

When Sunday school service ended there was a short pause before morning service began. In this pause, if it was good weather, the old folks might step outside a moment to talk among themselves. The sisters would almost always be dressed in white from crown to toe. The small children, on this day, in this place, and oppressed by their elders, tried hard to play without seeming to be disrespectful of God's house. But sometimes, nervous or perverse, they shouted, or threw hymn-books, or began to cry, putting their parents, men or women of God, under the necessity of proving—by harsh means or tender—who, in a sanctified household, ruled. The older children, like John or Roy, might wander down the avenue, but not too far. Their father never let John and Roy out of his sight, for Roy had often disappeared between Sunday school and morning service and had not come back all day.

The Sunday morning service began when Brother Elisha sat down at the piano and raised a song. This moment and this music had been with John, so it seemed, since he had first drawn breath. It seemed that there had never been a time when he had not known this moment of waiting while the packed church paused—the sisters in white, heads raised, the brothers in blue, heads back; the white caps of the women seeming to glow in the charged air like crowns, the kinky, gleaming heads of the men seeming to be lifted up—and the rustling and the whispering ceased and the children were quiet; perhaps someone coughed, or the sound of a car horn, or a curse from the streets came in; then Elisha hit the keys, beginning at once to sing, and everybody joined him, clapping their hands, and rising, and beating the tambourines.

The song might be: *Down at the cross where my Saviour died!*

Or: *Jesus, I'll never forget how you set me free!*

Or: *Lord, hold my hand while I run this race!*

They sang with all the strength that was in them, and clapped their hands for joy. There had never been a time when John had not sat watching the saints rejoice with terror in his heart, and wonder. Their singing caused him to believe in the presence of the Lord, indeed, it was no longer a question of belief, because they made that presence real. He did not feel it himself, the joy they felt, yet he could not doubt that it was, for them, the very bread of life—could not doubt it, that is, until it was too late to doubt. Something happened to their faces and their voices, the rhythm of their bodies, and to the air they breathed; it was as though wherever they might be became the upper room, and the Holy Ghost were riding on the air. His father's face, always awful, became more awful now; his father's daily anger was transformed into prophetic wrath. His mother, her eyes raised to heaven, hands arched before her, moving, made real for John that patience, that endurance, that long suffering, which he had read of in the Bible and found so hard to imagine.

On Sunday mornings the women all seemed patient, all the men seemed mighty. While John watched, the Power struck someone, a man or woman; they cried out, a long, wordless, crying, and, arms outstretched like wings, they began the Shout. Someone moved a chair a little to give them room, the rhythm paused, the singing stopped, only the pounding feet and the clapping hands were heard; then another cry, another dancer; then the tambourines began again, and the voices rose again, and the music swept on again, like fire, or flood, or judgment. Then the church seemed to swell with the Power it held, and, like a planet rocking in space, the temple rocked with the Power of God. John watched, watched the faces, and the weightless bodies, and listened to the timeless cries. One day, so everyone said, this Power would possess him; he would sing and cry as they did now, and dance before his King. He watched young Ella Mae Washington, the seventeen-year-old granddaughter of Praying Mother Washington, as she began to dance. And then Elisha danced.

At one moment, head thrown back, eyes closed, sweat standing on his brow, he sat at the piano, singing and playing; and then, like a great, black cat in trouble in the jungle, he stiffened and trembled, and cried out, *Jesus, Jesus, Oh Lord Jesus!* He struck on the piano one last, wild note, and threw up his hands, palms upward, stretched wide apart. The tambourines raced to fill the vacuum left by his silent piano, and his cry drew answering cries. Then he was on his feet, turning, blind, his face congested, contorted with this rage, and the muscles leaping and swelling in his long, dark neck. It seemed that he could not breathe, that his body could not contain this passion, that he would be, before their eyes, dispersed into the waiting air. His hands, rigid to the very fingertips, moved outward and back against his hips, his sightless eyes looked upward, and he began to dance. Then his hands closed into fists, and his head snapped downward, his sweat loosening the grease that slicked down his hair; and the rhythm of all the others quickened to match Elisha's rhythm; his thighs moved terribly against the cloth of his suit, his heels beat on the floor, and his fists moved beside his body as though he were beating his own drum. And so, for a while, in the center of the dancers, head down, fists beating, on, on, unbearably, until it seemed the walls of the church would fall for very sound; and then, in a moment, with a cry, head up, arms high in the air, sweat pouring from his forehead, and all his body dancing as though it would never stop. Sometimes he did not stop until he fell—until he dropped like some animal felled by a hammer—moaning, on his face. And then a great moaning filled the church.

There was sin among them. One Sunday, when regular service was over, Father James had uncovered sin in the congregation of the righteous. He had uncovered Elisha and Ella Mae. They had been "walking disorderly"; they were in danger of straying from the truth. And as Father James spoke of the sin that he knew they had not committed yet, of the unripe fig plucked too early from the tree—to set the children's teeth on edge—John felt himself grow dizzy in his seat and could not look at Elisha where he stood, beside Ella Mae, before the altar. Elisha hung his head as Father James spoke, and the congregation murmured. And Ella Mae was not so beautiful now as she was when she was singing and testifying, but looked like a sullen, ordinary girl. Her full lips were loose and her eyes were black—with shame, or rage, or both. Her grandmother, who had raised her, sat watching quietly, with folded hands. She was one of the pillars of the church, a powerful evangelist and very widely known. She said nothing in Ella Mae's defense, for she must have felt, as the congregation felt, that Father James was only exercising his clear and painful duty; he was responsible, after all, for Elisha, as Praying Mother Washington was responsible for Ella Mae. It was not an easy thing, said Father James, to be the pastor of a flock. It might look easy to just sit up there in the pulpit night after night, year in, year out, but let them remember the awful responsibility placed on his shoulders by almighty God—let them remember that God would ask an accounting of him one day for every soul in his flock. Let them remember this when they thought he was hard, let them remember that the word was hard, that the way of holiness was a hard way. There was no room in God's army for the coward heart, no crown awaiting him who put mother, or father, sister, or brother, sweetheart, or friend above God's will. Let the church cry amen to this! And they cried: "Amen! Amen!"

The Lord had led him, said Father James, looking down on the boy and girl before him, to give them a public warning before it was too late. For he knew them to be sincere young people, dedicated to the service of the Lord—it was only that, since they were young, they did not know the pitfalls Satan laid for the unwary. He knew that sin was not in their minds—not yet; yet sin was in the flesh; and should they continue with their walking out alone together, their secrets and laughter, and touching of hands, they would surely sin a sin beyond all forgiveness. And John wondered what Elisha was thinking—Elisha, who was tall and handsome, who played basketball, and who had been saved at the age of eleven in the improbable fields down south. *Had* he sinned? Had he been tempted? And the girl beside him, whose white robes now seemed the merest, thinnest covering for the nakedness of breasts and insistent thighs—what was her face like when she was alone with Elisha, with no singing when they were not surrounded by the saints? He was afraid to think of it, yet he could think of nothing else; and the fever of which they stood accused began also to rage in him.

After this Sunday Elisha and Ella Mae no longer met each other each day after school, no longer spent Saturday afternoons wandering through Central Park, or lying on the beach. All that was over for them. If they came together again it would be in wedlock. They would have children and raise them in the church.

This was what was meant by a holy life, this was what the way of the cross demanded. It was somehow on that Sunday, a Sunday shortly before his birthday, that John first realized that this was the life awaiting him—realized it consciously, as something no longer far off, but imminent, coming closer day by day.

John's birthday fell on a Saturday in March, in 1935. He awoke on this birthday morning with the feeling that there was menace in the air around him—that something irrevocable had occurred in him. He stared at a yellow stain on the ceiling just above his head. Roy was still smothered in the bedclothes, and his breath came and went with a small, whistling sound. There was no other sound anywhere; no one in the house was up. The neighbors' radios were all silent, and his mother hadn't yet risen to fix his father's breakfast. John wondered at his panic, then wondered about the time; and then (while the yellow stain on the ceiling slowly transformed itself into a woman's nakedness) he remembered that it was his fourteenth birthday and that he had sinned.

His first thought, nevertheless, was: "Will anyone remember?" For it had happened, once or twice, that his birthday had passed entirely unnoticed, and no one had said "Happy Birthday, Johnny," or given him anything—not even his mother.

Roy stirred again and John pushed him away, listening to the silence. On other mornings he awoke hearing his mother singing in the kitchen, hearing his father in the bedroom behind him grunting and muttering prayers to himself as he put on his clothes; hearing, perhaps, the chatter of Sarah and the squalling of Ruth, and the radios, the clatter of pots and pans, and the voices of all the folk nearby. This morning not even the cry of a bed-spring disturbed the silence, and John seemed, therefore, to be listening to his own unspeaking doom. He could believe, almost, that he had awakened late on that great getting-up morning; that all the saved had been transformed in the twinkling of an eye, and had risen to meet Jesus in the clouds, and that he was left, with his sinful body, to be bound in hell a thousand years.

He had sinned. In spite of saints, his mother and his father, the warnings he had heard from his ealiest beginnings, he had sinned with his hands a sin that was hard to forgive. In the school lavatory, alone, thinking of the boys, older, bigger, braver, who made bets with each other as to whose urine could arch higher, he had watched in himself a transformation of which he would never dare to speak.

And the darkness of John's sin was like the darkness of the church on Saturday evenings; like the silence of the church while he was there alone, sweeping, and running water into the great bucket, and over-turning chairs, long before the saints arrived. It was like his thoughts as he moved about the tabernacle in which his life had been spent; the tabernacle that he hated, yet loved and feared. It was like Roy's curses, like the echoes these curses raised in John: he remembered Roy, on some rare Saturday when he had come to help John clean the church, cursing in the house of God, and making obscene gestures before the eyes of Jesus. It was like all this, and it was like the walls that witnessed and the placards on the walls which testified that the wages of sin was death. The darkness of his sin was in the hardheartedness with which he resisted God's power; in the scorn that was often his while he listened to the crying, breaking voices, and watched the black skin glisten while they lifted up their arms and fell on their faces before the Lord. For he had made his decision. He would not be like his father, or his father's fathers. He would have another life.

For John excelled in school, though not, like Elisha, in mathematics or basketball, and it was said that he had a Great Future. He might become a Great Leader of His People. John was not much interested in his people and still less in leading them anywhere, but the phrase so often repeated rose in his mind like a great brass gate, opening outward for him on a world where people did not live in the darkness of his father's house, did not pray to Jesus in the darkness of his father's church, where he would eat good food, and wear fine clothes, and go to the movies as often as he wished. In this world John, who was, his father said, ugly, who was always the smallest boy in his class, and who had no friends, became immediately beautiful, tall, and popular. People fell all over themselves to meet John Grimes. He was a poet, or a college president, or a movie star; he drank expensive whisky, and he smoked Lucky Strike cigarettes in the green package.

It was not only colored people who praised John, since they could not, John felt, in any case really know; but white people also said it, in fact had said it first and said it still. It was when John was five years old and in the first grade that he was first noticed; and since he was noticed by an eye altogether alien and impersonal, he began to perceive, in wild uneasiness, his individual existence.

They were learning the alphabet that day, and six children at a time were sent to the blackboard to write the letters they had memorized. Six had finished and were waiting for the teacher's judgment when the back door opened and the school principal, of whom everyone was terrified, entered the room. No one spoke or moved. In the silence the principal's voice said:

"Which child is that?"

She was pointing at the blackboard, at John's letters. The possibility of being distinguished by her notice did not enter John's mind, and so he simply stared at her. Then he realized, by the immobility of the other children and by the way they avoided looking at him, that it was he who was selected for punishment.

"Speak up, John," said the teacher, gently.

On the edge of tears, he mumbled his name and waited. The principal, a woman with white hair and an iron face, looked down at him.

"You're a very bright boy, John Grimes," she said. "Keep up the good work."

Then she walked out of the room.

That moment gave him, from that time on, if not a weapon at least a shield; he apprehended totally, without belief or understanding, that he had in himself a power that other people lacked; that he could use this to save himself, to raise himself; and that, perhaps, with this power he might one day win that love which he so longed for. This was not, in John, a faith subject to death or alteration, nor yet a hope subject to destruction; it was his identity, and part, therefore, of that wickedness for which his father beat him and to which he clung in order to withstand his father. His father's arm, rising and falling, might make him cry, and that voice might cause him to tremble; yet his father could never be entirely the victor, for John cherished something that his father could not reach. It was his hatred and his intelligence that he cherished, the one feeding the other. He lived for the day when his father would be dying and he, John, would curse him on his deathbed. And this was why, though he had been born in the faith and had been surrounded all his life by the saints and by their prayers and their rejoicing, and though the tabernacle in which they worshipped was more completely real to him than the several precarious homes in which he and his family had lived, John's heart was hardened against the Lord. His father was God's minister, the ambassador of the King of Heaven, and John could not bow before the throne of grace without first kneeling to his father. On his refusal to do this had his life depended, and John's secret heart had flourished in its wickedness until the day his sin first overtook him.

In the midst of all his wonderings he fell asleep again, and when he woke up this time and got out of his bed his father had gone to the factory, where he would work for half a day. Roy was sitting in the kitchen, quarreling with their mother. The baby, Ruth, sat in her high chair banging on the tray with an oatmeal-covered spoon. This meant that she was in a good mood; she would not spend the day howling, for reasons known only to herself, allowing no one but her mother to touch her. Sarah was quiet, not chattering today, or at any rate not yet, and stood near the stove, arms folded, staring at Roy with the flat black eyes, her father's eyes, that made her look so old.

Their mother, her head tied up in an old rag, sipped black coffee and watched Roy. The pale end-of-winter sunlight filled the room and yellowed all their faces; and John, drugged and morbid and wondering how it was that he had slept again and had been allowed to sleep so long, saw them for a moment like figures on a screen, an effect that the yellow light intensified. The room was narrow and dirty; nothing could alter its dimensions, no labor could ever make it clean. Dirt was in the walls and the floorboards, and triumphed beneath the sink where roaches spawned; was in the fine ridges of the pots and pans, scoured daily, burnt black on the bottom, hanging above the stove; was in the wall against which they hung, and revealed itself where the paint had cracked and leaned outward in stiff squares and fragments, the paper-thin underside webbed with black. Dirt was in every corner, angle, crevice of the monstrous stove, and lived behind it in delirious communion with the corrupted wall. Dirt was in the baseboard that John scrubbed every Saturday, and roughened the cupboard shelves that held the cracked and gleaming dishes. Under this dark weight the walls leaned, under it the ceiling, with a great crack like lightning in its center, sagged. The windows gleamed like beaten gold or silver, but now John saw, in the yellow light, how fine dust veiled their doubtful glory. Dirt crawled in the gray mop hung out of the windows to dry. John thought with shame and horror, yet in angry hardness of heart: *He who is filthy, let him be filthy still*. Then he looked at his mother, seeing, as though she were someone else, the dark, hard lines running downward from her eyes, and the deep, perpetual scowl in her forehead, and the downturned, tightened mouth, and the strong, thin, brown, and bony hands; and the phrase turned against him like a two-edged sword, for was it not he, in his false pride and his evil imagination, who was filthy? Through a storm of tears that did not reach his eyes, he stared at the yellow room; and the room shifted, the light of the sun darkened, and his mother's face changed. Her face became the face that he gave her in his dreams, the face that had been hers in a photograph he had seen once, long ago, a photograph taken before he was born. This face was young and proud, uplifted, with a smile that made the wide mouth beautiful and glowed in the enormous eyes. It was the face of a girl who knew that no evil could undo her, and who could laugh, surely, as his mother did not laugh now. Between the two faces there stretched a darkness and a mystery that John feared, and that sometimes caused him to hate her.

Now she saw him and she asked, breaking off her conversation with Roy: "You hungry, little sleepyhead?"

"Well! About time you was getting up," said Sarah.

He moved to the table and sat down, feeling the most bewildering panic of his life, a need to touch things, the table and chairs and the walls of the room, to make certain that the room existed and that he was in the room. He did not look at his mother, who stood up and went to the stove to heat his breakfast. But he asked, in order to say something to her, and to hear his own voice:

"What we got for breakfast?"

He realized, with some shame, that he was hoping that she had prepared a special breakfast for him on his birthday.

"What you *think* we got for breakfast?" Roy asked scornfully. "You got a special craving for something?"

John looked at him. Roy was not in a good mood.

"I ain't said nothing to you," he said.

"Oh, I *beg* your pardon," said Roy, in the shrill, little-girl tone he knew John hated.

"What's the *matter* with you today?" John asked, angry, and trying at the same time to lend his voice as husky a pitch as possible.

"Don't you let Roy bother you," said their mother. "He cross as two sticks this morning."

"Yeah," said John, "I reckon." He and Roy watched each other. Then his plate was put before him: hominy grits and a scrap of bacon. He wanted to cry, like a child: "But, Mama, it's my birthday!" He kept his eyes on his plate and began to eat.

"You can *talk* about your Daddy all you want to," said his mother, picking up her battle with Roy, "but *one* thing you can't say—you can't say he ain't always done his best to be a father to you and to see to it that you ain't never gone hungry."

"I been hungry plenty of times," Roy said, proud to be able to score this point against his mother.

"Wasn't *his* fault, then. Wasn't because he wasn't *trying* to feed you. That man shoveled snow in zero weather when he ought've been in bed just to put food in your belly."

"Wasn't just *my* belly," said Roy indignantly. "He got a belly, too, I *know* it's a *shame* the way that man eats. I sure ain't asked him to shovel no snow for me." But he dropped his eyes, suspecting a flaw in his argument. "I just don't want him beating on me all the time," he said at last. "I ain't no dog."

She sighed, and turned slightly away, looking out of the window. "Your Daddy beats you," she said, "because he loves you."

Roy laughed. "That ain't the kind of love I understand, old lady. What you reckon he'd do if he didn't love me?"

"He'd let you go right on," she flashed, "right on down to hell where it looks like you is just determined to go anyhow! Right on, Mister Man, till somebody puts a knife in you, or takes you off to jail!"

"Mama," John asked suddenly, "is Daddy a good man?"

He had not known that he was going to ask the question, and he watched in astonishment as her mouth tightened and her eyes grew dark.

"That ain't no kind of question," she said mildly. "You don't know no better man, do you?"

"Looks to me like he's a mighty good man," said Sarah. "He sure is praying all the time."

"You children is young," their mother said, ignoring Sarah and sitting down again at the table, "and you don't know how lucky you is to have a father what worries about you and tries to see to it that you come up right."

"Yeah," said Roy, "we don't know how lucky we *is* to have a father what don't want you to go to movies, and don't want you to play in the streets, and don't want you to have no friends, and he don't want this and he don't want that, and he don't want you to do *nothing*. We so *lucky* to have a father who just wants us to go to church and read the Bible and beller like a fool in front of the altar and stay home all nice and quiet, like a little mouse. Boy, we sure is lucky, all right. Don't know what I done to be so lucky."

She laughed. "You going to find out one day," she said, "you mark my words."

"Yeah," said Roy.

"But it'll be too late, then," she said. "It'll be ' too late when you come to be . . . sorry." Her voice had changed. For a moment her eyes met John's eyes, and John was frightened. He felt that her words, after the strange fashion God sometimes chose to speak to men, were dictated by Heaven and were meant for him. He was fourteen—was it too late? And this uneasiness was reinforced by the impression, which at that moment he realized had been his all along, that his mother was not saying everything she meant. What, he wondered, did she say to Aunt Florence when they talked together? Or to his father? What were her thoughts? Her face would never tell. And yet, looking down at him in a moment that was like a secret, passing sign, her face did tell him. Her thoughts were bitter.

"I don't care," Roy said, rising. "When *I* have children I ain't going to treat them like this." John watched his mother; she watched Roy. "I'm *sure* this ain't no way to be. Ain't got no right to have a houseful of children if you don't know how to treat them."

"You mighty grown up this morning," his mother said. "You be careful."

"And tell me something else," Roy said, suddenly leaning over his mother, "tell me how come he don't never let me talk to him like I talk to you? He's my father, ain't he? But he don't never listen to me— no, I all the time got to listen to him."

"Your father," she said, watching him, "knows best. You listen to your father, I guarantee you, you won't end up in no jail."

Roy sucked his teeth in fury. "I ain't looking to go to no *jail*. You think that's all that's in the world is jails and churches? You ought to know better than that, Ma."

"I know," she said, "there ain't no safety except you walk humble before the Lord. You going to find it out, too, one day. You go on, hard-head. You going to come to grief."

And suddenly Roy grinned. "But you be there, won't you, Ma— when I'm in trouble?"

"You don't know," she said, trying not to smile, "how long the Lord's going to let me stay with you."

Roy turned and did a dance step. "That's all right," he said. "I know the Lord ain't as hard as Daddy. Is he, boy?" he demanded of John, and struck him lightly on the forehead.

"Boy, let me eat my breakfast," John muttered—though his plate had long been empty, and he was pleased that Roy had turned to him.

"That sure is a crazy boy," ventured Sarah, soberly.

"Just listen," cried Roy, "to the little saint! Daddy ain't never going to have no trouble with her—*that* one, she was born holy. I bet the first words she ever said was: 'Thank you, Jesus.' Ain't that so, Ma?"

"You stop this foolishness," she said, laughing, "and go on about your work. Can't nobody play the fool with you all morning."

"Oh, is you got work for me to do this morning? Well, I declare," said Roy, "what you got for me to do?"

"I got the woodwork in the dining-room for you to do. And you going to do it, too, before you set foot out of *this* house."

"Now, why you want to talk like that, Ma? Is I said I wouldn't do it? You know I'm a right good worker when I got a mind. After I do it, can I go?"

"You go ahead and do it, and we'll see. You better do it right."

"I *always* do it right," said Roy. "You won't know your old wood-work when *I* get through."

"John," said his mother, "you sweep the front room for me like a good boy, and dust the furniture. I'm going to clean up in here."

"Yes'm," he said, and rose. She *had* forgotten about his birthday. He swore he would not mention it. He would not think about it any more.

To sweep the front room meant, principally, to sweep the heavy red and green and purple Oriental-style carpet that had once been that room's glory, but was now so faded that it was all one swimming color, and so frayed in places that it tangled with the broom. John hated sweeping this carpet, for dust rose, clogging his nose and sticking to his sweaty skin, and he felt that should he sweep it forever, the clouds of dust would not diminish, the rug would not be clean. It became in his imagination his impossible, lifelong task, his hard trial, like that of a man he had read about somewhere, whose curse it was to push a boulder up a steep hill, only to have the giant who guarded the hill roll the boulder down again—and so on, forever, throughout eternity; he was still out there, that hapless man, somewhere at the other end of the earth, pushing his boulder up the hill. He had John's entire sympathy, for the longest and hardest part of his Saturday mornings was his voyage with the broom across this endless rug; and, coming to the French doors that ended the livingroom and stopped the rug, he felt like an indescribably weary traveler who sees his home at last. Yet for each dustpan he so laboriously filled at the doorsill demons added to the rug twenty more; he saw in the expanse behind him the dust that he had raised settling again into the carpet; and he gritted his teeth, already on edge because of the dust that filled his mouth, and nearly wept to think that so much labor brought so little reward.

Nor was this the end of John's labor; for, having put away the broom and the dustpan, he took from the small bucket under the sink the dustrag and the furniture oil and a damp cloth, and returned to the living-room to excavate, as it were, from the dust that threatened to bury them, his family's goods and gear. Thinking bitterly of his birthday, he attacked the mirror with the cloth, watching his face appear as out of a cloud. With a shock he saw that his face had not changed, that the hand of Satan was as yet invisible. His father had always said that his face was the face of Satan—and was there not something—in the lift of the eyebrow, in the way his rough hair formed a "V" on his brow —that bore witness to his father's words? In the eye there was a light that was not the light of Heaven, and the mouth trembled, lustful and lewd, to drink deep of the wines of Hell. He stared at his face as though it were, as indeed it soon appeared to be, the face of a stranger, a stranger who held secrets that John could never know. And, having thought of it as the face of a stranger, he tried to look at it as a stranger might, and tried to discover what other people saw. But he saw only details: two great eyes, and a broad, low forehead, and the triangle of his nose, and his enormous mouth, and the barely perceptible cleft in his chin, which was, his father said, the mark of the devil's little finger. These details did not help him, for the principle of their unity was undiscoverable, and he could not tell what he most passionately desired to know: whether his face was ugly or not.

The Pocketbook Game

ALICE CHILDRESS

Marge . . . Day's work is an education! Well, I mean workin' in different homes you learn much more than if you was steady in one place. . . . I tell you, it really keeps your mind sharp tryin' to watch for what folks will put over on you.

What? . . . No, Marge, I do not want to help shell no beans, but I'd be more than glad to stay and have supper with you, and I'll wash the dishes after. Is that all right? . . .

Who put anything over on who? . . . Oh yes! It's like this. . . . I been working for Mrs. E . . . one day a week for several months and I notice that she has some peculiar ways. Well, there was only one thing that really bothered me and that was her pocketbook habit. . . . No, not those little novels. . . . I mean her purse—her handbag.

Marge, she's got a big old pocketbook with two long straps on it . . . and whenever I'd go there, she'd be propped up in a chair with her handbag double-wrapped tight around her wrist, and from room to room she'd roam with that purse hugged to her bosom . . . yes, girl! This happens every time! No, there's nobody there but me and her. . . . Marge, I couldn't say nothin' to her! It's her purse, ain't it? She can hold onto it if she wants to!

I held my peace for months, tryin' to figure out how I'd make my point. . . . Well, bless Bess! Today was the day! . . . Please, Marge, keep shellin' the beans so we can eat! I know you're listenin', but you listen with your ears, not your hands. . . . Well, anyway, I was almost ready to go home when she steps in the room hangin' onto her bag as usual and says, "Mildred, will you ask the super to come up and fix the kitchen faucet?" "Yes, Mrs. E . . ." I says, "as soon as I leave." "Oh, no," she says, "he may be gone by then. Please go now." "All right," I says, and out the door I went, still wearin' my Hoover apron.

I just went down the hall and stood there a few minutes . . . and then I rushed back to the door and knocked on it as hard and frantic as I could. She flung open the door sayin', "What's the matter? Did you see the super?" . . . "No," I says, graspin' hard for breath, "I was almost downstairs when I remembered . . . I left my pocketbook!"

With that I dashed in, grabbed my purse and then went down to get the super! Later, when I was leavin' she says real timid-like, "Mildred, I hope that you don't think I distrust you because . . ." I cut her off real quick. . . . "That's all right, Mrs. E . . . , I understand. 'Cause if I paid anybody as little as you pay me, I'd hold my pocketbook too!"

Marge, you fool . . . lookout! . . . You gonna drop the beans on the floor!

from **Harlem Gallery**

MELVIN B. TOLSON

THE SEA-TURTLE AND THE SHARK

Strange but true is the story
of the sea-turtle and the shark—
the instinctive drive of the weak to survive
in the oceanic dark.
Driven,
riven
by hunger
from abyss to shoal,
sometimes the shark swallows
the sea-turtle whole.

The sly reptilian marine
withdraws,
into the shell
of his undersea craft,
his leathery head and the rapacious claws
that can rip
a rhinoceros' hide
or strip
a crocodile to fare-thee-well;
now,
the sea-turtle begins the churning seesaws
of his descent into pelagic hell;
then . . . *then,*
with ravenous jaws
that can cut sheet steel scrap,
the sea-turtle gnaws
. . . and gnaws . . . and gnaws . . .
his way in a way that appalls—
his way to freedom,
beyond the vomiting dark,
beyond the stomach walls
of the shark.

A Poem for Black Hearts

LeROI JONES

For Malcolm's eyes, when they broke
the face of some dumb white man. For
Malcolm's hands raised to bless us
all black and strong in his image
of ourselves, for Malcolm's words
fire darts, the victor's tireless
thrusts, words hung above the world
change as it may, he said it, and
for this he was killed, for saying,
and feeling, and being change, all
collected hot in his heart, For Malcolm's

heart, raising us above our filthy cities,
for his stride, and his beat, and his address
to the grey monsters of the world, For Malcolm's
pleas for your dignity, black men, for your life,
black men, for the filling of your minds
with righteousness, For all of him dead and
gone and vanished from us, and all of him which
clings to our speech, black god of our time.
For all of him, and all of yourself, look up,
black man, quit shuttering and shuffling, look up,
black man, quit whining and stooping, for all of him,
For Great Malcolm, a prince of the earth, let nothing in us rest
until we avenge ourselves for his death, stupid animals
that killed him, let us never breathe a pure breath if
we fail, and white men call us faggots till the end of
the earth.

from **Soul on Ice**
ELDRIDGE CLEAVER

Malcolm X had a special meaning for black convicts. A former prisoner himself, he had risen from the lowest depths to great heights. For this reason he was a symbol of hope, a model for thousands of black convicts who found themselves trapped in the vicious PPP cycle: prison-parole-prison. One thing that the judges, policemen, and administrators of prisons seem never to have understood, and for which they certainly do not make any allowances, is that Negro convicts, basically, rather than see themselves as criminals and perpetrators of misdeeds, look upon themselves as prisoners of war, the victims of a vicious, dog-eat-dog social system that is so heinous as to cancel out their own malefactions: in the jungle there is no right or wrong.

Rather than owing and paying a debt to society, Negro prisoners feel that they are being abused, that their imprisonment is simply another form of the oppression which they have known all their lives. Negro inmates feel that they are being robbed, that it is "society" that owes them, that should be paying them a debt.

America's penology does not take this into account. Malcolm X did, and black convicts know that the ascension to power of Malcolm X or a man like him would eventually have revolutionized penology in

America. Malcolm delivered a merciless and damning indictment of prevailing penology. It is only a matter of time until the question of the prisoner's debt to society versus society's debt to the prisoner is injected forcefully into national and state politics, into the civil and human rights struggle, and into the consciousness of the body politic. It is an explosive issue which goes to the very root of America's system of justice, the structure of criminal law, the prevailing beliefs and attitudes toward the convicted felon. While it is easier to make out a case for black convicts, the same principles apply to white and Mexican-American convicts as well. They too are victimized, albeit a little more subtly, by "society." When black convicts start demanding a new dispensation and definition of justice, naturally the white and Mexican-American convicts will demand equality of treatment. Malcolm X was a focus for these aspirations.

The Black Muslim movement was destroyed the moment Elijah cracked the whip over Malcolm's head, because it was not the Black Muslim movement itself that was so irresistibly appealing to the true believers. It was the awakening into self-consciousness of twenty million Negroes which was so compelling. Malcolm X articulated their aspirations better than any other man of our time. When he spoke under the banner of Elijah Muhammad he was irresistible. When he spoke under his own banner he was still irresistible. If he had become a Quaker, a Catholic, or a Seventh-Day Adventist, or a Sammy Davis-style Jew, and if he had continued to give voice to the mute ambitions in the black man's soul, his message would still have been triumphant: because what was great was not Malcolm X but the truth he uttered.

The whole truth which Malcolm uttered had vanquished the whole passel of so-called Negro leaders and spokesmen who trifle and compromise with the truth in order to curry favor with the white power structure. He was stopped in the only way such a man can be stopped, in the same way that the enemies of the Congolese people had to stop Lumumba, by the same method that exploiters, tyrants, and parasitical oppressors have always crushed the legitimate strivings of people for freedom, justice, and equality—by murder, assassination, and mad-dog butchery.

What provoked the assassins to murder? Did it bother them that Malcolm was elevating our struggle into the international arena through his campaign to carry it before the United Nations? Well, by murdering him they only hastened the process, because we certainly are going to take our cause before a sympathetic world. Did it bother the assassins that Malcolm denounced the racist strait-jacket demonology of Elijah Muhammad? Well, we certainly do denounce it and will continue to do so. Did it bother the assassins that Malcolm taught us to defend ourselves? We shall not remain a defenseless prey to the murderer, to the sniper and the bomber. Insofar as Malcolm spoke the truth, the truth will triumph and prevail and his name shall live; and insofar as those who opposed him lied, to that extent will their names become curses. Because "truth crushed to earth shall rise again."

So now Malcolm is no more. The bootlickers, Uncle Toms, lackeys, and stooges of the white power structure have done their best to denigrate Malcolm, to root him out of his people's heart, to tarnish his memory. But their million-worded lies fall on deaf ears. As Ossie Davis so eloquently expressed it in his immortal eulogy of Malcolm:

> If you knew him you would know why we must honor him: Malcolm was our manhood, our living, black manhood! This was his meaning to his people. And, in honoring him, we honor the best in ourselves. . . . However much we may have differed with him—or with each other about him and his value as a man, let his going from us serve only to bring us together, now. Consigning these mortal remains to earth, the common mother of all, secure in the knowledge that what we place in the ground is no more now a man—but a seed—which, after the winter of our discontent will come forth again to meet us. And we will know him then for what he was and is—a Prince—our own black shining Prince! —who didn't hesitate to die, because he loved us so.

We shall have our manhood. We shall have it or the earth will be leveled by our attempts to gain it.

from The Me Nobody Knows
Children's Voices from the Ghetto

EDITED BY STEPHEN M. JOSEPH

BLACK

R. C., AGE 16

Black we die
Black you cry
Black I cry
Does White they cry
Cause Black we die?
Why they kill me?

What crime you and me?
Oh, yes! Now I see.
Black is our skin and
We want to be free.
Yes black we be
That they can see
Of you and me
But what of the soul
That yearns to be free?
This they do not see in
You or I
But this is that
This cannot die.

ARTHUR JACKSON, AGE 15

I have felt lonely, forgotten or even left
out, set apart from the rest of the world.
I never wanted out. If anything I wanted in.

WHAT AM I?
CLOROX, AGE 17

I HAVE NO MANHOOD—WHAT AM I?

YOU HAVE MADE MY WOMAN HEAD OF THE HOUSE—WHAT AM I?

YOU HAVE ORIENTED ME SO THAT I HATE AND DISTRUST
MY BROTHERS AND SISTERS—WHAT AM I?

YOU MISPROUNCE MY NAME AND SAY I HAVE NO
SELF-RESPECT—WHAT AM I?

YOU GIVE ME A DILAPIDATED EDUCATION SYSTEM AND
EXPECT ME TO COMPETE WITH YOU—WHAT AM I?

YOU SAY I HAVE NO DIGNITY AND THEN DEPRIVE ME
OF MY CULTURE—WHAT AM I?

YOU CALL ME A BOY, DIRTY LOWDOWN SLUT—WHAT AM I?

NOW I'M A VICTIM OF THE WELFARE SYSTEM—
WHAT AM I?

YOU TELL ME TO WAIT FOR CHANGE TO COME, BUT 400
YEARS

HAVE PASSED AND CHANGE AIN'T COME—WHAT AM I?

I AM ALL OF YOUR SINS

I AM THE SKELETON IN YOUR CLOSETS

I AM THE UNWANTED SONS AND DAUGHTERS IN-LAWS AND
REJECTED BABIES
I MAY BE YOUR DESTRUCTION, BUT ABOVE ALL I AM, AS
YOU SO CRUDELY PUT IT, YOUR NIGGER.

OCTAVIUS WASHINGTON, AGE 15

Yesterday I was in the store. And then a little white boy came in the store and order some milk and a nigger. All the people in the store look at him. I said to myself, he made a mistake. He meant Hero.

But then again he said "may I have a nigger." He was looking at me. No respect. No respect.

LOCKED IN THE OUTSIDES
NELLIE HOLLOWAY, AGE 16

Here we go again, man,
I'm locked in the outsides of the white man's world
I hear them saying "We can work it out."
Yeah, they can work it out.
By giving us welfare and fixing the slums.
Of course, baby, how else
Listen to them laughing and declaring
"Give the niggers and spics some money,"
"Give them a shack to live in
And they'll be alright."
But don't pull tight, kid, don't fool me.
You! Boss man, you may
Give me a house and some bread
And I'll pretend I'm your perfect brother.
(A long time ago, huh,
Old times and all that)
Now I want my share of the deal.
You live in a nice Park Avenue house,
While I slave to keep you there,
You wear pearls and diamonds
And I, costume jewelry.
Like they say, "A man got to walk someday."
So it might as well be now.
Mr. Charlie is scared in his Bostonian shoes
And GGG suit

Now he hears about NOW.
He hears, "Black Power, Baby."
Yea, Yea, Black Power, NOW.
Not tomorrow or Monday,
But now.
You there, Mr. Yessir!
It's time to remember,
It's time to see just who you are messing with.
Not your little pink lipped,
Black faced slave,
But a man and a people who are going to win.
Who are going to have power.
So listen, Mr. White Man, listen good.
You may give me some money
And a new house.
But a new house just don't make a new man.

WHO LOOKS
NELL MOORE, AGE 14

Beneath the sidewalks
    to tunnels—
    merging
    separating—
    searching out the
        Earthy blackness;
Behind the neons
    proving
    camoflage
    for purple-veined faces;
Past the faces—
    hiding
    selves.

chapter 8

SCHOOL EXPERIENCES
AND EDUCATIONAL ATTAINMENT

I would like you to know my son, Mark, who is now five years old.
Although he has not yet attended kindergarten, he can both read and
write, and can accurately identify colors and forms with an acuity
beyond his years. He collects American flags, and pictures and ceramics
of our national emblem, the eagle. He learned from somewhere on his
own initiative the Pledge of Allegiance, which he recites with deep
fervor. He only asked me the definitions of those difficult words:
indivisible, liberty, justice. My precious, precocious Mark is very proud
of his white, Anglo-Saxon heritage. But, he's black: a beautifully carved
and polished piece of black American earth.

> —Cynthia N. Shepard
> "The World through
> Mark's Eyes"

Education in this country has traditionally provided the children
of minority groups with a ladder to work their way up and out of
the ghetto. Today, however, there is a growing criticism of current
educational practices, particularly among Negroes, as they assess
the effectiveness of the schools to perform this function for their
youngsters. The black community is not united in its view of the
school system. The Negro's perspective is very much conditioned
by, and is an outgrowth of, his views on his relationship to the
majority culture. There are those who argue that the American
Negro is a distinctive cultural group and as such should establish
black enclaves to preserve his identity. The integrationist, on the
other hand, sees only a socioeconomic disparity and argues for
an educational system that will provide the Negro with equal opportunities to find his place in American society. Even within this
dichotomy there are disparities. There are those who accept the
basic structure of the schools with its conventional liberal goals,
and those who seek basic changes in the allocation of power because they see education and politics as inextricably entwined.

Rather than accept "band-aid" approaches for the problems
of the urban disadvantaged, some educators see the four-walled
school concept as anachronistic; they have sought to expand the
physical boundaries through the establishment of "street academies"

259

and "storefront schools." These new entries in the academic market-place are founded on the promise that a change in control can lead to a change in the quality of the education. For these critics berate the "establishment" as having failed to teach a large number of Negro children to read and write. Furthermore, the schools have been ineffectual, they add, in assisting these young-sters to develop a positive self-concept. By the third grade, many of those children view themselves as failures and social rejects.

Whether the answer is urban coalition, community control, decentralization, modification of the existing system, or a combina-tion of any of these, the teacher still remains the most significant factor in establishing high quality education for all children. The success of any organizational plan in education is dependent upon the human qualities of those who implement it. If the criticism is valid that we are teaching nothing more than facts and concepts to some children, and not even that much to others, then teacher-education institutions might do well to seek out and train those individuals who are sensitive, authentic, "feelingful" people. To assume that large numbers of children cannot learn, and that it is not the responsibility of the school as a professional institution to work toward this goal is indeed a "cop out." Even to assume that environment is all, and that until we can restructure the entire society from 'womb to tomb' by eliminating economic depriva-tion and ghetto-ized living, is to activate the self-fulfilling prophecy. William H. Boyer and Paul Walsh write:

> Lacking definitive scientific evidence about human potentiali-ties, social policy should be based on moral considerations. We should base our policy on the most generous and promising assump-tions about human nature rather than the most niggardly and pessimistic.[1]

One's assumptions about human nature have far-reaching im-plications for all "disadvantaged" children. Taking a broad view of who are the disadvantaged in our schools may bring attention to the middle-class child, who is not achieving at the top of his class and who feels "identity-less" and deprived. Another disad-vantaged youngster is the white child enrolled in a school with a racist philosophy, though this may not be overtly articulated. These children have a sheltered, parochial view of the world and, if the racism is subtle, these children receive an education in the

---

[1] William H. Boyer and Paul Walsh, "Are Children Born Unequal?", *Saturday Review*, Oct. 19, 1968, p. 78.

superiority-inferiority syndrome. At this moment in time some are at the top of the heap; but they must guard their position zealously. For this irrational yardstick based on racial considerations may soon be replaced by another equally arbitrary measure.

For education to be relevant to living in a multiracial society, the white child must learn that he is not automatically superior, and the black youngster must appreciate his uniqueness and derive strength from his own sense of self. Children do not readily learn this from being "taught at." They learn from what Mario D. Fantini and Gerald Weinstein in the book, *The Disadvantaged*, call "The Hidden Curriculum." John Dewey had named it previously. In other words, children learn about life through experiencing it in the classroom environment. They learn about life through observing the model, the teacher. They believe behavior and learn about life by participating in a climate that demonstrates, rather than talks about, human values.

Teacher education has always placed considerable emphasis on human values, though the context has not usually been the literary experience. The selections that follow focus on basic human responses and seek to help the reader to comprehend appreciatively the feelings of the Negro. The work of art has the potentiality for challenging one's understanding and humanity, first, as individuals, second, as teachers. The dignity of a Malcolm X or the vigor of a Richard Wright may assist the prospective teacher to grow in empathic competence as he identifies with the human condition.

The readings in this unit should not intimidate the student into feeling that unsympathetic teaching is characteristic of the educational scene. The excerpts are selective, for the purposes of identifying subthemes, and they often portray the teacher unfavorably. There have been many white teachers who have been unusually compassionate and effective with black children though the evidence of this in Negro literature is minimal. It is therefore incumbent upon the reader to recognize the purposes of the selections, and to determine for himself whether the literature presents an accurate rendering of the real world.

The need for change in education is apparent, and already many attempts are being made to translate promising proposals into practical activity. Prospective teachers of Negro children must do considerable soul-searching as they prepare for the profession. But teachers, as well as those who seek to reform the system, must recognize that attitudinal change on the part of individuals is a long-range proposition and cannot be legislated. A multidimensional approach must be considered, and the potentialities of "the hidden curriculum" appreciated. The literary way of knowing may provide one route toward educational reforms.

I.   The readings in this chapter were selected for their relevance to the unit topic, *School Experiences and Educational Attainment*. Some of the subthemes developed in the selections are:

1.   The role of the school and the school officials
2.   The responsibilities of the school
3.   The roots of alienation from the schools
4.   Attitudes toward learning
5.   "The hidden curriculum"
6.   The education of the streets

II.   The following readings are suggested as supplementary references for this thematic unit:

1.   E. R. Braithwaite, *To Sir, With Love* (Englewood Cliffs, N.J.: Prentice-Hall, Inc., 1959). (novel)
2.   Charles Chesnutt, "The Bouquet," in *The Wife of His Youth* (Ann Arbor: University of Michigan Press, 1968). (short story)
3.   Septima Poinsette Clark, *Echo in My Soul* (New York: E. P. Dutton & Co., Inc., 1962). (autobiography)
4.   Mike Thelwell, "Direct Action," *The Best Short Stories by Negro Writers*, Langston Hughes, ed. (Boston: Little, Brown & Company, 1967). (short story)
5.   Mary Elizabeth Vroman, "See How They Run," in *The Best Short Stories by Negro Writers*, Langston Hughes, ed. (Boston: Little, Brown & Company, 1967). (short story)

QUESTIONS FOR DISCUSSION

1.   How are the extremes of Negro attitudes represented in these selections?
2.   How do you account for the author's preoccupation with self-expression in *Black Boy?*
3.   What value systems seem to be operating in "The Revolt of the Evil Fairies?"
4.   How do you feel about Nancy Lee's view of America in "One Friday Morning?"
5.   In these readings, what role do teachers play in shaping the black youngster's perceptions of the white world?

from **Black Boy**

RICHARD WRIGHT

In the immediate neighborhood there were many school children who, in the afternoons, would stop and play en route to their homes; they would leave their books upon the sidewalk and I would thumb through the pages and question them about the baffling black print. When I had learned to recognize certain words, I told my mother that I wanted to learn to read and she encouraged me. Soon I was able to pick my way through most of the children's books I ran across. There grew in me a consuming curiosity about what was happening around me and, when my mother came home from a hard day's work, I would question her so relentlessly about what I had heard in the streets that she refused to talk to me.

One cold morning my mother awakened me and told me that, because there was no coal in the house, she was taking my brother to the job with her and that I must remain in bed until the coal she had ordered was delivered. For the payment of the coal, she left a note together with some money under the dresser scarf. I went back to sleep and was awakened by the ringing of the doorbell. I opened the door, let in the coal man, and gave him the money and the note. He brought in a few bushels of coal, then lingered, asking me if I were cold.

"Yes," I said, shivering.

He made a fire, then sat and smoked.

"How much change do I owe you?" he asked me.

"I don't know," I said.

"Shame on you," he said. "Don't you know how to count?"

"No, sir," I said.

"Listen and repeat after me," he said.

He counted to ten and I listened carefully; then he asked me to count alone and I did. He then made me memorize the words twenty, thirty, forty, etc., then told me to add one, two, three, and so on. In about an hour's time I had learned to count to a hundred and I was overjoyed. Long after the coal man had gone I danced up and down on the bed in my nightclothes, counting again and again to a hundred, afraid that if I did not keep repeating the numbers I would forget them. When my mother returned from her job that night I insisted that she stand still and listen while I counted to one hundred. She was dumfounded. After that she taught me to read, told me stories. On Sundays

I would read the newspapers with my mother guiding me and spelling out the words.

I soon made myself a nuisance by asking far too many questions of everybody. Every happening in the neighborhood, no matter how trivial, became my business. It was in this manner that I first stumbled upon the relations between whites and blacks, and what I learned frightened me. Though I had long known that there were people called "white" people, it had never meant anything to me emotionally. I had seen white men and women upon the streets a thousand times, but they had never looked particularly "white." To me they were merely people like other people, yet somehow strangely different because I had never come in close touch with any of them. For the most part I never thought of them; they simply existed somewhere in the background of the city as a whole. It might have been that my tardiness in learning to sense white people as "white" people came from the fact that many of my relatives were "white"-looking people. My grandmother, who was white as any "white" person, had never looked "white" to me. And when word circulated among the black people of the neighborhood that a "black" boy had been severely beaten by a "white" man, I felt that the "white" man had had a right to beat the "black" boy, for I naïvely assumed that the "white" man must have been the "black" boy's father. And did not all fathers, like my father, have the right to beat their children? A paternal right was the only right, to my understanding, that a man had to beat a child. But when my mother told me that the "white" man was not the father of the "black" boy, was no kin to him at all, I was puzzled.

"Then why did the 'white' man whip the 'black' boy?" I asked my mother.

"The 'white' man did not *whip* the 'black' boy," my mother told me. "He *beat* the 'black' boy."

"But why?"

"You're too young to understand."

"I'm not going to let anybody beat me," I said stoutly.

"Then stop running wild in the streets," my mother said.

I brooded for a long time about the seemingly causeless beating of the "black" boy by the "white" man and the more questions I asked the more bewildering it all became. Whenever I saw "white" people now I stared at them, wondering what they were really like.

I began school at Howard Institute at a later age than was usual; my mother had not been able to buy me the necessary clothes to make me presentable. The boys of the neighborhood took me to school the first day and when I reached the edge of the school grounds I became terrified, wanted to return home, wanted to put it off. But the boys simply took my hand and pulled me inside the building. I was frightened speechless and the other children had to identify me, tell the teacher my name and address. I sat listening to pupils recite, knowing and understanding what was being said and done, but utterly incapable of opening my mouth when called upon. The students around me seemed so sure of themselves that I despaired of ever being able to conduct myself as they did.

On the playground at noon I attached myself to a group of older boys and followed them about, listening to their talk, asking countless questions. During that noon hour I learned all the four-letter words describing physiological and sex functions, and discovered that I had known them before—had spoken them in the saloon—although I had not known what they meant. A tall black boy recited a long, funny piece of doggerel, replete with filth, describing the physiological relations between men and women, and I memorized it word for word after having heard it but once. Yet, despite my retentive memory, I found it impossible to recite when I went back into the classroom. The teacher called upon me and I rose, holding my book before my eyes, but I could make no words come from me. I could feel the presence of the strange boys and girls behind me, waiting to hear me read, and fear paralyzed me.

Yet when school let out that first day I ran joyously home with a brain burdened with racy and daring knowledge, but not a single idea from books. I gobbled the cold food that had been left covered on the table, seized a piece of soap and rushed into the streets, eager to display all I had learned in school since morning. I went from window to window and printed in huge soap-letters all my newly acquired four-letter words. I had written on nearly all the windows in the neighborhood when a woman stopped me and drove me home. That night the woman visited my mother and informed her of what I had done, taking her from window to window and pointing out my inspirational scribblings. My mother was horrified. She demanded that I tell her where I had learned the words and she refused to believe me when I told her that I had learned them at school. My mother got a pail of water and a towel and took me by the hand and led me to a smeared window.

"Now, scrub until that word's gone," she ordered.

Neighbors gathered, giggling, muttering words of pity and astonishment, asking my mother how on earth I could have learned so much so quickly. I scrubbed at the four-letter soap-words and grew blind with anger. I sobbed, begging my mother to let me go, telling her that I would never write such words again; but she did not relent until the last soap-word had been cleaned away. Never again did I write words like that; I kept them to myself.

The Boy Who Painted Christ Black

JOHN HENRIK CLARKE

He was the smartest boy in the Muskogee County School—for colored children. Everybody even remotely connected with the school knew this. The teacher always pronounced his name with profound gusto as she pointed him out as the ideal student. Once I heard her say: "If he were white he might, some day, become President." Only Aaron Crawford wasn't white; quite the contrary. His skin was so solid black that it glowed, reflecting an inner virtue that was strange, and beyond my comprehension.

In many ways he looked like something that was awkwardly put together. Both his nose and his lips seemed a trifle too large for his face. To say he was ugly would be unjust and to say he was handsome would be gross exaggeration. Truthfully, I could never make up my mind about him. Sometimes he looked like something out of a book of ancient history . . . looked as if he was left over from that magnificent era before the machine age came and marred the earth's natural beauty.

His great variety of talent often startled the teachers. This caused his classmates to look upon him with a mixed feeling of awe and envy.

Before Thanksgiving, he always drew turkeys and pumpkins on the blackboard. On George Washington's birthday, he drew large American flags surrounded by little hatchets. It was these small master-pieces that made him the most talked-about colored boy in Columbus, Georgia. The Negro principal of the Muskogee County School said he would some day be a great painter, like Henry O. Tanner.

For the teacher's birthday, which fell on a day about a week before commencement, Aaron Crawford painted the picture that caused an uproar, and a turning point at the Muskogee County School. The moment he entered the room that morning, all eyes fell on him. Besides his torn book holder, he was carrying a large-framed concern wrapped in old newspapers. As he went to his seat, the teacher's eyes followed his every motion, a curious wonderment mirrored in them conflicting with the half-smile that wreathed her face.

Aaron put his books down, then smiling broadly, advanced toward the teacher's desk. His alert eyes were so bright with joy that they were almost frightening. The children were leaning forward in their seats, staring greedily at him; a restless anticipation was rampant within every breast.

Already the teacher sensed that Aaron had a present for her. Still smiling, he placed it on her desk and began to help her unwrap it. As the last piece of paper fell from the large frame, the teacher jerked her hand away from it suddenly, her eyes flickering unbelievingly. Amidst the rigid tension, her heavy breathing was distinct and frightening. Temporarily, there was no other sound in the room.

Aaron stared questioningly at her and she moved her hand back to the present cautiously, as if it were a living thing with vicious characteristics. I am sure it was the one thing she least expected.

With a quick, involuntary movement I rose up from my desk. A series of submerged murmurs spread through the room, rising to a distinct monotone. The teacher turned toward the children, staring reproachfully. They did not move their eyes from the present that Aaron had brought her. . . . It was a large picture of Christ—painted black!

Aaron Crawford went back to his seat, a feeling of triumph reflecting in his every movement.

The teacher faced us. Her curious half-smile had blurred into a mild bewilderment. She searched the bright faces before her and started to smile again, occasionally stealing quick glances at the large picture propped on her desk, as though doing so were forbidden amusement.

"Aaron," she spoke at last, a slight tinge of uncertainty in her tone, "this is a most welcome present. Thanks. I will treasure it." She paused, then went on speaking, a trifle more coherent than before. "Looks like you are going to be quite an artist. . . . Suppose you come forward and tell the class how you came to paint this remarkable picture."

When he rose to speak, to explain about the picture, a hush fell tightly over the room, and the children gave him all of their attention . . . something they rarely did for the teacher. He did not speak at first; he just stood there in front of the room, toying absently with his hands, observing his audience carefully, like a great concert artist.

"It was like this," he said, placing full emphasis on every word. "You see, my uncle who lives in New York teaches classes in Negro history at the Y.M.C.A. When he visited us last year he was telling me about the many great black folks who have made history. He said black folks were once the most powerful people on earth. When I asked him about Christ, he said no one ever proved whether he was black or white. Somehow a feeling came over me that he was a black man, 'cause he was so kind and forgiving, kinder than I have ever seen white people be. So, when I painted his picture I couldn't help but paint it as I thought it was."

After this, the little artist sat down, smiling broadly, as if he had gained entrance to a great storehouse of knowledge that ordinary people could neither acquire nor comprehend. The teacher, knowing nothing else to do under prevailing circumstances, invited the children to rise from their seats and come forward so they could get a complete view of Aaron's unique piece of art.

When I came close to the picture, I noticed it was painted with the kind of paint you get in the five and ten cent stores. Its shape was blurred slightly, as if someone had jarred the frame before the paint had time to dry. The eyes of Christ were deep-set and sad, very much like those of Aaron's father, who was a deacon in the local Baptist Church. This picture of Christ looked much different from the one I saw hanging on the wall when I was in Sunday School. It looked more like a helpless Negro, pleading silently for mercy.

For the next few days, there was much talk about Aaron's picture.

The school term ended the following week and Aaron's picture, along with the best handwork done by the students that year, was on display in the assembly room. Naturally, Aaron's picture graced the place of honor.

There was no book work to be done on commencement day and joy was rampant among the children. The girls in their brightly colored dresses gave the school the delightful air of Spring awakening.

In the middle of the day all the children were gathered in the small assembly. On this day we were always favored with a visit from a man whom all the teachers spoke of with mixed esteem and fear. Professor Danual, they called him, and they always pronounced his name with reverence. He was supervisor of all the city schools, including those small and poorly equipped ones set aside for colored children.

The great man arrived almost at the end of our commencement exercises. On seeing him enter the hall, the children rose, bowed courteously, and sat down again, their eyes examining him as if he were a circus freak.

He was a tall white man with solid gray hair that made his lean face seem paler than it actually was. His eyes were the clearest blue I have ever seen. They were the only life-like things about him.

As he made his way to the front of the room the Negro principal, George Du Vaul, was walking ahead of him, cautiously preventing anything from getting in his way. As he passed me, I heard the teachers, frightened, sucking in their breath, felt the tension rightening.

A large chair was in the center of the rostrum. It had been daintily polished and the janitor had laboriously recushioned its bottom. The supervisor went straight to it without being guided, knowing that this pretty splendor was reserved for him.

Presently the Negro principal introduced the distinguished guest and he favored us with a short speech. It wasn't a very important speech. Almost at the end of it, I remember him saying something about he wouldn't be surprised if one of us boys grew up to be a great colored man, like Booker T. Washington.

After he sat down, the school chorus sang two spirituals and the girls in the fourth grade did an Indian folk dance. This brought the commencement program to an end.

After this the supervisor came down from the rostrum, his eyes tinged with curiosity, and began to view the array of handwork on display in front of the chapel.

Suddenly his face underwent a strange rejuvenation. His clear blue eyes flickered in astonishment. He was looking at Aaron Crawford's picture of Christ. Mechanically he moved his stooped form closer to the picture and stood gazing fixedly at it, curious and undecided, as though it were a dangerous animal that would rise any moment and spread destruction.

We waited tensely for his next movement. The silence was almost suffocating. At last he twisted himself around and began to search the grim faces before him. The fiery glitter of his eyes abated slightly as they rested on the Negro principal, protestingly.

"Who painted this sacrilegious nonsense?" he demanded sharply.

"I painted it, sir." These were Aaron's words, spoken hesitantly. He wetted his lips timidly and looked up at the supervisor, his eyes voicing a sad plea for understanding.

He spoke again, this time more coherently. "Th' principal said a colored person has jes as much right paintin' Jesus black as a white person have paintin' him white. And he says. . . ." At this point he halted abruptly, as if to search for his next words. A strong tinge of bewilderment dimmed the glow of his solid black face. He stammered out a few more words, then stopped again.

The supervisor strode a few steps toward him. At last color had swelled some of the lifelessness out of his lean face.

"Well, go on!" he said enragedly, ". . . I'm still listening."

Aaron moved his lips pathetically but no words passed them. His eyes wandered around the room, resting finally, with an air of hope, on the face of the Negro principal. After a moment, he jerked his face in another direction, regretfully, as if something he had said had betrayed an understanding between him and the principal.

Presently the principal stepped forward to defend the school's prize student.

"I encouraged the boy in painting that picture," he said firmly. "And it was with my permission that he brought the picture into this school. I don't think the boy is so far wrong in painting Christ black. The artists of all other races have painted whatsoever God they worship to resemble themselves. I see no reason why we should be immune from that privilege. After all, Christ was born in that part of the world that had always been predominantly populated by colored people. There is a strong possibility that he could have been a Negro."

But for the monotonous lull of heavy breathing, I would have sworn that his words had frozen everyone in the hall. I had never heard the little principal speak so boldly to anyone, black or white.

The supervisor swallowed dumfoundedly. His face was aglow in silent rage.

"Have you been teaching these children things like that?" he asked the Negro principal, sternly.

"I have been teaching them that their race has produced great kings and queens as well as slaves and serfs," the principal said. "The time is long overdue when we should let the world know that we erected and enjoyed the benefits of a splendid civilization long before the people of Europe had a written language."

The supervisor coughed. His eyes bulged menacingly as he spoke. "You are not being paid to teach such things in this school, and I am demanding your resignation for overstepping your limit as principal."

George Du Vaul did not speak. A strong quiver swept over his sullen face. He revolved himself slowly and walked out of the room towards his office.

The supervisor's eyes followed him until he was out of focus. Then he murmured under his breath: "There'll be a lot of fuss in this world if you start people thinking that Christ was a nigger."

Some of the teachers followed the principal out of the chapel, leaving the crestfallen children restless and in a quandary about what to do next. Finally we started back to our rooms. The supervisor was behind me. I heard him murmur to himself: "Damn, if niggers ain't getting smarter."

A few days later I heard that the principal had accepted a summer job as art instructor of a small high school somewhere in south Georgia and had gotten permission from Aaron's parents to take him along so he could continue to encourage him in his painting.

I was on my way home when I saw him leaving his office. He was carrying a large briefcase and some books tucked under his arm. He had already said good-bye to all the teachers. And strangely, he did not look brokenhearted. As he headed for the large front door, he readjusted his hornrimmed glasses, but did not look back. An air of triumph gave more dignity to his soldierly stride. He had the appearance of a man who had done a great thing, something greater than any ordinary man would do.

Aaron Crawford was waiting outside for him. They walked down the street together. He put his arm around Aaron's shoulder affectionately. He was talking sincerely to Aaron about something, and Aaron was listening, deeply earnest.

I watched them until they were so far down the street that their forms had begun to blur. Even from this distance, I could see they were still walking in brisk, dignified strides, like two people who had won some sort of victory.

The Revolt of the Evil Fairies

TED POSTON

The grand dramatic offering of the Booker T. Washington Colored Grammar School was the biggest event of the year in our social life in Hopkinsville, Kentucky. It was the one occasion on which they let us use the old Cooper Opera House, and even some of the white folks came out yearly to applaud our presentation. The first two rows of the orchestra were always reserved for our white friends, and our leading colored citizens sat right behind them—with an empty row intervening, of course.

Mr. Ed Smith, our local undertaker, invariably occupied a box to the left of the house and wore his cutaway coat and striped breeches. This distinctive garb was usually reserved for those rare occasions when he officiated at the funerals of our most prominent colored citizens. Mr. Thaddeus Long, our colored mailman, once rented a tuxedo and bought a box too. But nobody paid him much mind. We knew he was just showing off.

The title of our play never varied. It was always Prince Charming and the Sleeping Beauty, but no two presentations were ever the same. Miss H. Belle LaPrade, our sixth-grade teacher, rewrote the script every season, and it was never like anything you read in the storybooks.

Miss LaPrade called it "a modern morality play of conflict between the forces of good and evil." And the forces of evil, of course, always came off second best.

The Booker T. Washington Colored Grammar School was in a state of ferment from Christmas until February, for this was the period when parts were assigned. First there was the selection of the Good Fairies and the Evil Fairies. This was very important, because the Good Fairies wore white costumes and the Evil Fairies black. And strangely enough most of the Good Fairies usually turned out to be extremely light in complexion, with straight hair and white folks' features. On rare occasions a darkskinned girl might be lucky enough to be a Good Fairy, but not one with a speaking part.

There never was any doubt about Prince Charming and the Sleeping Beauty. They were always lightskinned. And though nobody ever discussed those things openly, it was an accepted fact that a lack of pigmentation was a decided advantage in the Prince Charming and Sleeping Beauty sweepstakes.

And therein lay my personal tragedy. I made the best grades in my class, I was the leading debater, and the scion of a respected family in the community. But I could never be Prince Charming, because I was black.

In fact, every year when they started casting our grand dramatic offering my family started pricing black cheesecloth at Franklin's Department Store. For they knew that I would be leading the forces of darkness and skulking back in the shadows—waiting to be vanquished in the third act. Mamma had experience with this sort of thing. All my brothers had finished Booker T. before me.

Not that I was alone in my disappointment. Many of my classmates felt it too. I probably just took it more to heart. Rat Joiner, for instance, could rationalize the situation. Rat was not only black; he lived on Billy Goat Hill. But Rat summed it up like this:

"If you black, you black."

I should have been able to regard the matter calmly too. For our grand dramatic offering was only a reflection of our daily community life in Hopkinsville. The yallers had the best of everything. They held most of the teaching jobs in Booker T. Washington Colored Grammar School. They were the Negro doctors, the lawyers, the insurance men. They even had a "Blue Vein Society," and if your dark skin obscured your throbbing pulse you were hardly a member of the elite.

Yet I was inconsolable the first time they turned me down for Prince Charming. That was the year they picked Roger Jackson. Roger was not only dumb; he stuttered. But he was light enough to pass for white, and that was apparently sufficient.

In all fairness, however, it must be admitted that Roger had other qualifications. His father owned the only colored saloon in town and was quite a power in local politics. In fact, Mr. Clinton Jackson had a lot to say about just who taught in the Booker T. Washington Colored Grammar School. So it was understandable that Roger should have been picked for Prince Charming.

My real heartbreak, however, came the year they picked Sarah Williams for Sleeping Beauty. I had been in love with Sarah since kindergarten. She had soft light hair, bluish-gray eyes, and a dimple which stayed in her left cheek whether she was smiling or not.

Of course Sarah never encouraged me much. She never answered any of my fervent love letters, and Rat was very scornful of my one-sided love affair. "As long as she don't call you a black baboon," he sneered, "you'll keep on hanging around."

After Sarah was chosen for Sleeping Beauty, I went out for the Prince Charming role with all my heart. If I had declaimed boldly in previous contests, I was matchless now. If I had bothered Mamma with rehearsals at home before, I pestered her to death this time. Yes, and I purloined my sister's can of Palmer's Skin Success.

I knew the Prince's role from start to finish, having played the Head Evil Fairy opposite it for two seasons. And Prince Charming was one character whose lines Miss LaPrade never varied much in her many versions. But although I never admitted it, even to myself, I knew I was doomed from the start. They gave the part to Leonardius Wright. Leonardius, of course, was yaller.

The teachers sensed my resentment. They were almost apologetic. They pointed out that I had been such a splendid Head Evil Fairy for two seasons that it would be a crime to let anybody else try the role. They reminded me that Mamma wouldn't have to buy any more cheesecloth because I could use my same old costume. They insisted that the Head Evil Fairy was even more important than Prince Charming because he was the one who cast the spell on Sleeping Beauty. So what could I do but accept?

I had never liked Leonardius Wright. He was a goody-goody, and even Mamma was always throwing him up to me. But, above all, he too was in love with Sarah Williams. And now he got a chance to kiss Sarah every day in rehearsing the awakening scene.

Well, the show must go on, even for little black boys. So I threw my soul into my part and made the Head Evil Fairy a character to be remembered. When I drew back from the couch of Sleeping Beauty and slunk away into the shadows at the approach of Prince Charming, my facial expression was indeed something to behold. When I was vanquished by the shining sword of Prince Charming in the last act, I was a little hammy perhaps—but terrific!

The attendance at our grand dramtic offering that year was the best in its history. Even the white folks overflowed the two rows reserved for them, and a few were forced to sit in the intervening one. This created a delicate situation, but everybody tactfully ignored it.

When the curtain went up on the last act, the audience was in fine fettle. Everything had gone well for me too—except for one spot in the second act. That was where Leonardius unexpectedly rapped me over the head with his sword as I slunk off into the shadows. That was not in the script, but Miss LaPrade quieted me down by saying it made a nice touch anyway. Rat said Leonardius did it on purpose.

The third act went on smoothly, though, until we came to the vanquishing scene. That was where I slunk from the shadows for the last time and challenged Prince Charming to mortal combat. The hero reached for his shining sword—a bit unsportsmanlike, I always thought, since Miss LaPrade consistently left the Head Evil Fairy unarmed—and then it happened!

Later I protested loudly—but in vain—that it was a case of self-defense. I pointed out that Leonardius had a mean look in his eye. I cited the impromptu rapping he had given my head in the second act. But nobody would listen. They just wouldn't believe that Leonardius really intended to brain me when he reached for his sword.

Anyway, he didn't succeed. For the minute I saw that evil gleam in his eye—or was it my own?—I cut loose with a right to the chin, and Prince Charming dropped his shining sword and staggered back. His astonishment lasted only a minute, though, for he lowered his head and came charging in, fists flailing. There was nothing yellow about Leonardius but his skin.

The audience thought the scrap was something new Miss LaPrade had written in. They might have kept on thinking so if Miss LaPrade hadn't been screaming so hysterically from the sidelines. And if Rat Joiner hadn't decided that this was as good a time as any to settle old scores. So he turned around and took a sock at the male Good Fairy nearest him.

When the curtain rang down, the forces of Good and Evil were locked in combat. And Sleeping Beauty was wide awake and streaking for the wings.

They rang the curtain back up fifteen minutes later, and we finished the play. I lay down and expired according to specifications but Prince Charming will probably remember my sneering corpse to his dying day. They wouldn't let me appear in the grand dramatic offering at all the next year. But I didn't care. I couldn't have been Prince Charming anyway.

One Friday Morning

LANGSTON HUGHES

The thrilling news did not come directly to Nancy Lee, but it came in little indirections that finally added themselves up to one tremendous fact: she had won the prize! But being a calm and quiet young lady, she did not say anything, although the whole high school buzzed with rumors, guesses, reportedly authentic announcements on the part of students who had no right to be making announcements at all—since no student really knew yet who had won this year's art scholarship.

But Nancy Lee's drawing was so good, her lines so sure, her colors so bright and harmonious, that certainly no other student in the senior art class at George Washington High was thought to have very much of a chance. Yet you never could tell. Last year nobody had expected Joe Williams to win the Artist Club scholarship with that funny modernistic water color he had done of the high-level bridge. In fact, it was hard to make out there was a bridge until you had looked at the picture a long time. Still, Joe Williams got the prize, was feted by the community's leading painters, club women, and society folks at a big banquet at the Park-Rose Hotel, and was now an award student at the Art School—the city's only art school.

Nancy Lee Johnson was a colored girl, a few years out of the South. But seldom did her high-school classmates think of her as colored. She was smart, pretty, and brown, and fitted in well with the life of the school. She stood high in scholarship, played a swell game of basketball, had taken part in the senior musical in a soft, velvety voice, and had never seemed to intrude or stand out, except in pleasant ways, so it was seldom ever mentioned—her color.

Nancy Lee sometimes forgot she was colored herself. She liked her classmates and her school. Particularly she liked her art teacher, Miss Dietrich, the tall red-haired woman who taught her law and order in doing things; and the beauty of working step by step until a job was done; a picture finished; a design created; or a block print carved out of nothing but an idea and a smooth square of linoleum, inked, proofs made, and finally put down on paper—clean, sharp, beautiful, individual, unlike any other in the world, thus making the paper have a meaning nobody else could give it except Nancy Lee. That was the wonderful thing about true creation. You made something nobody else on earth could make—but you.

Miss Dietrich was the kind of teacher who brought out the best in her students—but their own best, not anybody else's copied best. For anybody else's best, great though it might be, even Michelangelo's, wasn't enough to please Miss Dietrich, dealing with the creative impulses of young men and women living in an American city in the Middle West, and being American.

Nancy Lee was proud of being an American, a Negro American with blood out of Africa a long time ago, too many generations back to count. But her parents had taught her the beauties of Africa, its strength, its song, its mighty rivers, its early smelting of iron, its building of the pyramids, and its ancient and important civilizations. And Miss Dietrich had discovered for her the sharp and humorous lines of African sculpture, Benin, Congo, Makonde. Nancy Lee's father was a mail carrier, her mother a social worker in a city settlement house. Both parents had been to Negro colleges in the South. And her mother had gotten a further degree in social work from a Northern university. Her parents were, like most Americans, simple, ordinary people who had worked hard and steadily for their education. Now they were trying to make it easier for Nancy Lee to achieve learning than it had been for them. They would be very happy when they heard of the award to their daughter—yet Nancy did not tell them. To surprise them would be better. Besides, there had been a promise.

Casually, one day, Miss Dietrich asked Nancy Lee what color frame she thought would be best on her picture. That had been the first inkling.

"Blue," Nancy Lee said. Although the picture had been entered in the Artist Club contest a month ago, Nancy Lee did not hesitate in her choice of a color for the possible frame, since she could still see her picture clearly in her mind's eye—for that picture waiting for the blue frame had come out of her soul, her own life, and had bloomed into miraculous being with Miss Dietrich's help. It was, she knew, the best water color she had painted in her four years as a high-school art student, and she was glad she had made something Miss Dietrich liked well enough to permit her to enter in the contest before she graduated.

It was not a modernistic picture in the sense that you had to look at it a long time to understand what it meant. It was just a simple scene in the city park on a spring day, with the trees still leaflessly lacy against the sky, the new grass fresh and green, a flag on a tall pole in the center, children playing, and an old Negro woman sitting on a bench with her head turned. A lot for one picture, to be sure, but it was not there in heavy and final detail like a calendar. Its charm was that everything was light and airy, happy like spring, with a lot of blue sky, paper-white clouds, and air showing through. You could tell that the old Negro woman was looking at the flag, and that the flag was proud in the spring breeze, and that the breeze helped to make the children's dresses billow as they played.

Miss Dietrich had taught Nancy Lee how to paint spring, people, and a breeze on what was only a plain white piece of paper from the supply closet. But Miss Dietrich had not said make it like any other spring-people-breeze ever seen before. She let it remain Nancy Lee's own. That is how the old Negro woman happened to be there looking at the flag—for in her mind the flag, the spring, and the woman formed a kind of triangle holding a dream Nancy Lee wanted to express. White stars on a blue field, spring, children, evergrowing life, and an old woman. Would the judges at the Artist Club like it?

One wet, rainy April afternoon Miss O'Shay, the girls' vice-principal, sent for Nancy Lee to stop by her office as school closed. Pupils without umbrellas or raincoats were clustered in doorways, hoping to make it home between showers. Outside the skies were gray. Nancy Lee's thoughts were suddenly gray, too.

She did not think she had done anything wrong, yet that tight little knot came in her throat just the same as she approached Miss O'Shay's door. Perhaps she had banged her locker too often and too hard. Perhaps the note in French she had written to Sallie halfway across the study hall just for fun had never gotten to Sallie but into Miss O'Shay's hands instead. Or maybe she was failing in some subject and wouldn't be allowed to graduate. Chemistry! A pang went through the pit of her stomach.

She knocked on Miss O'Shay's door. That familiarly solid and competent voice said, "Come in."

Miss O'Shay had a way of making you feel welcome, even if you came to be expelled.

"Sit down, Nancy Lee Johnson," said Miss O'Shay. "I have something to tell you." Nancy Lee sat down. "But I must ask you to promise not to tell anyone yet."

"I won't, Miss O'Shay," Nancy Lee said, wondering what on earth the principal had to say to her.

"You are about to graduate," Miss O'Shay said. "And we shall miss you. You have been an excellent student, Nancy, and you will not be without honors on the senior list, as I am sure you know."

At that point there was a light knock on the door. Miss O'Shay called out, "Come in," and Miss Dietrich entered. "May I be a part of this, too?" she asked, tall and smiling.

"Of course," Miss O'Shay said. "I was just telling Nancy Lee what we thought of her. But I hadn't gotten around to giving her the news. Perhaps, Miss Dietrich, you'd like to tell her yourself."

Miss Dietrich was always direct. "Nancy Lee," she said, "your picture has won the Artist Club scholarship."

The slender brown girl's eyes widened, her heart jumped, then her throat tightened again. She tried to smile, but instead tears came to her eyes.

"Dear Nancy Lee," Miss O'Shay said, "we are so happy for you." The elderly white woman took her hand and shook it warmly while Miss Dietrich beamed with pride.

Nancy Lee must have danced all the way home. She never remembered quite how she got there through the rain. She hoped she had been dignified. But certainly she hadn't stopped to tell anybody her secret on the way. Raindrops, smiles, and tears mingled on her brown cheeks. She hoped her mother hadn't yet gotten home and that the house was empty. She wanted to have time to calm down and look natural before she had to see anyone. She didn't want to be bursting with excitement—having a secret to contain.

Miss O'Shay's calling her to the office had been in the nature of a preparation and a warning. The kind, elderly vice-principal said she did not believe in catching young ladies unawares, even with honors, so she wished her to know about the coming award. In making acceptance speeches she wanted her to be calm, prepared, not nervous, overcome, and frightened. So Nancy Lee was asked to think what she would say when the scholarship was conferred upon her a few days hence, both at the Friday morning high-school assembly hour, when the announcement would be made, and at the evening banquet of the Artist Club. Nancy Lee promised the vice-principal to think calmly about what she would say.

Miss Dietrich had then asked for some facts about her parents, her background, and her life, since such material would probably be desired for the papers. Nancy Lee had told her how, six years before, they had come up from the Deep South, her father having been successful in achieving a transfer from the one post office to another, a thing he had long sought in order to give Nancy Lee a chance to go to school in the North. Now they lived in a modest Negro neighborhood, went to see the best plays when they came to town, and had been saving to send Nancy Lee to art school, in case she were permitted to enter. But the scholarship would help a great deal, for they were not rich people.

"Now Mother can have a new coat next winter," Nancy Lee thought, "because my tuition will all be covered for the first year. And once in art school, there are other scholarships I can win."

Dreams began to dance through her head, plans and ambitions, beauties she would create for herself, her parents, and the Negro people —for Nancy Lee possessed a deep and reverent race pride. She could see the old woman in her picture (really her grandmother in the South) lifting her head to the bright stars on the flag in the distance. A Negro in America! Often hurt, discriminated against, sometimes lynched—but always there were the stars on the blue body of the flag. Was there any other flag in the world that had so many stars? Nancy Lee thought deeply, but she could remember none in all the encyclopedias or geographies she had ever looked into.

"Hitch your wagon to a star," Nancy Lee thought, dancing home in the rain. "Who were our flag-makers?"

Friday morning came, the morning when the world would know —her high-school world, the newspaper world, her mother and dad. Dad could not be there at the assembly to hear the announcement, nor see her prize picture displayed on the stage, nor listen to Nancy Lee's little speech of acceptance, but Mother would be able to come, although Mother was much puzzled as to why Nancy Lee was so insistent she be at school on that particular Friday morning.

When something is happening, something new and fine, something that will change your very life, it is hard to go to sleep at night for thinking about it, and hard to keep your heart from pounding, or a strange little knot of joy from gathering in your throat. Nancy Lee had taken her bath, brushed her hair until it glowed, and had gone to bed thinking about the next day, the big day, when before three thousand students she would be the one student honored, her painting the one painting to be acclaimed as the best of the year from all the art classes of the city. Her short speech of gratitude was ready. She went over it in her mind, not word for word (because she didn't want it to sound as if she had learned it by heart), but she let the thoughts flow simply and sincerely through her consciousness many times.

When the president of the Artist Club presented her with the medal and scroll of the scholarship award, she would say:

"Judges and members of the Artist Club. I want to thank you for this award that means so much to me personally and through me to my people, the colored people of this city, who, sometimes, are discouraged and bewildered, thinking that color and poverty are against them. I accept this award with gratitude and pride, not for myself alone, but for my race that believes in American opportunity and American fairness—and the bright stars in our flag. I thank Miss Dietrich and the teachers who made it possible for me to have the knowledge and training that lie behind this honor you have conferred upon my painting. When I came here from the South a few years ago, I was not sure how you would receive me. You received me well. You have given me a chance and helped me along the road I wanted to follow. I suppose the judges know that every week here at assembly the students of this school pledge allegiance to the flag. I shall try to be worthy of that pledge, and of the help and friendship and understanding of my fellow citizens of whatever race or creed, and of our American dream of 'Liberty and justice for all!' "

That would be her response before the students in the morning. How proud and happy the Negro pupils would be, perhaps almost as proud as they were of the one colored star on the football team. Her mother would probably cry with happiness. Thus Nancy Lee went to sleep dreaming of a wonderful tomorrow.

The bright sunlight of an April morning woke her. There was

breakfast with her parents—their half-amused and puzzled faces across the table, wondering what could be this secret that made her eyes so bright. The swift walk to school; the clock in the tower almost nine; hundreds of pupils streaming into the long, rambling old building that was the city's largest high school; the sudden quiet of the homeroom after the bell rang; then the teacher opening her record book to call the roll. But just before she began, she looked across the room until her eyes located Nancy Lee.

"Nancy," she said, "Miss O'Shay would like to see you in her office, please."

Nancy Lee rose and went out while the names were being called and the word *present* added its period to each name. Perhaps, Nancy Lee thought, the reporters from the papers had already come. Maybe they wanted to take her picture before assembly, which wasn't until ten o'clock. (Last year they had had the photograph of the winner of the award in the morning papers as soon as the announcement had been made.)

Nancy Lee knocked at Miss O'Shay's door.

"Come in."

The vice-principal stood at her desk. There was no one else in the room. It was very quiet.

"Sit down, Nancy Lee," she said. Miss O'Shay did not smile. There was a long pause. The seconds went by slowly. "I do not know how to tell you what I have to say," the elderly woman began, her eyes on the papers on her desk. "I am indignant and ashamed for myself and for this city." Then she lifted her eyes and looked at Nancy Lee in the neat blue dress, sitting there before her. "You are not to receive the scholarship this morning."

Outside in the hall the electric bells announcing the first period rang, loud and interminably long. Miss O'Shay remained silent. To the brown girl there in the chair, the room grew suddenly smaller, smaller, smaller, and there was no air. She could not speak.

Miss O'Shay said, "When the committee learned that you were colored, they changed their plans."

Still Nancy Lee said nothing, for there was no air to give breath to her lungs.

"Here is the letter from the committee, Nancy Lee." Miss O'Shay picked it up and read the final paragraph to her.

"It seems to us wiser to arbitrarily rotate the award among the various high schools of the city from now on. And especially in this case since the student chosen happens to be colored, a circumstance which unfortunately, had we known, might have prevented this embarrassment. But there have never been any Negro students in the local art school, and the presence of one there might create difficulties for all concerned. We have high regard for the quality of Nancy Lee Johnson's talent, but we do not feel it would be fair to honor it with the Artist Club award." Miss O'Shay paused. She put the letter down.

"Nancy Lee, I am very sorry to have to give you this message."

"But my speech," Nancy Lee said, "was about. . . ." The words struck in her throat. ". . . America. . . ."

Miss O'Shay had risen; she turned her back and stood looking out the window at the spring tulips in the school yard.

"I thought, since the award would be made at assembly right after our oath of allegiance," the words tumbled almost hysterically from Nancy Lee's throat now, "I would put part of the flag salute in my speech. You know, Miss O'Shay, that part about 'liberty and justice for all.'"

"I know," said Miss O'Shay, slowly facing the room again. "But America is only what we who believe in it make it. I am Irish. You may not know, Nancy Lee, but years ago we were called the dirty Irish, and mobs rioted against us in the big cities, and we were invited to go back where we came from. But we didn't go. And we didn't give up, because we believed in the American dream, and in our power to make that dream come true. Difficulties, yes. Mountains to climb, yes. Discouragements to face, yes. Democracy to make, yes. That is it, Nancy Lee! We still have in this world of ours democracy to *make*. You and I, Nancy Lee. But the premise and the base are here, the lines of the Declaration of Independence and the words of Lincoln are here, and the stars in our flag. Those who deny you this scholarship do not know the meaning of those stars, but it's up to us to make them know. As a teacher in the public schools of this city, I myself will go before the school board and ask them to remove from our system the offer of any prizes or awards denied to any student because of race or color."

Suddenly Miss O'Shay stopped speaking. Her clear, clear blue eyes looked into those of the girl before her. The woman's eyes were full of strength and courage. "Lift up your head, Nancy Lee, and smile at me."

Miss O'Shay stood against the open window with the green lawn and the tulips beyond, the sunlight tangled in her gray hair, and her voice an electric flow of strength to the hurt spirit of Nancy Lee. The Abolitionists who believed in freedom when there was slavery must have been like that. The first white teachers who went into the Deep South to teach the freed slaves must have been like that. All those who stand against ignorance, narrowness, hate, and mud on stars must be like that.

Nancy Lee lifted her head and smiled. The bell for assembly rang. She went through the long hall filled with students, toward the auditorium.

"There will be other awards," Nancy Lee thought. "There're schools in other cities. This won't keep me down. But when I'm a woman, I'll fight to see that these things don't happen to other girls as this has happened to me. And men and women like Miss O'Shay will help me."

She took her seat among the seniors. The doors of the auditorium closed. As the principal came onto the platform, the students rose and turned their eyes to the flag on the stage.

One hand went to the heart, the other outstretched toward the flag. Three thousand voices spoke. Among them was the voice of a dark girl whose cheeks were suddenly wet with tears, ". . . one nation indivisible, with liberty and justice for all."

"That is the land we must make," she thought.

from The Autobiography of Malcolm X

CHAPTER TWO
MASCOT

On June twenty-seventh of that year, nineteen thirty-seven, Joe Louis knocked out James J. Braddock to become the heavyweight champion of the world. And all the Negroes in Lansing, like Negroes everywhere, went wildly happy with the greatest celebration of race pride our generation had ever known. Every Negro boy old enough to walk wanted to be the next Brown Bomber. My brother Philbert, who had already become a pretty good boxer in school, was no exception. (I was trying to play basketball. I was gangling and tall, but I wasn't very good at it—too awkward.) In the fall of that year, Philbert entered the amateur bouts that were held in Lansing's Prudden Auditorium.

He did well, surviving the increasingly tough eliminations. I would go down to the gym and watch him train. It was very exciting. Perhaps without realizing it I became secretly envious; for one thing, I know I could not help seeing some of my younger brother Reginald's lifelong admiration for me getting siphoned off to Philbert.

People praised Philbert as a natural boxer. I figured that since we belonged to the same family, maybe I would become one, too. So I put myself in the ring. I think I was thirteen when I signed up for my first bout, but my height and raw-boned frame let me get away with claiming that I was sixteen, the minimum age—and my height of about 128 pounds got me classified as a bantamweight.

They matched me with a white boy, a novice like myself, named Bill Peterson. I'll never forget him. When our turn in the next amateur bouts came up, all of my brothers and sisters were there watching, along with just about everyone else I knew in town. They were there not so much because of me but because of Philbert, who had begun to build up a pretty good following, and they wanted to see how his brother would do.

I walked down the aisle between the people thronging the rows of seats, and climbed in the ring. Bill Peterson and I were introduced, and then the referee called us together and mumbled all of that stuff about fighting fair and breaking clean. Then the bell rang and we came out of our corners. I knew I was scared, but I didn't know, as Bill Peterson told me later on, that he was scared of me, too. He was so scared I was going to hurt him that he knocked me down fifty times if he did once.

He did such a job on my reputation in the Negro neighborhood that I practically went into hiding. A Negro just can't be whipped by somebody white and return with his head up to the neighborhood, especially in those days, when sports and, to a lesser extent show business, were the only fields open to Negroes, and when the ring was the only place a Negro could whip a white man and not be lynched. When I did show my face again, the Negroes I knew rode me so badly I knew I had to do something.

But the worst of my humiliations was my younger brother Reginald's attitude: he simply never mentioned the fight. It was the way he looked at me—and avoided looking at me. So I went back to the gym, and I trained—hard. I beat bags and skipped rope and grunted and sweated all over the place. And finally I signed up to fight Bill Peterson again. This time, the bouts were held in his hometown of Alma, Michigan.

The only thing better about the rematch was that hardly anyone I knew was there to see it; I was particularly grateful for Reginald's absence. The moment the bell rang, I saw a fist, then the canvas coming up, and ten seconds later the referee was saying *"Ten!"* over me. It was probably the shortest "fight" in history. I lay there listening to the full count, but I couldn't move. To tell the truth, I'm not sure I wanted to move.

That white boy was the beginning and the end of my fight career. A lot of times in these later years since I became a Muslim, I've thought back to that fight and reflected that it was Allah's work to stop me: I might have wound up punchy.

Not long after this, I came into a classroom with my hat on. I did it deliberately. The teacher, who was white, ordered me to keep the hat on, and to walk around and around the room until he told me to stop. "That way," he said, "everyone can see you. Meanwhile, we'll go on with class for those who are here to learn something."

I was still walking around when he got up from his desk and turned to the blackboard to write something on it. Everyone in the classroom was looking when, at this moment, I passed behind his desk, snatched up a thumbtack and deposited it in his chair. When he turned to sit back down, I was far from the scene of the crime, circling around the rear of the room. Then he hit the tack, and I heard him holler and caught a glimpse of him spraddling up as I disappeared through the door.

With my deportment record, I wasn't really shocked when the decision came that I had been expelled.

I guess I must have had some vague idea that if I didn't have to go to school, I'd be allowed to stay on with the Gohannas' and wander around town, or maybe get a job if I wanted one for pocket money. But I got rocked on my heels when a state man whom I hadn't seen before came and got me at the Gohannas' and took me down to court.

They told me I was going to a reform school. I was still thirteen years old.

But first I was going to the detention home. It was in Mason Michigan, about twelve miles from Lansing. The detention home was where all the "bad" boys and girls from Ingham County were held, on their way to reform school—waiting for their hearings.

The white state man was a Mr. Maynard Allen. He was nicer to me than most of the state Welfare people had been. He even had consoling words for the Gohannas' and Mrs. Adcock and Big Boy; all of them were crying. But I wasn't. With the few clothes I owned stuffed into a box, we rode in his car to Mason. He talked as he drove along, saying that my school marks showed that if I would just straighten up I could make something of myself. He said that reform school had the wrong reputation; he talked about what the word "reform" meant—to change and become better. He said the school was really a place where boys like me could have time to see their mistakes and start a new life and become somebody everyone would be proud of. And he told me that the lady in charge of the detention home, a Mrs. Swerlin, and her husband were very good people.

They were good people. Mrs. Swerlin was bigger than her husband, I remember, a big, buxom, robust, laughing woman, and Mr. Swerlin was thin, with black hair, and a black mustache and a red face, quiet and polite, even to me.

They liked me right away, too. Mrs. Swerlin showed me to my room, my own room—the first in my life. It was in one of those huge dormitory-like buildings where kids in detention were kept in those days—and still are in most places. I discovered next, with surprise, that I was allowed to eat with the Swerlins. It was the first time I'd eaten with white people—at least with grown white people—since the Seventh Day Adventist country meetings. It wasn't my own exclusive privilege, of course. Except for the very troublesome boys and girls at the detention home, who were kept locked up—those who had run away and been caught and brought back, or something like that—all of us ate with the Swerlins sitting at the head of the long tables.

They had a white cook-helper, I recall—Lucille Lathrop. (It amazes me how these names come back, from a time I haven't thought about for more than twenty years.) Lucille treated me well too. Her husband's name was Duane Lathrop. He worked somewhere else, but he stayed there at the detention home on the weekends with Lucille.

I noticed again how white people smelled different from us, and how their food tasted different, not seasoned like Negro cooking. I began to sweep and mop and dust around in the Swerlins' house, as I had done with Big Boy at the Gohannas'.

They all liked my attitude, and it was out of their liking for me that I soon became accepted by them—as a mascot, I know now. They would talk about anything and everything with me standing right there hearing them, the same way people would talk freely in front of a pet canary. They would even talk about me, or about "niggers," as though I wasn't there, as if I wouldn't understand what the word meant. A hundred times a day, they used the word "nigger." I suppose that in their own minds they meant no harm; in fact they probably meant well. It was the same with the cook, Lucille, and her husband, Duane. I remember one day when Mr. Swerlin, as nice as he was, came in from Lansing, where he had been through the Negro section, and said to Mrs. Swerlin right in front of me, "I just can't see how those niggers can be so happy and be so poor." He talked about how they lived in shacks, but had those big, shining cars out front.

And Mrs. Swerlin said, me standing right there. "Niggers are just that way. . . ." That scene always stayed with me.

It was the same with the other white people, most of them local politicians, when they would come visiting the Swerlins. One of their favorite parlor topics was "niggers." One of them was the judge who was in charge of me in Lansing. He was a close friend of the Swerlins. He would ask about me when he came, and they would call me in, and he would look me up and down, his expression approving, like he was examining a fine colt, or a pedigreed pup. I knew they must have told him how I acted and how I worked.

What I am trying to say is that it just never dawned upon them that I could understand, that I wasn't a pet, but a human being. They didn't give me credit for having the same sensitivity, intellect, and understanding that they would have been ready and willing to recognize in a white boy in my position. But it has historically been the case with white people, in their regard for black people, that even though we might be *with* them, we weren't considered *of* them. Even though they appeared to have opened the door, it was still closed. Thus they never did really see *me*.

This is the sort of kindly condescension which I try to clarify today, to those integration-hungry Negroes, about their "liberal" white friends, these so-called "good white people"—most of them anyway. I don't care how nice one is to you; the thing you must always remember is that almost never does he really see you as he sees himself, as he sees his own kind. He may stand with you through thin, but not thick; when the chips are down, you'll find that as fixed in him as his bone structure is his sometimes subconscious conviction that he's better than anybody black.

But I was no more than vaguely aware of anything like that in my detention-home years. I did my little chores around the house, and everything was fine. And each weekend, they didn't mind my catching a ride over to Lansing for the afternoon or evening. If I wasn't old enough, I sure was big enough by then, and nobody ever questioned my hanging out, even at night, in the streets of the Negro section.

I was growing up to be even bigger than Wilfred and Philbert, who had begun to meet girls at the school dances, and other places, and introduced me to a few. But the ones who seemed to like me, I didn't go for—and vice versa. I couldn't dance a lick, anyway, and I couldn't see squandering my few dimes on girls. So mostly I pleasured myself these Saturday nights by gawking around the Negro bars and restaurants. The jukeboxes were wailing Erskine Hawkins' "Tuxedo Junction," Slim and Slam's "Flatfoot Floogie," things like that. Sometimes, big bands from New York, out touring the one-night stands in the sticks, would play for big dances in Lansing. Everybody with legs would come out to see any performer who bore the magic name "New York." Which is how I first heard Lucky Thompson and Milt Jackson, both of whom I later got to know well in Harlem.

Many youngsters from the detention home, when their dates came up, went off to the reform school. But when mine came up—two or three times—it was always ignored. I saw new youngsters arrive and leave. I was glad and grateful. I knew it was Mrs. Swerlin's doing. I didn't want to leave.

She finally told me one day that I was going to be entered in Mason Junior High School. It was the only school in town. No ward of the detention home had ever gone to school there, at least while still a ward. So I entered their seventh grade. The only other Negroes there were some of the Lyons children, younger than I was, in the lower grades. The Lyons and I, as it happened, were the town's only Negroes. They were, as Negroes, very much respected. Mr. Lyons was a smart, hardworking man, and Mrs. Lyons was a very good woman. She and my mother, I had heard my mother say, were two of the four West Indians in that whole section of Michigan.

Some of the white kids at school, I found, were even friendlier than some of those in Lansing had been. Though some, including the teachers, called me "nigger," it was easy to see that they didn't mean any more harm by it than the Swerlins. As the "nigger" of my class, I was in fact extremely popular—I suppose partly because I was kind of a novelty. I was in demand, I had top priority. But I also benefited from the special prestige of having the seal of approval from that Very Important Woman about the town of Mason, Mrs. Swerlin. Nobody in Mason would have dreamed of getting on the wrong side of her. It became hard for me to get through a school day without someone after me to join this or head up that—the debating society, the Junior High basketball team, or some other extracurricular activity. I never turned them down.

And I hadn't been in the school long when Mrs. Swerlin, knowing I could use spending money of my own, got me a job after school washing the dishes in a local restaurant. My boss there was the father of a white classmate whom I spent a lot of time with. His family lived over the restaurant. It was fine working there. Every Friday night when I got paid, I'd feel at least ten feet tall. I forget how much I made, but it seemed like a lot. It was the first time I'd ever had any money to speak of, all of my own, in my whole life. As soon as I could afford it, I bought a green suit and some shoes, and at school I'd buy treats for the others in my class—at least as much as any of them did for me.

English and history were the subjects I liked most. My English teacher, I recall—a Mr. Ostrowski—was always giving advice about how to become something in life. The one thing I didn't like about history class was that the teacher, Mr. Williams, was a great one for "nigger" jokes. One day during my first week at school, I walked into the room and he started singing to the class, as a joke, "Way down yonder in the cotton field, some folks say that a nigger won't steal." Very funny. I liked history, but I never thereafter had much liking for Mr. Williams. Later, I remember, we came to the textbook section on Negro history. It was exactly one paragraph long. Mr. Williams laughed through it in practically a single breath, reading aloud how the Negroes had been slaves and then were freed, and how they were usually lazy and dumb and shiftless. He added, I remember, an anthropological footnote on his own, telling us between laughs how Negroes' feet were "so big that when they walk, they don't leave tracks, they leave a hole in the ground."

I'm sorry to say that the subject I most disliked was mathematics.

I have thought about it. I think the reason was that mathematics leaves no room for argument. If you made a mistake, that was all there was to it.

Basketball was a big thing in my life, though. I was on the team; we traveled to neighboring towns such as Howell and Charlotte, and wherever I showed my face the audiences in the gymnasiums "niggered" and "cooned" me to death. Or called me "Rastus." It didn't bother my teammates or my coach at all, and to tell the truth, it bothered me only vaguely. Mine was the same psychology that makes Negroes even today, though it bothers them down inside, keep letting the white man tell them how much "progress" they are making. They've heard it so much they've almost gotten brainwashed into believing it—or at least accepting it.

After the basketball games, there would usually be a school dance. Whenever our team walked into another school's gym for the dance, with me among them, I could feel the freeze. It would start to ease as they saw that I didn't try to mix, but stuck close to someone on our team, or kept to myself. I think I developed ways to do it without making it obvious. Even at our own school, I could sense it almost as a physical barrier, that despite all the beaming and smiling, the mascot wasn't supposed to dance with any of the white girls.

It was some kind of psychic message—not just from them, but also from within myself. I am proud to be able to say that much for myself, at least. I would just stand around and smile and talk and drink punch and eat sandwiches, and then I would make some excuse and get away early.

They were typical small-town school dances. Sometimes a little white band from Lansing would be brought in to play. But most often, the music was a phonograph set up on a table, with the volume turned up high, and the records scratchy, blaring things like Glenn Miller's "Moonlight Serenade"—his band was riding high then—or the Ink Spots, who were also very popular, singing "If I Didn't Care."

I used to spend a lot of time thinking about a peculiar thing. Many of these Mason white boys, like the ones at the Lansing school— especially if they knew me well, and if we hung out a lot together—would get me off in a corner somewhere and push me to proposition certain white girls, sometimes their own sisters. They would tell me that they'd already had the girls themselves—including their sisters—or that they were trying to and couldn't. Later on, I came to understand what was going on: If they could get the girls into the position of having broken the terrible taboo by slipping off with me somewhere, they would have that hammer over the girls' heads, to make them give in to them.

It seemed that the white boys felt that I, being a Negro, just naturally knew more about "romance," or sex, than they did—that I instinctively knew more about what to do and say with their own girls.

I never did tell anybody that I really went for some of the white girls, and some of them went for me, too. They let me know in many ways. But anytime we found ourselves in any close conversations or potentially intimate situations, always there would come up between us some kind of a wall. The girls I really wanted to have were a couple of Negro girls whom Wilfred or Philbert had introduced me to in Lansing. But with these girls, somehow, I lacked the nerve.

From what I heard and saw on the Saturday nights I spent hanging around in the Negro district I knew that race-mixing went on in Lansing. But strangely enough, this didn't have any kind of effect on me. Every Negro in Lansing, I guess, knew how white men would drive along certain streets in the black neighborhoods and pick up Negro streetwalkers who patrolled the area. And, on the other hand, there was a bridge that separated the Negro and Polish neighborhoods, where white women would drive or walk across and pick up Negro men, who would hang around in certain places close to the bridge, waiting for them. Lansing's white women, even in those days, were famous for chasing Negro men. I didn't yet appreciate how most whites accord to the Negro this reputation for prodigious sexual prowess. There in Lansing I never heard of any trouble about this mixing, from either side. I imagine that everyone simply took it for granted, as I did.

Anyway, from my experience as a little boy at the Lansing school, I had become fairly adept at avoiding the white-girl issue—at least for a couple of years yet.

Then, in the second semester of the seventh grade, I was elected class president. It surprised me even more than other people. But I can see now why the class might have done it. My grades were among the highest in the school. I was unique in my class, like a pink poodle. And I was proud; I'm not going to say I wasn't. In fact, by then, I didn't really have much feeling about being a Negro, because I was trying so hard, in every way I could, to be white. Which is why I am spending much of my life today telling the American black man that he's wasting his time straining to "integrate." I know from personal experience. I tried hard enough.

"Malcolm, we're just so *proud* of you!" Mrs. Swerlin exclaimed when she heard about my election. It was all over the restaurant where I worked. Even the state man, Maynard Allen, who still dropped by to see me once in a while, had a word of praise. He said he never saw anybody prove better exactly what "reform" meant. I really liked him— except for one thing: he now and then would drop something that hinted my mother had let us down somehow.

Fairly often, I would go and visit the Lyons, and they acted as happy as though I was one of their children. And it was the same warm feeling when I went into Lansing to visit my brothers and sisters, and the Gohannas'.

I remember one thing that marred this time for me: the movie "Gone with the Wind." When it played in Mason, I was the only Negro in the theater, and when Butterfly McQueen went into her act, I felt like crawling under the rug.

Every Saturday, just about, I would go into Lansing. I was going on fourteen, now. Wilfred and Hilda still lived out by themselves at the old family home. Hilda kept the house very clean. It was easier than my mother's plight, with eight of us always under foot or running around. Wilfred worked wherever he could, and he still read every book he could get his hands on. Philbert was getting a reputation as one of the better amateur fighters in this part of the state; everyone really expected that he was going to become a professional.

Reginald and I, after my fighting fiasco, had finally gotten back on good terms. It made me feel great to visit him and Wesley over at Mrs. Williams'. I'd offhandedly give them each a couple of dollars to just stick in their pockets, to have something to spend. And little Yvonne and Robert were doing okay, too, over at the home of the West Indian lady, Mrs. McGuire. I'd give them about a quarter apiece; it made me feel good to see how they were coming along.

None of us talked much about our mother. And we never mentioned our father. I guess none of us knew what to say. We didn't want anybody else to mention our mother either, I think. From time to time, though, we would all go over to Kalamazoo to visit her. Most often we older ones went singly, for it was something you didn't want to have to experience with anyone else present, even your brother or sister.

During this period, the visit to my mother that I most remember was toward the end of that seventh-grade year, when our father's grown daughter by his first marriage, Ella, came from Boston to visit us. Wilfred and Hilda had exchanged some letters with Ella, and I, at Hilda's suggestion, had written to her from the Swerlins'. We were all excited and happy when her letter told us that she was coming to Lansing.

I think the major impact of Ella's arrival, at least upon me, was that she was the first really proud black woman I had ever seen in my life. She was plainly proud of her very dark skin. This was unheard of among Negroes in those days, especially in Lansing.

I hadn't been sure just what day she would come. And then one afternoon I got home from school and there she was. She hugged me, stood me away, looked me up and down. A commanding woman, maybe even bigger than Mrs. Swerlin, Ella wasn't just black, but like our father, she was jet black. The way she sat, moved, talked, did everything, bespoke somebody who did and got exactly what she wanted. This was the woman my father had boasted of so often for having brought so many of their family out of Georgia to Boston. She owned some property, he would say, and she was "in society." She had come North with nothing, and she had worked and saved and had invested in property that she built up in value, and then she started sending money to Georgia for another sister, brother, cousin, niece or nephew to come north to Boston. All that I had heard was reflected in Ella's appearance and bearing. I had never been so impressed with anybody. She was in her second marriage; her first husband had been a doctor.

Ella asked all kinds of questions about how I was doing; she had already heard from Wilfred and Hilda about my election as class president. She asked especially about my grades, and I ran and got my report cards. I was then one of the three highest in the class. Ella praised me. I asked her about her brother, Earl, and her sister, Mary. She had the exciting news that Earl was a singer with a band in Boston. He was singing under the name of Jimmy Carleton. Mary was also doing well.

Ella told me about other relatives from that branch of the family. A number of them I'd never heard of; she had helped them up from Georgia. They, in their turn, had helped up others. "We Littles have to stick together," Ella said. It thrilled me to hear her say that, and even more, the way she said it. I had become a mascot; our branch of the family was split to pieces; I had just about forgotten about being a Little in any family sense. She said that different members of the family were working in good jobs, and some even had small businesses going. Most of them were homeowners.

When Ella suggested that all of us Littles in Lansing accompany her on a visit to our mother, we all were grateful. We all felt that if anyone could do anything that could help our mother, that might help her get well and come back, it would be Ella. Anyway, all of us, for the first time together, went with Ella to Kalamazoo.

Our mother was smiling when they brought her out. She was extremely surprised when she saw Ella. They made a striking contrast, the thin near-white woman and the big black one hugging each other. I don't remember much about the rest of the visit, except that there was a lot of talking, and Ella had everything in hand, and we left with all of us feeling better than we ever had about the circumstances. I know that for the first time I felt as though I had visited with someone who had some kind of physical illness that had just lingered on.

A few days later, after visiting the homes where each of us were staying, Ella left Lansing and returned to Boston. But before leaving she told me to write to her regularly. And she suggested that I might like to spend my summer holiday visiting her in Boston. I jumped at that chance.

That summer of 1940, in Lansing, I caught the Greyhound bus for Boston with my cardboard suitcase, and wearing my green suit. If someone had hung a sign, "HICK," around my neck, I couldn't have looked much more obvious. They didn't have the turnpikes then; the bus stopped at what seemed every corner and cowpatch. From my seat in—you guessed it—the back of the bus, I gawked out of the window at white man's America rolling past for what seemed a month, but must have been only a day and a half.

When we finally arrived, Ella met me at the terminal and took me home. The house was on Waumbeck Street in the Sugar Hill section of Roxbury, the Harlem of Boston. I met Ella's second husband, Frank, who was now a soldier; and her brother, Earl, the singer who called himself Jimmy Carleton; and Mary, who was very different from her older sister. It's funny how I seemed to think of Mary as Ella's sister, instead of her being, just as Ella is, my own half-sister. It's probably because Ella and I always were much closer as basic types; we're dominant people, and Mary had always been mild and quiet, almost shy.

Ella was busily involved in dozens of things. She belonged to I don't know how many different clubs; she was a leading light of local so-called "black society." I saw and met a hundred black people there whose big-city talk and ways left my mouth hanging open.

I couldn't have feigned indifference if I had tried to. People talked casually about Chicago, Detroit, New York. I didn't know the world contained as many Negroes as I saw thronging downtown Roxbury at night, especially on Saturdays. Neon lights, nightclubs, poolhalls, bars, the cars they drove! Restaurants made the streets smell—rich, greasy, down-home black cooking! Jukeboxes blared Erskine Hawkins, Duke Ellington, Cootie Williams, dozens of others. If somebody had told me then that some day I'd know them all personally, I'd have found it hard to believe. The biggest bands, like these, played at the Roseland State Ballroom, on Boston's Massachusetts Avenue—one night for Negroes, the next night for whites.

I saw for the first time occasional black-white couples strolling around arm in arm. And on Sundays, when Ella, Mary, or somebody took me to church, I saw churches for black people such as I had never seen. They were many times finer than the white church I had attended back in Mason, Michigan. There, the white people just sat and worshiped with words; but the Boston Negroes, like all other Negroes I had ever seen at church, threw their souls and bodies wholly into worship.

Two or three times, I wrote letters to Wilfred intended for everybody back in Lansing. I said I'd try to describe it when I got back.

But I found I couldn't.

My restlessness with Mason—and for the first time in my life a restlessness with being around white people—began as soon as I got back home and entered the eighth grade.

I continued to think constantly about all that I had seen in Boston, and about the way I had felt there. I know now that it was the sense of being a real part of a mass of my own kind, for the first time.

The white people—classmates, the Swerlins, the people at the restaurant where I worked—noticed the change. They said, "You're acting so strange. You don't seem like yourself, Malcolm. What's the matter?"

I kept close to the top of the class, though. The topmost scholastic standing, I remember, kept shifting between me, a girl named Audry Slaugh, and a boy named Jimmy Cotton.

It went on that way, as I became increasingly restless and disturbed, through the first semester. And then one day, just about when those of us who had passed were about to move up to 8-A, from which we would enter high school the next year, something happened which was to become the first major turning point of my life.

Somehow, I happened to be alone in the classroom with Mr. Ostrowski, my English teacher. He was a tall, rather reddish white man and he had a thick mustache. I had gotten some of my best marks under him, and he had always made me feel that he liked me. He was, as I have mentioned, a natural-born "advisor," about what you ought to read, to do, or think—about any and everything. We used to make unkind jokes about him: why was he teaching in Mason instead of somewhere else, getting for himself some of the "success in life" that he kept telling us how to get?

I know that he probably meant well in what he happened to advise me that day. I doubt that he meant any harm. It was just in his nature as an American white man. I was one of his top students, one of the school's top students—but all he could see for me was the kind of future "in your place" that almost all white people see for black people.

He told me, "Malcolm, you ought to be thinking about a career. Have you been giving it thought?"

The truth is, I hadn't. I never figured out why I told him, "Well, yes, sir, I've been thinking I'd like to be a lawyer." Lansing certainly had no Negro lawyers—or doctors either—in those days, to hold up an image I might have aspired to. All I really knew for certain was that a lawyer didn't wash dishes, as I was doing.

Mr. Ostrowski looked surprised, I remember, and leaned back in his chair and clasped his hands behind his head. He kind of half-smiled and said, "Malcolm, one of life's first needs is for us to be realistic. Don't misunderstand me, now. We all here like you, you know that. But you've got to be realistic about being a nigger. A lawyer—that's no realistic goal for a nigger. You need to think about something you *can* be. You're good with your hands—making things. Everybody admires your carpentry shop work. Why don't you plan on carpentry? People like you as a person—you'd get all kinds of work."

The more I thought afterwards about what he said, the more uneasy it made me. It just kept treading around in my mind.

What made it really begin to disturb me was Mr. Ostrowski's advice to others in my class—all of them white. Most of them had told him they were planning to become farmers. But those who wanted to strike out on their own, to try something new, he had encouraged. Some, mostly girls, wanted to be teachers. A few wanted other professions, such as one boy who wanted to become a county agent; another, a veterinarian; and one girl wanted to be a nurse. They all reported that Mr. Ostrowski had encouraged what they had wanted. Yet nearly none of them had earned marks equal to mine.

It was a surprising thing that I had never thought of it that way before, but I realized that whatever I wasn't, I *was* smarter than nearly all of those white kids. But apparently I was still not intelligent enough, in their eyes, to become whatever *I* wanted to be.

It was then that I began to change—inside.

I drew away from white people. I came to class, and I answered when called upon. It became a physical strain simply to sit in Mr. Ostrowski's class.

Where "nigger" had slipped off my back before, wherever I heard it now, I stopped and looked at whoever said it. And they looked surprised that I did.

I quit hearing so much "nigger" and "What's wrong?"—which was the way I wanted it. Nobody, including the teachers, could decide what had come over me. I knew I was being discussed.

In a few more weeks, it was that way, too, at the restaurant where I worked washing dishes, and at the Swerlins'.

One day soon after, Mrs. Swerlin called me into the living room, and there was the state man, Maynard Allen. I knew from their faces that something was about to happen. She told me that none of them could understand why—after I had done so well in school, and on my job, and living with them, and after everyone in Mason had come to like me—I had lately begun to make them all feel that I wasn't happy there anymore.

She said she felt there was no need for me to stay at the detention home any longer, and that arrangements had been made for me to go and live with the Lyons family, who liked me so much.

She stood up and put out her hand. "I guess I've asked you a hundred times, Malcolm—do you want to tell me what's wrong?"

I shook her hand, and said, "Nothing, Mrs. Swerlin." Then I went and got my things, and came back down. At the living room door I saw her wiping her eyes. I felt very bad. I thanked her and went out in front to Mr. Allen, who took me over to the Lyons'.

Mr. and Mrs. Lyons, and their children, during the two months I lived with them—while finishing eighth grade—also tried to get me to tell them what was wrong. But somehow I couldn't tell them, either.

I went every Saturday to see my brothers and sisters in Lansing, and almost every other day I wrote to Ella in Boston. Not saying why, I told Ella that I wanted to come there and live.

I don't know how she did it, but she arranged for official custody of me to be transferred from Michigan to Massachusetts, and the very week I finished the eighth grade, I again boarded the Greyhound bus for Boston.

I've thought about that time a lot since then. No physical move in my life has been more pivotal or profound in its repercussions.

If I had stayed on in Michigan, I would probably have married one of those Negro girls I knew and liked in Lansing. I might have become one of those state capitol building shoeshine boys, or a Lansing Country Club waiter, or gotten one of the other menial jobs which, in those days, among Lansing Negroes, would have been considered "successful"—or even become a carpenter.

Whatever I have done since then, I have driven myself to become a success at it. I've often thought that if Mr. Ostrowski had encouraged me to become a lawyer, I would today probably be among some city's professional black bourgeoisie, sipping cocktails and palming myself off as a community spokesman for and leader of the suffering black masses, while my primary concern would be to grab a few more crumbs from the groaning board of the two-faced whites with whom they're begging to "integrate."

All praise is due to Allah that I went to Boston when I did. If I hadn't, I'd probably still be a brainwashed black Christian.

❖   ❖   ❖

. . . The Deep South white press generally blacked me out. But they front-paged what I felt about Northern white and black Freedom Riders going *South* to "demonstrate." I called it "ridiculous"; their own Northern ghettos, right at home, had enough rats and roaches to kill to keep all of the Freedom Riders busy. I said that ultra-liberal New York had more integration problems than Mississippi. If the Northern Freedom Riders wanted more to do, they could work on the roots of such ghetto evils as the little children out in the streets at midnight, with apartment keys on strings around their necks to let themselves in, and their mothers and fathers drunk, drug addicts, thieves, prostitutes. Or the Northern Freedom Riders could light some fires under Northern city halls, unions, and major industries to give more jobs to Negroes to remove so many of them from the relief and welfare rolls, which created laziness, and which deteriorated the ghettos into steadily worse places for humans to live. It was all—it *is* all—the absolute truth; but what did I want to *say* it for? Snakes couldn't have turned on me faster than the liberal.

Yes, I will pull off that liberal's halo that he spends such efforts cultivating! The North's liberals have been for so long pointing accusing fingers at the South and getting away with it that they have fits when they are exposed as the world's worst hypocrites.

I believe my own life *mirrors* this hypocrisy. I know nothing about the South. I am a creation of the Northern white man and his hypocritical atttiude toward the Negro.

The white Southerner was always given his due by Mr. Muhammad. The white Southerner, you can say one thing—he is honest. He bares his teeth to the black man; he tells the black man, to his face, that Southern whites never will accept phony "integration." The Southern white goes further, to tell the black man that he means to fight him every inch of the way—against even the so-called "tokenism." The advantage of this is the Southern black man never had been under any illusion about the opposition he is dealing with.

You can say for many Southern white people that, individually, they have been paternalistically helpful to many individual Negroes. But the Northern white man, he grins with his teeth, and his mouth has always been full of tricks and lies of "equality" and "integration." When one day all over America, a black hand touched the white man's shoulder, and the white man turned, and there stood the Negro saying, "Me, too. . . ." why, that Northern liberal shrank from that black man with as much guilt and dread as any Southern white man.

Actually, America's most dangerous and threatening black man is the one who has been kept sealed up by the Northerner in the black ghettos—the Northern white power structure's system to keep talking democracy while keeping the black man out of sight somewhere, around the corner.

The word "integration" was invented by a Northern liberal. The word has no real meaning. I ask you: in the racial sense in which it's used so much today, whatever "integration" is supposed to mean, can it precisely be defined? The truth is that "integration" is an *image*, it's a foxy Northern liberal's smoke-screen that confuses the true wants of the American black man. Here in these fifty racist, and neo-racist states of North America, this word "integration" has millions of white people confused, and angry, believing wrongly that the black masses want to live mixed up with the white man. That is the case only with the relative handful of these "integration"-mad Negroes.

I'm talking about these "token-integrated" Negroes who flee from their poor, downtrodden black brothers—from their own self-hate, which is what they're really trying to escape. I'm talking about these Negroes you will see who can't get enough of nuzzling up to the white man. These "chosen few" Negroes are more white-minded, more anti-black, then even the white man is.

Human rights! Respect as *human beings*! That's what America's black masses want. That's the true problem. The black masses want not to be shrunk from as though they are plague-ridden. They want not to be walled up in slums, in the ghettos, like animals. They want to live in an open, free society where they can walk with their heads up, like men, and women!

Few white people realize that many black people today dislike and avoid spending any more time than they must around white people. This "integration" image, as it is popularly interpreted, has millions of vain, self-exalted white people convinced that black people want to sleep in bed with them—and that's a lie! Or you can't *tell* the average white man that the Negro man's prime desire isn't to have a white woman—another lie! Like a black brother recently observed to me, "Look, you ever smell one of them *wet*?"

The black masses prefer the company of their own kind. Why, even these fancy, bourgeois Negroes—when they get back home from the fancy "integrated" cocktail parties, what do they do but kick off their shoes and talk about those white liberals they just left as if the liberals were dogs. And the white liberals probably do the very same thing. I can't be sure about the whites, I am never around them in private—but the bourgeois Negroes know I'm not lying.

I'm telling it like it *is*! You *never* have to worry about me biting my tongue if something I know as truth is on my mind. Raw, naked truth exchanged between the black man and the white man is what a whole lot more of is needed in this country—to clear the air of the racial mirages, clichés, and lies that this country's very atmosphere has been filled with for four hundred years.

In many communities, especially small communities, white people have created a benevolent image of themselves as having had so much "good-will toward our Negroes," every time any "local Negro" begins suddenly letting the local whites know the truth—that the black people are sick of being hind-tit, second-class, disfranchised, that's when you hear, uttered so sadly, "Unfortunately now because of this, our whites of goodwill are starting to turn against the Negroes. . . . It's so regrettable . . . progress *was* being made . . . but now our communications between the races have broken down!"

What are they talking about? There never was any *communication.* Until after World War II, there wasn't a single community in the entire United States where the white man heard from any local Negro "leaders" the truth of what Negroes felt about the conditions that the white community imposed upon Negroes.

You need some proof? Well, then, why was it that when Negroes did start revolting across America, virtually all of white America was caught up in surprise and even shock? I would hate to be general of an army as badly informed as the American white man has been about the Negro in this country.

This is the situation which permitted Negro combustion to slowly build up to the revolution-point, without the white man realizing it. All over America, the local Negro "leader," in order to survive as a "leader," kept reassuring the local white man, in effect, "Everything's all right, everything's right in hand, boss!" When the "leader" wanted a little something for his people: "Er, boss, some of the people talking about we sure need a better school, boss." And if the local Negroes hadn't been causing any "trouble," the "benevolent" white man might nod and give them a school, or some jobs.

The white men belonging to the power structures in thousands of communities across America know that I'm right! They know that I am describing what has been the true pattern of "communications" between the "local whites of good-will" and the local Negroes. It has been a pattern created by domineering, ego-ridden whites. Its characteristic design permitted the white man to feel "noble" about throwing crumbs to the black man, instead of feeling guilty about the local community's system of cruelly exploiting Negroes.

But I want to tell you something. This pattern, this "system" that the white man created, of teaching Negroes to hide the truth from him behind a facade of grinning, "yessir-bossing," foot-shuffling and head-scratching—that system has done the American white man more harm than an invading army would do to him.

Why do I say this? Because all this has steadily helped this American white man to build up, deep in his psyche, absolute conviction that he *is* "superior." In how many, many communities have, thus, white men who didn't finish high school regarded condescendingly university-educated local Negro "leaders," principals of schools, teachers, doctors, other professionals?

The white man's system has been imposed upon non-white peoples all over the world. This is exactly the reason why wherever people who are anything but white live in this world today, the white man's governments are finding themselves in deeper and deeper trouble and peril.

Let's just face truth. Facts! Whether or not the white man of the world is able to face truth, and facts, about the true reasons for his troubles—that's what essentially will determine whether or not *he* will now survive.

Today we are seeing this revolution of the non-white peoples, who just a few years ago would have frozen in horror if the mighty white nations so much as lifted an eyebrow. What it is, simply, is that black and brown and red and yellow peoples have, after hundreds of years of exploitation and imposed "inferiority" and general misuse, become, finally, do-or-die sick and tired of the white man's heel on their necks.

How can the white American government figure on selling "democracy" and "brotherhood" to non-white peoples—if they read and hear every day what's going on right here in America, and see the better-than -a-thousand-words photographs of the American white man denying "democracy" and "brotherhood" even to America's native-born non-whites? The world's non-whites know how this Negro here has loved the American white man, and slaved for him, tended to him, nursed him. This Negro has jumped into uniform and gone off and died when this America was attacked by enemies both white and non-white. Such a faithful, loyal non-white as *this*—and *still* America bombs him, and sets dogs on him, and turns fire hoses on him, and jails him by the thousands, and beats him bloody, and inflicts upon him all manner of other crimes.

Of course these things, known and refreshed every day for the rest of the world's non-whites, are a vital factor in these burnings of ambassadors' limousines, these stonings, defilings, and wreckings of embassies and legations, these shouts of "White man, go home!" these attacks on White Christian missionaries, and these bombings and tearing down of flags.

Is it clear why I have said that the American white man's malignant superiority complex has done him more harm than an invading army? . . .

Bibliography

Abramson, Doris. "Negro Playwrights in America." *Columbia Forum*, 12:11–17, Spring 1969.

Adoff, Arnold, ed. *Black on Black: Commentaries by Negro Americans.* New York: Crowell-Collier and Macmillan, Inc., 1968.

Alexander, S. *Art and the Material.* New York: Longmans, Green & Co., Inc., 1925.

Attaway, William. *Blood on the Forge.* New York: Doubleday & Company, Inc., 1941.

Baker, Augusta. *Books about Negro Life for Children*, rev. ed. New York: The New York Public Library, 1961.

Baldwin, James. *Go Tell It on the Mountain.* New York: Dell Publishing Company, Inc., 1968.

Bone, Robert A. *The Negro Novel in America*, rev. ed. New Haven: Yale University Press, 1966.

Bontemps, Arna, ed. *American Negro Poetry.* New York: Hill & Wang, Inc.

Boyer, William H., and Walsh, Paul. "Are Children Born Unequal?" *Saturday Review*, October 19, 1968.

Braithwaite, M. H. *To Sir with Love.* Englewood Cliffs, N.J.: Prentice-Hall, Inc., 1959.

Brennan, Joseph Gerard. "Morals or Literature: The Abstractive Fallacy." *English Journal*, 58:226–229, February 1969.

Brooks, Gwendolyn. *Annie Allen.* New York: Harper & Row, Publishers, 1949.

———. *A Street in Bronzeville.* New York: Harper & Row, Publishers, 1945.

———. *In the Mecca.* New York: Harper & Row, Publishers, 1968.

Brown, John. *Slave Life in Georgia: A Narrative of the Life, Sufferings, and Escape of John Brown, A Fugitive Slave.* Ed. by L. A. Chamerovzow, 2d ed., London: W. M. Watts, 1855.

Brown, Claude. *Manchild in the Promised Land.* New York: Crowell-Collier and Macmillan, Inc., 1965.

Brown, Sterling, Arthur B. Davis, and Ulysses Lee, eds. *The Negro Caravan.* New York: Dryden Press, 1943.

Chapman, Abraham, ed. *Black Voices.* New York: New American Library of World Literature, Inc., 1968.

Chapman, Abraham, ed. *The Negro in American Literature and a Bibliography of Literature by and about Negro Americans.* Oshkosh: Wisconsin State University, 1966.

Chesnutt, Charles. *The Wife of His Youth.* Ann Arbor: University of Michigan Press, 1968, pp. 60–93.

Childress, Alice. "The Pocketbook Game." *The Best Short Stories by Negro Writers.* Ed. by Langston Hughes. Boston: Little, Brown & Company, 1967, pp. 205–206.

Clark, Kenneth B. *Dark Ghetto: Dilemmas of Social Power.* New York: Harper & Row, Publishers, 1965, p. 31.

Clark, Septima Poinsette, with LeGette Blythe. *Echo in My Soul.* New York: E. P. Dutton & Co., Inc., 1962.

Clarke, John Henrik, ed. *American Negro Short Stories.* New York: Hill & Wang, Inc., 1966.

Cleaver, Eldridge. *Soul on Ice.* New York: McGraw-Hill, Inc., 1968.

Crosby, Muriel, ed. *Reading Ladders for Human Relations.* 4th ed. Washington, D. C.: American Council on Education, 1963.

Crow, Lester D., Walter I. Murray, and Hugh H. Smythe, eds. *Educating the Culturally Disadvantaged Child: Principles and Programs.* New York: David McKay Company, Inc., 1966.

Cruse, Harold. *The Crisis of the Negro Intellectual.* New York: William Morrow & Company, Inc., 1967.

Cullen, Countee. *On These I Stand: An Anthology of the Best Poems of Countee Cullen.* New York: Harper & Row, Publishers, 1947.

————. "Yet Do I Marvel." *American Negro Poetry.* Ed. by Arna Bontemps. New York: Hill & Wang, Inc., 1968, p. 88.

Davis, Ossie. "On Malcolm X." *The Autobiography of Malcolm X.* New York: Grove Press, Inc., 1966.

Demby, William. *Bettlecreek.* New York: Holt, Rinehart and Winston, Inc., 1950.

Dodds, Barbara. *Negro Literature for High School Students.* Champaign: National Council of Teachers of English, 1968.

Douglass, Frederick. *Narrative of the Life of Frederick Douglass, An American Slave: Written by Himself.* Garden City: Doubleday & Company, Inc., 1963.

————. "What to the Slave is the Fourth of July?" *Black on Black: Commentaries by Negro Americans.* Ed. by Arnold Adoff. New York: Crowell-Collier and Macmillan, Inc., 1968, pp. 1–6.

DuBois, W. E. B. *The Souls of Black Folk.* Greenwich: Fawcett Publications, 1968.

Dunbar, Paul Laurence. *The Complete Poems of Paul Laurence Dunbar.* New York: Dodd, Mead & Company, Inc., 1965.

Early, Margaret J. "Stages of Growth in Literary Appreciation." *Teaching English in Today's High Schools: Selected Readings.* Ed. by Dwight Burton and John S. Simmons. New York: Holt, Rinehart and Winston, Inc., 1967, pp. 75–85.

Ellison, Ralph. *Invisible Man.* New York: New American Library of World Literature, Inc., 1947.

Emanuel, James A., and Theodore L. Gross, eds. *Dark Symphony: Negro Literature in America.* New York: The Free Press, 1968.

Fiske, Edward B. "Baldwin Accuses Christian Church of Betraying Negro." *New York Times,* July 8, 1968, pp. 1, 23.

Frazier, R. Franklin. *Black Bourgeoisie.* New York: The Free Press, 1957.

Gordone, Charles. "Yes, I Am a Black Playwright, But . . .," *New York Times,* Jan. 26, 1969, p. 11.

Greene, Maxine. "Against Invisibility: English for the Probing Black and White Young." *Negro American Literature Forum,* 2:39–45, Fall 1968.

Gloster, Hugh. *Negro Voices in American Fiction*. New York: Russell and Russell, 1965.

Hansberry, Lorraine. *A Raisin in the Sun*. New York: New American Library of World Literature, Inc., 1966.

Hass, Glenn, and Kimball Wiles, eds. *Readings in Curriculum*. Boston: Allyn and Bacon, Inc., 1965.

Heilman, Robert B. "Literature and Growing Up." *Teaching English in Today's High Schools: Selected Readings*. Ed. by Dwight Burton and John S. Simmons. New York: Holt, Rinehart and Winston, Inc., 1965, pp. 37–52.

Hill, Herbert, ed. *Anger, and Beyond: The Negro Writer in the United States*. New York: Harper & Row, Publishers, 1968.

Homans, George C. *The Human Group*. New York: Harcourt Brace Jovanovich, Inc., 1950, p. 5.

Hughes, Langston. *The Best of Simple*. New York: Hill & Wang, Inc., 1961.

Hughes, Langston, ed. *The Best Short Stories by Negro Writers, An Anthology from 1899 to the Present*. Boston: Little, Brown & Company, Inc., 1967.

———. *The Panther and The Lash*. New York: Alfred A. Knopf, 1967.

———. *Selected Poems by Langston Hughes*. New York: Alfred A. Knopf, 1967.

Hughes, Langston, and Arna Bontemps, eds. *The Poetry of the Negro, 1746–1949*. Garden City: Doubleday & Company, Inc., 1949.

Jackson, Miles M., Jr., ed. *A Bibliography of Negro History and Culture for Young Readers*. Pittsburgh: University of Pittsburgh Press, 1960.

Jersild, Arthur T. *When Teachers Face Themselves*. New York: Teachers College Press, Columbia University, 1955.

Johnson, James Weldon. *The Autobiography of an Ex-Colored Man*. New York: Sherman, French and Company, 1912.

———. *God's Trombones: Seven Negro Sermons in Verse*. New York: The Viking Press, Inc., 1968.

Jones, LeRoi, and Larry Neal, eds. *Black Fire: An Anthology of Afro-American Writing*. New York: William Morrow & Company, Inc., 1968.

———. *The Dutchman and the Slave*. New York: William Morrow & Company, Inc., 1964.

Joseph, Stephen M., ed. *The Me Nobody Knows: Children's Voices from the Ghetto*. New York: Avon Books, 1969.

Kamarck, Edward L. "Art or Social Protest." *Arts in Society*, 5:viii–ix, Fall–Winter, 1968.

Killens, John O. "The Black Writer and the Revolution." *Arts in Society*, 5:397–399, Fall–Winter, 1968.

Koblitz, Minnie W. *The Negro in Schoolroom Literature: Resource Materials for the Teacher of Kindergarten through Sixth Grade*. New York: Center for Urban Education, 1966.

Lester, Julius. *To Be a Slave*. New York: The Dial Press, Inc., 1968.

Littlejohn, David. *Black on White: A Critical Survey of Writing by American Negroes*. New York: Grossman Publishers, 1966.

Locke, Alain. *The New Negro: An Interpretation*. New York: Albert & Charles Boni, Inc., 1925.

Malcolm X, with assistance of Alex Haley. *The Autobiography of Malcolm X*. New York: Grove Press, Inc., 1966.

Margolies, Edward. *Native Sons: A Critical Study of Twentieth-Century Negro American Authors*. Philadelphia: J. B. Lippincott Company, 1969.

Mayer, Milton. "There Used To Be Negroes." *The Gadfly*. Chicago: The Great Books Foundation, Fall, 1969.

McKay, Claude. *Selected Poems of Claude McKay*. New York: Bookman Associates, 1953.

Meltzer, Milton, ed. *In Their Own Words: A History of the American Negro 1619–1865*. 3 vol. New York: Thomas Y. Crowell Company, 1963.

Miller, Elizabeth, comp. *The Negro in America: A Bibliography*. Cambridge: Harvard University Press, 1966.

Moody, Anne. *Coming of Age in Mississippi: An Autobiography*. New York: The Dial Press, Inc., 1968.

O'Connell, Mary Sheila. "Images of Canadians in Children's Realistic Fiction." Doctor of Education Project Report. New York: Teachers College, Columbia University, 1966. 407 pp. typewritten.

Parker, Elizabeth Ann. "A Manual for Elementary-School Teachers on Teaching Prose Fiction Abilities." Doctor of Education Project Report. New York: Teachers College, Columbia University, 1966. 257 pp. typewritten.

Pool, Rosey E., ed. *Beyond the Blues: New Poems by American Negroes*. London: Headley Brothers Ltd., 1962.

Redding, Saunders. *On Being Negro in America*. Indianapolis: Bobbs-Merrill Company, Inc., 1951.

————. *To Make a Poet Black*. Chapel Hill: University of North Carolina Press, 1939.

Rollins, Charlemae, ed. *We Build Together: A Reader's Guide to Negro Life and Literature for Elementary and High School Use*. Champaign: National Council of Teachers of English, 1967.

Rowan, Carl T. *South of Freedom*. New York: Alfred A. Knopf, 1952.

Ryan, Margaret. *Teaching the Novel in Paperback*. New York: Crowell-Collier and Macmillan, Inc., 1963.

Shepard, Cynthia N. "The World through Mark's Eyes." *Saturday Review*, 52:61, January 18, 1969.

Sterling, Dorothy. "The Soul of Learning." *The English Journal*, 57:166–180, February, 1968.

Tolson, M. B. *Harlem Gallery*. New York: Twayne Publishers, Inc., 1965.

Toomer, Jean. *Cane*. New York: Liveright, Publishers, 1951.

Vassa, Gustavus. "The Interesting Narrative of the Life of Olaudah Equiano, or Gustavus Vassa the African, Written by Himself, 1791." *In Their Own Words: A History of the American Negro*. Ed. by Milton Meltzer. New York: Thomas Y. Crowell Company, 1964, pp. 3–10.

Walker, David. "Walker's Appeal, in Four Articles: Together with a Preamble to the Coloured Citizens of the World." *In Their Own Words:*

A History of the American Negro 1619–1865. Ed. by Milton Meltzer. New York: Thomas Y. Crowell Company, 1967.

Walker, Margaret. *For My People.* New Haven and London: Yale University Press, 1968.

Warren, Robert Penn. *Who Speaks for the Negro?* New York: Random House, Inc., 1965.

Wellek, René, and Austin Warren. *Theory of Literature.* 3d ed. New York: Harcourt Brace Jovanavich, Inc., 1956.

Wright, Richard. *Black Boy.* New York: Harper & Row, Publishers, 1945.

———. *Native Son.* New York: Harper & Row, Publishers, 1966.

———. *Eight Men.* New York: Pyramid Books, 1969.